UML and the Unified Process

Table of Contents

UML and the Unified Process

Liliana Favre
Universidad Nacional del Centro de la Provincia de Buenos Aires
Argentina

IRM Press
Publisher of innovative scholarly and professional
information technology titles in the cyberage

Hershey • London • Melbourne • Singapore • Beijing

Acquisitions Editor: Mehdi Khosrow-Pour
Senior Managing Editor: Jan Travers
Managing Editor: Amanda Appicello
Development Editor: Michele Rossi
Copy Editor: Joyce Gouger
Typesetter: Amanda Appicello
Cover Design: Kory Gongloff
Printed at: Integrated Book Technology

Published in the United States of America by
        IRM Press (an imprint of Idea Group Inc.)
        1331 E. Chocolate Avenue, Suite 200
        Hershey PA 17033-1117
        Tel: 717-533-8845
        Fax: 717-533-8661
        E-mail: cust@idea-group.com
        Web site: http://www.irm-press.com

and in the United Kingdom by
        IRM Press (an imprint of Idea Group Inc.)
        3 Henrietta Street
        Covent Garden
        London WC2E 8LU
        Tel: 44 20 7240 0856
        Fax: 44 20 7379 3313
        Web site: http://www.eurospan.co.uk

        Library of Congress Cataloging-in-Publication Data

Favre, Liliana.
    UML and the unified process / Liliana Favre.
        p. cm.
Includes bibliographical references and index.
    ISBN 1-931777-44-6
    1. Application software--Development. 2. UML (Computer science) 3.
Computer software--Development. 4. Software engineering. 5. Web site
development. I. Title.
    QA76.76.A65F39 2003
    005.1--dc21
                                                        2002156230

eISBN 1-931777-60-8

British Cataloguing in Publication Data
A Cataloguing in Publication record for this book is available from the British Library.

Preface

This book provides a set of readings on the state-of-the-art and the state-of-the-practice of the Unified Modeling Language (UML) and the Unified Process (UP).

UML is a language for specifying, visualizing, constructing and documenting software- intensive systems. It is a unifier of proven software modeling languages that appeared in the early 1990s. UML incorporates the object-oriented community's consensus on core modeling concepts and includes an additional expressiveness to handle problems that previous languages (Booch, OMT, OOSE) did not fully address. It emerged in response to a call for a standard object-oriented and design method by the Object Management Group (OMG) in 1997. Currently, the OMG/UML standard is version 1.4 and the evolution of UML will result in version 2.0.

The UML notation includes diagrams that provide multiple perspectives of the system under analysis or development. It is layered architecturally and organized by packages. The model's elements are defined in terms of their abstract syntax, well-formed rules (using the Object Constraint Language and precise text) and precise text. The formalization of UML is still an open problem. Many works have been done to formalize parts of the language and it is difficult to see how to integrate the works in order to define a formal semantics for UML.

Although UML does not prescribe any particular development process, various companies are working on processes to provide advice on the use of UML in the software development life cycle.

The OMG presented the "Software Process Engineering Metamodel" (SPEM) as a standard in November 2001. This metamodel is used to describe a concrete software development process or a family of related software development processes that use the UML notation. SPEM has a four-layered architecture of modeling for describing performing process, process model, process metamodel and MetaObject facility. Several processes fit SPEM. The most popular of these is the Rational Unified Process (RUP), developed and marketed by Rational Software. It is a software development process based on UML that is use-driven, architecture-centered, iterative and risk-driven. It provides a disciplined approach to assigning tasks and responsibilities within a development organization. RUP is organized around four phases: inception, elaboration, construction and transition and core workflows: requirements, capture, analysis, design, implementation and test. Various industry sectors around the world use RUP in different applications: telecommunications, transportation, aerospace, defense, manufacturing and financial services.

UML and UP are having a significant impact on the software development industry. However, numerous practical difficulties have been detected with their use. As a result, they must evolve further by looking toward extension practitioners and researchers to address specific concerns, then incorporate their feedback. In this direction, many innovations are concerned with the development of new theories and practices that are required to clarify and to make precise its semantics and reasons underlying properties of UML models. New theories and practices also transform software modeling and designs into code and enable object-oriented visual modeling tool interoperability.

There are still important issues to be solved in a satisfactory way. Techniques that currently exist in UML CASE tools provide little support for validating models in the design stages and are insufficient for completed, automated code generation. Little work has been done in order to investigate the use of well-proven and accepted requirements, techniques and models for the business and requirements of UP models. Some problems have been detected in the process of MDA methods that require flexible code generation mechanisms. Modeling of a performance-oriented, parallel and distributed application in UML is still an open problem.

This book collects insightful contributions from both industry and academia, illustrating how UML can be used, identifying open problems with UML and UP and suggesting solutions. The different chapters present perspectives on the UML and UP with respect to the following topics:

- Extensions and restrictions of UML and UP,
- Business process and modeling,
- Semantics,
- Mapping of UML models to frameworks, databases, formal languages and programming languages,
- Software components,
- Profiles,
- Security.

As an edited collection, this book should be of interest to practitioners, researchers and instructors of UML and UP.

ORGANIZATION OF THE BOOK

The book is organized into 19 chapters. A brief description of each chapter follows.

Chapter 1 provides a critical look at UML. The evaluation is done using a general framework for understanding the quality of models and modeling languages in the information systems. The authors argue that although being an improvement over its predecessors, UML still has many limitations and deficiencies related to both the expressiveness and comprehensiveness of the language.

Chapter 2 describes a generic framework for tailoring general purpose and model-based methodologies in order to deliver domain-specific models and to ensure utilization of existing knowledge possessed within the actual domain. By applying the tailoring framework, a domain-specific reference model is presented that consists of UML profiles, reusable models and patterns..

Chapter 3 analyzes the possibility of applying UML to design an inter-firm, on-line business model using UML. The proposed framework comprises such principal elements as value, business players and relationships among players, with each specified in terms of representative attributes and incorporating related notations. The business model is then visualized by value and structure diagrams.

Chapter 4 describes an approach for specifying business components. The authors propose a general and layered structure of software contracts for business components and show the shortcomings of common specification approaches. They introduce a formal notation for the specification of business components based on temporal extensions of the OCL.

Chapter 5 evaluates UML's support for reuse using a modeling framework based on semiotic theory. This chapter explores the nature of modeling abstractions that could support the negotiation between stakeholders. The authors analyze two scenarios: one based on composable, functional abstractions and the other using structural abstractions as the basis for component compositions.

Chapter 6 describes a strategy that is based on natural, language-oriented requirements models to define the RUP business model through the business use case and business object models. The strategy proposes a set of activities and heuristics to define conceptual object models starting with models belonging to the client-oriented requirements baseline. The author argues that the use of heuristics in the business model definition encourages pre- through post-traceability between models.

Chapter 7 introduces an approach that is concerned with non-functional features of software systems. The authors examine an extension of UML to capture non-functional information in a way that is similar to its counterpart:, the functional information. The NoFun (non-functional) language and the software Quality Standard ISO/IEC9126 are the bases used to achieve some organization about non-functional concepts.

Chapter 8 explores the use of RSL, the language of the RAISE method, to provide formal foundation for UML class diagrams. An automated tool to transform UML class diagrams to RSL is described. Through analysis of the semantics of UML class diagrams and their formal specification in RSL, abstract templates are obtained, which guide the implementation of a translator tool.

Chapter 9 presents the basis of a rigorous process for systematic, object-oriented code generation starting from UML static models. The authors propose an integration of UML, algebraic specifications and Eiffel code. The overall aim of this chapter is to describe the transformation of different kinds of associations to code and the generation of Eiffel assertions.

Chapter 10 describes a step-by-step process for transforming UML class diagrams into entity relation diagrams, which can be used to make objects persistent. The authors also show the possibility of using UML notation to draw entity relation diagrams.

Chapter 11 presents a rigorous approach to specify and check dependency relations between UML models. The authors classify relationships between UML models along three different dimensions: artifact dimension, activity dimension and iteration dimension, and propose a formal description of them. The goal of the proposed formalization is to provide formal foundations for tools that perform intelligent analysis on models used to assist software engineers throughout the development process.

Chapter 12 reviews IS modeling techniques and presents a new technique called "info-mathics" for describing formally hierarchical system architectures. The authors analyze the practical implications of their technique in system analysis and design. They argue that this technique is similar to other engineering techniques applied in well-developed industries.

Chapter 13 proposes the use of Business Process Diagrams (BPD), which are based on UML's activity diagrams. The authors show how to derive BPD from the business process language of the Event-driven Process Chain (EPC) using Petri nets as a common process metamodel. The authors show examples of business processes and their representation as EPCs and BPDs.

Chapter 14 presents an extension of the UML metamodel with evolutionary stereotypes. An evolutionary stereotype allows the designer to create new classes of UML metamodels with their respective semantics. The authors propose to incorporate evolutionary stereotypes in the tools of modeling so that the developers can modify the UML metamodel. The authors argue that evolutionary stereotypes allow for the automatic generation of code, maintaining the consistence of the UML model.

Chapter 15 describes an extension of the UML activity diagram from workflow. It shows a proposal for the integration of UML with the WfMC (Workflow Management Coalition), Interface 1. The main goal of this approach is to allow UML modeling tools to generate artifacts that represent the workflow process and can be translated to the standard WfMC format. The authors analyze the limitations of UML activity diagrams in modeling an automated organizational process according to the WfMC standard, and then propose how the UML metamodel should be extended to overcome such limitations.

Chapter 16 presents some particularly useful stereotypes to be used in business systems. The authors exemplify their usage with both design drawings and implementation code in C++.

Chapter 17 introduces the CORAS methodology, in which UML and UP are combined to support a model-based, risk assessment on security-critical systems. The authors argue that modeling techniques such as UML contribute to increased understanding by the different stakeholders involved during a risk assessment.

Chapter 18 recommends a set of extensions through a UML profile to support development dealing with safeguarding. The authors take into account three aspects of safeguarding: the business expertise, the interface and the code itself. They show how CORAS can be used for better understanding, documentation and communication during the different phases of the risk management process.

Chapter 19 introduces an extension of RUP with a method that supports the progressive and separate implementation of three different aspects: persistence, distribution and concurrence control. The authors define the software process resulting from the inclusion of this method into RUP, modifying some aspects of the latter. The proposed modifications consider dynamic and static aspects.

Acknowledgments

The editor would like to acknowledge the help of all individuals involved in the collation and review process of the book, without whose support the project could not have been satisfactorily completed. A further special note of thanks goes to all of the staff at Idea Group, Inc., whose contributions throughout the whole process, from inception of the initial idea to final publication, have been invaluable.

Special thanks also go to the publishing team at Idea Group, Inc. In particular, the editor thanks Amanda Appicello, who continuously prodded, via e-mail, in order to keep the project on schedule, and to Mehdi Khosrow-Pour, whose enthusiasm motivated me to initially accept his invitation to take on this project.

In closing, I wish to thank all of the authors for their insights and excellent contributions to this book. In addition, this book would not have been possible without the ongoing professional support from Mehdi Khosrow-Pour and the staff at Idea Group, Inc.

Liliana Favre
Editor
INTIA, Universidad Nacional del Centro de la Provincia de Buenos Aires
Tandil, Argentina

Chapter I

Evaluating UML Using a Generic Quality Framework

John Krogstie
SINTEF Telecom and Informatics and
IDI, NTNU, Norway

ABSTRACT

Many researchers have evaluated different parts of UML™ and have come up with suggestions for improvements to different parts of the language. This chapter looks at UML (version 1.4) as a whole, and contains an overview evaluation of UML and how it is described in the OMG™ standard. The evaluation is done using a general framework for understanding quality of models and modeling languages in the information systems field. The evaluation is based on both practical experiences and more theoretical evaluations of UML. Based on the evaluation, we conclude that although being an improvement over it is predecessors, UML still has many limitations and deficiencies, both related to the expressiveness and comprehensibility of the language. Although work is well underway for the next version of UML (version 2.0), not all of the important problems seem to be addressed in the upcoming new version of the language.

INTRODUCTION

According to Booch, Rumbaugh and Jacobson (1999), developing a model for an industrial-strength software system before its construction is regarded increasingly as a necessary activity in information systems development. Good models are essential for communication among the members of project teams, and to assure that it is possible to implement the system.

Modeling has been a cornerstone in many traditional software development methodologies for decades. The use of object-oriented modeling in analysis and design started to become popular in the late 1980s, producing a large number of different languages and approaches. Lately, UML has taken a leading position in this area, partly through the standardization of the language within the Object Management Group (OMG).

In this chapter, we give an assessment of UML (version 1.4), highlighting both the positive aspects and the areas where improvement is needed. We first present the evaluation framework. We then evaluate the language quality of UML. In earlier work, we had also looked at how UML, in combination with the modeling techniques found in one UML-tool Rational Rose®, can support the development of models of high quality (Krogstie, 2001b). In this chapter, we look at language quality in more detail than has been reviewed in previous work.

BACKGROUND ON THE EVALUATION FRAMEWORK

Most existing UML evaluations focus narrowly on what we call language quality, either by:

- Evaluating UML relative to an existing approach, and highlighting those areas where the other approach is better than UML.
- Looking upon detailed aspects of the language and presenting improvements for these areas.
- Using a framework for assessing limited aspects of language quality such as expressiveness in a certain context.

Even those using a general evaluation framework look upon the language quality features as goals to achieve. Contrary to this, Krogstie, Sindre, and Lindland (Krogstie, Lindland, & Sindre 1995; Krogstie & Sølvberg, 2000) have developed a framework for discussing the quality of models in general, motivating the focus on language quality as a means to achieve models of high quality.

The framework:

- Distinguishes between quality goals and the means to achieve these goals. Language quality goals are one type of means, but means can also be related to modeling processes, techniques, and tools. Even if it can be argued from both activity theory and decision theory that the interrelationships between goals and means are being determined through the preference function of the modeler, we have found that most modeling techniques, in practice, contribute primarily to a specific model quality goal.
- Is closely linked to linguistic and semiotic theory. In particular, the core of the framework (including the discussion on syntax, semantics, and pragmatics), is parallel to the use of these terms in the semiotic theory of Morris. It is further based on the use of semiotic theory within the information systems field by Stamper (1998).

- Is based on a constructivistic, world-view, which recognizes that models are usually created as part of a dialogue among the participants involved in modeling.

Further details on the framework can be found in Carlsen, Krogstie, Sølvberg and Lindland (1997), Krogstie (1999), and Krogstie and Sølvberg (2000) where several modeling approaches, including OMT (Object Modeling Technique) and approaches for workflow modeling, have been evaluated. What one is able to evaluate using the framework, is the *potential* of a modeling approach to support the creation of models of high quality. Used in this way, we only utilize parts of the total framework as will be illustrated below. How the framework can be specialized for requirements specification models is discussed in Krogstie (2001a).

The main concepts of the framework and its relationships are shown in Figure 1 and are explained below. Quality has been defined as referring to the correspondence between statements belonging to the following sets:

- **G**, the normally, organizationally-motivated goals of the modeling task.
- **L**, the language extension (i.e., the set of all statements that are possible to make according to the graphemes, vocabulary, and syntax of the modeling languages used.
- **D**, the domain (i.e., the set of all statements that can be stated about the situation at hand). Enterprise domains are socially constructed and are more or less inter-subjectively agreed upon. That the world is socially constructed does not make it any less important to model that world.
- **M**, the externalized model (i.e., the set of all statements in someone's model of part of the perceived reality written in a language).
- K_s, the relevant explicit knowledge of the set of stakeholders involved in modeling (the audience **A**). A subset of the audience is those actively involved in modeling; and, their knowledge is indicated by K_M.
- **I**, the social actor interpretation (i.e., the set of all statements that the audience thinks an externalized model consists of).
- **T**, the technical actor interpretation (i.e., the statements in the model as "interpreted" by different model activators) (i.e., modeling tools).

The main quality types are indicated by solid lines between the sets as described briefly next.

- Physical quality has two goals: Externalization, that the knowledge **K** of the domain **D** of some social actor has been externalized by the use of a modeling language, and internalizeability, that the externalized model **M** is persistent and available, thereby enabling the audience to make sense of it.
- Empirical quality deals with predicable error frequencies identified when a model is read or written by different users, through coding (e.g., shapes of boxes), and by HCI-ergonomics for documentation and modeling tools.
- Syntactic quality is the correspondence between the model **M** and the language extension **L** of the language in which the model is written.

Figure 1: Framework for discussing the quality of models

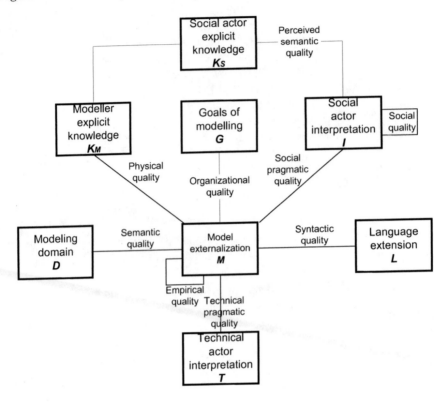

- Semantic quality is the correspondence between the model *M* and the domain *D*. The framework contains two semantic goals: validity, which means that all statements made in the model are correct relative to the domain, and completeness, which means that the model contains all statements that are found in the domain.
- Perceived semantic quality is the similar correspondence between the audience interpretation *I* of a model *M,* his or her current knowledge *K* of the domain *D*, and what can actually be checked during quality control/validation.
- Pragmatic quality is the correspondence between the model *M* and the audience interpretation of the model (*I*). We differentiate between social pragmatic quality (i.e., to what extent people understand the models) and technical pragmatic quality (i.e., to what extent tools can be constructed to understand the models).
- Social quality has as its defined goal, the agreement among audience members' interpretations (*I*).
- The organizational quality of the model relates to the premise that all statements in the model either directly or indirectly contribute to fulfilling the goals of modeling (i.e., organizational goal validity), and that all the goals of modeling are addressed through the model (i.e., organizational goal completeness).

Figure 2: Language quality in the quality framework

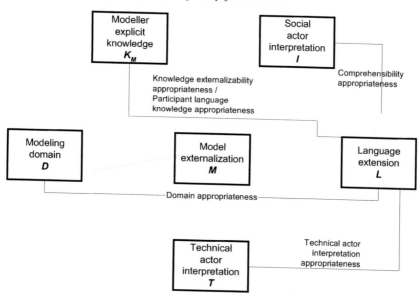

Language quality relates the modeling languages that have been used to the other sets. It is distinguished between two types of criteria:

- Criteria for the underlying (i.e., conceptual) basis of the language (i.e., what is typically represented in the meta-model).
- Criteria for the external (visual) representation of the language (i.e., the notation and the concrete syntax).

Five areas for language quality are identified with aspects related to both the meta-model and the notation as illustrated in Figure 2.

Domain Appropriateness

Ideally, the conceptual basis must be powerful enough to express anything in the domain (i.e., not having construct deficit) (Wand & Weber, 1993). On the other hand, you should *not* be able to express things that are not in the domain (i.e., what is termed construct excess) (Wand & Weber, 1993).

The only requirement to the external representation is that it does not destroy the underlying basis. This means that it is possible to visually represent a concept in the basis and that the visual representation has a corresponding, underlying basis.

One approach to evaluating domain appropriateness, which will be used here, is to look at how the modeling perspectives found useful for the relevant modeling tasks are covered. Seven general modeling perspectives have been identified for information systems modeling (Krogstie & Sølvberg, 2000). These seven general modeling perspectives are: structural, functional, behavioral, rule-oriented, object-oriented, language-action-oriented, and role and actor-oriented. More detailed evaluations of languages within these perspectives can be based on evaluation frameworks (Embley, Jackson, & Woodfield, 1995; Iivari, 1995; Wieringa, 1998). Another approach is to base an evaluation on an ontological theory, see example in Opdahl, Henderson-Sellers and Barbier (1999) that uses the ontology presented by Wand and Weber (1993). Domain appropriateness is primarily a means to achieve physical quality, and through this mechanism, to potentially achieve semantic quality.

Participant Language Knowledge Appropriateness

This area relates participant knowledge to the language. The conceptual basis should correspond as much as possible to the way that individuals perceive reality. This will differ from person to person according to his or her previous experience. Thus, it will initially be dependent directly on participants during a modeling effort. On the other hand, the knowledge of the participants is not static (i.e., it is possible to educate persons in the use of a specific language). In such an instance, one should base the language on experiences with languages used for the relevant types of modeling, and languages that have been previously used successfully in similar tasks. Participant language knowledge appropriateness is primarily a means to achieve physical quality (for those actively modeling) and pragmatic quality (for those interpreting the models made).

Knowledge Externalizability Appropriateness

This area relates language to the participant knowledge. The goal is to ensure that there are no statements in the explicit knowledge of the participant that cannot be expressed in the language. As this is highly dependent on the participants, we do not look into this aspect of language quality in this paper. Knowledge externalizability appropriateness is primarily a mean to achieve physical quality.

Comprehensibility Appropriateness

This area relates language to the social actor interpretation. The conceptual basis states the following:

- The phenomena of the language should be easily distinguishable from each other. This is the same as what is covered by construct redundancy (Wand & Weber, 1993).
- The number of phenomena should be reasonable. While there are an infinite number of statements that might be made (vs. domain appropriateness), these have to be dealt with through a limited number of phenomena classes. This means that:
  - The phenomena must be general rather than specialized.
  - The phenomena must be composable, which means that related statements can be grouped in a natural way.
  - The language must be flexible in precision.
- If the number of phenomena must be large, they should be organized hierarchically and/or in sub-languages, making it possible to approach the framework at different levels of abstraction or from different perspectives.
- The use of phenomena should be uniform throughout the whole set of statements that can be expressed within the language. Using the same construct for different phenomenon or different constructs for the same function (depending on the context), will tend to make the language confusing vs. construct overloading (Wand & Weber, 1993).

- The language must be flexible in its level of detail. Statements must be easily extendible by other statements that provide more details. Details must also be easily hidden.

The following aspects are important for the external representation:
- Symbol discrimination should be easy.
- Distinguishing what symbols in a model any graphical mark is part of should be easy (what Goodman terms "syntactic disjointness") (1976).
- Use of symbols should be uniform (e.g., a symbol should not represent one phenomenon in one context and another phenomenon in a different context). Similarly, different symbols should not be used for the same phenomenon in different contexts. Goodman (1976) argues that the last aspect is less important; however, if many different representations of the same concept are used, the number of simple shapes that can be easily distinguished is exhausted.
- Symbolic simplicity should be a goal.
- Use of emphasis in the notation should be consistent with the relative importance of the statements in the given model.
- Composition of symbols should be made in an aesthetically-pleasing way. A counter-example illustrating this would be a process modeling language mandating that all inflow enter the same side of the process symbol, resulting in a model that has many unnecessary crossing or long lines.

Comprehensibility appropriateness is primarily a means to achieve empirical, and subsequently, pragmatic quality.

Technical Actor Interpretation Appropriateness

This area relates language to the technical actor interpretations. For the technical actors, it is especially important that the language lend itself to automatic reasoning. This requires formality (i.e., both formal syntax and semantics). Formal semantics can be operational, logical, or both; but, formality is not sufficient since the reasoning must also be efficient for practical use. This is covered by what we termed analyzability (i.e., to have exploited the mathematical semantics) and executability (i.e., to have exploited the operational semantics). The power of formal semantics lies in three aspects (Wieringa, 1998):

1. The process of making a more formal specification may reveal errors and ambiguities at an early stage.
2. Formal as well as automated proofs may be available.
3. The remaining (or unprovable) rules may be translated into executable constraints in some imperative language.

Different aspects of technical actor interpretation appropriateness are a means to achieve syntactic, semantic, and pragmatic quality (through formal syntax, mathematical semantics, and operational semantics, respectively).

In addition to aspects related directly to the language, the quality of the official model of a modeling language (the language model, which is what Prasse (1999) covers under documentation) should be looked at. A modeling language is described (e.g., in a notation guide and in a semantic description) vs. how UML is described by OMG.

A notation guide typically contains structured text and example models, which are often in some type of hypertext-structure.

The semantic description typically contains a meta-model (in a given language or set of languages) and a set of structured text describing the meta-model.

Different types of meta-model users have very different needs:

- Users of the language need the language model primarily to develop their domain models.
- Adapters of the language need to understand the existing language in order to adapt it to more specific needs through meta-modeling.
- Tool developers need to understand the notations and meta-model semantics in order to support the use of the language by building modeling tools that incorporate the different techniques required to achieve high quality models as summarized in Table 1.

The first user-group identified above is the primary focus in most cases. A look at the language model across the levels of quality offers the following:

Physical quality

- Externalization refers to a modeling language that is typically described in text and models. It is important that the meta-modeler ensures that the language model, including the language description, can be updated in a controlled way.
- Internalizability means that the relevant parts of the descriptions are available for those who need it in an efficient way (e.g., all users have access to the notation guide for those parts of the language they want to use).

Empirical quality

For empirical quality, a range of means for readability has been devised, (e.g., number of different readability indexes) for informal textual models. Other general guidelines include not mixing different fonts, colors etc. in a paragraph that is on the same level within the overall text. For graphical models in particular, layout modifications have been found to improve the comprehensibility of models. Thus for the textual part, the structure and readability of the text can be assessed. For meta-models and example models it can be judged whether the models are made aesthetically pleasing.

Syntactic quality

There is one syntactic goal of syntactic quality, syntactical correctness, which means that all statements in the model are in accordance with the syntax and vocabulary of the language. Syntactic errors are of two kinds: syntactic invalidity, in which words or graphemes that are not part of the language are used, and syntactic incompleteness, in which the model or text lacks the constructs or parts needed to obey the language's grammar. For the textual part of the language model, it should be verified that it is according to the language and structure chosen. Similarly, the model examples and meta-models must follow the chosen syntax.

Semantic quality

The focus of semantic quality is semantic completeness (i.e., that all parts of the language are described in text and in the meta-model). Semantic validity of the language model focuses on whether the different descriptions are consistent both within and with each other. The language model should only describe the modeling language, and nothing more. It should be noted that in most language models, the domain is to a larger degree given "objectively" (e.g., in the definition by UML by what has been agreed upon through the standardization process).

Pragmatic quality

Pragmatic quality refers to the inclusion of a means to make it easier to understand the modeling language through the language model. This can include the use of indexes,

Table 1: Goals and means in the quality framework

Quality type	Goals	Means *Model and language properties*	*Activities and tool support*
Physical	Externalization	Domain appropriateness Participant language knowledge appropriateness Knowledge externalizeability appropriateness Language extension	Statement insertion Meta-model adaptation Language extension
	Internalizeability	Persistence Availability	DB activities Repository
Empirical	Minimal error frequency	Comprehensibility appropriateness Aesthetics	Diagram layout Readability index
Syntactic	Syntactic correctness	Formal syntax	Error prevention Error detection Error correction
Semantic	Feasible validity Feasible completeness	Formal semantics Modifiability Analyzability	Statement delete Driving quest. Model reuse Model testing Consistency
Pragmatic	Feasible comprehension	Operational semantics Executability	Inspection Visualization Filtering Rephrasing Paraphrasing Explanation Execution Animation Simulation
Perceived semantic	Feasible perceived validity Feasible perceived comp.	Variety	Participant training
Social	Feasible agreement	Inconsistency handling	Model int. Conflict res.
Organizatonal	Goal validity Goal completeness	Traceability Tracedness	Based on modeling goal

cross-references, and glossaries. It can also be done through tutorials, by linking of the model of modeling language to the use of the language in a modeling environment, etc.

Social quality

Social quality is an aspect that is relevant both in connection to the development of a standard language, and in connection to meta-modeling extensions. The representation of a language and its appropriateness can be disliked; therefore, good examples (e.g., use in the notation guide) is very important here.

Organizational quality

In regards to organizational quality, the model of the modeling language helps create efficient use of the modeling language for those tasks where it is meant to be used (e.g., minimize training time, etc.).

The quality of the language used for meta-modeling can be used to further evaluate according to the five criteria above.

As mentioned, many means might be useful on several levels. The means have been as we have positioned them here, within the area where they are believed to have the most effect. This part of the framework is summarized in Table 1 as an extended version of the framework found in (Krogstie, 2001b).

EVALUATION

Before presenting the evaluation, we will position UML in relation to the sets of the quality framework.

Domain

According to (OMG, 2001), UML is a language used for specifying, visualizing, constructing, and documenting the artifacts of software systems. It is also used for business modeling and other non-software systems. In other words, UML is meant to be used in the analysis of business and information, specification of requirements and design. UML is meant to support the modeling of (object-oriented) transaction systems, real-time systems and safety-critical systems. In addition, UML is used for the meta-modeling of UML itself. For those areas related directly to the modeling domain, the discussion has been differentiated according to the different domains.

Language

We have based the evaluation on UML (version 1.4) (OMG, 2001). Defined profiles were not looked at, rather the concentration was the core language. Additionally, a detailed evaluation of OCL was not performed. The language model evaluated is the official OMG-standard, in its textual form, including pictures of the different views of the meta-models and example models. Although many UML books and tutorials that are linked to the different available UML tools exist, and can improve the understanding and use of the language, we have looked only and specifically at the OMG standard in this evaluation.

The sets "Knowledge", "Model", and "Interpretation" must be judged from case to case in the practical application of modeling languages and tools. Additionally, when weighting the different criteria against each other, it must be done in respect to the specific modeling task to be supported by the language, such as has been done, e.g., by Arnesen and Krogstie (2002) and Østbø (2000).

When using the quality framework in such an evaluation, the following should be kept in mind:

- It is possible to make good models in a poor modeling language.
- It is possible to make poor models in a comparatively good modeling language.
- Some deficiencies will always be found in any language and tool support; however, it is useful to know the weak spots in order to avoid the related, potential problems. In general, such deficiencies should be addressed with the use of modeling techniques and an overall methodology. None of these areas are addressed in UML.

The primary aim of this evaluation is to help people using UML to recognize the existing weaknesses. This evaluation has also been used to provide input on areas that should be addressed in later versions of the standard.

The basis for the evaluation is in addition to the framework:

- UML (version 1.4) language specification (OMG, 2001).
- Practical experience using UML by the author and by others in industrial and academic settings who were interviewed by the author.
- Other evaluations found in the literature (Bergner, Rausch, & Sihling, 1998; Bézivin & Muller, 1998; Castellani, 1999; France & Rumpe, 1999; Jézéquel, Hussman, & Cook, 2002, Ovum, 1998; Prasse, 1998, Siau & Cao, 2001).

Due to the limitation on the length of a paper of this kind and the breadth of this evaluation, there is only room for presenting the major results. See Østbø (2000) for a more detailed description of using the framework for evaluating UML.

Language Quality of UML

The UML semantics (based on the meta-model) is the basis for evaluating the conceptual basis; whereas, the notation guide is used as a basis for the evaluation of the external representation.

Domain Appropriateness

Looking briefly on the coverage of the seven main modeling perspectives in information systems modeling, we find:

- The object-oriented perspective is relevant primarily during analysis of information and design (Davis, 1995). UML has, not surprisingly, been found to be a very good support for modeling according to an object-oriented perspective, although with a limited modeling capability regarding responsibilities.
- The structural perspective is relevant primarily during analysis of information and design. This perspective is also well supported, although not as well as in

languages made specifically for this purpose (Halpin, 2001). Traditional abstraction mechanisms such as aggregation, classification, and generalization are provided; but, other object-oriented (OO) modeling languages and different languages for semantic data modeling have a more precise representation of these abstraction mechanisms (Barbier et al., 2001). The area of volumetrics is only partly supported.

- The behavioral perspective can be useful in all domains, but is particularly used within design. UML supports the behavioral perspective using Statecharts, but does not support the refinement of Statecharts in a satisfactory way (Hitz & Kappel, 1998).

- The functional (i.e., process) perspective is supported on a high level through use case modeling (a.k.a. 0-level DFD), which is a language that has been highly criticized for not being well defined (Hitz & Kappel, 1998; Genova, Llorens & Quintana, 2002). Whereas Use-cases are meant for requirements modeling, activity diagrams can be used for simple procedural descriptions by showing control flow and the production of data or objects in a process flow. This is useful for design. Many IT modelers have also attempted using activity diagrams for business models. Hommes and van Reijswoud (1999) argue that the modeling concepts in the business process domain are not easily mapped to UML. The lack of, e.g., traditional dataflow in activity diagrams has been noted as one of the problems. However, if it is possible to make use of the activity diagram for visualization and understanding of process models (Arnesen 2002), it may be beneficial as long as the current semantics in UML are not exploited. The semantics of activity diagrams will probably be changed substantially in UML (version 2.0) to enable activity diagrams to be better suited for business process modeling.

- The actor-role perspective can be relevant in analysis of business and design. It is partly covered using the Collaboration Diagrams. Using roles in sequence diagrams or "swimlanes" in Activity Diagrams, allows for a role-oriented view. However, there is no intuitive way to represent organizational and group structures in UML, which would be very useful for analyzing organizations and organizational structures.

- Single rules can be used in all domains. It is possible to formulate single, static rules in OCL. There are some general problems with constraints that are expressed in an OO modeling framework (Høydalsvik & Sindre, 1993). Temporal and deontic constraints are hard to express. The same problem applies to non-functional requirements, such as Quality of Service (QoS) (Aagedal, 2002), performance (Pllana & Fahringer, 2002), reliability, or security requirements (Lodderstedt, Basin & Doser, 2002). There are also technical problems with visibility of, e.g., private attributes used in constraints. There is no support for goal-hierarchies (Mylopoulos, Chung, & Tu, 1999), a technique used primarily to analyze businesses and specify requirements.

- The language-action perspective, which is most useful for the analysis of businesses, is not supported.

A meta-model of UML is defined (using UML), and extension mechanisms exist, which can make the language more applicable in specific domains. UML contains only lightweight extension mechanisms such as stereotypes, constraints, and tagged values (compared to meta-classes, which are regarded as heavyweight extension mechanisms). Atkinson, Kühne and Henderson-Sellars (2002) highlights additional problems with the existing extension mechanisms.

Most of UML is useful primarily during design. Its language mechanisms should not be used for analysis and requirements specification, even in areas where the transition from analysis to design is "seamless". (There is extensive evidence demonstrating that this transition is far from seamless even when using object-oriented modeling in all domains, especially for business systems (Davis, 1995; Høydalsvik & Sindre, 1993; Lauesen, 1998)). Proper guidelines for avoiding this are not consistently provided, and there is no support for avoidance using analysis and design concepts in the same model. It is generally believed that a good method should help in keeping information about what a system should do separated from how that functionality should be implemented in a specific implementation environment. The connections between such models should also be possible to express (Ovum, 1998). UML gives limited support in this regard.

Although comprehensive, UML cannot be used to specify complete applications. Its limitations are that it does not yet provide an action language in the main language (Mellor, Tockey, Arthaud, & LeBlanc, 1998) to support the analysis of complete specifications, and that it lacks some constructs for, e.g., architecture (Hilliard, 1999), real-time systems (André, Peraldi-Frati, & Rigault, 2002; Flake & Mueller, 2002), user-interfaces (Kovacevic, 1998), hypermedia (Baumeister, Koch, & Mandel, 1998) , and Web-development (Hennicker & Koch, 2001). Also, for emerging areas such as mobile agents (Klein, 2001) and mobile information systems (Kosiuczenko, 2002), several extensions have been suggested.

There are also mismatches between the underlying basis and the external representation. In sequence diagrams, for instance, the following characters are semantically vacant (Morris & Spanoudakis, 2001):

- Time axis.
- Swimlane.
- Sequence number labeling an arrow.
- Lifeline.
- Lifeline split into two or more concurrent lifelines.
- Activation box.
- Construction marks.
- Slanted, downward arrow.
- Arrows leaving a single point labeled with guard conditions that are not mutually exclusive.

Examples of concrete constructs in the meta-model, without representation in the notation (e.g., namespace and model), are also found.

Comprehensibility Appropriateness

Some main observations on comprehensibility appropriateness are:

- UML can be argued to be overly complex, with a total of 233 different concepts (Castellani, 1999).

  In Keng and Cao (2001), a detailed comparison using the complexity metrics devised by Rossi and Brinkkemper (1994) is presented. The various diagrams in UML are not distinctly different from the diagrams in other OO methods. Although UML has more diagramming techniques when compared to other OO methods, each of the diagramming techniques, when taken in isolation, is no more complex than techniques found in other OO methods. In fact, for most of the metrics, the majority of UML diagrams rank in the middle for complexity with the exception of class diagrams, which are more complex than similar diagrams found in other approaches. On the overall method level, UML stands out noticeably as being the most complex according to most of the metrics. Compared to other OO-methods, UML consist of three to19 times more object types, two to 27 more relationship types, and two to nine times more property types. As a result, UML is two to 11 times more complex than other OO methods.

- With so many concepts, it is not surprising that some redundancy and overlap are witnessed. Some examples are:

  - The concepts "Signal" and "Operation call" are almost identical.
  - Differentiating between the use of types and the use of classes is poorly defined.
  - Guards, preconditions, post conditions, constraints, multiplicity, and invariants are all different types of rules. However, these terms might be so well established that in practice, they cause few problems.

- Break of uniformity are common and several examples of this can be found. For instance, a transition in an activity diagram represents a flow of control, whereas a transition in a Statechart diagram symbolizes a change of state.

- Symbol differentiation can create confusion, as in the examples below:

  - Both classes and objects are shown using rectangles.
  - Slightly slanted arrows may not be distinguishable from horizontal arrows in sequence diagrams.
  - Nothing in the sequence diagram notation distinguishes between the name of a signal and the name of an operation.
  - Use cases, states in statecharts and activities in activity diagrams are all shaped more or less like an ellipse.
  - The same symbol is used for choice in activity diagrams, aggregation, and n-ary associations.

- UML contains several possibilities for adding (often small) adornments to the models. In addition, such adornments are often difficult to see and comprehend. Moreover, when sensed, adornments can often be difficult to link back to the right concept. Morris and Spanoudakis (2001) for instance have identified the following problems in relation to syntactic disjointness in sequence diagrams alone:

  - Name of arrow / timing label.
  - Sequence number labeling an arrow / timing label / name of arrow.

- Text label next to activation box or in the left margin / timing label / name of arrow / sequence number labeling an arrow.
- Guard condition attached to x-arrow/ name of arrow /timing label.
- Iteration condition attached to arrow-x / name of arrow / timing label.
- As the predecessor to the structural model in UML, OMT had quite a few deficiencies in regards to the uniform use of symbols, some of which have been addressed as noted below:
  - Contrary to OMT, UML has a uniform way of showing cardinality (i.e., multiplicity).
  - Associations in UML are shown in two ways as compared with the four ways of showing associations in OMT.
  - Different symbols are used for external and internal roles: pin-man if it is external to the system or rectangle if it is internal to the system.
  - An interface is shown in two different ways: as a circle or as a class-symbol.

Many of these deficiencies are relatively unproblematic, as different aspects are the focus in different models. Irrespective, having too many deficiencies makes it more difficult to learn the language and comprehend the models that are made using the language. This is specifically important in models used to analyze business and information and requirements specification, which are meant to be comprehended by many people with different backgrounds.

- In the structural model, the emphasis is classes and objects as identified through the size of the symbols, which is sensible. Most of the usage of filled symbols found in OMT is removed, with the exception of full aggregation, which is an intuitive use of this effect. Because the class-symbols receive different sizes and shapes, dependent on the number of attributes and operations that are defined, potentially makes class-symbols visually complex. This is out-weighed by the fact that the diagrams are in fact much simpler than if these concepts are represented separately (as done in many languages for structural modeling). The same positive remark can be made on the onion-notation inherited through adopting Harel's Statecharts. The possibility of grouping classes/objects in packages as well as in composite classes and objects is also potentially a positive aspect in this connection, which is an improvement over its predecessors.
- Some symbols are unnecessarily complex (e.g., the components in Components Diagrams). There are historical reasons for this: it makes it easier for people used to the Booch notation to recognize these symbols. For those unfamiliar with the Booch-notation, this is mostly negative.

Participant Language Knowledge Appropriateness

It can be argued that for those who are familiar with the main OO-modeling concepts and main OO modeling-languages, the core of UML should not represent too steep of a learning curve. We should also note that almost all CS and IS degrees now include a course or more where UML is lectured and used. On the other hand , we have noted the complexity of UML under comprehensibility appropriateness. The large number of constructs in UML is due partly to its diverse diagramming techniques (Keng & Cao,

2001). Constructs in use case diagrams are very different from constructs in class diagrams. Class diagrams are also very different from activity diagrams or Statecharts. This diversity causes problems. First, there are more constructs to learn. Second, the knowledge and experience gained in using one diagramming technique cannot be transferred to another diagramming technique in UML. Sometimes, as indicated above, one concept can have different semantics in different diagrams. This can be very confusing for a novice user.

Technical Actor Interpretation Appropriateness

The UML-syntax is rigorously defined, and the language is described through a meta-model made in the structural model of UML with accompanying OCL rules and natural language descriptions of the semantics. Using UML to model UML means that some of the definitions are circular, and this leaves UML (formally speaking) undefined. This would be unproblematic if most practitioners already understood the meaning of the concepts (classes, inheritance, and associations) that are involved. To illustrate that this can be problematic, we can point to how the concept "inheritance" is used in three different ways in the literature (Taivalsaari, 1996). UML supports one of these. There are significant improvements in the meta-model of UML (version 1.4) compared with the first version of the language, although it falls short of a strict meta-modeling approach (Kobryn, 1999). UML (version 1.4) has neither a formal mathematical nor an operational semantics, and there isn't any support for the generation of design models from analysis models or implementation models from design models. OCL also offers the potential for some of the analysis and consistency checking that a formally-defined mathematical semantics would provide. However, it is unclear what tool support will be developed. Other groups have proposed extending Z to provide a formal semantics to UML (Evans, 1998). A formal (i.e., operational) action language would also be useful for supporting a wider repertoire of modeling techniques (Mellor, Tockey, Arthaud, & LeBlanc, 1998).

Quality of the UML Language Model

As indicated above, we base quality of the UML language model on the standard document from OMG (OMG, 2001). This is a textual document with inline, static models. As indicated in the preface of the document, the audience of the document is OMG, standards' organizations, book authors, trainers, and tool builders rather than modelers, who are referred to reference manuals (e.g., Booch, 1999). The relevant parts of the documents (in particular part 2 - UML Semantics and part 3 - UML Notation Guide) are several hundred pages long, therefore, only some highlights of the evaluation are presented here.

Physical Quality

OMG's specification of UML (version 1.4) is primarily externalized as a several hundred-page document that includes example models and a meta-model in UML. It is available in PDF format for anyone visiting the OMG Web site, thus is not easily available for update if there is a need to develop extensions.

Empirical Quality

As the model is not available in, e.g., Microsoft® Word, we have not conducted a detailed evaluation of the readability of the text. This seems to be reasonably good when looking at text samples. The meta-models and example models also seem to be of good empirical quality from a graph aesthetics point of view.

Syntactic Quality

Both the semantics chapter and the notation guide have detailed structuring and typographic guidelines that are largely followed. The text is written in correct American English. Model examples and meta-models appear to be according to the UML syntax.

Semantic Quality

The description of the notation and semantics is fairly complete. However, there are several inconsistencies in the language, due partly to the inheritance of sometimes meaningless (or at least undefined) properties resulting from how the meta-model was made. As examples, a constraint is a model element that constraints other model elements (potentially including a constraint), and any model element (including a constraint) might have a state model. Circularities in the definitions are also found (Castellani, 1999).

Pragmatic Quality

The pragmatic quality of the model is somewhat poor, as in order to understand the meaning of a given concept, three to four different places have to be looked at. This is cumbersome to work with in a flat text, when there are limited direct references. Some help is provided through the consistent structuring, the index, table of contents, and glossary. Much additional support could be provided if the language model was available, e.g., in a hypertext structure, or linked to a modeling tool.

Social Quality

The model is developed using the OMG-standardization process. The membership roster of OMG, about 800 strong, includes virtually every large company in the computer industry as well as hundreds of smaller companies. Most of the companies that shape enterprise and Internet computing today are represented on OMG's board of directors.

Any company may join OMG and participate in the process of setting standards. The one-company/one-vote policy ensures that every company has an effective voice in the process. This also makes it possible to achieve good backing of the standards that have been developed using the process.

Organizational Quality

The goals of the language and language model are described in the introductory chapters, where these goals are also partly linked to specific concepts in the language. It is difficult, however, to track all of the different parts of the modeling language back to the goals. This would be possible only if a more hypertext or model-oriented way of representing the language model was chosen.

CONCLUSION AND FURTHER WORK

Many improvements can be found in UML as compared to its predecessors. Due to its strong support, UML is probably the best general modeling language to adopt as a basis for object-oriented development if not another language with good support tools is being used in a satisfactory way. Another positive aspect of UML, when compared to early work on OOA/OOD, is the inclusion of use-cases (Hitz & Kappel, 1998). Thanks to the inclusion of use-cases, the first step in object-oriented development does *not* encompass finding objects in the problem domain, but rather it encompasses the identification of the system functionality as required by the users. Most of the incidental problems, such as inconsistencies in the language descriptions found in earlier versions of UML, seem to be addressed in UML (version 1.4), but there are still major concerns:

A major lesson learned after the introduction of CASE tools, based on structured approaches, can be summarized by "No methodology – no hope" (Parkinson, 1990). This is a major point also made by OVUM (1998). Even if it has not been possible to agree on a standard process, process guidelines need to be outlined and included – even if the best that can be done is to describe a number of alternatives. This step would have helped users to understand UML. Rational Unified Process (RUP) is looked upon by many as a candidate for such a methodology, although is also highly criticized by some (Hesse, 2001). Particularly problematic for RUP is the logical/physical confusion within the UML-definition. As discussed by Davis (1995), there are fundamental differences between the models as it relates to analysis, design, and requirements specification. Our investigation has also illustrated that while there is a perceived need to extend the expressiveness and formality of the language, the language has several weaknesses regarding comprehensibility appropriateness. Additionally, it is already looked upon as difficult to comprehend, and having a steep learning curve (France & Rumpe, 1999). It has been suggested that a successful response to these challenges will require that the OMG adopt a sculpting approach (where "less is more"), rather than a mudpacking approach. This leaves an open question as to what should be kept in the core of UML, what should be kept as part of internally consistent, but separate profiles, or what should be kept in standard model libraries. In connection to the work on UML (version 2.0), several proposals are competing, and it is still early to judge what the final result will be (results will be probably be available in early 2003). A review of the 800-page proposals of the consortium, including Rational Rose, for a new UML infrastructure and superstructure, offer little hope that the next version of UML will be particularly easier to learn and use, especially because some have a strong need for backward consistency.

In our opinion, the main strength of UML is currently its use in the creation of design models for traditional object-oriented systems. This domain (with the extension and necessary elaboration of use cases or other means of expressing functionality in order to say something sensible about system requirements) should probably define the scope for the core language. Profiles should then be developed just as rigorously for extensions using a full meta-modeling approach, and tools should enable the use of those extra profiles that are deemed necessary for the modeling activity at hand, in addition to situated meta-modeling.

This work will be followed up and updated as new versions of UML and tools supporting modeling with UML are made available. In the future, we will also look at how different UML-based methodologies help in addressing the problematic areas still found in UML.

REFERENCES

Aagedal, J. Ø. & Ecklund, E. F. (2002). Modeling QoS: Towards a UML profile. In J.-M. Jézéquel, H. Hussman & S. Cook (Eds.), UML 2002 - The Unified Modeling Language, 5ᵗʰ International Conference, Dresden Germany, September/October. Springer Verlag LNCS 2460.

André, C., Peraldi-Frati, M-A. & Rigault, J-R. (2002). Integrating the synchronous paradigm into UML: Application to control-dominated systems. In J.-M. Jézéquel, H. Hussman & S. Cook (Eds.), UML 2002 - The Unified Modeling Language, 5ᵗʰ International Conference, Dresden Germany, September/October. Springer Verlag LNCS 2460.

Arnesen, S. & Krogstie, J. (2002). Assessing enterprise modeling languages using a generic quality framework, Proceedings of EMMSAD '02. Toronto, Canada.

Atkinson, C., Kühne, T. & Henderson-Sellers, B. (2002). Stereotypical encounters of the third kind. In J.-M. Jézéquel, H. Hussman & S. Cook (Eds.), UML 2002 - The Unified Modeling Language, 5ᵗʰ International Conference, Dresden Germany, September/ October. Springer Verlag LNCS 2460.

Barbier, F., Henderson-Sellers, B, Opdahl, A. L. & Gogolla, M. (2001). The whole-part relationship in the Unified Modeling Language: A new approach. In K. Siau & T. Halpin (Eds.), Unified Modeling Language: System Analysis, Design and Development Issues. Hershey, PA: Idea Group Publishing.

Baumeister, H., Koch, N., & Mandel, L. (1999). Towards a UML extension for hypermedia design. In R. France & B. Rumpe (Eds.), UML '99 – The Unified Modeling Language – Beyond the Standard. Springer Verlag, pp. 614-629.

Bergner, K., Rausch, A., & Sihling, M. (1998). Critical look upon UML 1.0. In M. Schader & A. Korthaus (Eds.), The Unified Modeling Language – Technical Aspects and Applications. Physica-Verlag: Heidelberg.

Bézivin, J. & Muller, P-A (Eds.) (1998). UML'98- Beyond the notation. June 3-4, Mulhouse, France: Springer-Verlag.

Booch, G., Rumbaugh, J. & Jacobson, I (1999). The Unified Modeling Language: User Guide. Addison-Wesley.

Carlsen, S., Krogstie, J., Sølvberg, A., & Lindland, O.I. (1997). Evaluating flexible workflow systems. In J. F. Nunamaker, & R. H. Sprague (Eds.), Proceedings of the Thirtieth Annual Hawaii International Conference on System Sciences (HICCS'97). Volume II Information Systems- Collaboration Systems and Technology, January (pp. 230-239).

Castellani, X. (1999). Overview of models defined with charts of concepts. In E. Falkenberg, K. Lyytinen, & A. Verrijn-Stuart (Eds.), Proceedings of the IFIP8.1 working conference on Information Systems Concepts (ISCO4); An Integrated Discipline Emerging, September 20-22, Leiden: The Netherlands (pp. 235-256).

Davis, A. (1995). Object-oriented requirements to object-oriented design: An easy transition? Journal of Systems and Software 30(1/2), July/August (pp. 151-159).

Embley, D. W., Jackson, R. B., & Woodfield, S. N. (1995). OO system analysis: Is it or isn't it? IEEE Software 12 (3), July (pp. 19-33).

Evans, A., France, R., Lano, K., & Rumpe, B.(1998). Developing the UML as a formal modeling language. In J. Bézivin & P.-A. Muller (Eds.), UML '98- Beyond the Notation. June 3-4, Mulhouse, France: Springer-Verlag, pp. 346-348.

Flake, S. & Mueller, W. (2002). A UML profile for real-time constraints with the OCL. In J.-M. Jézéquel, H. Hussman & S. Cook (Eds.), UML 2002 - The Unified Modeling Language, *5th International Conference, Dresden Germany, September/October.* Springer Verlag LNCS 2460.

France, R. & Rumpe, B. (Eds.) (1999). *UML '99 – The Unified Modeling Language – Beyond the Standard.* Springer Verlag.

Génova, G. Llorens, J. & Quintana, V. (2002). Digging into use case relationships. In J.-M. Jézéquel, H. Hussman & S. Cook (Eds.), UML 2002 - The Unified Modeling Language, *5th International Conference, Dresden Germany, September/October.* Springer Verlag LNCS 2460.

Goodman, N. (1976). Languages of art: An approach to a theory of symbols. Hackett: Indianapolis.

Halpin, T. (2001). Supplementing UML with concepts from ORM. In K. Siau & T. Halpin (Eds.), *Unified Modeling Language: System Analysis, Design and Development Issues.* Hershey, PA: Idea Group Publishing.

Hennicker, R. & Koch, N. (2001). Systematic design of Web applications with UML. In K. Siau & T. Halpin (Eds.), *Unified Modeling Language: System Analysis, Design and Development Issues.* Hershey, PA: Idea Group Publishing.

Hesse, W. (2001). RUP: A process model for working with UML. In K. Siau & T. Halpin (Eds.), *Unified Modeling Language: System Analysis, Design and Development Issues.* Hershey, PA: Idea Group Publishing.

Hilliard, R. (1999). Using the UML for architectural description. In R. France & B. Rumpe (Eds.), *UML '99 – The Unified Modeling Language – Beyond the Standard.* Springer Verlag, pp. 32-48.

Hitz, M. & Kappel, G. (1998). Developing with UML – Some pitfalls and workarounds. In J. Bézivin & P.-A. Muller (Eds.), *UML '98- Beyond the Notation.* June 3-4, Mulhouse, France: Springer-Verlag, pp. 9-20.

Hommes, B-J. & van Reijswoud, V. (1999). The quality of business process modeling techniques. In E. Falkenberg, K. Lyytinen, & A. Verrijn-Stuart (Eds.), *Proceedings of the IFIP8.1 working conference on Information Systems Concepts (ISCO4); An Integrated Discipline Emerging, September 20-22,* Leiden: The Netherlands (pp. 117-126).

Høydalsvik, G. M. & Sindre, G. (1993). On the purpose of object-oriented analysis. In A. Paepcke (Ed.), *Proceedings of the Conference on Object-Oriented Programming Systems, Languages, and Applications (OOPSLA'93), September* (pp. 240-255), ACM Press.

Iivari, J. (1995). Object-orientation as structural, functional, and behavioral modeling: A comparison of six methods for object-oriented analysis. *Information and Software Technology 37 (3)* (pp. 155-163).

Jézéquel, J.-M., Hussmann, H. & Cook, S. (2002). UML 2002 - The Unified Modeling Language, *5th International Conference, Dresden Germany, September/October.* Springer Verlag LNCS 2460.

Kobryn, C. (1999). UML 2001. A standardization odyssey. *Communication of the ACM 42 (10), October* (pp. 29-37).

Kovacevic, S.(1998). UML and user interface modeling. In J. Bézivin & P.-A. Muller (Eds.), *UML '98- Beyond the Notation.* June 3-4, Mulhouse, France: Springer-Verlag, pp. 253-266.

Klein, C. (2001). Extension of the Unified Modeling Language for mobile agents. In K. Siau & T. Halpin (Eds.), *Unified Modeling Language: System Analysis, Design and Development Issues*. Hershey, PA: Idea Group Publishing.

Kosiuczenko, P. (2002). Sequence diagrams for mobility. *Workshop Proceedings ER'2002*, Tampere, Finland: Springer-Verlag.

Krogstie, J. (1999). Using quality function deployment in software requirements specification. In A. L. Opdahl, K. Pohl, & E. Dubois (Eds.), *Proceedings of the Fifth International Workshop on Requirements Engineering: Foundations for Software Quality (REFSQ'99), June 14-15* Heidelberg, Germany (pp. 171-185).

Krogstie, J. (2001a). A semiotic approach to quality in requirements specifications. *In Proceedings of IFIP 8.1. Working Conference on Organizational Semiotics, Montreal, Canada, July 2001* (pp. 23-25).

Krogstie, J. (2001b). Using a semiotic framework to evaluate UML for the development of models of high quality. In K. Siau & T. Halpin (Eds.), *Unified Modeling Language: System Analysis, Design and Development Issues*. Hershey, PA: Idea Group Publishing.

Krogstie, J. & Sølvberg, A. (2000). Information systems engineering : Conceptual modeling in a quality perspective. *Draft of Book, Information Systems Groups, NTNU*, Trondheim, Norway.

Krogstie, J., Lindland, O.I., & Sindre, G. (1995). Defining quality aspects for conceptual models. In E. D. Falkenberg, W. Hesse, & A. Olive (Eds.). *Proceedings of the IFIP8.1 working conference on Information Systems Concepts (ISCO3); Towards a consolidation of views, March 28-30*, Marburg, Germany (pp. 216-231).

Lauesen, S. (1998). Real-life object-oriented systems. *IEEE Software 15(2)* (pp. 76-83).

Lodderstedt, T., Basin, D. & Doser, J. (2002). Secure UML: A UML-based modeling language for model-driven security. In J.-M. Jézéquel, H. Hussman & S. Cook (Eds.), UML 2002 - The Unified Modeling Language, *5th International Conference, Dresden Germany, September/October*. Springer Verlag LNCS 2460.

Mellor, S. J., Tockey, S. R., Arthaud, P., & LeBlanc, P. (1998). An action language for UML. In J. Bézivin & P.-A. Muller (Eds.), *UML '98- Beyond the Notation*. June 3-4, Mulhouse, France: Springer-Verlag, pp. 307-318.

Morris, S. & Spanoudakis, G. (2001). UML: An evaluation of the visual syntax of the language. *HICSS 34*.

Mylopoulos, J., Chung, L., & Tu, E. (1999). From object-oriented to goal-oriented requirements analysis. *Communications of the ACM. 42 (1), January* (pp. 31-37).

OMG (2001). Unified Modeling Language v 1.4. OMG Web site on the World Wide Web: http://www.omg.org

Opdahl, A., Henderson-Sellers, B., & Barbier, F. (1999). An ontological evaluation of the OML metamodel. In E. Falkenberg, K. Lyytinen, & A. Verrijn-Stuart (Eds.), *Proceedings of the IFIP8.1 working conference on Information Systems Concepts (ISCO4); An Integrated Discipline Emerging, September 20-22 , Leiden* (pp. 217-232). The Netherlands.

Ovum (1998). Ovum evaluates: CASE products. Guide to UML.

Østbø, M. (2000). Anvendelse av UML til dokumentering av generiske systemer (In Norwegian). Unpublished *Master Thesis, 20 Juni*. Høgskolen i Stavanger, Norway.

Parkinson, J. (1990). Making CASE work. In K. Spurr and P. Layzell (Eds.) *CASE on Trial* (pp. 213-242). John Wiley & Sons.

Pllana, S. & Fahringer, T. (2002). On customizing the UML for modeling performance-oriented applications. In J.-M. Jézéquel, H. Hussman & S. Cook (Eds.), *UML 2002 - The Unified Modeling Language, 5th International Conference, Dresden Germany, September/October*. Springer Verlag LNCS 2460.

Prasse, M. (1998). Evaluation of object-oriented modeling languages. A comparison between OML and UML. In M. Schader, & A. Korthaus (Eds.). *The unified modeling language – Technical aspects and applications* (pp. 58-78). Physica-Verlag: Heidelberg.

Rossi, M. & Brinkkemper, S. (1994). Complexity metrics for system development methods and techniques. *Information Systems 21 (2)* (pp. 209-227).

Siau, K. & Cao, Q. (2001). Unified Modeling Language (UML) - A complexity analysis. *Journal of Database Management, Jan-Mar 2001*.

Siau, K. & Halpin, T. (2001). *Unified Modeling Language: System Analysis, Design and Development Issues*. Hershey, PA: Idea Group Publishing.

Stamper, R. K. (1998). Organizational semiotics. In J. Minger & F. Stowell (Eds.), *Information Systems: An Emerging Discipline?* (pp. 267-283). McGraw-Hill.

Taivalsaari, A. (1996). On the notion of inheritance. *ACM Computing Survey 28 (3) September* (pp. 438-479).

Wand, Y. & Weber, R. (1993). On the ontological expressiveness of information systems analysis and design grammars. *Journal of Information Systems 3(4)* (pp. 217-237).

Wieringa, R. (1998). A Survey of structured and object-oriented software specification methods and techniques. *ACM Computing Survey 30 (4) December* (pp. 459-527).

Chapter II

A Generic Framework for Defining Domain-Specific Models

Arnor Solberg
SINTEF Telecom and Informatics, Norway

Jon Oldevik
SINTEF Telecom and Informatics, Norway

Audun Jensvoll
EDBTelesciences, Norway

ABSTRACT

How do you tailor a general-purpose system development methodology to appropriately fit the specific needs of your company and the actual domain or product-family you are working with? Moreover, how do you alter a general-purpose methodology to utilize the domain knowledge possessed by your company? This chapter describes a generic framework for tailoring general-purpose, model-based methodologies in order to deliver domain-specific models.

INTRODUCTION

As a result of the widespread popularity of UML, many companies have invested in introducing a UML-based methodology. There are many general-purpose, UML-based methodologies on the market today. Among the most popular are UP(Jacobson, 1999), RUP (Rational, 1996), Catalysis (D'Souza, 1998), Select perspective (Allen, 1998), and KOBRA (Atkinson, 2000). Typically, these general-purpose software system development methodologies do not immediately fulfil a company's need. That is why many consultants, researchers, and others are in the business of helping companies to introduce these methodologies as well as to customize general-purpose methodologies as appropriate for the actual company and its purpose. A common way of customizing a general-purpose methodology is by removing, adding, and/or merging defined tasks, phases, roles, and models/artifacts of the methodology. The customization is typically tuned based on different criteria such as domain, kind of customers, market (e.g., in-house or off-the-shelf), quality demands, size of the company, and size of the software development teams. Although introduction of a general-purpose methodology typically requires a customization effort, there does not seem to be any standard and formalized way of customizing. The aim of the customization is typically to get a methodology that fits the purpose, fits the company, and fits the people who are going to use it and make the software development efficient. A key to achieving this is to get the methodology to support a process that delivers the wanted artifacts/models (including specifications, documentation, executable increments, and the final products) comprising the right quality. As a result, how should you, in a standard and formalized way, customize a general-purpose methodology to produce domain-specific artifacts/models?

In our research group at SINTEF[1], we have for some time worked with customizing methodologies to satisfy specific needs. Customization has been accomplished by utilizing experience attained through the usage of a set of different OO-based methodologies, such as RUP (Rational, 1996), UP (Jacobson, 1999), OOram (Reenskaug, 1996), Select Perspective (Allen, 1998), Catalysis (D'Souza, 1998) and Open Process (Graham, 1997), as well as self-developed methodologies. This has been combined with general methodology expertise and experience as input to a collaborative process with superusers (users equal developers who will use the methodology). By massaging this input using an iterative and incremental process, we have analysed the company's need, existing methodology (or practice) used by the company, company's culture, particularities of the domain, customers, market etc., to output a tailored methodology. Some results of this work have been the Business Object Methodology (BOM) (Solberg, 1999) and the Magma methodology handbook (Hallsteinsen, 2000). Recently we have been working with Telenor[2] and EDB4Tel[3] with a methodology called TeMOD (Solberg, 2001). This methodology is now in widespread use within the Telenor group. What we discovered during our work with developing TeMOD for Telenor was that even if we gained substantial benefits from tailoring general-purpose methodologies to the needs of the company, the company itself is quite diverse. Thereby, a need was expressed for more tailoring of TeMOD to fit the purpose of different domains and product families within the Telenor group. A main request was to obtain a methodology that was tailored to utilize existing domain knowledge. However, one of the goals of making TeMOD was to use a common methodology throughout the company to achieve a common way of developing and specifying systems. Therefore, it was clear that we didn't want to end up with a set of proprietary, special-purpose methodologies (i.e., one for each domain and system development group). *Our challenge became keeping TeMOD as the common methodology for the company, producing specifications in a standard way, and simultaneously getting TeMOD to support specific needs and utilize the existing domain knowledge.*

The most popular general-purpose, UML-based software engineering methodologies have both diversities and commonalties. One frequent commonality is that they are model-driven. A model-driven methodology signifies that the methodology prescribes a set of models to be produced during the system development process. Model-driven methodologies have gained increasing popularity, particularly even more so after the MDA (OMG, 2001) initiative was launched. TeMOD is indeed a model-driven methodology. Our approach to the challenge described above, was to identify a generic framework that provided utilities for tailoring model-driven methodologies in general, in order to utilize the domain knowledge possessed by the company and to produce domain-specific models. Using the framework, the tailoring will only affect the expression of the models that are prescribed by the general-purpose methodology.

FRAMEWORK DESCRIPTION

By applying the tailoring framework, a domain-specific, reference model is produced. The reference model describes the extensions of the actual, general-purpose methodology made for a specific domain. It consists of:

- UML profiles.
- Existing (reusable) models.
- Patterns.

The set of UML profiles, existing models, and patterns defined in a reference model are developed, structured, and aligned according to the general-purpose software engineering methodology chosen. UML profiles are used for defining domain concepts and reference architecture, existing models are prepared for reuse, and patterns are used to describe standard solutions for recurring problems within the domain. Thus, tailoring a software engineering methodology using the framework, constitutes a leveraging of the methodology in an environment of domain concepts, defined reference architecture, existing models, and patterns. The profiles are the most stable asset as they define the overall, reusable concepts within the domain. The existing models and patterns are typically changing; but, presumably they constitute a valuable and growing pool of reusable assets.

Figure 1 shows the structure of the framework usage. The tailoring framework defines how to build appropriate UML profiles, patterns, and existing models. It also defines how to use the reference model in correspondence along with the chosen, general-purpose methodology. The domain-specific, reference model is built using the tailoring framework and is structured according to the chosen methodology. The profile maker and pattern modeller are mainly responsible for building the domain-specific, reference model. The system modeller uses the chosen methodology's prescribed models and process, as well as the reference model for the actual domain, to build a concrete model. The system modeller might also feed back the reusable models to be part of the reference model. Those models will then be categorized according to the chosen methodology and become an existing model of the domain-specific, reference model.

Figure 1 indicates use of a general-purpose methodology (xx methodology), which specifies three main models as the outcome of the development process: a business model, an architecture model, and a platform-specific model. The yy reference model (supporting the yy domain or yy product-family) is structured according to the xx methodology and specifies a set of UML profiles, patterns, and existing models in accordance with the model architecture of the xx methodology (i.e., business, architecture, and platform-specific). The concrete zz model consists of a business model, an architecture model, and a platform-specific model produced according to the xx-methodology and the yy reference model.

Figure 1: Example of framework usage

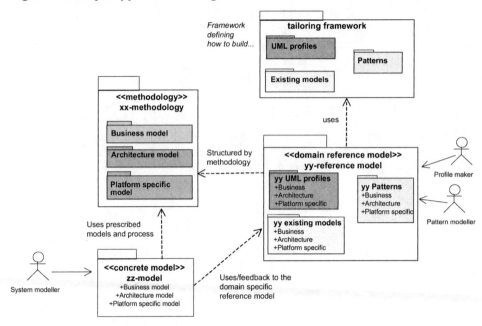

In the example of Figure 1, the domain reference model includes UML profiles, patterns, and existing models at all model levels (i.e., business, architecture and platform-specific). This is not required. However, the tailoring framework requires that the constituents of the domain reference model should be structured according to the model architecture of the chosen, general-purpose methodology. This will ensure commonality and standardization across domain-specific, reference models.

Multiple relationships are not shown in the figure. The tailoring framework is generic and might be used to customize all UML-based, model-driven methodologies (including UP, RUP, Select Perspective, BOM, and TeMOD). In principle, an infinite set of domain reference models supporting a specific domain or product-family might be developed as customization of a particular methodology (thus, a one-to-many relationship between methodology and reference model). There are also one-to-many relationships between a methodology and concrete model as well as between a domain reference model and concrete model.

It is also plausible to use the tailoring framework to extend or specialize a specific domain reference model (i.e., to support a sub-domain).

UML Profiles

The framework prescribes the common techniques for defining UML profiles using the UML-extension mechanisms, stereotypes, and tagged values, all of which extend the concepts that can be worked with in the UML world. Using the UML extension mechanisms imply that the developed models still conform to the UML standard.

The UML profiles of the framework describe the essential concepts from the domain in question. These profiles (i.e., the concepts defined in these profiles,e.g., the stereotypes), can be used as first class modelling concepts when defining concrete models.

Figure 2: Reference architecture, UML profile and usage example

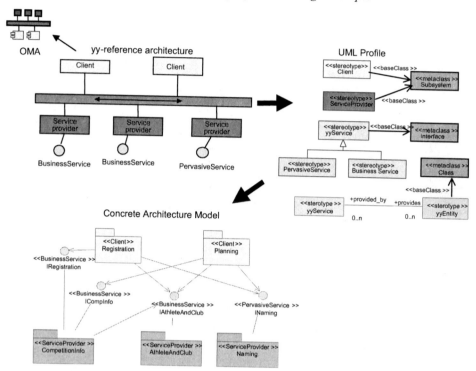

The framework suggests building a profile defining the reference architecture used within the domain or product-family. Such a profile will give essential support when modelling concrete system architectures. Figure 2 shows an example of defining the reference architecture for the yy domain by a UML profile. The architecture model prescribed by the general-purpose methodology is then customised to support the reference architecture of the domain or product-family. The figure shows the yy reference architecture for the yy domain or the yy product-family. This reference-architecture is similar in nature to a standard business-architecture like the OMA[4]. The UML profile extends the UML with the appropriate architectural concepts, which then become employed as first class modelling concepts in the concrete architecture model as shown in Figure 2.

Detailing of the UML profile might be done in a tabular form as shown below (for the yyService and the yyEntity).

Stereotype	Metamodel base	TaggedValues	Description	Constraints
yyService	Interface	Transactional network-accessible	A service access interface; corresponds to a yyservice from the architecture profile.	self.allOppositeAssociationEnd s -> forAll (a | a.type.oclIsTypeOf (yyService) or a.type.oclIsTypeOf (yyEntity))
yyEntity	Class	Persistent	Represents information provided through a yyservice.	self.allOppositeAssociationEnd s -> forAll(a | a.type.oclIsTypeOf(yyEntity))

Similarly, UML profiles might be made for all the model levels defined by the chosen methodology, e.g., for the xx methodology indicated in Figure 1 we might have domain profiles for the business, architecture, and the platform-specific level that define the vocabulary to be used for modelling each of these levels, respectively.

A Profile Example

The profile that follows describes the concepts of a domain of architectures that we called Fleksit. The profile defines the concepts and stereotypes used for all model levels (i.e., business model, architecture model, and platform-specific model). Figure 3 shows the profile packages.

The Fleksit profile is subdivided into what can be called sub-profiles. Sub-profiles typically match sub-domains within the main domain that are natural separations of concerns (and typically may be used individually). We recommend separating concerns according to the method model architecture (in the case of TeMOD, this is business, architecture, and platform-specific).

Figure 3: Profile packages (sub-profiles)

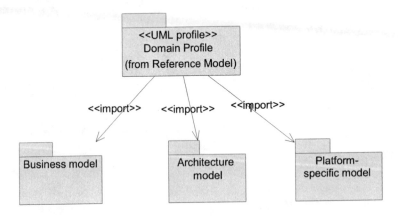

Business Level Profile

The business level metamodel and profile typically describe common business level concepts and the relationships among them. Figure 4 shows a business level profile for the Fleksit reference model. The relationships to the UML metamodel are omitted in Figure 4 for readability. Instead, these are described in a separate diagram as shown in Figure 5.

The metamodel description "business model package" describes some concepts that are important when describing a Fleksit business case. The *customer* establishes a *service contract* with a *service owner* for usage of a *service*. The service contract may be related to a higher-level *business agreement*. A service contract is always maintained by a *maintainer*, and the maintenance responsibilities are defined in a *service level agreement (SLA)*.

The profile for the business model package is described in Figure 5, which relates each of the business concepts to its respective UML metamodel base.

Figure 4: Metamodel for the business model package

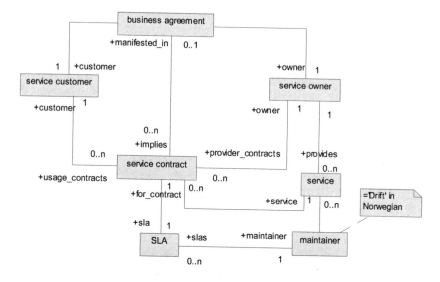

Figure 5: Business model profile

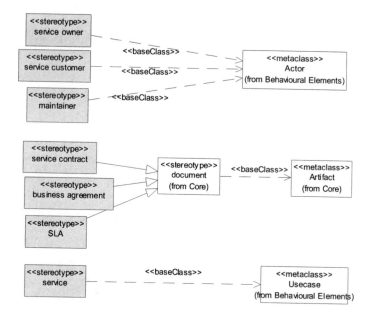

The tabular specification of the business model stereotypes is described on the next page. It details each concept in terms of textual descriptions, constraints, and tagged values.

Stereotype	Metamodel Base	Tagged Values	Description	Constraints
Service owner	Actor		The legal owner of a Fleksit service.	
Service customer	Actor		The legal user/buyer of a Fleksit service.	
Maintainer	Actor		The legal authority for maintenance, installation, etc., of a service.	
Service contract	Document		The contract established between a service owner and a service customer.	
Business agreement	Document		The high-level business agreement between the business parties.	
SLA	Document		The service level agreement.	
Service	Use Case		The service in question.	

Architecture Level Profile

The architecture level contains the concepts service provider, service user, Fleksit service, Fleksit basis service, and Fleksit business service, as depicted in Figure 6. A service provider represents a component that offers a set of Fleksit services. A service user is a client of a service provider (i.e., uses one or more of its Fleksit services ,which are interfaces).

Figure 6: Architecture package metamodel

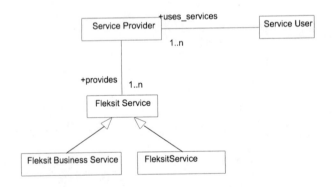

Stereotype specifications for the architecture model are shown below.

Stereotype	Metamodel Base	TaggedValues	Description	Constraints
Service provider	Subsystem		The component that provides a service.	
Service user	Subsystem		The component that uses a service.	
Fleksit service	Interface		A Fleksit service interface (abstract).	
Fleksit basis service	Fleksit service		A Fleksit basis service, e.g., naming service	
Fleksit business service	Fleksit service		A Fleksit business service, e.g., customer service.	

Figure 7: Architecture package profile

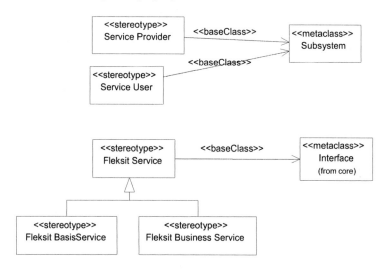

Figure 8: Architectural services and entities

The stereotypes for the architecture package are depicted in Figure 7. Service provider and service user are stereotypes of the UML subsystem. Fleksit service (and its subtypes) are stereotypes of the UML interface.

The profile defines the reference architecture of the Fleksit platform. Part of the architecture includes the component interfaces, identified in this reference architecture as a Fleksit service and Fleksit entity (aka. entity). A Fleksit service represents the interface of an architecture component. Each service provides a set of entities, which represent the information flowing though the interface. Figure 8 shows the metamodel concepts.

Figure 9 shows the model profile for services and entities and its base class relation. A Fleksit service is stereotyped as an interface. A Fleksit entity is stereotyped as a class.

Figure 9: Interface model package profile

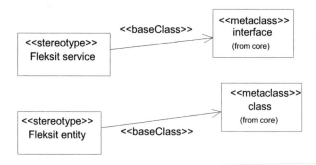

The detailed specifications for services and entities are shown in the table below.

Stereotype	Metamodel base	Tagged Values	Description	Constraints
Fleksit service interface	Interface		A service access interface; corresponds to a Fleksit service from the architecture profile.	self.allOppositeAssociationE nds -> forAll (a | a.type.oclIsTypeOf (Fleksit service) or a.type.oclIsTypeOf (Fleksti entity))
Fleksit entity	Class		Represents information flowing in a service.	self.allOppositeAssociationE nds -> forAll(a | a.type.oclIsTypeOf(Entity))

Figure 10: Profile (stereotype) usage

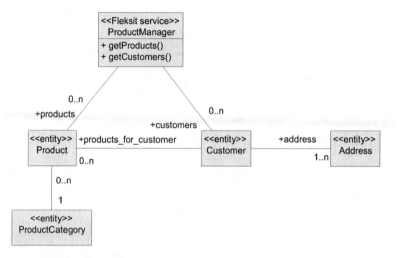

Figure 10 illustrates the use of the profile in a concrete model. The model shows a <<Fleksit service>> named "Product Manager" that manages a set of "Product" and "Customer" <<entities>>.

An example of a platform-specific profile is the standardized UML profile for EJB. This will not be shown here, but its specification can be found at Java Community Process.

Patterns

Patterns represent a special kind of existing model that describes a recurring problem and suggest a general solution to that problem. The tailoring framework is used to define patterns and categorize them according the actual model architecture of the chosen methodology. For the xx methodology in Figure 1, there might be business model patterns, architecture model patterns, and platform-specific model patterns. A pattern is employed by instantiating it (as a template) into a concrete model. The concrete model defines who or what is fulfilling the responsibilities that are defined by the roles in the pattern.

The tailoring framework includes a framework for pattern definition and use. This pattern framework includes some special notation (defined in an UML profile) and a template for pattern description.

The pattern structure technique of UML collaboration is used as a basis to define the pattern. The pattern structure technique is used for viewing the collaboration as a single entity from the outside. The collaboration details are further defined using a UML activity diagram or UML sequence diagram. A simple example describing a pattern for a naming service and the usage of the pattern is shown in Figure 11.

A UML collaboration describes the collaboration of roles. A role is a placeholder for a set of objects that can fulfil the responsibilities of that role. Roles can be specified in two ways in UML: instance level and specification level. Instance level role collaborations are described in terms of collaboration diagrams with objects, links, and message stimuli. Specification level collaborations are described by "ClassifiersRoles" and "AssociationRoles".

UML has defined a naming convention denoting roles, which is a simple way to indicate a role. The general syntax is:

ObjectName '/' ClassifierRoleName ':' ClassifierName [',' ClassifierName]*

This convention can be used on both instance-level and specification-level collaborations.

A collaboration can be considered a set of roles collaborating to fulfill a mission as defined by the unified responsibilities of the roles in the collaboration. Collaborations as a concept have been proven useful in several recognized methodology approaches. Catalysis (D'Souza, 1998) uses collaborations and collaboration refinements for analysis, design, and reuse purposes. OORam (Reensaug, 1996) uses role models to describe collaborations of roles and synthesis to refine and reuse existing models. Lately, the UML community also embraces this view of collaborations.

The top left of Figure 11 show the pattern structure in terms of roles collaborating to fulfil a mission defined by the unified responsibilities of the roles in the collaboration. The naming pattern defined includes three roles: "Name Binder", "Name Client," and "Naming Handler".

A collaboration is modelled as a use case stereotyped with <<collaboration>>. The roles are modelled as UML actors with role names. These roles can be either external or internal to the pattern. External roles are parameterised when the pattern is used. The worker stereotype defined in RUP is used to denote internal actors. The "Naming Handler" is an internal role in the example. The semantics of the collaboration "use case" are the same as a UML collaboration pattern structure (a use case realization).

The sequence diagram at the top right of Figure 11 defines the behavior of the pattern by specifying interactions between roles. Certain conventions for describing behavior in a UML sequence diagram are defined when describing a pattern using the following framework:

- Messages sent to a role are described in the standard UML manner. These may or may not be messages that exist as a part of that role's protocol. Using '//' as prefix for a method denotes that this method is not explicitly located in the interface (i.e., it may be an analysis operation only or a reference to existing behavior pattern).
- Return values are always specified explicitly with a special message-sending convention (i.e., the message name is the value of the return and it is packed in curly braces, e.g., {IObjectType}).

Figure 11: Pattern description and usage

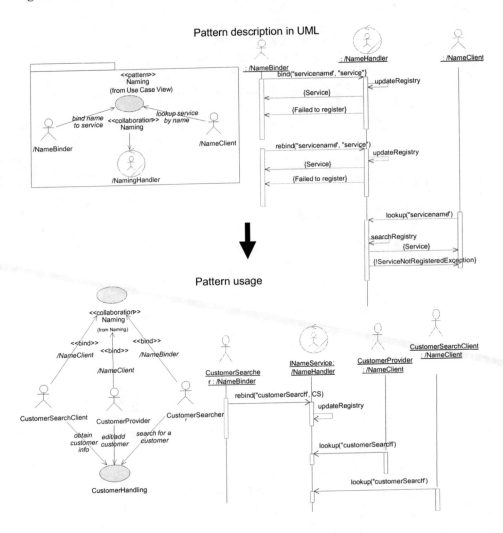

- Errors or exceptions are specified to the extent considered necessary. The convention is the same as for method returns, except that an exclamation mark (!) is used to indicate the nature of an exception (e.g., {!IOException}).

In order to use a pattern, the desired external roles of the pattern must be instantiated. This is done by using a specialized *"binding"* relationship that binds the pattern collaboration source to the roles that instantiate the designated roles of the pattern. The role parameters are bound by the role/name specified on the binding relation (e.g., '/NameClient'). The lower left area of Figure 11 shows how a pattern can be instantiated by binding the roles from the pattern. There are no limits as to how many roles can be bound to other roles or actors.

The sequence diagram at the lower right in Figure 11 shows an example of synthesizing a pattern onto a specific architecture.

The framework provides a template for the pattern description as shown below:

Name
Names the pattern after the solution it proposes. The pattern name can be composed of verb phrases that stress the action implied or can use descriptive nouns.

Problem description
Provides a thumbnail description of the problem that the pattern is solving (text description).

Parameterised structure
Identifies the roles participating in the collaboration and the collaboration symbol (the use case view) (UML use case diagram).

Behavior
Describes the behavioral details of the collaboration (UML activity or sequence diagram).

Example
Provides an example of usage.

Existing Models

Existing models represent already defined, concrete models that can be reused by package importing and referencing. In the same way as used for the UML profiles and patterns, the tailoring framework prescribes that the existing models should be categorized and structured according to the model architecture of the chosen general-purpose methodology. An example of typical usage of an existing model is to reuse an existing interface by inheritance or reference.

An existing model is reused in terms of package import, where the namespace defined by the package becomes available. All public artifacts (use cases, actors, interfaces, classes, etc.) become available to the import package. Alternatively, elements from an existing model can be used simply by scoped naming or UML pathnames (e.g., nnCore::PervasiveServices::NamingService::INaming, which refers to the INaming interface contained in the package structure implied).

The general mechanism for reuse of a either a pattern or standard model is by import of the package that defines the model. Package import makes the model elements defined in that package available by model elements, meaning interfaces, classes, etc. In principle, we can then reference interfaces, etc., from that package.

Package import is straightforward in UML. It is done with the <<import>> dependency stereotype between packages.

CONCLUSIONS

In this paper, we have described a generic framework for customizing general-purpose methodologies for the purpose of providing better support for specific needs within a domain or product-family. An important aspect of our framework has been to ensure utilization of the existing knowledge possessed within the actual domain.

The tailoring framework introduces a need for new roles that are responsible for developing and maintaining reference models. The developers must also learn to use the actual reference model appropriately. Thus, successful introduction of the tailoring framework requires a well-defined process with careful consideration of the relevant risks.

The framework has already been used within the Telenor group and several benefits have been identifies in its application:

- Domain knowledge use: The knowledge possessed within the domain is used to establish and maintain models

- Model reuse: The reference model advocates model-level reuse, which leverages existing models and patterns of best practice to solve recurring problems within the domain. Current tool support is rather immature; therefore, there is still potential for substantial efficiency improvement of model development with sufficient tool support.

- Reuse at the right level: It has been proven that efficient reuse within a product-family community or within a fairly small, scoped domain is easier to gain as opposed to general purpose reuse within widely scoped domains. It is then easier to build a reusable asset library that is accessible by users. The reuse task is also more straightforward (i.e., does not imply a lot of tailoring).

- Consistency in a set of models: Customizing a general-purpose methodology with stereotypes, common domain models, or common patterns will ensure that the models more consistent.

- Standardization: The reference model functions as the "standard" for the specific domain, without contradicting the prescriptions of the general-purpose methodology, which function as the standard for a set of domains (i.e., the enterprise as a whole).

- Additional semantics: The use of stereotypes and pattern descriptions can help make the models more powerful and expressive for readers and modellers.

- Code generation preparation: Code generation can be made more powerful when defining reference models and when the defined UML-profiles, patterns, and existing models are utilized. This might be accomplished by stereotyping a certain kind of interfaces, data types, or other aspects that help the code generator perform sophisticated code generation. This requires a customized code generator, which introduces overhead and administration in some aspects of development. However, it might substantially increase the efficiency of development and also make the system development less error-prone.

Another interesting aspect we experienced is that the tailoring framework might be used as a vehicle for successful introduction of a common, general-purpose methodology within an enterprise. As the customizations make the general-purpose methodology more appropriate for the different domains within the enterprise, it is more acceptable for the different groups of system developers (i.e., users). The users are also typically involved in the customization, which can provide a feeling of ownership to the introduced methodology.

FUTURE WORK

In the future, we plan to work further with the tailoring framework in cooperation with Telenor and EDB4Tel. We will follow up the usage of the framework within those companies and investigate the experiences attained. General aspects of the framework, as well as tool support, will be main focus in the COMBINE (COMBINE, 2002) project and the DAIM project (DAIM, 2002). We will also work further with the framework as part of the CAFÉ (CAFÉ, 2002) project.

REFERENCES

Allen, Paul & Frost, Stuart (1998). Component-based development for enterprise systems, applying the SELECT perspective. *SIGS Book and Multimedia.*

Atkinson, C., Bayer, J., Bunse, C., Kamsties, E., Laitenberger, O., Laqua, R., Muthig, D., Paech, B., Wust, J., & Zettel, J. (2002). Component-based product line engineering with UML. Addison-Wesley.

CAFÉ (2001). From concept to application in system-family engineering, on the World Wide Web: http://www.extra.research.philips.com/euprojects/cafe/.

COMBINE (1999). COMponent-based INteroperable enterprise system development. *ESPRIT V project IST,* 1999-20893.

D'Souza, Desmond & Wills, Alan C. (1998). The catalsysis approach. ISBN 0-201-31012-0, on the World Wide Web: http://www.catalysis.org.

DAIM (2000). Distributed architecture, internet, and multimedia. *A research project sponsored by the Norwegian Research Council.*

Graham, Ian, Henderson-Sellers, Brian & Youness,i Houman (1997). The OPEN process specification. Addison Wesley, ISBN 0-201-33133-0.

Hallsteinsen, Svein O, Solberg, Arnor, Skyllstad, Geir, Neple, Tor & Berre ,Arne Jørgen (2000). The magma software engineering handbook, ver 1.0. Magma - *A technology development project initiated by PROFF; The Software Industry Association of Norway.*

Jacobson, Ivar, Booch, Grady & Rumbaugh, James (1999). The unified software development process.Addison-Wesley.

Java Community Process, *UML profile for EJB,* JSR 26, on the World Wide Web: http://www.jcp.org/jsr/detail/26.jsp.

MAGMA. (2000). On the World Wide Web: http://www.ikt-norge.no, > *Prosjekter* > *MAGMA* (Web pages in Norwegian, but the MAGMA Software Engineering Handbook in English can be downloaded).

OBOE - Open business object environment. *Esprit IV project 23233,* on the World Wide Web: http://www.opengroup.org/public/oboe/Home.html.

OMG (2001). EDOC profile – UML-profile for enterprise distributed object computing, on the World Wide Web: http://www.omg.org/techprocess/meetings/schedule/UML_Profile_for_EDOC_RFP.html.

OMG (2001). Model driven architecture specification, on the World Wide Web: http://www.omg.org/mda Addison Wesley. ISBN 0-201-33133-0.

Rational (1996). The rational development process. ISBN 0134529308.

Reenskaug, Trygve, Wold & Lehne (1996). Working with objects. The OOram software engineering method, Manning: Prentice Hall. ISBN 0-13-452930-8.

Solberg, Arnor & Berre, Arne Jørgen (1999). The business object methodology, deliverable of the OBOE[10] project.

Solberg, Arnor & Oldevik, Jon (2001). Telenor methodology for interface modelling with UML, version 3.02, August 2001.

ENDNOTES

[1]   Independent Norwegian Institute for Applied Research.

[2]   The major Norwegian telecom company (http://www.Telenor.com).

[3]   Company offering administrative software product on the international telecom industry market, owned 50% by Telenor (http://www.EDB4Tel.com).

[4]   Object Management Architecture defined by OMG (Object Management Group, http://www.omg.org).

Chapter III

On the Application of UML to Designing On-line Business Model

Yongtae Park
Seoul National University, Korea

Seonwoo Kim
Seoul National University, Korea

ABSTRACT

The applicability of UML is not restricted to software development, but can be extended to other process modeling tasks. This chapter introduces a framework for designing an inter-firm, on-line business model using UML. The framework comprises such principal elements as value, business players, and relationship among players, with each specified in terms of representative attributes and related notations. The business model is then visualized by value diagram and structure diagram. An illustrative case is employed to show how the proposed framework is applied. By nature, the current research is exploratory; therefore, for the purpose of illustration, it deals with a rather simple business form. As a result, extension and elaboration of the framework may be required to accommodate the complexity and diversity of a real world business.

INTRODUCTION

Since its introduction in 1997, the Unified Modeling Language (UML) has attracted widespread attention and become the standard modeling language for software engineering. In nature, the applicability of UML is not restricted to software development, but can be extended to other process modeling tasks. However, attempting business model design using UML is as yet unexplored. A notable exception to this is due to the seminal work by Eriksson and Penker (2000). They noted the limitation of the conventional documentation method of business modeling and proposed the possibility of, and rationale for, employing object-oriented techniques to describe a business and to suggest a comprehensive guideline for UML-based business modeling.

Their work widened the applicability of UML to business modeling; however, the utility is still limited because the framework is mainly for intra-firm business, rather than for inter-firm business. Furthermore, the possibility of expansion is open to the on-line business model that has gained in recent popularity (Timmers, 1998; Rappa, 1999). In this chapter, we suggest a framework for designing an inter-firm, on-line business model using UML. The framework comprises such principal elements as value, business players, and relationship among players. The characteristics of each element are explained in terms of representative attributes and related notations. The business model of interest is then visualized by two major forms of diagram: value diagram and structure diagram. Finally, we adopt a real case to illustrate how the proposed framework is applied.

CONCEPTUAL ARCHITECTURE OF FRAMEWORK

Broadly, the conceptual architecture of the framework is divided into two stages: definition stage and design stage. In the definition stage, values and players involved in the business are defined and the relationship between the values and players are identified. In the design stage, value and structure diagrams are drawn to describe the overall nature of the business model. Figure 1 exhibits the conceptual architecture of the framework.

Figure 1: Conceptual architecture of framework

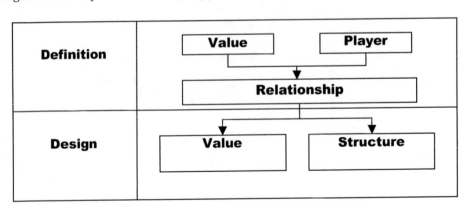

DESIGN OF BUSINESS MODEL
Definition of Major Elements

As explained before, the major elements of a business model are value, player, and relationship. These are also summarized in Table 1. If necessary, other elements may be added to provide a full explanation of the business. In this chapter only a selective set of elements are used as the objective of the current work is to show an illustrative approach for UML-based business modeling rather than give a full account of business model *per se*.

Value

The value of business is operationally defined as either a service or a product. A service is materialized as value because it uses real-time interaction between players. A product is changed to value when it is transferred to customers in a packaged form. In the case of on-line businesses, it is also critical to identify whether a value is in physical or digital form because form determines the method of transaction, transfer, and use. In the context of UML, the value can be considered as an object with a name, attributes, and functions. Hence, as shown in Table 2, we employ the same notation of object as used in UML (D'souza al., 1999; Eriksson and Penker, 2000; Sigfried, 1996).

Player

In general, players in a business model can be described by their name, role, and number of players. The names of players may be specified as either proper nouns or

Table 1: Elements of a business model

Elements	Description
Value	A product or service produced, transferred, and used to achieve a specific goal.
Player	A person or a group who participates in the business process.
Relationship	Relationship between players.

Table 2: Classification and notation of values

Value	Form of value	Notation	Examples
Service	Physical	PS	fedex.com (on-line order-based delivery)
	Digital	DS	etrade.com (on-line financial services provider)
Product	Physical	PP	amazon.com (on-line book seller)
	Digital	DP	MP3.com (on-line contents provider)

Table 3: Typical roles of players

Roles	Description
Main player	A player who designs and constructs business model.
Customer	A player who uses or buys the values provided by main player.
Supplier	A player who provides (part of) values to main player.
Distributor	A player who buys and resells values provided by main player.
Logistics	A player who delivers values from one player to another.
Agent	A player who facilitates the flow of values between players.
Indirect revenue Source	A player who utilizes additional values produced in interaction between other players and provides some revenue to main player.

Figure 2: Notation of player in a business

Name : Number (Single, Multiple, Unspecific)
Roles

sequential numbers. In an on-line business, the role of players can be classified into seven typical ones: supplier, main player, distributor, logistics, customer, indirect revenue source, and agent. A brief description of each role is presented in Table 3. It is not uncommon for only part of the roles to be required to form a business model. The number of players needed to undertake a specific role is also important in the business model. The number of players can be specified as single, multiple, and unspecific. Figure 2 shows the notation of players involved in a business.

Relationship

The relationship between players is defined as the way in which values are transferred. Broadly, there are two ways to transfer values: One is to transfer the ownership of value to buyer or user. The other is merely to grant a right to use without ownership. In an on-line business, how value is transferred (physically or electronically) is also important. Table 4 summarizes typical forms of relationship among players.

Table 4: Relationship between players

Ownership	Transmission	Relationship	Notation
Ownership transfer	Physically	Physical transfer of ownership	⟶
	Electronically	Electronic transfer of ownership	┈┈▶
Without ownership transfer	Physically	Physical use	⟶●
	Electronically	Electronic use	┈┈●

Value Diagram

Once the details of the major elements are determined, the next step is to draw a value diagram of the business model. In a sense, a value diagram is a micro diagram, vis-à-vis the structure diagram, in that it only exhibits the players who are involved in the business in order to obtain the kinds of values. Therefore, it provides basic information on the commercial viability of the business model. The value diagram encompasses values with attributes and functions, players, benefits, and relationships between them. Specifically, it shows how the value provides benefits to participating players. It also delineates the relationships between values and players. The value diagram, in nature, is similar to the use case diagram in UML. Thus, in this chapter, we basically adopt the notation of the use case diagram in UML. However, we revise this to some extent to accommodate specific needs. Figure 3 portrays a typical form of value diagram.

Figure 3: Illustration of value diagram

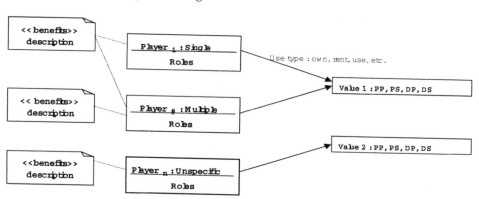

Table 5: Four typical ways of payment

Way of payment	Description	Notation
/product	Revenue is paid per product.	→
/use number	Revenue is paid per number of use.	→
/use time	Revenue is paid per use time.	→
/license	Revenue is paid per license.	→

Figure 4: Illustration of structure diagram

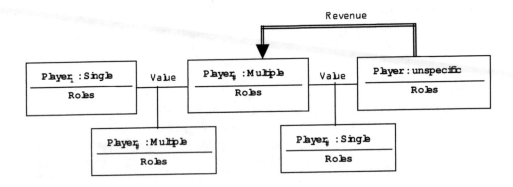

Structure Diagram

The structure diagram depicts the overall structure of the business model. It is a macro diagram, as compared to a value diagram, as it exhibits the overall picture of the business. Therefore, the structure diagram also includes the major components of value diagram but, at the same time, describes the position of individual components, the sequence and direction of the transaction, and the contents of flow in the business. In drawing a structure diagram, the method of payment deserves attention. As summarized in Table 5, we propose four ways of payment. Note that a double line is used to differentiate the revenue flow from the value flow. Figure 4 illustrates a typical form of structure diagram.

ILLUSTRATION OF A CASE

For the purpose of illustration, we have adopted a real world example and explained how the proposed framework works. The on-line company in our example buys physical comic books. The company digitalizes the comic books and sells them to unspecified end-users through the Internet or several portal sites. The company transfers ownership of the contents when it sells books to portal sites. However, when selling to unspecified end-users, the company just grants a right to view the contents without the option to download. The illustration is composed of five steps, which have been presented here as either tables or figures.

Step 1: To Define Value

Value	Form of values	Description
Comics contents	PP, DP	Forms of value change
Payment system	DS	Agent for transaction

Step 2: To Define Players

Player	Number	Role of player
Main player	Single	Main player
Customer	Unspecific	Customer
Comics production	Multiple	Supplier
Portal site	Multiple	Distributor
Credit card co.	Multiple	Agent
Advertiser	Multiple	Indirect revenue source

Step 3: To Define Relationship

Producers physically transfer ownership of the comic book contents to a main player. The main player then changes the form of value and transfers the contents with ownership to portal sites. This player also provides advertisers with advertising pages, who are restricted to electronic use. The credit card company owns the payment system while customers and the main player uses the payment system without transferring ownership.

Step 4: Value Diagram

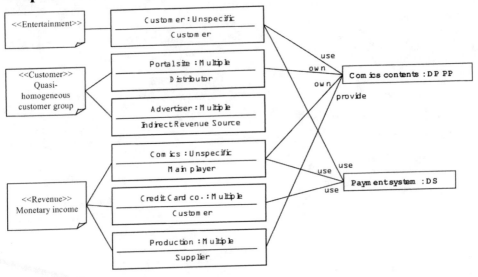

Step 5: Structure Diagram

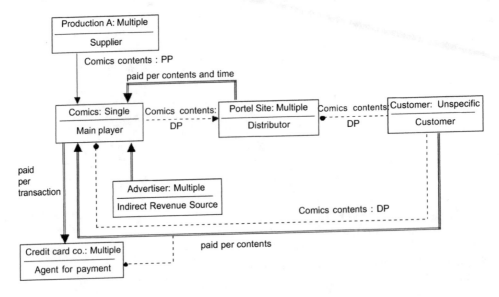

CONCLUSIONS AND FUTURE WORK

In this chapter, we examined the possibility of applying UML to designing an inter-firm, on-line business model. The utility of UML is not restricted to software development and can be extended to many modeling tasks, as long as the characteristics of objects can be specified and the process of modeling can be more or less formally determined. Therefore, it is expected that the proposed framework will be of help in designing complex, on-line businesses and identifying potential problems in advance.

However, the current research is exploratory and for the purpose of illustration, the research deals with a rather simple business form. In reality, more complex and diverse (in terms of the roles of players and relationships between players) may exist. As a result, extension and elaboration of the current research is required in the future. UML *per se* is a static modeling language that lacks dynamic simulation tools. In that regard, one of the promising future research themes is to integrate a UML-based static design module with a simulation-based dynamic experiment module in order to evaluate the commercial viability and technical feasibility of business models.

REFERENCES

D'souza, D. (1999). Objects, components, and frameworks with UML. Massachusetts: Addison Wesley.

Eriksson, H-E. & Penker, M. (2000). Business modeling with UML – Business patterns at work. New York: John Wiley & Sons.

Rappa, M. (1999). Business models on the Web. E-commerce Learning Center @ North Carolina State University, On the World Wide Web: http://ecommerce.ncsu.edu

Sigfried, S. (1996). Understanding object-oriented software engineering. New York: IEEE Press.

Timmers, P. (1998). Business models for electronic markets. Electronic Markets. 8(2). (pp. 3-8).

Chapter IV

Specification of Business Components Using Temporal OCL

Stefan Conrad
University of Düsseldorf, Germany

Klaus Turowski
University of Augsburg, Germany

ABSTRACT

Compositional, plug-and-play-like reuse of black box components requires sophisticated techniques to specify components, especially when combined with third party components that are traded on component markets to individual customer's business application systems. As in established engineering disciplines, like mechanical engineering or electrical engineering, formal documentation of business components that become part of contractual agreements are needed. With this initial problem, we explain the general, layered structure of software contracts for business components and show shortcomings of common specification approaches. Furthermore, we introduce a formal notation for the specification of business components that extends the Object Constraint Language (OCL) and allows for a broader use of the Unified Modeling Language (UML) with respect to the layered structure of software contracts for business components.

INTRODUCTION

Compositional, plug-and-play-like reuse of black box components requires sophisticated techniques to specify components, especially when combined with third party components that are traded on component markets to individual customer's business application systems. As in established engineering disciplines, like mechanical engineering or electrical engineering, formal documentation of business components that become part of *contractual agreements* are needed. With this initial problem, we explain the general, layered structure of software contracts for business components and show shortcomings of common specification approaches. Furthermore, we introduce a formal notation for the specification of business components that extends the Object Constraint Language (OCL) and allows for a broader use of the Unified Modeling Language (UML) with respect to the layered structure of software contracts for business components.

The remainder of the chapter remains as follows. After providing background information in the next section, we discuss the necessity of a multi-level notation standard. Thereafter, we explain how the OCL can be used to specify business components. Using this as a basis, we proceed to the main thrust of our chapter - the temporal extension of OCL. Finally, we present our conclusions and provide an outlook.

SOFTWARE CONTRACTS FOR BUSINESS COMPONENTS

Combining off-the-shelf software components that are offered by different vendors to individual customer's business application systems is a goal that is followed up for a lengthy time. By achieving this goal, advantages of individually-programmed software that is combined with standardized, off-the-shelf software could come together. In this context, we are speaking about *compositional reuse* techniques. Compositional reuse represents special kinds of reuse techniques as *generative* techniques or *code and design scavenging* (Sametinger, 1997, pp. 25-28). The emphasis on compositional reuse stems from our *guiding model,* which is the compositional, plug-and-play-like reuse of black box components that are traded on a component market. In general, a guiding model is an ideal future state that might not be reached completely.

Corresponding with our guiding model, a company that (e.g., needs new software for stock keeping), could buy a suitable software component on the component market and further integrate it into its business application system with little effort. Brown and Wallnau (1996, pp. 11-14) explain the steps that are generally necessary to do so (e.g., technical and semantic adaptation or composition). Expected improvements, which should come along with using software components, concern cost efficiency, quality, productivity, market penetration, market share, performance, interoperability, reliability, or software complexity, cf., e.g., Orfali, Harkey, and Edwards (1996 S. pp. 29-32).

According to Fellner and Turowski (2000, pp. 3-4), the term *component* is defined as follows: A component consists of different (software-) artifacts. It is reusable, self-contained, and marketable; provides services through well-defined interfaces; hides its implementation, and can be deployed in configurations unknown at the time of development. A *business component* is a component that implements a certain set of services out of a given business domain. Refer to Szyperski (1998, pp. 164-168) and Fellner and Turowski (2000) for an in-depth discussion of various other component approaches given in literature.

To use business components according to our guiding model, it is necessary to standardize them as detailed in a discussion on standardizing business components (cf., Turowski, 2000). Furthermore, we must describe the component's interface and behavior in a consistent and unequivocal way. In short, we have to *specify* them. Specification becomes more and more important with respect the to third party composition of business components, as the specification might be the only support available for a composer who combines business components from different vendors for an application system.

Software contracts offer a good solution to meet the special requirements of specifying business components. Software contracts go back to Meyer, who introduced contracts as a concept in the *Eiffel* programming language. He called it *programming by contract* (Meyer, 1988) and later extended it to the concept of *design by contract* (Meyer, 1992). Furthermore, similar concepts are described in Wilkerson and Wirfs-Brock (1989) or Johnson and Wirfs-Brock (1990).

Software contracts are obligations to which a service donator (e.g., a business component) and a service client agree. The service donator guarantees:

- A service it offers (e.g., *calculate balance* or *determine demand*).
- Certain conditions, which have to be met by the service client (e.g., the provision of data necessary to process the service).
- Guaranteed quality performance (e.g., with a predetermined storage demand or with an agreed upon response time).
- The service has certain external characteristics (e.g., the specified interface).

Beugnard, Jézéquel, Plouzeau, and Watkins (1999, pp. 38-40) describes a general model for software contracts for components with four tiers. The authors distinguish between syntactic, behavioral, synchronization, and quality-of-service levels. Business components need to be specified on each level.

Figure 1: Software contract levels

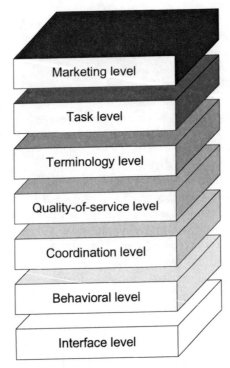

Figure 1 shows contract levels according to Turowski (2002). By (logically) subdividing the synchronization level into inter- and intra-component coordination levels, as an extension to Beugnard et al. (1999), this approach allows for an additional specification of a synchronization demand that exists between different business components. Furthermore, the terminology, task, and marketing level allows for the specification of business related issues.

Basic agreements are concluded at the interface (or syntactic) level. Typical parts of these agreements concern the names of services (offered by a business component); names of public-accessible attributes, variables, or constant values; specialized data types (in common and based upon standardized data types); signatures of services; and declaration of error messages or exception signals. To accomplish this, we use (e.g., programming languages or *Interface Definition Languages* (IDL)) like the IDL that was proposed by the Object Management Group (OMG) (OMG, 2002 S. 3.1-3.74). The resulting agreement guarantees that service client and service donator can communicate with each other. However, emphasis is placed on enabling communication technically. Semantic aspects remain unconsidered.

Agreements at the behavioral level serve as a closer description of a business component's behavior. These agreements enhance the basic agreements of the interface level, which mainly describe the syntax of an interface. Agreements at the interface level do not describe how a given business component acts in general or in borderline cases.

As an example, we could define an invariant condition for a business component "*stock keeping*" at behavioral level, which would say that the reordering quantity for each (stock) account has to be higher than the minimum inventory level. Known approaches to specify behavior are based on approaches to *algebraic specification* of abstract data types, cf., e.g., Ehrig and Mahr (1985). To describe behavior, the specification of an abstract data type is extended by conditions. These conditions describe the abstract data type's behavior in general (as *invariant conditions*) or at specific times (*pre-conditions* or *post-conditions*). In general, conditions are formulated as equations and as the axioms that they become part of through the specification of an abstract data type (Ehrig & Mahr, 1985). The *Object Constraint Language* (OCL) (OMG, 2001, pp. 6.1-6.50) is an example of a widespread notation that specifies facts at the behavioral level. It complements the *Unified Modeling Language* (UML) (OMG, 2001).

Agreements at the *intra-component* coordination (synchronization) level regulate the sequence in which services of a specific business component may be invoked, as well as regulate the synchronization demand between its services. Here, e.g., we may specify that a minimum inventory level has to be set before it is allowed to book on a (stock) account for the first time, or we may specify that it is not allowed to carry through on more than one bookkeeping entry at the same time, for the same account.

At the *inter-component* coordination level are agreements that regulate the sequence in which services of *different* business components may be invoked. Here, e.g., we may define that a certain service, which belongs to a business component *shipping*, and which refers to a certain order, may only be processed after a service belonging to a business component, *sales*. Also, that it refers to the same order and has been processed at any time before. It should be noted that the differentiation between an intra- and inter-component coordination level depends on the identification of business components rather than their granularity. The granularity of a business component depends on the number of services it offers.

Various approaches exist to specify business components at the coordination level. These approaches are based, e.g., on using *process algebras*, *process calculi* (cf., e.g., Hennessy, 1988), or *temporal logics* cf., e.g., Alagar and Periyasamy (1998, pp. 79-131). In addition, (semi-formal) graphical notations are used. These notations are mostly graphical notations used in the context of business process modeling. Besides extended event-driven process chains (eEPC) (Keller, Nüttgens, & Scheer, 1992, pp. 32-35) and approaches that use eEPC as a basis, e.g. (Rittgen, 1999), Petri net based notations are in use, e.g., Jaeschke, Oberweis, and Stucky (1994). In particular, object-oriented software development methods like Rumbaugh, Blaha, Premerlani, Eddy, and Lorensen (1991), Coleman (1993), or Booch (1994) provide such modeling means.

Non-functional characteristics of business components are described as an extension of functional characteristics. Non-functional characteristics are specified at the quality-of-service level. An Example of these characteristics is the distribution of the response time of a service or its availability. For further non-functional requirements and their definition cf., e.g., (Jalote, 1997, pp. 73-158).

In all levels mentioned thus far, the specification of business components uses *technical terms*, which have a domain-specific functional meaning (semantic), e.g., *stock*, *inventory level*, or *account*. Often these terms do not have unequivocal meanings or definitions and hence, have to be specified to guarantee their unequivocal use. The terminology level serves as a central registry for all of these terms and keeps all terms that are useful for the specification and their definitions in a dictionary. In order to achieve a high quality of specification, norm language reconstruction is used to specify the respective issues (Ortner, 1997). The same technique is used to specify issues at the task level. In the task level, we explain what *business tasks* are supported or automatically done through services offered by a business component.

At the marketing level, features of the business component that are important from a *business-organizational* point of view are specified using tables (e.g., legal or contract terms, version, coarse business domain, or vendor contact persons).

NECESSITY OF A MULTI-LEVEL NOTATION STANDARD

Using software contracts of the type explained in section 1 opens a way to a systematic specification of business components. Therefore, software contracts become a foundation for the third party composition of business components, which must conform to our guiding model. In an extreme case, employers of software components must be able to decide based solely on the method of use specification.

Besides arranging the agreements' contents according to contract levels (in the context of systematic specification of business components), it is helpful to use a well-known and well-accepted formal notation, which can be used for more than one contract level. We call a notation *formal* if the syntax and semantics of the notation are unequivocal and consistent. For this reason, formal notations seem to be particularly suited for specifying software contracts, which must have these characteristics for use by third parties.

The OMG IDL, as part of the *Common Object Request Broker Architecture* (CORBA) (OMG, 2002), has gained more and more acceptance as a standardized notation for the interface level. It uses a so-called "*IDL compiler*" to translate the interface's specification into concrete programming languages. UML (together with the OCL) is the additional means (recommended by the OMG) to specify facts that belong to the behavioral level. Furthermore, the UML (together with the OCL) is especially recommended for specifying components, e.g., Allen and Frost (1998) or D'Souza and Wills (1999). However, the OCL is only conditionally suited to specifying facts at the coordination level(s). With this initial problem, we propose a way to extend the OCL with some additional temporal operators to be able to formally specify facts at the coordination level as well.

We point out that some authors tend to criticize the formal specification of (parts of) business application systems. The authors' main arguments reflect the comparably higher effort and decreased, general understandability with formal approaches . As an example illustrating the weaknesses of formal approaches, the authors often discuss the algebraic specifications of abstract data types, cf., e.g., Biethahn, Mucksch, and Ruf (1991, pp. 288-291) and the references cited. These authors also mention the very good separation of the inside versus the outside view as an important advantage of the algebraic specification of abstract data types. This factor has been gaining in importance with respect to the specification of black box components.

Operational and *verbal* specifications are discussed as more practicable alternatives to algebraic specification. For operational specification, specification is done using the declarative capabilities of programming languages (Ferstl & Sinz, 1998, pp. 293-294). By using declarative capabilities, the interface and behavioral levels may be specified (dependent on the programming language chosen). For verbal specification, natural language is used. Due to its inherent fuzziness, natural language is only conditionally suited for specifying business components. For example, natural language may be used in addition to a formal specification or together with specialized methods such as norm language reconstruction (Ortner, 1997) (as we propose to use on terminology and task level).

USING OCL TO SPECIFY BUSINESS SOMPONENTS

In the following, an example is explained in order to show how to use the OCL in specifying business components on the behavioral level. In order to complete the example with respect to the contract levels given in section 1, we first explain what agreements are necessary at the interface level. For our example, we use the OMG IDL as interface definition language (OMG, 2002 S. 3.1-3.74).

Figure 2 shows examples for the specification of the interface of different business components at the interface level. The figure depicts parts of the interfaces of the business components "*OrderProcessing*," "*ProductionPlanning*," and "*ProductionControl*." The business components support business tasks from the area of production planning and control (PPC), cf., e.g., Scheer (1994).

First, the name of the service donator is defined with the keyword "`interface`." This keyword creates a name space, which allows for an unequivocal definition of contained names. `OrderProcessing::PrintInvoice`, for example, indicates

Figure 2: Specification of business components at the interface level

```
interface  OrderProcessing  {
     . . .
     struct  OrderPosition  {
         double   Quantity;
         double   PiecePrice;
         double   Discount;
         . . .
     };

     struct  Order  {
         . . .
         boolean            TechnicallyPracticable;
         boolean            Delivered;
         double             InvoiceAmount;
         double             Discount;
         . . .
         sequence  <OrderPosition>  OrderPositions;
     };
     . . .
     void  AcceptCustomerOrder(in  Order  a);
     void  CancelOrder(in  Order  a);
     void  PrintInvoice(in  Order  a);
     . . .
};

interface  ProductionPlanning  {
     . . .
     ProductionPlan  RoughPlanning(in  Period  p);
     . . .
};

interface  ProductionControl  {
     . . .
     ProductionsPlan  Scheduling(in  Period  p,  in
         ProductionPlan  pp);
     . . .
};
```

that a service "*PrintInvoice*" should be invoked as a part of a business component, "*OrderProcessing.*"

In addition, we need to define data types, structured data types, and exceptions, which we will not explain further in the context of our example.

In Figure 3, we extend our example to specify requirements at behavioral level by using the OCL. The OCL is part of the UML. The OCL was also adopted by the OMG as standardized notation. With standardization, the OCL is the recommended extension of the OMG IDL to specify requirements at the behavioral level.

First, we fix the specification's reference context. The context is underlined. The first condition in Figure 3, e.g., refers to the business component "*OrderProcessing*" as a whole. Conditions appear as pre-conditions (keyword pre), post-conditions (keyword post), or as invariant conditions (no keyword).

Figure 3: Examples for the specification of business components at behavioral level using OCL

```
OrderProcessing
    self.Order->forAll(a:Order  |  a.TechnicallyPracticable  =
    True)

OrderProcessing::PrintInvoice(at:Order)
    pre  :  self.Order->exists(a:Order  |  a  =  at  and
       at.Delivered  =  True)
    post:  at.InvoiceAmount  =  at.OrderPositions-
       >iterate(p:Position;  b:Amount  =  0  |
              b  +  p.Quantity  *  p.PiecePrice  *  (1  -  p.Discount)
          )  *  (1  -  at.Discount)
```

For purposes of our example, order processing encompasses the management of orders. The symbolic term "*Order*" references orders. Thus, the first invariant condition ensures that all orders, which are held by the business component "*OrderProcessing*," are technically practicable.

Other requirements relate to the service "*PrintInvoice*." For this reason, : : restricts the conditions' context(s). In addition, parameters may be enumerated to describe a service's behavior in more detail. Take, for example, the service "*PrintInvoice*." In order to specify this service in more detail, the parameter "*at*" was typed, which is of type "*order*." (The types used in the example correspond to those defined in Figure 2.)

We use a pre-condition for the service "*PrintInvoice*." The pre-condition ensures that an invoice can be printed if, and only if, the corresponding order was delivered prior to print processing. There is also a post-condition that explains in detail how the invoice amount was calculated.

In principle, all such requirements are local to their respective context. The context may be the business component that offers the respective service. We could suppose that, e.g., pre- conditions for services, which are part of a single business component, may relate to services or objects of the same business component. Business components are not isolated, rather, they are collaborative. For that reason, services and properties of other business components are published as interfaces. Thus, all published services and properties of other business components become part of the context of one particular business component. Furthermore, it is possible to refer to other business components while specifying pre, post, and invariant conditions for a particular business component. Thus, characteristics of one particular business component may influence (or restrict) the behavior of another business component(s).

Being able to describe characteristics that have spread to different business components poses questions: In which business components should these character-istics be specified, and is it necessary to specify these characteristics redundantly? These aspects go beyond the concern of our contribution and for this reason we have omitted a detailed discussion of it.

TEMPORAL EXTENSION OF OCL

In the previous section we discussed how OCL could be employed for specifying business components. OCL seems to be an ideal approach for describing properties of business components declarative and independent of specific implementations. Thereby, OCL can be used as an integral part of software contracts. OCL allows for describing the properties of states (which must hold for each single state of the system or component) and for describing pre- and post-conditions of services offered by a business component. By means of pre- and post- conditions, the applicability (or executability) of services can be restricted. Furthermore, the result of a service (i.e., the effect of its execution) can be specified by referring to the state of its invocation (using @pre).

Thus, introducing @pre and @post for explicitly referencing the values of the states, directly before and after a service execution, allows for specifying certain kinds of conditions. In the context of database systems (such conditions are usually called transitional integrity constraints) cf., e.g., Lipeck, Gertz, and Saake (1994). In addition to this comparison with integrity constraints in database systems, OCL, also allows for specifying static integrity constraints (without @pre and @post). In this widely-used classification of integrity constraints, the class of temporal constraints remains, which cannot be described by means of OCL (except in a few cases where it may be possible to translate into transitional constraints). Temporal constraints not only describe state transitions that are triggered by calling services, but also describe complete life spans of objects or large parts of evolution within a business component.

Some restricted kinds of temporal constraints can also be described by means of state charts, which is the part of UML used for modeling behavior of objects) or other models of state machines, which basically correspond to regular expressions. However, certain temporal constraints cannot be represented by state machines at all (e.g., the constraint that after executing a certain service A another service B cannot be invoked unless a service C has been executed). Another state machine might be found to fulfill this constraint; however, it is always a concrete implementation restricting the behavior of the system more than the temporal constraint requires. For our purposes, we want to specify the general properties business components have to meet rather than certain implementations.

Temporal constraints are a means to declaratively describe properties of components at the interface level. The required view from outside on to components is essentially the reason why state machines do not provide an adequate level of description for us. A state machine's *operational* character is inappropriate for that level of specification – especially in comparison to temporal logic's *descriptive* character that allows for a significant reduction of specification effort. Consequently, we focus here on temporal integrity constraints as the means of description.

Within the application area, which was introduced before, the following temporal integrity constraints offer examples:

- A service "*Scheduling*" can only provide a result for a certain period of time if a service "*RoughPlanning*" was already executed for the same period.
- The execution of a service "*PrintInvoice*" for a certain order requires that the exact order be entered using a service "*AcceptCustomerOrder*" and that other orders in between have not been canceled by executing the service "*CancelOrder.*"

Figure 4: State based specification using (linear) temporal logics

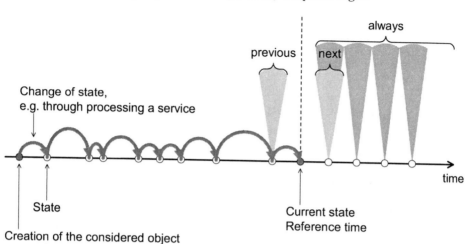

After executing the service "*AcceptCustomerOrder*," we could also require that an invoice be written for that order by means of the service "*PrintInvoice*" or that the order must be eventually canceled by invoking the service "*CancelOrder*."

Extending OCL seems to be a good approach for specifying such properties. The fact that OCL is a standardized notation based on a well-known declarative formalism and with a clear (and formal) semantics, provides the motivation for this. We do not intend to create our own specification formalism for temporal integrity constraints. Therefore, it is reasonable to look for a nominal, but sufficiently expressive, extension of OCL that is consistent with OCL.

The basic possibilities for describing temporal properties are depicted in Figure 4. On the time axis, the different states of an object (which are the subjects of our description) at different instants of time are given. Starting from the current state of the object, different statements can be made about the object. For instance, we can describe properties of the state directly before or after the current one by means of the temporal operator *previous* and *next*, resp. Using the (future tense temporal) operator, *always*, we can state properties of all future states. The current state has been reached by executing all state-changing operations (services in our context) in their temporal order beginning with the initial state of the object (the initial state is usually given when creating the object). The temporal distances between all pairs of consecutive states don't need to be the same. In this way we use only an abstract notion of discrete time when representing the order of changes.

A large number of approaches to describing such temporal properties is based on temporal logics — for a survey see, e.g., Manna and Pnueli (1992) or Emerson (1990). In Lipeck and Saake (1987), a temporal logic for formulating temporal integrity constraints was developed, which has since been adapted and extended for the object-oriented modeling language, TROLL (Jungclaus, Saake, Hartmann, & Sernadas, 1996). The temporal operators by which we extend OCL and for which all semantic foundations can also be found in Lipeck and Saake (1987) are as follows:

Past tense temporal operators:

- `sometime_past` φ
  Starting from the current state, i.e., the state which is currently observed, sometime in the past φ must have been valid (i.e., there is a past state in which φ held).

- `always_past` φ
  Starting from the current state, φ was valid always in the past (i.e., in all past states).

- φ `always_since_last` ψ
  Starting from the last state, in which ψ held for the last time, φ held in all states up to the current one.

- φ `sometime_since_last` ψ
  Since the state in which ψ held for the last time, there was a state (before the current state) in which φ held.

Future tense temporal operators:

- `sometime` φ
  Starting from the current state, there will be (at least) one future state in which φ will be valid.

- `always` φ
  Starting from the current state, φ will hold in all future states.

- φ `until` ψ
  Starting from the current state, φ will hold in all future states until there is a state in which ψ is fulfilled.

- φ `before` ψ
  Starting from the current state, there will be a future state in which φ will be valid before a state will be reached in which ψ will hold.

Besides these past tense and future tense temporal operators, which are always interpreted relative to a current state, we need to designate a special operator for referring to the initial state (of the system or business component):

- initially φ
  In the initial state, φ holds.

By means of this operator, it is possible to specify the initial state of the system (i.e., to provide initial values for some state variables).

Before we consider examples for temporal constraints in our application area using the temporal extension of OCL, the necessity of offering past tense and future tense temporal operators has to be discussed. Taking a purist view, one could claim that one kind of temporal operator (i.e., past tense or future tense) would be sufficient. Although this already is not completely right with regard to expressive power, the main reason for having both kinds of operators is for the methodology. Using each kind of temporal operator in an adequate way essentially improves the readability and thereby, the comprehensibility of specifications. For instance, pre-conditions for services (i.e., constraints restricting the applicability of services) should be formulated only by using past tense temporal operators. It is obvious that the execution of a service must not depend on future states.

By allowing post conditions to include future tense temporal operators, we slightly change or extend the notion of post condition. In the literature, and in particular for object-oriented languages, the notion of post condition usually refers to a property fulfilled by the state yielded by executing a method. A temporal logic formula as post condition also refers to other future states. Nevertheless, from a logical point of view, this property formulated in temporal logic can also be considered a property of that state.

It might be useful for expressing certain properties to explicitly refer to the state immediately before or after the execution of a method. However, we abstain from introducing an additional operator (e.g., *before* or *after*) for that purpose in order to keep our extension of the original OCL as small and clear as possible. Using *@pre* (already offered by the original OCL) within a post condition allows for referring to the state immediately before executing the method. The introduction of *before* and *after* as their own temporal operators would result in no additional expressive power.

A further issue of importance is that the grammar of OCL has to be extended corresponding to the temporal operators we add. Considering the grammar for OCL given in (OMG, 2001, pp. 6.46-6.49) we need only very few minor changes and additions. In detail these are as follows:

*   An additional alternative temporalExpression is introduced into the rule for relationalExpression.

*   For temporalExpression, a rule is added in which temporal expressions are constructed in two different ways: using a unary temporal operator like (always) or a binary one (like until).

*   In two additional rules, the unary and binary temporal operators are defined (unaryTemporalOperator and BinaryTemporalOperator).

The complete extended grammar is given as an appendix.

Obviously, our extension seamlessly fits into the existing grammar for OCL without requiring significant changes. Thereby, integration into existing tools supporting OCL should not cause severe problems.

Figure 5 shows formulations of the temporal (integrity) constraints introduced verbally at the beginning of this section. The temporal extension of OCL sketched before is now used to express these constraints. The first statement is a pre-condition for executing the service, *Scheduling,* for a certain period of time. It is required that for the

Figure 5: Specification of temporal properties using the extended OCL

```
ProductionPlanning::Scheduling(p:Period)
    pre  :  sometime_past( RoughPlanning(p) )

OrderProcessing::PrintInvoice(at:Order)
    pre  :  sometime_past( AcceptCustomerOrder(at) )  and
            not( CancelOrder(at) sometime_since_last
            AcceptCustomerOrder(at) )

OrderProcessing::AcceptCustomerOrder(at:Order)
    post:  sometime( PrintInvoice(at) )  or  sometime(
            CancelOrder(at) )
```

same period of time a service, *RoughPlanning,* was already executed. Here, we assume that the service, *RoughPlanning, is* provided by another business component, as is known in the component, *ProductionPlanning,* by declaring its interface description.

The second statement in Figure 5 is a pre-condition for the service *PrintInvoice* in the business component *OrderProcessing.* This pre-condition expresses that, before this service can be invoked, the service *AcceptCustomerOrder* must have been executed for the same order and additionally, since acceptance of this order, there has been no cancellation of this order (by executing the service *CancelOrder*).

The third temporal property is a post condition for the service *AcceptCustomerOrder.* In addition to the previous statement, it is required that after accepting an order by a customer, sometime later either an invoice has to be printed for exactly this order by executing the service *PrintInvoice* or this order must eventually be cancelled by executing the service *CancelOrder.*

The second and third statements express different properties. On the one hand, the pre-condition for *PrintInvoice* does not forbid that the service *AcceptCustomerOrder* can be executed without the conditions that an invoice will ever be printed or a cancellation will ever occur for that order. On the other hand, the post condition for *AcceptCustomerOrder* does not exclude the execution of the service *PrintInvoice* for a certain order, although this order has never been accepted by means of the service *AcceptCustomerOrder.*

Finally, we have to discuss the issue of formal semantics for this extension of OCL by temporal operators. As already mentioned, the semantic foundations (i.e., a complete definition of the formal semantics for a temporal logic with past and future tense temporal operators) are given, e.g., in Lipeck and Saake (1987) such that we refrain from repeating these definitions here. In contrast to Lipeck and Saake (1987), we did not introduce the operators *next* (referring to the subsequent state) nor *previous* (referring to the previous state). This is due to the well-known semantic problems, which are caused by these two operators when composing independently specified systems of components. In general, we implicitly obtain concurrent processes in the composed system where no global synchronization of local states is given. As a consequence, considering a common global state "*next* operator" in the specifications of different components may, e.g., refer to different local states that do not necessarily belong to any one global state cf., also Conrad (1995) or Mokkedem and Méry (1994). Although there are several proposals for solving these kinds of problems (besides the references mentioned before — see also Conrad (1996) and Sørensen, Hansen, and Løvengreen (1994), it is not yet clear which approach is the most adequate. In addition, there is the fact that their incorporation into a specification framework still needs an in-depth investigation from a methodological point of view.

CONCLUSIONS AND OUTLOOK

The usage of business components offers a possibility to customize business application systems incorporating both the advantages of standardized software and individually-developed software. However, this requires the standardization of business components and subsequently, a specification of these components. After deriving basic requirements for specifications of business components by investigating the paradigm of software contracts, we present a proposal for extending OCL by temporal operators. Based on a widespread notational standard, it is now possible to specify across several software contract levels, thereby avoiding a change of methods while respecting the particular requirements of business components.

It should be noted that our proposal - in contrast to OCL itself - is not standardized by the OMG. Considering the fact that such extensions by temporal properties are indispensable in specifying business components, our proposal might be an essential first step towards a later standardization. In fact, it has become part of a recommendation of the business components working group of the German Informatics Society (GI) (cp., Turowski, 2002).

We obtain practical experience towards practicality and usability of our approach in the context of in house projects, which concern the development of business components for the application domain, production planning, and control. After an introductory tutorial, the notation's extension was well accepted by project participants. Problems that arose were primarily due to an inaccurate understanding of dependencies of the application domain. Consequently, in some cases we could observe an inadequate specification. Further practical experiences are documented in Ackermann (2001) or Fettke, Loos, and Tann (2001).

REFERENCES

Ackermann, J. (2001). *Fallstudie zur Spezifikation von Fachkomponenten.* Paper presented at the 2. Workshop Modellierung und Spezifikation von Fachkomponenten: Workshop im Rahmen der vertIS (verteilte Informationssysteme auf der Grundlage von Objekten, Komponenten und Agenten) 2001 Bamberg, Deutschland, 05. Oktober 2001, Tagungsband, Bamberg.

Alagar, V. S., & Periyasamy, K. (1998). *Specification of Software Systems.* New York: Springer.

Allen, P., & Frost, S. (1998). *Component-Based Development for Enterprise Systems: Applying The Select Perspective.* Cambridge: Cambridge University Press.

Beugnard, A., Jézéquel, J.-M., Plouzeau, N., & Watkins, D. (1999). Making Components Contract Aware. *IEEE Computer, 32*(7), 38-44.

Biethahn, J., Mucksch, H., & Ruf, W. (1991). *Ganzheitliches Informationsmanagement: Daten- und Entwicklungsmanagement* (Vol. 2). München: Oldenbourg.

Booch, G. (1994). *Object-oriented analysis and design with applications* (2 ed.). Reading: Addison-Wesley.

Brown, A. W., & Wallnau, K. C. (1996). Engineering of Component-Based Systems. In A. W. Brown (Ed.), *Component-Based Software Engineering: Selected Papers from the Software Engineering Institute* (pp. 7-15). Los Alamitos, California: IEEE Computer Society Press.

Coleman, D. (1993). *Object-Oriented Development: The Fusion Method.* Englewood Cliffs: Prentice Hall.

Conrad, S. (1995). *Compositional Object Specification and Verification.* Paper presented at the Proceedings of the International Conference on Software Quality (ICSQ'95), Maribor.

Conrad, S. (1996). A Basic Calculus for Verifying Properties of Interacting Objects. *Data and Knowledge Engineering, 18*(2), 119-146.

D'Souza, D. F., & Wills, A. C. (1999). *Objects, Components, and Frameworks with UML: The Catalysis Approach*. Reading: Addison-Wesley.

Ehrig, H., & Mahr, B. (1985). *Fundamentals of Algebraic Specification 1: Equations and Initial Semantics*. Berlin: Springer.

Emerson, E. A. (1990). Temporal and Modal Logic. In J. v. Leeuwen (Ed.), *Handbook of Theoretical Computer Science* (Vol. B, pp. 995-1072). Amsterdam: Elsevier Science Publishers, North-Holland.

Fellner, K., & Turowski, K. (2000). *Classification Framework for Business Components*. Paper presented at the Proceedings of the 33rd Annual Hawaii International Conference On System Sciences, Maui, Hawaii.

Ferstl, O. K., & Sinz, E. J. (1998). *Grundlagen der Wirtschaftsinformatik* (3 ed. Vol. 1). München: Oldenbourg.

Fettke, P., Loos, P., & Tann, M. v. d. (2001). *Eine Fallstudie zur Spezifikation von Fachkomponenten eines Informationssystems für Virtuelle Finanzdienstleister – Beschreibung und Schlussfolgerungen*. Paper presented at the 2. Workshop Modellierung und Spezifikation von Fachkomponenten: Workshop im Rahmen der vertIS (verteilte Informationssysteme auf der Grundlage von Objekten, Komponenten und Agenten) 2001 Bamberg, Deutschland, 05. Oktober 2001, Tagungsband, Bamberg.

Hennessy, M. (1988). *Algebraic Theory of Processes*. Cambridge: MIT Press.

Jaeschke, P., Oberweis, A., & Stucky, W. (1994). *Deriving Complex Structured Objects for Business Process Modelling*. Paper presented at the Entity-Relationship Approach - ER'94, Proceedings of the 13th International Conference on the Entity-Relationship Approach, Manchester.

Jalote, P. (1997). *An Integrated Approach to Software Engineering*. New York: Springer.

Johnson, R. E., & Wirfs-Brock, R. J. (1990). Surveying Current Research in Object-Oriented Design. *Communications of the ACM, 33*(9), 104-124.

Jungclaus, R., Saake, G., Hartmann, T., & Sernadas, C. (1996). Troll: A Language for Object-Oriented Specification of Information Systems. *ACM Transactions on Information Systems, 14*(2), 175-211.

Keller, G., Nüttgens, M., & Scheer, A.-W. (1992). Planungsinseln - Vom Konzept zum integrierten Informationsmodell. *HMD, 29*(168), 25-39.

Lipeck, U. W., & Saake, G. (1987). Monitoring Dynamic Integrity Constraints Based on Temporal Logic. *Information Systems, 12*(3), 255-269.

Lipeck, U. W., Gertz, M., & Saake, G. (1994). Transitional Monitoring of Dynamic Integrity Contraints. *Bulletin of the IEEE Technical Committee on Data Engineering, 17*(2), 38-42.

Manna, Z., & Pnueli, A. (1992). *The Temporal Logic of Reactive and Concurrent Systems: Specification* (Vol. 1). Berlin: Springer.

Meyer, B. (1988). *Object-Oriented Software Construction*. Englewood Cliffs: Prentice Hall.

Meyer, B. (1992). Applying "Design by Contract". *IEEE Computer, 25*(10), 40-51.

Mokkedem, A., & Méry, D. (1994). *A Stuttering Closed Temporal Logic for Modular Reasoning about Concurrent Programs*. Paper presented at the Proceedings of the First International Conference on Temporal Logic (ICTL'94), Bonn.

OMG (Ed.). (2001). *OMG Unified Modeling Language Specification, Version 1.4, Septermber 2001*. Needham.

OMG (Ed.). (2002). *The Common Object Request Broker: Architecture and Specification: Version 3.0, July 2002*. Framingham: OMG.

Orfali, R., Harkey, D., & Edwards, J. (1996). *The Essential Distributed Objects Survival Guide*. New York: John Wiley & Sons.

Ortner, E. (1997). *Methodenneutraler Fachentwurf: Zu den Grundlagen einer anwendungsorientierten Informatik*. Stuttgart: Teubner.

Rittgen, P. (1999). *Objektorientierte Analyse mit EMK*. Paper presented at the Modellierung betrieblicher Informationssysteme: Proceedings der MobIS-Fachtagung 1999 (MobIS'99), Bamberg.

Rumbaugh, J., Blaha, M., Premerlani, W., Eddy, F., & Lorensen, W. (1991). *Object-Oriented Modeling and Design*. Englewood Cliffs, NY: Prentice Hall.

Sametinger, J. (1997). *Software Engineering with Reusable Components*. Berlin: Springer.

Scheer, A.-W. (1994). *Business Process Engineering: Reference Models for Industrial Enterprises* (2 ed.). Berlin: Springer.

Sørensen, M. U., Hansen, O. E., & Løvengreen, H. H. (1994). *Combining Temporal Specification Techniques*. Paper presented at the Proceedings of the First International Conference on Temporal Logic (ICTL'94), Bonn.

Szyperski, C. (1998). *Component Software: Beyond Object-Oriented Programming* (2 ed.). Harlow: Addison-Wesley.

Turowski, K. (2000). Establishing Standards for Business Components. In K. Jakobs (Ed.), *Information Technology Standards and Standardisation: A Global Perspective* (pp. 131-151). Hershey: Idea Group Publishing.

Turowski, K. (Ed.). (2002). *Vereinheitlichte Spezifikation von Fachkomponenten: Memorandum des Arbeitskreises 5.10.3 Komponentenorientierte betriebliche Anwendungssysteme, Februar 2002*. Augsburg: Universität Augsburg.

Wilkerson, B., & Wirfs-Brock, R. J. (1989). A Responsibility-Driven Approach. *SIGPLAN Notices, 24*(10), 72-76.

APPENDIX
(GRAMMAR OF TEMPORAL OCL)

```
expression                := logicalExpression
ifExpression              := "if" expression
                             "then" expression
                             "else" expression
                             "endif"
logicalExpression         := relationalExpression
                             ( logicalOperator relationalExpression )*
relationalExpression      := temporalExpression
                             | additiveExpression
                             ( relationalOperator additiveExpression )?
temporalExpression        := unaryTemporalOperator logicalExpression
                             | logicalExpression
                             binaryTemporalOperator logicalExpression
additiveExpression        := multiplicativeExpression
                             ( addOperator multiplicativeExpression )*
multiplicativeExpression  := unaryExpression
                             ( multiplyOperator unaryExpression )*
unaryExpression           := ( unaryOperator postfixExpression )
                             | postfixExpression
postfixExpression         := primaryExpression ( ( "." | "->" ) propertyCall)*
primaryExpression         := literalCollection
                             | literal
                             | pathName timeExpression? qualifier?
                             propertyCallParameters?
                             | "(" expression ")"
                             | ifExpression
propertyCallParameters    := "(" ( declarator )? ( actualParameterList )? ")"
literal                   := string | number | enumLiteral
enumLiteral               := name "::" name ( "::" name )*
simpleTypeSpecifier       := pathName
literalCollection         := collectionKind "{"
                                  ( collectionItem ("," collectionItem )* )? "}"
collectionItem            := expression ( ".." expression )?
propertyCall              := pathName ( timeExpression )? ( qualifiers )?
                             propertyCallParameters?
qualifiers                := "[" actualParameterList "]"
declarator                := name ( "," name )*
                             ( ":" simpleTypeSpecifier )?
                             ( ";" name ":" typeSpecifier "=" expression )?
                             "|"
pathName                  := name ( "::" name )*
timeExpression            := "@" "pre"
actualParameterList       := expression ( "," expression )*
logicalOperator           := "and" | "or" | "xor" | "implies"
collectionKind            := "Set" | "Bag" | "Sequence" | "Collection"
relationalOperator        := "=" | ">" | "<" | ">=" | "<=" | "<>"
addOperator               := "+" | "-"
multiplyOperator          := "*" | "/"
unaryOperator             := "-" | "not"
```

```
typeName            := charForNameTop charForName*
name                := charForNameTop charForName*
charForNameTop      := /* Characters except inhibitedChar and ["0"-"9"];
                       the available characters shall be determined
                       by the tool implementers ultimately. */
charForName         := /* Characters except inhibitedChar; the available
                       characters shall be determined by the tool
                       implementers ultimately. */
inhibitedChar       :=   "\" | ", KT " | "\'" | "(" | ")" | "*" | "+" | ","
                       | "." | "/" | ":" | ";" | "<" | "=" | ">" | "@"
                       | "\\" | "[" | "]" | "{" | "}" | "|"
number              := "0"-"9" (["0"-"9"])*
                       ("." ["0"-"9"] (["0"-"9"])* )?
                       ( ("e"|"E") ) ( "+"|"-")? ["0"-"9"] (["0"-"9"])*
                       )?
string              := "'" ( (~["'","\\","\n","\r"])
                            | ("\\"
                            ( ["n","t","b","r","f","\\","'","\""]
                              | ["0"-"7"] (["0"-"7"] (["0"-"7"])? )? )?
                              )
                              )
                            )*
                       "'"
unaryTemporalOperator := "sometime_past" | "always_past"
                       | "sometime" | "always" | "initially"
binaryTemporalOperator := "sometime_since_last" | "always_since_last"
                       | "until" | "before"
```

Chapter V

Negotiating Early Reuse of Components – A Model-Based Analysis

J. A. Sykes
Swinburne University of Technology, Australia

ABSTRACT

Unless existing components are considered during formulation of a system specification, the amount of component reuse that is possible may be limited. In order to increase the amount of reuse, it may be necessary to alter the functionality or performance of the system from that originally envisioned. Tension between stakeholders thus exists. Reuse of components also significantly changes the specification activity because it must now deal with component specifications as input models, which is not necessarily the case when reuse is not the goal. These issues are investigated using a modeling framework based on semiotic theory. The nature of modeling abstractions that could support the negotiation between stakeholders is also explored. Two scenarios are examined: one based on the idea of functional abstractions that can be composed and the other one using structural abstractions of the kind available in the UML as the basis of component composition. Even though at this stage, there are no good examples of functional abstractions that can be composed, it is concluded that functional abstractions are the best prospect for supporting collaboration and negotiation.

INTRODUCTION

Reuse of existing software components is becoming more attractive to system developers as a way of shortening development time, reducing costs, or producing software of higher quality or greater complexity.

However, as Wallnau et al. (2001) have noted, the decision to reuse components constrains the choices open to system designers and alters the nature of the design process. Instead of being able to specify subsystems in a relatively free way, designers must choose from the limited, although possibly large, number of ways that those components could be combined. Furthermore, in order to make such choices, designers must be able to rationalize the ways that different combinations of components would behave. This differs from the top-down, problem-solving approach to design that is possible when subsystems can be specified in a less constrained way.

The possibility that decisions to reuse components could be made quite early in the development process has been discussed previously. Herzum and Sims (2000) envision maturity of the component industry as meaning that components of large granularity will be reusable at the enterprise level by developers with limited technical skills. These components will be supported by suitable software tools to manage deployment, configuration, etc. How such components should be represented, in order to enable their composition by domain experts rather than software experts, then becomes an issue. This point has been explored by Sykes and Gupta (2001), who discussed the need for functional abstractions that support the composition of components during require-ments specification. The authors also noted the lack of suitable abstractions at present in the Unified Modeling Language (UML).

A related issue, which is addressed in this chapter, is tension. Taking component behavior into account during the formulation and specification of system requirements introduces a tension between the desire to specify a system that precisely meets some user's requirement and the possibility of implementing the system sooner or more inexpensively if some component that is already available is used, even if it does not exactly meet the requirement.

The approach adopted is to regard the formulation of the specification for a system that will incorporate existing components as a negotiation between stakeholders, who will make use of models of the system and the candidate components through their collaboration.

The modeling aspects are discussed using the modeling framework described in the next section. The framework, which is based on semiotic theory, is an extension of that used in Sykes and Gupta (2001). Here it has been extended with concepts about interactive systems in order to deal with the nature of components as subsystems.

The modeling framework is used to examine the role of specifications in a develop-ment process that reuses existing components. Terminology from the Unified System Development Process (USDP) has been used for this part of the work, mainly because the USDP is well-documented (Jacobson et al., 1999) and is now quite widely known.

Other characteristics of the USDP that make it an appropriate context for the work, are first, its architectural focus on subsystems, which makes it compatible with the use of components. Second is the fact that it is model-based, which makes it possible to use the modeling framework for studying it.

The process through which the use of existing components can influence the formulation of a system specification is investigated using the modeling framework. This extends an earlier discussion in Sykes and Gupta (2001) and also puts it in a more general context (i.e., in terms of the participants involved in the collaboration).

CHARACTERIZING MODELS AND MODELING

The process of modeling is a purposeful, subjective human activity. It involves perception (of the thing to be modeled), conceptualization (thinking about the thing to be modeled in a particular way), and action (actual creation of the model).

One way to study the modeling process is via the semiotic triangle. Based on the semiotic triangle, a so-called modeling triangle was used by Brinkkemper (1990) to study the formalization of information system modeling. More recently, it was used to investigate the conceptual modeling process (Gupta and Sykes, 2001). This approach has now been extended with ideas about mental models and the system development notion of modeling purpose, in order to create a general theoretical framework for analyzing information systems modeling and development processes. In this form, it has been used for an initial examination of early reuse decisions in component-based development (Sykes and Gupta, 2001).

The Semiotic Triangle

The semiotic triangle (also called the meaning triangle) deals with the process by which a human observer is able to claim that some sign or symbol stands for (i.e., means) some perceived thing (see Figure 1). It is important as it shows how meaning relies on a two-stage process involving human perception and conceptualization, which therefore, makes it subjective. The meaning of a sign is determined by the observer rather than the thing being observed (i.e., referent) or by the sign itself.

Figure 1: Meaning triangle

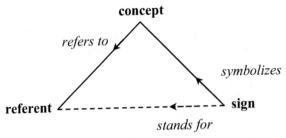

Figure 2: Two meaning triangles representing communication between two observers

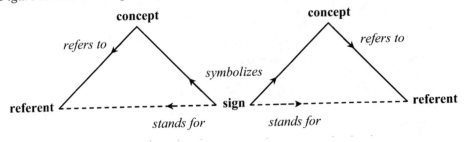

When two observers communicate, they do so by using signs. In this sense, natural language is considered to be a system of signs. The semiotic triangle shows that it is only the sign that is indisputably common to both observers. The other elements (referent and concept) could be different for each observer (Figure 2).

The Modeling Triangle

The modeling triangle is a form of the semiotic triangle in which the sign, the conceptualization, and the referent are systems rather than simple signs or icons (See Figure 3). In the form of the modeling triangle presented in Brinkkemper (1990), the term *concrete system* is used for the system that is to be modeled. In Gupta and Sykes (2001) and Sykes and Gupta (2001), the term *perceived system* is used instead, because it reflects the fact that conceptualization is preceded by perception, and it avoids the connotation that the system being modeled is a tangible thing existing in the real world. It can be a system that the observer imagines, one that exists only in the observer's "mind's eye," as it were. This is the situation that must exist during requirements specification for a new system.

Figure 3 names four of the relationships that can exist between pairs of models (i.e., systems). In Brinkkemper's version of the triangle, two relationships for the lower (i.e., dashed) side of the triangle are given, and relationships between systems of the same kind are also named. In Figure 3, the dashed side of the triangle is not named in terms of relationships on the grounds that it is better to regard it as representing the results of applying the other relationships. Thus conceptualization followed by representation is called "*model creation*," and realization followed by application is called "*model interpretation*." Relationships between systems of the same kind are called "*translation*" (i.e., between symbolic systems), "*mapping*" (i.e., between conceptual systems) and "*empirical model*" (i.e., between perceived systems), as in Brinkkemper's version.

The modeling triangle shows that two sets of ideas need to be clearly established for a modeling activity to be successful, namely:

- The notation (corresponding to the representation side of the triangle).
- The abstractions (corresponding to the conceptualization side of the triangle).

Figure 3: Modeling triangle

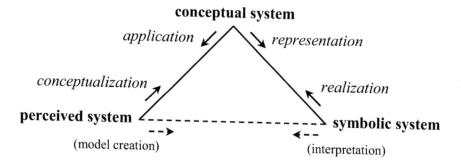

If the model is to serve as a means of communication between developers, developers must agree about abstractions and notations and have a clear understanding about which notations represent which abstractions.

Components as Subsystems

In terms of the classification of systems used by Ackoff (1999), subsystems and components, which are a special kind of subsystem, are examples of *open systems*. An open system is one that is not independent of its surroundings. As Ackoff explains, an open system requires certain kinds of environmental conditions in order to perform its intended or "defining" function. The *environment* of a system consists of those things that the system cannot control, but includes things that can affect system properties or performance. Some systems can, to some extent, affect their environment. The environment of such systems is divided into a *transactional part* (i.e., the part that the system can affect but not control), and a *contextual part* (i.e., the part that it can neither affect nor control.

The purpose of a component is to interact with (affect) the other components and subsystems that constitute its environment. Thus it is clear that the environment of a component must have a transactional part. Systems that are open and that also have a transactional part to their environment are called *interactive systems*.

One of the characteristics of interactive systems is that they are specified via their external behavior. External behavior is not modeled explicitly, rather it emerges from the interaction between the system and its environment (Goldin et al., 2001). One consequence of this is that an interactive system cannot be fully understood unless its environment is known. The extent to which the environment of an interactive system is known can be used to distinguish between the general case of a subsystem and the special case of a subsystem that is also a component.

The partitioning of a larger system that occurs during top-down design produces subsystems that should not be thought of as components. Only one instance of each subsystem might be built, and each subsystem will exist in only one environment, which can be well specified and understood.

There will also be many instances in which a subsystem is also a component (if it is a successful component) and these instances will be used in different environments.

Thus, a component is a subsystem that has many potential behaviors. The behavior of a particular component will not be fully describable until an instance of it has been put into some environment. In other words, the goal of reuse means that it would be necessary to describe all possible environments for a component in order to completely specify it.

Mental Models

The notion of mental models aims to account for the different ways that humans attempt to understand complex systems (Preece et al., 1994). People who have a notion about how a system is internally structured, may be able to explain the behavior of that system by mentally "executing" their mental model of it. This kind of mental model is called a *"structural mental model"* (i.e., a "how-it-works" model). Other people may have no idea of how the system is structured internally, but instead understand its use in terms of how it responds when operated. This kind of mental model is called a *"functional mental model"* (i.e., a "how-to-use-it" model).

These ideas are relevant for system development. It appears that software experts tend to prefer structural mental models, while application users are more likely to prefer a functional, mental model of a software application.

Mental models can also be characterized as either normative or descriptive. A normative mental model represents a person's ideas about how a system ought to behave, while a descriptive mental model represents the system's actual behavior.

These distinctions are also relevant for system development work. A normative model represents a system yet to be built (a so-called "to-be" model) and a descriptive model represents an existing system (a so-called "as-is" model).

The Modeling Framework

A summary of the factors that should be considered for any shared modeling activity is as follows:

- *Participants:* Who is involved in the modeling activity? What are their preferred styles of mental models?

- *Purpose:* What is the purpose of the modeling activity? Is it descriptive or normative? Is it to create a specification, or to create a model that can be implemented as executable software (i.e., *a translation*)?

- *Perceived system:* What is the perceived system? If the modeling is normative in purpose, how will agreement be reached about the perceived (imaginary) system?

- *Abstractions:* What sets of abstractions best suit the purpose of the modeling activity; the knowledge, skills and interests of the participants; and the kinds of mental models they prefer?

- *Symbols:* What sets of symbols will be used to represent the conceptualized system? Do all participants understand the notations, and can they relate them to the set of abstractions?

SPECIFICATIONS AS INPUT AND OUTPUT MODELS

In Jacobson et al. (1999), the USDP is described as an *architecture-centric* process. This means that the system under development is viewed as a collaboration of subsystems in which each subsystem is specified by means of a set of use cases.

Thus specifications exist, or are needed, for at least two levels, namely: the specifications of the system under development; and, at one or more lower levels, specifications of the constituent parts (i.e., the subsystems).

The USDP is also a *model-based* development process, meaning that it consists of a sequence of modeling activities. Each modeling activity can be described in terms of the *output models* that result from it and the *input models* that the modelers need during the development steps.

Early in a development process, one goal is to prepare a system specification. In the case of the USDP, this occurs during the inception and elaboration phases. During these periods, the specification is an output model. Later in a development process the system specification serves as an input model (e.g., during the construction and transition phases of the USDP).

It is recognized by the USDP that a system specification is in a sense never finished, because it can continue to evolve throughout development. Nevertheless, progression from the elaboration phase to the construction phase can be seen as the point in the USDP where the role of the system specification changes from being an output model to being (primarily) an input model.

It is also useful to consider whether the roles played by the specifications of subsystems can change in a similar way. In order to do so, it is necessary to take into account the possibility of the reuse of existing components.

Development Process without Reuse

Figure 4 shows some models in a development process in which there is no reuse of existing components. Models are represented as rectangles: drawn with either a solid line for an input model or a broken line for an output model.

In Figure 4(a), which shows models in the elaboration phase of the USDP, the system under development is shown as an input model and the specifications of both the system and its subsystems appear as output models. The input model is the vision, or private, imaginary model of the proposed system that exists in the mind of each developer.

The purpose of the elaboration phase, viewed as a modeling activity, is to transform this vision of the proposed system into a representation that exists in the real world where it can be communicated and shared.

In Figure 4(b), which shows models in the construction phase, the specifications are the input models and the output model is a representation of the system under development. There will generally be other input models as well, such as class models.

*Figure 4: Specifications as input and output models in an architecture-centric development process **without reuse** of existing components*

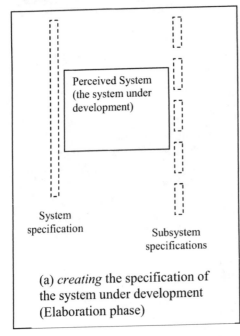 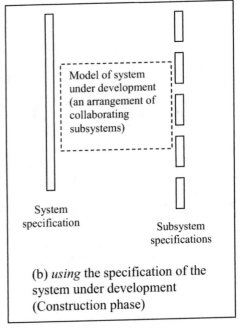

(a) *creating* the specification of the system under development (Elaboration phase)

(b) *using* the specification of the system under development (Construction phase)

*Figure 5: Specifications as input and output models in an architecture-centric development process **using some existing components***

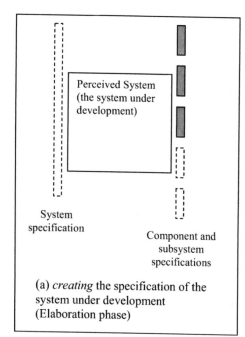

(a) *creating* the specification of the system under development (Elaboration phase)

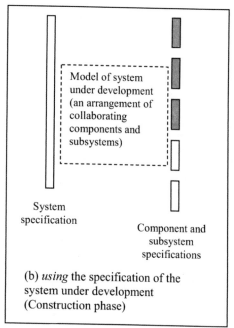

(b) *using* the specification of the system under development (Construction phase)

Development Process with Reuse of Existing Components

Figure 5 shows a development process in which some of the subsystems that will comprise the system under development are existing components (shown as "black-boxes"). Presumably, the specifications of those components will already exist as well. These specifications will be available as input models throughout the entire development process. This is indicated in Figure 5(a) by drawing the components with a solid line to show that they exist during the elaboration phase. Specifications of non-component subsystems are shown in the same way that they were in Figure 4 for the development process without reuse; namely, as output models during elaboration and as input models during construction.

Early and Late Reuse

Actual reuse of an existing component occurs during the construction phase of software development, when a developer chooses to handle some part of the construction phase as a "buy" instead of a "build." The reuse occurs as the result of a *reuse decision*. Such a decision can occur during construction, but it can also occur at an earlier stage of the development process.

This is possible because, prior to construction, the system specification is still an output model. Because of this, the way is open for it to be influenced by knowledge about existing components that might be useful.

Thus a distinction between early and late reuse can be made that is based on when the reuse decision is made, rather than when the actual reuse occurs.

An *early reuse decision* occurs when knowledge of a component's behavior is taken into account in the formulation of the system specification. For example, a decision to specify a use case in a way in which some or all of its steps could be handled by an existing component would be an early reuse decision.

When a specification has not been influenced by knowledge about existing components, only *late reuse decisions* are possible. In these circumstances, the designer's choices are constrained to attempts to match existing components to a specification that has been prepared without any consideration of the possibilities for reuse.

Thus, the making of reuse decisions can be a requirements-focused activity, occurring during the inception and elaboration phases. It seems reasonable to suggest that by making reuse decisions as early as possible in the development process, the amount of actual reuse can be increased.

For this to happen, it must be possible to evaluate the choice of components and the way in which they are to be assembled before the construction phase begins. Models provide the means for doing this.

INFLUENCING THE SYSTEM SPECIFICATION

Participants

If there is to be reuse, preparation of a specification requires knowledge about the environment in which the system will function, knowledge about systems of the kind being envisioned and how they operate in general, and knowledge of available components.

It some instances, one person possesses all this knowledge. The more likely situation is that two or more participants will be involved. This is also a more interesting case to study, because the participants will need to communicate.

Whenever two participants in a software development project are communicating via a model, there are four steps in each communication act, as shown in Figure 2. The communication acts are steps in a process aimed at bringing the developers' understandings about the model into alignment.

The success of the developers' communication depends on their knowledge of, and ability to effectively use, a set of concepts and a set of notations to express those concepts (representing two sides of the semiotic triangle).

The term "mindset" is used here to refer to the combined effects of the participant's:

- Available abstractions (the conceptualizations they know about and can use).
- Available notations (the symbolic systems they are able to use effectively).
- Preference for a structural or a functional style of mental model.

Modeling is likely to be least problematic when the participants share (understand and agree on the):

- Perceived system.
- Set of abstractions to be used in conceptualizing the system.
- Notation to be used to represent the conceptual system.

Collaborative modeling will be more difficult the more these conditions are altered. Serious misunderstandings are possible if the participants have significantly different mindsets.

The discussion here is concerned with how the participants will communicate during the negotiation about the system specification. In Sykes and Gupta (2001) two participant roles named "Client" and "Analyst" were used. These roles are replaced here by "Environment Designer" and "System Designer," respectively. This has been done to make the discussion more general, to emphasize that the essential nature of the activity is design, and as a reminder that the system under development is an open, interactive system (i.e., interaction with its environment is important).

It is assumed that the mindset of the Environment Designer comprises:

- Detailed knowledge about the environment in which the system will operate.
- A preference for a structural, mental model of the environment.
- A preference for functional, mental models of systems of the kind being developed.

It is assumed that the mindset of the System Designer comprises:

- Detailed knowledge of systems of the kind being developed.
- Some general knowledge of the environment.
- A preference for structural, mental models of systems.

The System Designer could also be expected to know about techniques and tools for building systems and the availability and characteristics of components that could be used.

For example, if the system under development is a software application that will operate as part of a business process, a business analyst/systems analyst could fill the role of Environment Designer and a software developer such as an analyst/programmer could fill the role of System Designer. If the system under development is a subsystem forming part of a software application, a system architect could fill the role of Environment Designer and a programmer could fill the role of System Designer.

Negotiating Early Reuse

Figure 6, which is based on two modeling triangles joined via two common symbolic systems, shows the modeling transitions and communications that occur as the Environment Designer and the System Designer collaborate in the preparation of a symbolic system. They need to agree that the symbolic system "stands for" the perceived system, and in this case, specifies it.

To examine more closely the process via which the participants negotiate the preparation of a specification for a system that will reuse existing components, Figure 6 has to be related to Figure 5(a). This can be done as follows.

The perceived system in Figure 5(a) does not yet exist, even though it is shown as an input model in the figure. It is depicted this way because the participants must imagine

Figure 6: Transitions between perceived, conceptual and symbolic systems, and communication between Environment Designer and System Designer, during a system specification modeling activity

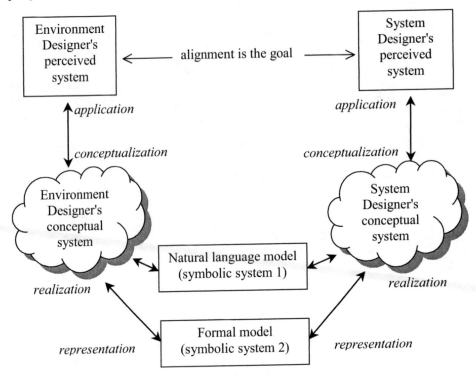

the system at this early stage. It thus corresponds to *both* views of the perceived system shown in Figure 6 (i.e., the Environment Designer's perceived system *and* the System Designer's perceived system).

The system specification in Figure 5(a) corresponds to the formal model (symbolic system 2) shown in Figure 6.

Interactions between the Environment Designer and the System Designer are aimed at accomplishing the following tasks:

1. Bringing their respective, perceived systems into alignment.
2. Preparing a specification (model) of the behavior of the perceived system.
3. Deciding what parts of that behavior will be implemented by means of existing components (which also requires an understanding of the behaviors of those components).

The validity of any agreement that the Environment Designer and System Designer might reach about the correctness of the formal model in Figure 6 is likely to be in doubt unless it can be established that the formal model "stands for" the same perceived system. The participants need some way of discovering that the other perceives the "same" system. The process via which participants bring their respective perceptions of the two imagined systems into alignment is therefore of interest.

This process will normally comprise a number of iterations, each consisting of *model creation* by one participant followed by *model interpretation* by the other participant. It is assumed that either the Environment Designer or the System Designer can originate a model.

Essentially what is being sought is agreement about correspondence between elements in the symbolic model of the perceived system and elements in the perceived system itself (i.e., the *meaning* of elements in the symbolic model in terms of the proposed system).

As the meaning triangle shows, the association between sign and referent is comprised of two associations. The association between referent and concept results from the observer's scheme of abstraction. The association between concept and sign results from the observer's scheme of notation.

Thus, the alignment between perceived systems being sought by the Environment Designer and the System Designer can be achieved only if they concur with their respective schemes of abstraction and notation.

Assuming that the model is to be expressed formally, the Environment Designer and System Designer have to make explicit (a) their agreed upon scheme of abstraction, and (b) their agreed upon scheme of *formal* notation that will link model elements to system elements.

It is, therefore, necessary to consider the abstractions and notations that are likely to be familiar to both the Environment Designer and the System Designer. Is it assumed that each of the designers is familiar with abstractions about the real world, and that they have a natural language in common that will provide the notational scheme for communicating about those abstractions.

Beyond that, it must be considered what kind of abstractions will be used for:
- Discussing the environment.
- Specifying components.
- Expressing the formal system specification (symbolic system 2 in Figure 6).
- Composing components.

For genuine collaboration and negotiation to be possible, at least one of these sets of abstractions must be familiar to both the participants.

Two of the many possible collaboration scenarios will now be described.

Reasoning Using Intermediate Structural Abstractions

This scenario is based on the assumption that the only abstractions shared by the participants are those that can describe the behavior of the system in functional terms, such as use cases. The Environment Designer and the System Designer collaborate by assessing a functional model of the system (its specification) that has been produced by the System Designer.

The System Designer obtains the functional model from the component specifications using an indirect process that involves the preparation of one or more intermediate, structural models of the proposed system. Structural models provide the means by which the behaviors of various arrangements of the components are composed. For example, in the case of software components that offer services by means of objects instantiated from classes in the component, the System Designer could prepare interaction diagrams, such as a UML collaboration diagram, in order to try out various arrangements of components (i.e., various designs for the system).

In order for the Environment Designer to be able to participate in the preparation of the specification, the System Designer has to convert each structural model into a functional model that the Environment Designer can comprehend. For example, a set of use cases could be prepared.

The Environment Designer need not know about the components, and does not participate in the preparation of the structural model. Thus, this approach is a rather one-sided collaboration. The responsibility for creating designs (i.e., for selecting and composing components), rests almost entirely with the System Designer. The Environment Designer may only participate in the evaluation.

Reasoning Using Composable, Functional Abstractions

In this scenario, the goal is to use the same kinds of abstractions throughout the specification process. As it is necessary that the specification be expressed in functional terms, any other abstractions used should also be functional.

In order to perform the composition step using functional abstractions, abstractions must also be composable. That is, it must be possible to combine the behavioral representations of two components in a straightforward way to obtain a combined description of behavior that is expressed in the same way as the separate behaviors.

This approach was discussed in Sykes and Gupta (2001) for the case of a business application (i.e., the system was a software application and the environment was a business domain). In that discussion, some UML diagrams proposed for use in component-based development were evaluated for usefulness in supporting early reuse decisions. The component diagram was considered unsuitable due to its focus on implementation and its lack of detail about component behavior. Packages representing component interfaces, which have been proposed in various forms as suitable for CBD modeling, were judged to be better than the component diagram because they can provide more detail about behavior. However, when used in conjunction with a layered architectural view of the software system, these packages invited a structural view of the system that was thought likely to be incompatible with the Environment Designer's preference for a functional mental model. Use cases, which offer a functional view of a system, were considered too detailed and unwieldy to be easily composable.

CONCLUSION

Reuse of components changes the specification activity because reuse must deal with component specifications as input models. This is not necessarily (nor often) the case when subsystems are specified in a top-down fashion (i.e., without reuse).

Analysis of the issues from a modeling perspective revealed that a direct approach in which the Environment Designer and System Designer could collaborate more or less as equals requires that the system and its subsystems (components) be specified in functional terms. Preferably the functional terms used are those favored by the Environment Designer. Additionally, the abstractions used must be composable so that the composition can be performed directly (i.e., without having to transform the component specifications into another form in order to model the combined behavior.)

At this stage, no suitable abstractions seem to be available. The closest approximation appears to be the UML use case. However, the usual kind of text format in which use cases are written are not readily composable.

In order to use what the UML already offers, functional specifications of components can be used as inputs to an intermediate modeling activity that produces a structural interaction model that represents the composition of collaborating components.

This not only necessitates a further transformation to obtain the functional style of system specification preferred by the Environment Designer, but it can also limit the Environment Designer's contribution to the process. This occurs if the functional abstractions used to specify components, or the structural abstractions used to compose them, are not understood by the Environment Designer. The Environment Designer is then reliant on the System Designer to choose the components, perform the structural composition, and then interpret results in functional terms for the Environment Designer.

The analysis presented here supports the view that it worthwhile continuing to search for composable, functional abstractions suitable for modeling components and systems.

REFERENCES

Ackoff, R. L. (1999). *Re-creating the Corporation: A Design of Organizations for the 21st Century*. Oxford University Press.

Brinkkemper, S. (1990). Formalisation of information systems modelling. Ph.D. thesis, University of Nijmegen, Netherlands.

Goldin, D., Keil, D. & Wegner, P. (2001). An interactive viewpoint on the role of UML. In Siau, K. & Halpin, T. (Eds.), *Unified Modeling Language: Systems Analysis, Design and Development Issues*. Hershey, PA: Idea Group Publishing.

Gupta, P. & Sykes, J. A. (2001). The conceptual modelling process and the notion of a concept. In Rossi, M. & Siau, K. (Eds.), *Information modelling for the new millennium*. Hershey, PA: Idea Group Publishing.

Herzum, P. & Sims, O. (2000). *Business Component Factory: A Comprehensive Overview of Component-Based Development for the Enterprise*. John Wiley & Sons, Inc.

Jacobson, I., Booch, G., & Rumbaugh, J. (1999). *The Unified Software Development Process*. Addison-Wesley.

Preece, J. et al. (1994). *Human-Computer Interaction*. Addison-Wesley.

Sykes, J. A. & Gupta, P. (2001). UML Modeling Support for Early Reuse Decisions in Component-Based Development. In Siau, K. & Halpin, T. (Eds.), *Unified Modeling Language: Systems Analysis, Design and Development Issues*. Hershey, PA: Idea Group Publishing.

Wallnau, K. C., Hissam, S. A. & Seacord, R. C. (2002). *Building Systems from Commercial Components*. Addison-Wesley.

Chapter VI

Enhancing RUP Business Model with Client-Oriented Requirements Models

María Carmen Leonardi
INTIA, Universidad Nacional del Centro de la Provincia de Buenos Aires
Argentina

ABSTRACT

This chapter presents a strategy for the construction of RUP business models using client-oriented requirements models that are written in natural language. The RUP business model, whose objective is to understand the context of the system, is represented with business use cases and a business objects model. As there is no concrete strategy for its development, an integration of client-oriented requirements models and strategies that enhance the construction process of the business model, while keeping the RUP philosophy of using the language of the customer for the first stages of development, are proposed in this chapter. These models describe the context of the system from a different perspective through the use of a lexical model to describe the vocabulary, a model of scenarios to describe the behavior, and a business rules model to describe the policies of the organization. These models are manipulated through a set of heuristics in order to define the UP business model and to enhance traceability between the models. We use a case study to exemplify the strategy throughout the entire chapter.

INTRODUCTION

Unified Process, well known as RUP (Jacobson et al., 1999), is one of the object-oriented methodologies used more frequently at the present time. UP is an iterative, incremental, and use cases-driven methodology. As any methodology, RUP starts with the requirements capture stage, in which RUP considers that *"the major challenge is that the customer, who we assume to be primarily a non-computer specialist, must be able to read and understand the result of requirements capture. To meet this challenge we must use the language of the customer to describe these results. As a consequence, we should be very careful when introducing formality and structure and when introducing details about the system's internal working, in the results"* (Jacobson et al., 1999, p. 113). As part of this early requirements definition stage, RUP proposes the task of defining the system context to acquire the knowledge of the organization in which the software will operate. The system context is defined through a business model, more concretely, a *Business Use-Cases model* and a *Business Objects Model*. There are no concrete strategies for the model development; for this reason, we highlight the necessity of integrating client-oriented requirements models and strategies to enhance the construction process of the business model and keep the RUP philosophy of using the language of the customer for this stage. We adapted the strategy presented in Leonardi (2001) to be used in the context of RUP. This strategy proposes a set of activities and heuristics to define a conceptual objects model starting from natural language-oriented requirements models belonging to the *client-oriented requirements baseline* (Leite & Oliveira, 1995; Leite et al., 1997). These models describe the overall context — also known as Universe of Discourse or *UofD* (Leite & Oliveira, 1995) — in which the software will be developed and operated from different perspectives as follows: through a lexical model known as LEL (Leite & Franco, 1993) to describe the vocabulary; through a scenarios model (Leite et al., 1997) to describe the behavior, and through a business rules model (Leite & Leonardi, 1998) to describe the policies of the organization. The strategy enhances traceability between the models. Specifically, the use of the heuristics allows for pre-*traceability* (Gotel & Finkelstein, 1994) between the RUP business model and LEL and scenarios and business rule models.

The chapter is organized in the following way: First, the requirements baseline models are presented; this is followed by a section that briefly introduces the RUP business model; next, a definition strategy of the business models construction starting from requirements baseline models is described; the chapter then deals with the traceability aspects of the strategy. We conclude with a comparison of other works, and provide a general conclusion and summary of future work.

We will use a case study to exemplify the strategy through the entire chapter. The case study is "Car Purchase Saving Plan Administrator" case. The objective of the administration is the "making up" of groups of subscribers to buy automobiles through a saving and bid system. In order to be a subscriber of a group, the applicant will complete an application form. If he or she is accepted, the applicant will subscribe to a plan according to an adhesion contract. There are different types of plans. The subscriber has to pay a monthly installment, which gives the subscriber the right to participate in monthly acts of "Draw or Bid." The subscriber may bid money each month with some money by using a bid envelope. The subscriber becomes a grantee when he or she obtains the automobile by any of these two mechanisms. In this particular case, he or she will request the car by means of a special form and pay a special fee in order to receive the car. The grantee can opt for an automobile of a higher or lower value based on a set of existing rules. The subscriber can transfer his or her rights of the plan to another person and can reject the plan or be separated by the administration. He or she will have to pay for a life insurance. A group can be dissolved by decision of the adherents (e.g., discontinuing the manufacture of the car) or by the administration if there is a lack of group members or irregularities in payments. The full case and the requirements-related models may be obtained in Leonardi (2001).

THE CLIENT-ORIENTED REQUIREMENTS BASELINE

The requirements baseline (Leite & Oliveira,1995; Leite et al., 1997) is a structure that incorporates sentences about the desired system. Sentences are written in a natural language and follow defined patterns. The basic idea behind the baseline is that it is perennial. The baseline is developed during the requirements engineering process, but keeps evolving as the software construction process evolves. The baseline is geared towards the *UofD*. This strategy is similar to the one recommended by Jackson (1983) when he stated:

> "The traditional practice in software development has been to ignore the application domain and focus the attention on the machine. Requirements are about the phenomena of the application domain, not about the machine. To describe them exactly, we describe the required relationships among the phenomena of the problem context."

The *requirements baseline* is structured as follows:

* A lexicon model.
* A basic model.
* A business rule model.
* A scenarios model.
* A hypertext view.
* A configuration view.

The hypertext view and the configuration view support the evolution and the presentation of the other views. In this work we use the lexicon model, the scenario model, and the business rule model. These models are described in the following sub-sections.

Language Extended Lexicon

The Language Extended Lexicon (LEL) (Leite & Franco, 1993) is a structure that allows for the representation of significant terms of the *UofD (Universe of Discourse)*. The purpose of the lexicon is to help understand the application vocabulary and its semantics, leaving the comprehension of the problem for a future step. This lexicon unifies the language and allows communication with customers. LEL is composed of a set of symbols that represent the basis of an application language. Symbols are generally words or phrases that customers repeat or emphasize. The lexicon is a series of symbols with the following structure: *symbol name*, i.e., a word or phrase and a set of synonyms, *notions* that describe the denotation of the symbol, and *behavioral responses or impacts,* that describe the symbol connotation, i.e., how the symbols impact the *UofD*. In the description of notions and impacts, there are two basic rules that must be followed simultaneously: the "closure principle," which encourages the use of LEL symbols in other LEL symbols (thus forming a graph), and the "minimum vocabulary principle," in which the use of symbols external to the application language is minimized, and the ones used refer to a very small and well accepted general core. LEL defines a general classification for the symbol: objects (passive entities), subjects (active entities), and verbal phrases and states. Figure 1 shows the heuristics to define each type of symbol.

Figure 1: Heuristics to represent LEL terms

Subject	Notions: who the subject is.
	Behavioral responses: register actions executed by the subject.
Object	Notions: define the object and identify other objects with which the former has a relationship.
	Behavioral responses: describe the actions that may be applied to this object.
Verb	Notions: describe who executes the action, when it happens, and procedures involved in the action.
	Behavioral responses: describe the constraints on the happening of an action, which are the actions triggered in the environment and new situations that appear as consequences.
State	Notions: what it means and the actions that triggered the state.
	Behavioral responses: describe situations and actions related to it.

Figure 2: LEL terms examples

- **Subscriber**
Notions:
- He is an **Applicant** accepted by the **Administrator**.
- He belongs to a **group**.
Behavioral responses:
- To pay a **monthly installment**.
- **To transfer the plan**.
- **To bid**.
- **To reject the car**.
- **To give up saving plan**.

- **Group**
Notions:
- Set of **subscriber** that want to obtain a **Car** through a particular **Saving Plan**.
- Initially the quantity of **subscribers** of a group must doubles the quantity of **installments** of the corresponding saving **plan**.
Behavioral Responses:
- To **dissolve group**.
- To accept or to reject the **change of a Car type**.

- **Monthly installment | installment**
Notions:
- **Monthly amount** that **subscribers** and **grantees** have to pay.
- It is calculated by adding the **commercial installment** to the **life insurance**.
Behavioral responses:
- It is paid by the **grantee** or **subscriber**.
- The **Administration** calculates the installment.
- It is paid in a Bank.
- ....

The LEL construction process is carried out by means of two elicitation techniques: interviews and reading. The first interviews are non-structured and aim at collecting candidate symbols. Reading documents related to the application can also be used to find symbols. After the first interviews and readings, a list of symbols having the most frequently-used words is defined. These symbols are then generally classified. The next stage is to describe each symbol, using notions and behavioral responses that have been determined, and to then validate this with customers. The first LEL version, which will be polished to unify the syntax in order to attain a consistent and homogeneous LEL, is obtained as a result of the validation interviews. Figure 2 shows an example of the Car purchase installment plan contract Administrator case. Bold words represent other terms defined in the LEL, following the "closure principle" previously mentioned.

Scenario Model

A scenario describes *UofD* situations (Leite et al., 1997). Scenarios use natural language for basic representation and are naturally connected to LEL. Figure 3 describes the components of a scenario.

Notions of "*constraint*" and "*exception*" are added to some scenario components. A *constraint* refers to non-functional requirements and may be applied to context, resources, or episodes. An *exception*, applied to episodes, causes serious disruptions in the scenario, asking for a different set of actions which may be described separately as an exception scenario.

Figure 3: Scenario components

Title: identifies a scenario. In the case of a sub-scenario, the title is the same as the sentence containing the episode.
Objective: describes the purpose of the scenario.
Context: defines geographical and temporal locations and preconditions.
Resources: identify passive entities with which actors work.
Actors: detail entities actively involved in the scenario, generally a person or an organization.
Set of episodes: each episode represents an action performed by actors using resources. An episode may be explained as a scenario; this enables a scenario to be split into sub-scenarios.

Figure 4 shows two scenarios of the proposed case study. Words in bold represent LEL symbols. Thus, both models are connected by means of the hypertext view of the *requirements baseline.*

The scenario construction process (Leite et al., 2000) starts from the application lexicon, producing a first version of the scenarios derived exclusively from the LEL. These scenarios are improved using other sources of information and are organized in order to obtain a consistent set of scenarios that represent the application. During or after these activities, the scenarios are verified and validated with the clients/users to detect Discrepancies, Errors, and Omissions (DEO). The process is composed of five activities. The first activity is the *Derive* activity, which aims to generate the derived candidate scenarios from the information of the LEL by using the scenario meta-model and applying the derivation heuristics. The derivation process consists of three steps: identifying the

Figure 4: A scenario corresponding to the payment

> **Title**:   To pay installment.
> **Objective**: The **subscriber** has to pay the **monthly installment** corresponding to his **saving plan**.
> **Context**:   The payment is done in the **Bank**. Restriction: installment is not due.
> **Actors**:   **Subscriber, Bank, Administration**.
> **Resources**: **Payment receipt**.
> **Episodes**:
> The **subscriber** gives the **Bank** employee the **payment receipt** with the correspondent amount.
> The **Bank** employee returns the stamped **payment receipt**.
> The **Bank** sends the payment voucher to the Administration.
>
> **Title**:   To transfer plan.
> **Objective**: To change the owner of a plan.
> **Context**:   The **subscriber** decides to transfer the **saving plan**. *Restrictions*: The **subscriber** should have all the **installments** paid.
> **Actors**:   **Administration, subscriber, group**.
> **Resources**: **authentic communication**.
> **Episodes**:
> The **subscriber** sends an **authentic communication** informing the change of the owner of the **saving plan**.
> The **Administration** registers the modifications caused for new adherent in the **group**.
> The **Administration** deletes the **subscriber** from the **group**.

actors of the *UofD*, identifying the candidate scenarios, and creating scenarios using the lexicon. The *Describe* activity aims to improve the candidate scenarios by adding information from the *UofD* by using the scenario meta-model, the LEL symbols, and application of the description heuristics. The result is a set of fully described scenarios. This activity should be planned and usually relies on structured interviews, observations, and document reading. The *Organize* activity is the most complex and more systematized activity in our scenario construction process. It is based on the idea of *integration scenarios* (i.e., artificial descriptions with the sole purpose of making the set of scenarios more understandable and manageable). Integration scenarios give a global vision of the application. Each integration scenario episode corresponds to a scenario. *Verify* activity is performed at least twice during the scenario building process: The first Verify is performed over the fully described scenario set and the second Verify is performed after the Organize activity. This is done following a checklist with verification heuristics. As a consequence of this activity, two DEO lists are produced: One is used for the Describe activity and the other one is used during the LEL construction process. The verification is divided into three activities: intra scenarios, inter scenarios, and verification (against the LEL verification). Using the verification DEO lists, the scenarios and the LEL are modified. If major corrections are needed, a new verification could be required. Finally, scenarios are *Validated* with stakeholders, usually accomplished by performing structured interviews or conducting meetings.

Business rule model

We define business rules as statements about the enterprise's way of doing business (Leite & Leonardi, 1998). Organizations have policies in order to satisfy the business objectives, satisfy customers, make good use of resources, and conform to laws

Figure 5: Business rule taxonomy

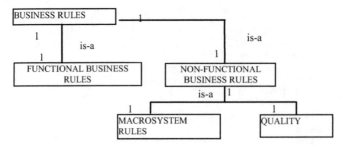

or general business conventions. The business rule model distinguishes between functional rules and non-functional rules as shown in Figure 5.

Each type of rule is described in the following sub-sections. The syntax of the rules follows our approach of using restricted, natural language to express entries in our client-oriented requirements baseline.

Non-functional Rules

Non-functional business can be further classified as general or macrosystem rules and quantity rules. We exemplify each type below:

Macrosystem Rules: This type of rule describes policies that constraints the behavior or structure of the organization. It has the following pattern:

[Property]+Non-verb Phrase+Relation+ [Property] +Non-verb Phrase

where:
- Property is a phrase denoting a characteristic of a Non-verb Phrase.
- Non-verb Phrase is a phrase, which should be an entry in the LEL.
- Relation is a Verbal Phrase.
- Property and relation may be an entry in the LEL.
- A combination of property and relation with a Non-verb Phrase may be an entry in the LEL.

The following are examples of the case study. The bold words are LEL terms.

The **grantee** may reject the **car** up to three times.
A **subscriber** may belong to one or more **groups**.

Quality Rules: Quality rules are demands of the organization on the characteristics of its processes or products. They usually reflect general policies related to quality standards or quality expectations of the organization. They have the following pattern:

Non-verb Phrase + [SHOULD | SHOULD NOT | MUST | MUST NOT] + Verbal Phrase + Property + [BECAUSE + Cause]

where:
- Property is a phrase denoting a quality characteristic.
- Non-verb Phrase is a phrase, which should be an entry in the LEL.
- Property and Verbal Phrase may be an entry in the LEL.
- A combination of a property and relation with a Non-verb Phrase may be an entry in the LEL.
- Cause is a sentence, and as such, may have a combination of a Non-verb Phrase with a Verbal Phrase.

Example:

The **authentic notice** to the winner of the **bid** or **Draw** MUST be sent as soon as possible BECAUSE the **subscriber** has short term to accept or not.

Functional Rules: Functional rules are general policies regarding organizational functionality. They follow the following pattern:

Non-verb Phrase + Verbal Phrase + [Non-verb Phrase]

where:
- Non-verb Phrase is a phrase, which should be an entry in the LEL.
- Verbal Phrase may be an entry in the LEL.
- A combination of a Verbal Phrase with a Non-verb Phrase may be an entry in the LEL.

Example:

The **Administrator** monthly **draws** and **bids** two **cars**

The business rules construction process (Leonardi et al., 1998) begins with the identification of the sources of information. Organization documents, such as ISO-required documents (Schmauch, 1995) and organizational models (Yu, 1995; Fiorini et al., 1997) are generally the best sources. If the company does not have any documentation, other techniques such as observation, interviews, and meetings should be used to acquire the information. We categorize the sentences that appear in the sources by considering their purpose in the organization. We try to distinguish sentences referring to: limits, responsibilities, and rights. To decide if a sentence is a business rule, we analyze if it is determined by a decision of the organization (for internal or external reasons) or if it is an inherent sentence to the functionality of the *UofD* (in which case it is not considered a rule). Taking the concept of stability we determine the stability of each sentence. We use the degree of stability of a sentence, not only to determine if it is a rule as (Diaz et al., 1997), but also to attach that information to the rule to help in the construction of architecture adaptable to the organizational changes. Business rules are classified and documented following the presented syntax patterns, connecting them with the corresponding LEL symbols. After documentation, the model is verified against the set of scenarios and the LEL. For the verification process, we use a set of questions of the type: a) For a given rule, e.g., which is the context of the organization in which this rule is applied? What is the associated behavior? What are the consequences produced by the application of the rule? and b) For a particular scenario, e.g., are there any policies that can modify the behavior of the episodes? Finally, the model is validated with the stakeholders in order to detect elicitation errors or organizational conflicts. It is an informal validation with the help of a syntactic-oriented procedure that identifies subsets of related rules given by the use of LEL symbols.

THE BUSINESS MODEL OF RUP

As a previous activity to the analysis stage, and with the objective of understanding the context in which the system will be implemented, RUP proposes the construction of a business model (Jacobson et al., 1999). Business modeling is a technique for understanding the business processes of an organization by identifying the business or domain objects involved in the business, and also establishing the competencies required in each process: the workers, their responsibilities, and the operations they will perform. This activity is supported by two kinds of UML models: use cases models and object models, both of them defined in the business-specific extension to UML:

- A *business use cases model* (BUC): This model describes the business processes of an organization in terms of *business use cases* and business *actors* corresponding to business processes and customers, respectively. BUC are descriptions of the business system from the perspective of their use.
- A *business-objects model*: This is an interior model of the business. It defines how each business use cases is realized by a set of workers who are using a set of *business entities* and work units. Each realization can be shown in an interaction diagram (collaboration or sequence) or an activity diagram (Rumbaugh et al., 1999). The business entities are shown using a class diagram.

Business model definition consists of the two following steps:

- Definition of the *business use cases* starting from the business actors.
- Definition of the *business-object model* by identifying the workers and the business entities that together realize the business use cases. Business rules and other regulations imposed on the business are associated with the objects. The workers found in business modeling are used as the starting point to derive a first set of actors and use cases for the information system to be built. This allows for tracing every use case of the information system back to its origin in the business.

As we observe, RUP does not present any concrete heuristics to be used in the business model definition. Therefore, we believe that the incorporation of the client-oriented requirements models and a set of heuristics to manipulate and guide them in the business model construction, may enhance the early requirements stage of RUP, improving in consequence, the overall process. The use of heuristics encourages the pre-traceability of the *business uses cases* and the *business objects*, relating them to their origins described in the different models of the *requirements baseline*.

A CONSTRUCTION PROCESS OF THE RUP BUSINESS MODEL BASED ON NATURAL LANGUAGE ORIENTED REQUIREMENTS MODELS

This section describes the strategy for the construction of the RUP starting from the *requirements baseline* models. The first step is to define the business uses cases starting from the scenarios model and follow with the construction of the *business objects* models. Following a similar philosophy to RDD (Wirfs, 1995), RBM (Cockburn, 1999), our proposal begins with the definition of the classes and its responsibilities, leaving for a later stage the static aspects of the objects (attributes and associations). Finally, we describe the realizations of the business uses cases (i.e., the responsibilities and collaborations among the classes that allow them to perform each business uses cases). The activities of the strategy are:

* Business use-cases model definition.
* Business classes identification and definition.
* Business object diagram definition.
* Business use cases model realization.

For each activity we present, in the following sub-sections, a set of heuristics to be used as a guide in developing the RUP models based on the *requirements baseline* models. The heuristics are defined by the following pattern:

Identity: An abbreviation will be used to identify each heuristic. All the heuristics related to the CRCs definition begin with HC, the heuristics related to the business uses cases with HUC, and those related to the logical model with HM. Identity is used for the traceability relationships created from the application of the heuristics.

Description: Each heuristic will be described and justified. The heuristic may contain sub-heuristics, which are identified with an order corresponding to the heuristic that they belong to.

Example: Each heuristic will be exemplified using the case study presented in the introduction.

Business use-cases model definition

As we mentioned, the first step is to define the business use cases through the following heuristic:

* **HUC1:** DEFINING BUSINESS USE CASES FROM SCENARIOS

  Description: Both business use cases as scenarios describe situations of business systems without considering the existence of the software. Business use cases are defined directly from the scenarios. The actors and the workers of the business use cases are the actors in the scenarios that correspond to the LEL subject. Although in the LEL an explicit classification of who the client and the worker of the organization are does not exist, these may be deduced from the notions of the LEL term. In the same way, as business use cases are identified from actors, scenarios are derived from the LEL subject. Some conceptual differences exist among the business use cases and the scenarios. The actors of the scenarios can interact among them. Additionally, scenarios may have some type of inter-action, through the preconditions, in addition to the IS-A and USES interaction proposed by Jacobson et al. (1999). By definition, the business use case does not possess these characteristics (one of the deficiencies of UML as a requirements specification language pointed out by Glinz (2000)). Therefore, we can obtain the business use cases from the scenarios in a straightforward way.

Example: All the scenarios of the case study become the business use cases:

Title: To pay due installment.
Objective: The **subscriber** has to pay the **monthly installment** corresponding to his saving **plan**.
Context: The payment is done in the **Administrator** building. Restriction: the **installment** is due.
Actors: **Subscriber, Administrator**.
Resources: **Payment receipt**.
Episodes:
The **subscriber** gives to the Administrator employee the **payment receipt** with the amount corresponding to the actualized **monthly installment** plus the due amount.
The **Administrator** employee returns the stamped **payment receipt**.

Business classes identification and definition

Once the business use cases are defined, the next step is to define the business classes. It is important to remark that when the *UofD* is analyzed, entities that participate actively and entities that are used to carry out some action can be distinguished. This distinction is reflected in the classification of actor or resource as considered in the scenario model and as object- or subject-considered in the LEL. As the business classes define the *UofD*, they will have these same distinction. Therefore, we can consider primary and secondary classes. Although from the object-oriented paradigm there is no distinction between kinds of objects, heuristics to define them are different. Inside the *UofD* they have different semantics: the primary classes are those that represent the active entities of the *UofD* and the secondary classes are the ones that represent the passive entities.

- **HC1:** MODELING LEL SUBJECTS AS PRIMARY CLASSES
  Description: LEL subjects correspond to actors and workers in the business use case. They represent individuals or a part of the organization. Within the scope of conceptual modeling, these entities are those that carry out the main actions of the organization. For this reason, their representation as classes is automatic.

Example: Subscriber is a LEL term that is an actor of the scenarios with a relevant behavior for the *UofD*. He is the client of the Administrator and a member of a group for a particular saving plan. Therefore, when applying HC1, this term is modeled as a class.

- **HC2:** DETERMINING RESPONSIBILITIES FROM BEHAVIORAL RESPONSES OF THE SUBJECT LEL TERMS

  Description: As each primary class is modeled from the LEL subject, all the behavioral responses define actions performed by the term. Each impact is then defined as a responsibility of the correspondent class. A particular case exists when the impact defines a verbal phrase that has been modeled as a term of the LEL. This term will be analyzed for being able or not able to be modeled as a class in the identification of the secondary classes. As a first solution, the term will be modeled as a responsibility of the primary class. It will also collaborate with the class that represents the action.

  Example: In the LEL term subscriber (modeled as a class by applying HC1), several behavioral responses appear (e.g., to pay a monthly installment or to transfer the plan). Both represent significant behavior; therefore, they are modeled as responsibilities of the class.

The following heuristics guide in the definition of the secondary class (i.e., those that represent resources so that primary classes can perform their responsibilities). They are passive entities inside the *UofD;* generally data repositories. In the context of RUP, they are known as business entities. Although some heuristics are related to LEL symbols that represent states, it is important to remark that the LEL symbols representing states are an exception in the LEL definition.

- **HC3:** DEFINITION OF BUSINESS ENTITIES FROM OBJECTS, STATES, AND VERBAL PHRASES OF THE LEL

  Description: A list with the terms of the LEL that represent objects, verbal phrases, and states is built. Most of these terms appear previously in each one of the responsibilities of the defined primary classes. However, new terms can appear that are not directly related to the previously-defined classes. Each term is analyzed to determine if it will be modeled or not modeled as an object.

  HC3.1: LEL OBJECTS AS ATTRIBUTES OR CLASSES

  Description: Behavioral responses of the LEL object are analyzed. If the term does not represent a relevant behavior for the *UofD*, it is modeled as an attribute. To determine the primary class that will contain the attribute, the notions and impacts of the terms corresponding to the defined classes are analyzed. Business use cases in which the term appears may be revised in case of doubt. One way of deciding if it will be modeled as an attribute, is to analyze whether the impacts of the term are describing actions similar to some primitive class (e.g., Integer, String). That is to say that, although it is a characteristic abstraction of the system in terms of objects, it is not worth modeling as a new class (Meyer, 1997).

If the term represents a significant behavior for the *UofD*, it will be modeled as a class because it modeled a necessary resource for primary classes to perform their responsibilities.

Example: The LEL term Monthly installment does not represent a behavior that justifies its modeling as a class; therefore, it will be modeled as an attribute of Administration class. On the other hand, the term Authentic Communication is a term that represents a communication mechanism used inside the Administration. For this reason, it is modeled as a class to distinguish the different communication forms from the entities that use them.

HC3.2: VERBAL PRASES AS CLASSES OR RESPONSIBILITIES

Description: If the term corresponds to an action, it may be modeled as an individual class or as a responsibility of a previously-defined class. Typical examples of action classes are the bank transactions as either deposit or extraction, each having its own attributes that justify modeling as a class. If this is the case, it is modeled like a class. Otherwise, it will be modeled as one or more responsibilities of the objects involved. The abuse of modeling behavior as classes in the first stages of development is one of the main causes of a bad definition of classes (Meyer, 1997). If a class is described for the capacity to perform only one action, would it not be more appropriately modeled as a responsibility of another class? Modeling the action as a class may be justified if it represents a complex behavior, or if it keeps properties that correspond to the action rather than any other class (i.e., as mentioned in the examples of bank transactions).

Example: The LEL term, to bid, has a group of impacts that justifies representation as a class as it describes one of the main actions of the Administration. It is also necessary to keep characteristic information of the bid that cannot be stored in another class. For this reason, it is modeled as class bid. Class bid will collaborate with the Administration. However, the term, To Expel Adherent, has no impacts that justify class modeling. Therefore it remains as a responsibility of the Administration class.

HC3.3: STATES LIKE CLASSES OR ATTRIBUTES

Description: If the term corresponds to a state, then by definition (see Figure 1), it affects the *UofD* either as a whole or through some of its entities that are reflected as LEL terms. The fact that it was modeled as a different term implies that it has notions or impacts that characterize and distinguish it from the term that it affects. If the affected LEL term was modeled as a class, the term is analyzed to determine whether the state can become an attribute (with a new responsibility that modifies it). If it has impacts that can be modeled as responsibilities, then it is a candidate for modeling as a different class.

- **HC4:** DEFINING RESPONSIBILITIES OF THE SECONDARY CLASSES USING THE LEL

Description: As with the primary classes, the impacts of the LEL terms corresponding to the previously-defined classes are analyzed. It is necessary to keep in mind the category of the LEL term (see Figure 1) as the meaning of the impacts depend on each LEL term category.

HC4.1: DETERMINING RESPONSIBILITIES OF THE OBJECTS' TERMS OF THE LEL

Description: The impacts of an object term describe what actions can be applied to it. In terms of the object-oriented paradigm, this does not necessarily imply that the object will always be responsible for responding to these actions. This depends on the semantics of the impact. In general, there will always be a responsibility associated with the impact; but, sometimes the objects are a resource for other objects without an associated responsibility. In this case, it is necessary to find another term for the impact that represents this class or to analyze the group of business use cases where this term appears to look for the actions associated to this impact and to determine the involved classes.

Example: If we consider the impact, It is filled by the applicant, of the LEL term Application, we realize that a responsibility should be defined for the class Application that allows it to be filled (in this case, a basic responsibility). In addition, it is necessary to define a responsibility "toCompleteApplication" for the Applicant class.

HC4.2: DETERMINING THE RESPONSIBILITIES OF THE LEL TERMS' VERBAL PHRASE

Description: Behavioral responses of the verbal phrase describe restrictions of the action and new actions. If behavioral responses are a restriction, they can derive as new responsibilities as well as affect existing responsibilities (this case is analyzed during static diagram definition). If modeled as an action, the response should be analyzed to determine whether there is an LEL term in the impact that is the performer of the action. In this case, a collaboration exists between both classes. If this is not the case, the impact will be modeled as the responsibility of the class that is representing the verb.

Example: In analyzing the LEL term, Draws, to define the responsibilities of the corresponding class, it is seen that the impact ..is defined the winner adherent... is a responsibility of the class. On the other hand, the impact ..the adherent who won the draw may reject the car... establishes two actions: a rejection action for the Adherent class and an acceptance action of rejection for the Draw class, which have to evaluate this rejection collaborating with the Administration class.

HC4.3: DETERMINING THE RESPONSIBILITIES OF THE TERMS CORRESPONDING TO STATES

Description: If the term is a state, some of the two previous heuristics is applied (HC4.1 and HC4.2) depending on the classification of the term affected by the state.

Once we obtain the candidate business classes and their main responsibilities, the following step is taken to refine the responsibilities as they appear in a general way as extracted from the impacts of the correspondent LEL terms. To accomplish this, business use cases and business rules are used following the heuristics mentioned next.

- **HC5:** REFINING RESPONSIBILITIES ANALYZING THE BUSINESS USE CASES MODEL

  Description: A list with the business use cases is built where each one of the defined classes appears. When identifying the responsibilities starting from the LEL impacts, responsibilities can be very general. Therefore, it is necessary to refine them using the business use cases, thereby defining the associated sub-responsibilities (later on these sub-responsibilities may be defined as methods). The episodes are analyzed and the responsibilities are refined with the actions that the class carries out to fulfill that responsibility. When refining the responsibilities, it can be detected that in most of the cases, the actions of the responsibility are carried out by other classes. Subsequently, the corresponding action is defined, the collaboration is specified in the class, and it is verified whether some responsibility that can carry out the collaboration exists in the other class.

  Example: Analyzing the scenario, to bid, in which the responsibility "bid of Adherent" appears, it is determined that this responsibility can be refined as "toCreateEnvelopes" and "ToSendEnvelope." The first responsibility collaborates with the "bidEnvelope" class, while the other responsibility collaborates with Administration class. It is verified that for both classes there are responsibilities that allow for the fulfillment of this collaboration. In this case, a responsibility "toCreateEnvelope" is added to the "bidEnvelope" class.

  HC5.1: ANALYZING STRUCTURES OF THE BUSINESS USE CASES THAT INDICATE ALTERNATIVE COURSES OF ACTION

  Description: In order to evaluate different behavioral alternatives, whether there are exceptions, restrictions, or conditional clauses associated with each responsibility appearing in the business uses cases should be analyzed. In such cases the responsibility is refined, or new responsibilities are generated, to be able to carry out the behavior detailed in the alternative course.

  Example: When analyzing the "ToEvaluateBid" scenario is observed, a conditional sentence, "... If there are similar offers, the order settled down in the Draw is taken into account to choose the subscriber... " In this case, the responsibility "toEvaluateBid" of Bid class is refined in order to obtain the order of the draw from the Draw class.

As a result of the application of the presented heuristics, we complete the classes and their responsibilities. Classes may be modeled with CRC's cards (i.e., cards that represent the responsibilities and collaborations of each defined class) (Beck & Cunningham, 1989). We extend the representation in order to define the justification (the applied heuristic) and the context (the business use cases in which the responsibility appears). This extended notation allows traceability of the models. Figure 6 shows the extended CRC for the subscriber class.

- **HC6:** USING FUNCTIONAL RULE MODEL TO COMPLETE THE CLASSES

  Description: Functional rules define the organization's behavior; therefore, in general, the rules will be modeled as responsibilities. As a consequence, we analyze if each rule has been modeled as a responsibility of the class corresponding with some of the LEL terms that appear in the rule.

Figure 6: Subscriber class

Name class: Subscriber Justification: HC1: He is an actor of the scenarios with a relevant behavior for the UofD (is the client of the **Administration**, a member of a special **saving plan group**)		
Responsibilities	**Collaborations**	**Context** (BUC)
1. To pay **monthly installment**. 2. To transfer the **plan**. 3. **To bid**. 4. **To reject** the **car**. 5. **To give up** the saving plan.	1. **Bank, Administrator.** 2. **Saving plan, Authentic notice.** 3. **Administrator.** 4. **Car, Administrator, raffle, Authentic notice.** 5. **Saving plan, Authentic notice, Administrator.**	1. To pay installment; To pay due installment. 2. To transfer the plan. 3. To bid. 4. To reject the car. 5. To give up the saving plan.

Example: The rule "**Administration** should call to a **Meeting of subscribers in case of discontinuation of the car**" reflects an obligation of the Administration; however, it was not previously modeled as a responsibility of the corresponding class. A new responsibility is defined to represent it.

HC6.1: MODELING BUSINESS RULES AS CLASSES

Description: In some particular situations, it is a good modeling practice to define business rules as classes, depending on semantics and relevance. To do this, we can group functional and non-functional business rules that represent a particular activity of the *UofD*. We analyze the complexity, stability (Leonardi et al., 1998), and the importance of the activity inside the *UofD*. We then decide whether it is convenient to model the group in an independent way. In this case, a new class is defined to model these rules, which is connected with the involved classes. Defining business rules as classes improves the understanding and maintenance of the future system (Diaz et al., 1997). If a rule changes, the associated rules that are encapsulated in the same object can be analyzed without affecting the entire system. Classes representing rules can be specialized independently from the objects they affect. It is also possible to have an activation mechanism in the class that reflects the dynamism of the rules without affecting the conceptual objects involved. The disadvantage of modeling business rules as classes is that the complexity of the object model increases because new objects and relationships are added to it. For this reason, this heuristic is strongly dependent on the rules being modeling with respect to the *UofD*.
Example: The following set of rules represents some policies related to payment.
1.   **Administration** should calculate **installment**.
2.   If case of **no fulfillment of group**, the **Administration** proceeds to the **liquidation of the group**.

3. The no fulfillment on the payment of the **monthly installment** of a **subscriber** determines the liquidation of **interests punishments**.

4. **Subscriber** can choose among a list of Banks to pay the **installment**.

5. If **subscriber rejects to the plan**, **Administration** will return his payments diminished in 2%.

6. The **subscriber** should pay the **monthly installment** within the first five days of the month.

7. The **subscriber** should pay his installment by means of the **payment receipt**.

8. The **subscriber** pays in the selected Bank.

9. The **subscriber** pays the **due installment** in the **Administration**.

10. The **grantee** should pay his installment by means of the **payment receipt**.

11. If unpaid **installments** of the **group** are 60% or more, **Administration** defines the **no fulfillment of the group**.

12. The **applicant** should pay the payments corresponding to the **application** in the **Administration**.

Figure 7: Business rule based class

Name: Payment Administration
Justification: it reflects a set of rules that describes aspects related to payment: definition, due payments, modifications to payment mechanism (HC6.1)

Responsibilities	Collaborators	Context
todeterminePaymentMechanism	**subscriber Administration**	(init)
TogetPaidAccordingRule	**subscriber**	to pay installment
TogetPaidBank		
ToGetPaidAdministratation	**Administration subscriber Bank**	to pay installment
ToGetDueInstallment		
	subscriber grantee	to pay due installment
TocalculatePunishmentInterests		
	subscriber	to pay due installment
ListOfBanks		
	subscriber	to pay due installment
ToGePayAdmision		
	Applicant Administration	to applicant Admission
ToGetPayAdjudication		
	Applicant Administration	Adjudication
ToDetermineNonFullfimentGroup		
	grantee	to Dissolve Group
....		
	Group Administration	....
	....	

This group of rules defines an important behavior for the organization since it determines the mechanism of carrying out the payments and the control of the non-fulfillment of the group, an individual subscriber, or grantee. They are internal rules, since it is the Administration who determines the payment policies. These internal rules affect the adherent and grantees. Although this behavior can be performed by the Administration, due to its importance, it can be modeled by another class that collaborates with the Administration. In this way, the changes related to the payment policies are managed by this class without affecting the Administration. Figure 7 shows the corresponding class.

Business Objects Diagram Definition

Once the classes and their responsibilities have been identified, structural aspects of the classes are modeled. In this strategy, we define a class diagram for the primary classes and the business entities or secondary classes to enhance the proposal of RUP to define an object model for the business entities. This diagram defines the *UofD*. As such, it presents no software limits (a task left for the analysis stage, where the actors of the system are defined and the use cases of the system are identified from the business use cases). The following heuristics guide in the definition of the attributes, methods, and relationships among classes.

- **HM1:** DEFINITION OF CLASSES AND THEIR ATTRIBUTES USING THE CANDIDATES CLASSES AND THE LEL

  Description: Each class candidate becomes a class of the object diagram. For each class, we analyze the notions of the corresponding LEL term, searching for the characteristic properties. It is also necessary to analyze the responsibilities of the class since new attributes can appear, enabling the class to perform the action of the responsibility. Two things can happen:

  HM1.1: HANDLING OF SIMPLE PROPERTIES
  Description: The property is modeled directly as an attribute of the component, since in the LEL, it represents the name of the property.

  HM1.2: HANDLING OF PROPERTIES THAT REPRESENT DIFFERENT VALUES
  Description: In the LEL term, several properties appear modeling different states or concrete values of the term. In this case it is possible to choose one of two alternatives:
  - The first alternative is to define an attribute whose domain is the group of values that appear in the term.
  - The second alternative is to define a Boolean attribute for each property. If it can be detected that some non-functional rules affect these values, then it is better to model as an independent attribute to be able to reflect the rule.

- **HM2:** DEFINITION OF THE METHODS
  Description: Each responsibility is a candidate to be modeled as a method. However, as with the attributes, the following things may happen:

HM2.1: ANALYZING RESPONSIBILITIES RELATED TO THE SAME ATTRIBUTE

Description: Several responsibilities of a class can modify the same attribute in different ways. The Software Engineer decides to define a method for each responsibility or to define only one method for managing the different alternatives through parameters. Although this is a design decision that depends on the software engineer, it is possible to obtain information that helps to make a better decision (for example, how many times each method candidate is used or if there is some rule that affects a particular responsibility) through the business use cases, business rules, and LEL models.

HM2.2: ANALYZING THE DIVISION OF A RESPONSIBILITY

Description: A responsibility may be split within several methods, since it defines actions that are also performed by other responsibilities of the same class. For this reason, it is better to isolate this action and transform it into a method.

HM2.3: DEFINING PARAMETERS OF A RESPONSIBILITY ANALYZING THE BUSINESS USE CASES

Description: In order to define the parameters of the methods, the group of business use cases containing the responsibility of each class is analyzed. For each one of them, the data used to perform the method is analyzed and new attributes are defined in case there is no previous definition.

HM2.4: INCORPORATING BASIC METHODS TO CLASSES

Description: To complete the definition of methods, the basic methods of access and modification, which were not defined in previous stages, are described. This takes into account any disregard for those attributes that represent a property that can not be modified explicitly.

HM2.5: FACTORING OF RESPONSIBILITIES

Description: Although in the definition of the responsibilities the services of each class were expressed concretely, it should be analyzed if similar responsibilities exist when defining the methods and thinking of an object-oriented solution. To do this, it is necessary to "think" the responsibilities in a generic form, i.e., if a certain responsibility is for example, "printXX," and another responsibility is "printMM," the method will be "print." This strategy decreases the number of methods of a class, improving the future object-oriented design (Cockburn, 1999).

Figure 8 shows a partial description of a class with the heuristics that created or modified some of its attributes and methods.

As illustrated by the example, there are some attributes and methods modified or created by heuristics (**HM4**) related to the application of business rules (as we will see later on in this section).

- **HM3:** DEFINITION OF RELATIONSHIPS AMONG CLASSES USING THE LEL

  Description: The notions of the LEL terms that correspond to each defined class are analyzed in order to detect other LEL terms that have been defined as classes.

Figure 8: Class definition

Administration   (**HM1**)
⇒   Attributes
    – Name
    – Address
    – Saving Plans (**HM1.1**)
    – AdmissionFee (**HM3.1**)
    – AllowedRejectAmount (**HM4.1**)
    – MinimalCardinaltyGroup
⇒   Methods
    - Transfer (cft) (**HM2/ HM2.3**)
          cft.applicant?.changeData(cft)
          self.eliminateSubscriber

    – analizeRejectOfCar(adh) (**HM4.3**)
          If (adh.#Reject?.<= AllowedRejectAmount)
            toEliminateSubscriber(adh)
        ....

    – toAcceptAdmission (solAdh)
          pre: today() <= solAdh.data +10 or toAcceptAdmission =true (**HM5.3**)
  ....

    – toEliminateSubscriber (adh) (**HM2/ HM4.3**)
          adh.group? toEliminate (adh)
          If adh.group? .#Adh? <= MinimalCardinaltyGroup
            adh.group?.Savingplan? toEliminateGroup(adh.group?.)

    – toGiveCar(grt)
          pre: today() <= grt. BidDate +60 (**HM4.3**)
        ....
    – toFormGroup (gr)
    –   pre:gr.subscribers->size>=gr.savingPlan. MinimalCardinaltyGroup (**HM4.3**)
    – toChangeTypeOfCar
       (AuthenticComunication.new) notify (self, group,"changeCar") (**HM4.3**)
    –   ....

In this case, an association relationship is determined between the classes. Cardinality of the associations can be deduced starting from the LEL notions that mention the association. The following sub-heuristics consider the different types of relationships:

HM3.1: DETERMINING INHERITANCE RELATIONSHIPS

> **Description:** In this stage, inheritance relationships reflect real relationships among terms of the *UofD*. The notions and the impacts of each LEL term for which a class was built are analyzed. Relationships can be identified in two ways:

- In the notion of the LEL terms, it is suggested explicitly that this term is a specialization / generalization of another LEL term. This concept is generally expressed as a linguistic pattern identified by Juristo (Juristo et al., 1998) as *bottom-up verbs* and *top-down verbs*: "to be, to be a type, to be a class, it can be." Other types of verbs can be "to specialize, to generalize or to refine."

- Similar behavioral responses appear in different LEL terms suggesting a common behavior that can be modeled as an inheritance relationship. However, this is not common. Through the "closure principle," engineers model explicitly the relationships between the two LEL terms, obviating in consequence, the repetition of impacts.

HM3.2: DEFINING PART-OF RELATIONSHIPS

Description: This relationship is identified if reference "that the class is formed by other classes" appears explicitly in the notions of the LEL term that is considered the container. These notions contain verbs of the type "component_composition_verb" (Juristo et al., 1998): "to consist / to contain / to have / to possess / to include / to form, to compose, to divide" (these three last in passive voice). Likewise, the notions of the "component" term must suggest that the component is involved in the "part-of" relationship, which is identified with the content_composition_verb (Juristo et al., 1998): "it is part, it belongs, it is a component, it is included," among others. Behavioral responses of the LEL term of the container class are analyzed in order to determine if the class participates in the creation or destruction of the components. It is difficult to detect the type of composition (shared aggregation or simple aggregation vs. not shared aggregation or composition), following the UML terminology, since the semantics of this relationship is still under discussion (Henderson Sellers & Barbier, 1999). In this sense, only dependence of existence can be deduced from the notions and impacts or in the related business use cases. This determines if the life of the LEL term that corresponds to the component class is bound to the life of the class that contains it.

HM3.3: DETERMINING ASSOCIATION RELATIONSHIPS

Description: Determining association relationships can be accomplished by analyzing the collaborations among the classes. Any collaboration among classes that does not represent a relationship of the previous type represents an association. The verb that figures in the responsibility (categorized as *general* verb) in Juristo et al. (1998) determines the name for the relationship.

Example: Starting from the LEL terms of Figure 2, the following analysis can be carried out: in the first notion of **Subscriber**, the bottom-up/top-down verb "is" appears connecting the subscriber class with an **Applicant** via inheritance relationship (**HM3.1**). The second notion has the verb "to belong" of the type *content-composition-verb*. In the same way found in the

LEL term group, the first notion suggests a composition relationship. This indicates a composition relationship between **Group** and **Adherent** (**HM3.2**).

- **HM4:** APPLYING NON-FUNCTIONAL RULE MODEL TO THE OBJECT DIAGRAM

Description: The Macrosystem, non-functional rules model introduces modifications in the object diagrams in order to reflect the non-functional business rules that affect the structure and behavior of the organization. The aim of the incorporation of these rules in the business object model is the identification of the components, and more concretely, the methods, attributes, classes, and relationships among classes that are affected by each rule. Rules may be expressed using the OCL (Warner & Kleppe, 1999). Taking into account that the rules are anchored to the LEL by the use of the LEL symbols, (from an object-oriented point of view), rules will affect classes, attributes, or responsibilities that arise from the LEL symbols that appear in the original rules. Quality rules will be applied further, during the software limits definition, which is out of the scope of this chapter.

HM4.1: TO ANALYZE RULES THAT AFFECT A CLASS

Description: The rule can affect the class as a whole or the attributes of the class:

- In the first situation, the only characteristic of the class that can be affected is cardinality, since any other characteristic would imply an attribute, class, or method. This is not a frequent situation. Cardinality may be expressed in OCL with the method size of collection. (className.size -> quantity of instances of the class).
- If the rule affects an attribute, it is marked in the class as an invariant. Responsibilities implicit in the rule or related to a functional rule should be sought. In this case, sub-heuristic HM4.3 will be applied.

Example: The business rule " ...A subscriber can reject the car up to three times ..." is expressed in the same way:

Context : Subscriber
    #Rejections <= 3

This restriction may be enhanced by adding an attribute in the **Administration** class, (**AllowedRejectAmount=3**), therefore any change in the particular value affects only the class **Administration** and the rest of the classes use this attribute.

Context : Subscriber
    #Rejections <= Administration. AllowedRejectAmount

HM4.2: ANALYZING RULES THAT AFFECT SEVERAL CLASSES

Description: Rule may affect the classes as a whole or the attributes of the classes.

- In the first case, rule affects the cardinality of some type of relationship between the two classes (composition or association). These relationships were previously generated. If this is not the case, it should be added. Cardinality restriction is indicated in the relationship.

- If the rule affects the attributes, it can be modeled as an OCL expression over the corresponding attributes.

Example: The rule "...The quantity of members of a **group** doubles the quantity of **installments** of the elected **plan**..." determines the minimum quantity of **Subscribers** of a **Group**. This may be expressed in the following way:

```
context: SavingPlan
    minimalGroupSize := self.#installment * 2
context: Group
    (Subscribers.size + Grantee.size) >= SavingPlan.minimalGroupSize
```

HM4.3: ANALYZING RULES THAT AFFECT METHODS

Description: If the rule has associated some class responsibility, the methods associated to the rule should be sought. In each method, pre- and post- conditions are added to reflect the rule. Whether it is necessary to add an attribute into the class that contains the method should be analyzed.

Example: Continuing with the example of the sub-heuristic HM5.1, the rule "...If the subscriber rejects the car three times the Administration expel him of the Group..." indicates the behavior associated with the rejection. It is indicated in the corresponding method.

```
Subscriber:
    toRejectCar
    post= pre@#reject = 3 implies subscriber.Group ->
    includes (subscriber) =
        false
```

Realization of the business uses cases

The next step is to describe the *business use cases* based on the previously-defined classes. As indicated in this chapter, business uses cases realizations may be defined by means of interaction diagrams (collaboration or sequence) or activity diagrams. The heuristics may be used as informal validation mechanisms. By applying heuristics, the business use cases are "executed" and the engineer may analyze if the defined classes and their responsibilities may carry out the behavior of the BUC.

- **HBOM1:** MODELING BUSINESS USE CASES AS ACTIVITY DIAGRAM

Description: Activity diagrams emphasize the sequential and concurrent steps inside a process, taking into account the actors who perform the behavior. Activity diagrams describe the order of the activities and optionally, the inputs / outputs by means of the flow of objects. There is no explicit assignment of responsibilities to the object. However, the swimlane of the activity diagram can be used to organize the activities with a particular criterion. In this context, activities are grouped, taking into account the primary classes. The secondary classes remain as activities (if it is a class that represents an action) or as input / output of the activities.

For each business use cases:
For each episode:
1.   Are actors and workers of the BUC represented as primary classes?

> To define a swimlane for each class, start with the class that unchains the business use cases. The name of the swimlane is the name of the primary class.

Else:

> To define the corresponding primary classes and return to this process.

2.   Is each activity of the episode represented in the responsibilities of the corresponding primary classes?

> 2.1. To write the activity with the name assigned for that responsibility in the swimlane of the corresponding class.
> 2.2. The resources used in the activity can be used as input or output values, indicating the changes of state through a flow of objects.
> 2.3. To indicate the beginning/end sign control indicating the concurrent activities for concurrent episodes.
> 2.4. To indicate the corresponding "guards" and the alternative actions with the class responsibilities if conditional sentences or context restrictions exist.

Else:

> To add responsibilities and return to this process.

- **HBOM2:** MODELING BUSINESS USE CASES AS SEQUENCE DIAGRAMS
  Description: The sequence diagrams show the interaction of the objects in a sequence of time, defining the interchange of messages between the objects. This diagram is one of the most used by UML in order to specify the use cases.

For each business use cases:
For each episode:
1.   Are actors and workers represented as primary classes?

> To create a line with the name of the primary class.

Else:

> To define the corresponding primary classes and return to this process.

2.   Are the resources of the episode modeled as secondary classes?

> 2.1. To create a line with the name of the secondary class to represent the "rol" in the activity.
> 2.2. To use the special notation if the object is created as a consequence of that message.

Else:

> To define the corresponding classes and return to this process.

3.   Is each activity of the episode represented in the responsibilities of the corresponding class?

> 3.1. To create an arrow with the message from the class requiring the services to the class performing it (both represented with lines).

3.2. To define the input in the message and the output in the dotted line that it returns to the class.

3.3. To indicate corresponding "guards" in each alternative arrows if conditional sentences or context restrictions exist.

Else:

To add responsibilities and return to the process.

- **HBOM3:** TO MODEL THE USE CASES THROUGH COLLABORATION DIAGRAMS
  Description: These diagrams show the interactions of the objects organized by "rol" (i.e., squares representing instances and their associations inside collaboration) showing explicitly the relationships among the rol.

For each business use cases:
For each episode:

1. Are actors and workers represented as primary classes?

    To create a slot with the name of the primary class to represent the rol.

    Else:

    To define the corresponding primary classes and return to this process.

2. Are the resources of the episode modeled as secondary classes?

    2.1. To create a slot with the name of the class to represent the rol.

    2.2. If the object is created as a consequence of a message, to place in the slot the key word " new."

    Else:

    To define the corresponding classes and to reassume this process.

3. To define the links corresponding to the object's associations. To analyze this association (obtained in HM3) and define a line that indicates the navigability.

4. Is each activity of the episode represented in the responsibilities of the corresponding class?

    4.1. To create and numerate an arrow with the message sent by the requester class to the performer class.

    4.2. To define the parameters in the message among brackets.

    4.3. To indicate sub-responsibilities by means of a relative-nested numeration to the message that contains them if the responsibility has sub-responsibilities (obtained in the heuristic HC5).

    4.4. To add a letter to the numbers of messages if the episodes are concurrent.

    4.5. To indicate the corresponding "guards" as predecessors of the names of the messages if conditional sentences or context restrictions exist.

    Else:

    To add responsibilities and to return to this process.

Example: Figure 9 shows the realization of "To transfer the saving plan" business use case (Figure 4) modeled as a sequence diagram following HBOM2.

Figure 9: Sequence diagram corresponding to "To transfer the plan" business use case

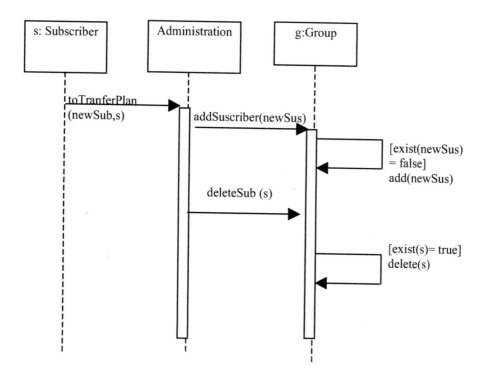

TRACEABILITY BETWEEN BASELINE REQUIREMENTS MODELS AND UML BUSINESS MODELS

Requirements traceability has been defined as "the ability to describe and follow information about the life of a requirement in both a forwards and backwards direction, known as pre and post traceability" (Gotel & Finkelstein, 1994). This strategy identifies and maintains the trace relationships generated by the application of the heuristics, enhancing the UML trace relationship that only relates models of different development stages. In our proposal, trace relates models of the business model stage.   More precisely, trace relates object diagrams and use cases with the LEL terms, scenarios, and business rules that generate or modify them. It also shows relationships between class candidates and their responsibilities with the UML classes, methods, and attributes.

Figure 10: Traceability relationships among requirements baseline models and UML business models

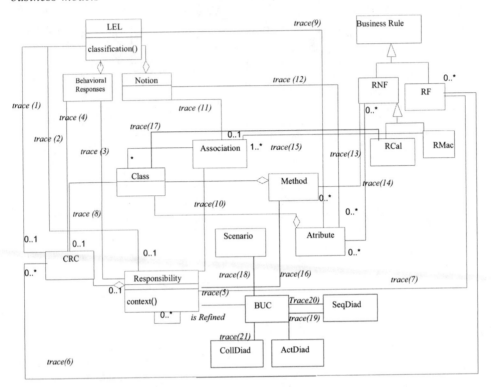

Figure 10 shows the meta-model of the models and their components as used in this strategy. The involved classes are:

- Classes corresponding to the *requirements baseline* models: LEL (with its components, behavioral responses, and notions), scenario and business rules (with its hierarchy of RF for the functional rules and RNF for the non-functional rules, which in turn are divided into Rcal and Rmac to distinguish the quality rules from the general ones).
- Classes that represent the models and their components, corresponding to the definition of the candidates classes, CRC and Responsibility.
- Classes that represent the models and their components, corresponding to the definition of the RUP conceptual model, Class, Association, Method, and Attribute.
- Classes that represent the business use cases model and their realizations, BUC, ActDiag, SeqDiag and CollDiag.

The trace relationships of Figure 10 correspond to the relationships generated by the application of a particular heuristic between the origin model and the created or modified model. For example, trace(1) relates the candidate class with the LEL term that originated it by applying heuristic HC1. Figures 11 and 12 show the semantic of each

Figure 11: Forward trace relationships corresponding to candidate classes

Destination / Source	CRC	Responsibility	Refined Responsibility	Business Use Case
Subject LEL term	mandatory modeling (1/1) HC1 (trace 1)			
Object or state LEL term	optional modeling (0,1/ 0,1) HC3.1 HC3.3 (trace 1)			
Verbal Phrase LEL	optional modeling (0,1/ 0,1) HC3.2 (trace 1)	optional modeling (0,1/ 0,1) HC3.2 (trace 2)		
Behavioral responses of LEL term	optional modeling (0,1/ 0,1) HC4 (trace 4)	optional modeling (0,1/ 0,1) HC2 HC4 HC5 (trace 3)		
Scenario				mandatory modeling (1/1) HBUC1 (trace 18)
Functional rule	optional modeling (0,+/ 0,+) HC6.2 (trace 6)	optional modeling (0,+/ 0,+) HC6 (trace 7)	optional modeling (0,+/ 0,+) HC6 (trace 7)	

Figure 12: Trace forward relationships of the conceptual model

Destination / Source	Conceptual Class	Method	Attribute	Association
CRC	to become to (1/1) HM1 (trace 8)			
Responsibility		optional modeling (0,+/ 0,+) HM2 (trace 16)		optional modeling (0,1/ 0,1) HM3.3 (trace 10)
Refined responsibility		optional modeling (0,1/ 0,1) HM2.3 (trace 16)		optional modeling (0,1/ 0,1) HM3.3 (trace 10)
object or state LEL term			optional modeling (0,1/ 0,1) HC1.2 (trace 9)	
Notions of LEL			Origin (0+ / 1+) HM1 (trace 12)	optional modeling (0,1/ 0,1) [1] HM3.1 HM3.2 (trace 11)
Macrosystem NF rule	to affect (0+/0+) HM4.1 HM4.2 (trace 17)	to create (0+/0+) or to affect (0+/0+) HM4.3 (trace 13)	to create (0+/0+) or to affect (0+/0+) HM4.1 HM5.2 (trace 14)	to affect (0+/0+) HM4.2 (trace 15)

trace relationship among the generated models. The left column of the figures represents the "Origin" of the relationship and the superior row the "Destination." Each cell indicates information about a particular trace relationship. Forward relationships (Davis, 1993) are considered in the figures; however, backward relationships can also be obtained by starting from there. For each relationship, the following items are indicated:

- Semantic of the relationship, i.e., how the origin affects the destination (e.g., creation, mandatory modeling, optional modeling, to become to, appears in context, to affect to).
- Cardinality of the origin, i.e., how many components were used to create or to modify the new component?
- Cardinality of the destination, i.e., how many components were created or affected?
- Heuristic that originated the trace relationship.
- Trace relationship corresponding to the Figure 10.

Modeling the Trace Relationships: A Trace View

Following a similar philosophy as used in the configuration view (Leite & Oliveira,1995), the strategy defines a trace view to reflect the relationships among the classes of Figure 10 generated by the application of the heuristics. Figure 13 defines the trace view.

An instance of a trace view relates instances of the classes presented in Figure 10 that are generated by the relationships between the classes as a result of the heuristics. These relationships are formally defined using the navigational context concept presented in the object-oriented hypermedia development methodology proposed by (Rossi, 1996). A navigational context is a group of nodes that are related with some criteria (in this strategy a trace relationship) that can be navigated in a certain way. In this strategy, classes of Figure 10 are the nodes that will be navigated through the trace views. The navigational context returns a group (sometimes unitary) of components that fulfills the condition defined in the context for the input parameter. This group of

Figure 13: Trace view

Trace View:
Name: Indicates the semantics of the relationship mentioned in Figures 11 and 12.
Justification: Explains the reason of that relationship, i.e., the heuristic that generated the trace relationship.
Responsible: Indicates the author of the application of the heuristic.
Origin: Identifies instance of any class of Figure 10 that generates the relationship; also, input parameter of the navigational context.
Destination: Identifies instance of any class of Figure 10. (Note: it always retrieves the container class of the involved class, for example if a trace relationship relates an impact and a responsibility, Destination retrieves the candidate class that contains the responsibility.)
Cardinality of Destination: Reflects quantity of instances generated

components corresponds to the attribute destination of the trace view (Figure 13). The syntax of a navigational /context is defined as:

$$Trace_n: Context_{name} (input\ parameter) = \{\ output\ parameter\ class\ /\ conditional\ sentence\ \}$$

where:

- n indicates the trace number indicated in Figure 10.
- Name is the name of the semantics expressed in Figures 11 and 12.
- The input parameter determines the instance of a class that generates the relationship.
- The output parameter class indicates the class that the retrieved instances belong to.
- The conditional sentence represents the different trace conditions that instances must satisfy with respect to the input parameter.

The variables used in the definition of the navigational context are:
- t is an instance of the LEL class.
- crc is an instance of the candidateClass(CRC) class.
- i is an instance of the Impact class.
- buc is an instance of the BUC class.
- fr is an instance of the RF class.
- r is an instance of the Responsibility class.
- n it is an instance of the Notion class.
- rnfc is an instance of the RCal class.
- rnfm it is an instance of the RMac class.
- at is an instance of the Attribute class.

We exemplify some of the forward navigational contexts generated by the relationships detailed in Figures 11 and 12. The examples are instances of the ViewTrace.

- Trace1: Context mandatory modeling (t) = {crc / t.clasification= Subject AND mandatory modeling (t,crc)}

This context retrieves all the primary classes. Figure 14 shows two instances of the trace view for this context. The first context is evaluated for the LEL term, t = Subscriber, retrieving the class originated through the heuristic HC1. The same situation

Figure 14: Instances of trace view created by HC1

Trace:	*Trace:*
Name: mandatory modeling	Name: mandatory modeling
Justification: HC1	Justification: HC1
Source: Subscriber ε **LEL**	Source: **Administration** ε **LEL**
Destination: Subscriber ε **CRC**	Destination: **Administration** ε **CRC**
Cardinality: 1	Cardinality: 1

happens for the second instance of the example that shows the relationship among the term t = administration and its corresponding class.

- Trace2: Context optionally modeling (t) = {crc / res ε Responsibility, t.clasification = Verbal Phrase, part-of (crc, res) AND optionally modeling (t,Res)}

This context retrieves the classes that possess responsibilities that are LEL terms. Figure 15 shows two instances generated by the heuristic HC2. The first instance is the result of applying the context for the LEL term, t = Reject Subscriber that became a responsibility of the Administration class. The second instance corresponds to the application of the context for t = to Reject Car related to Subscriber class, with the responsibility generated by the term.

Figure 15: Instances of trace view created by HC2

Trace:	*Trace:*
Name: optional modeling	Name: optional modeling
Justification: HC2	Justification: HC2
Source: to Expel Subscriber ε **LEL**	Source: to **Reject Car** ε **LEL**
Destination: **Administration ε class** (responsibility: **toExpelSubscriber**)	Destination: Subscriber ε **Class** (responsibility: **toRejectCar**)
Cardinality: 1	Cardinality: 1

- Trace 5: Context appears in context (buc) = { crc/ crc ε CRC, res ε Responsibility part-of (crc, res) AND res context includes (buc)}

The method context of responsibility class analyzes if the responsibility contains the business use case, according to the extended CRC notation (see Figure 7).

Given a business use case, this context retrieves all classes that have responsibilities that appear in it. Figure 16 shows an example, For buc = "to Pay due Monthly Installment" the context returns a group of classes indicated in destination = {Subscriber, Administration.....} since they have responsibilities that appear in this business use case.

Figure 16: Instances of trace view created by HC5

Trace:
Name: appears in context
Justification: HC5
Source: to Pay due Monthly Installment ε **BUC**
Destination: { subscriber ε **class** (**resp**: to pay due installment)
Administration ε class (resp: to get paid due installment)
.... }
Cardinality: N

- Trace 9: Context optionally modeling (t) = {cl / t.clasification = Object, cl ε ConceptualClass, at ε Attribute, part-of (cl, at) AND optionally modeling (t, at) }

This context returns all the classes that possess attributes that are LEL terms. Figure 17 shows examples. The first instance shows the attribute, monthly installment Fee of class Saving Plan, which was generated starting from the LEL term, t = monthly installment applying the HM1.2. The second instance shows how the term, t = admission installment, becomes an attribute of the Administration class.

Figure 17: Instances created by HM1.2

Trace:	*Trace:*
Name: optional modeling Justification: HM1.2 Source: **monthly installment ε LEL** Destination: Saving Plan **ε Class** **(attribute: monthyInstallment)** Cardinality: 1	Name: optional modeling Justification: HM1.2 Source: admission installment **ε LEL** Destination: **Administration** **ε Class** **(attribute: admissionFee)** Cardinality: 1

All the trace relationships have inverse relationships (**backward relationships**) to allow pre-traceability (i.e., given a component of the RUP object model, the origin that justifies its existence is obtained). For example:

- Trace 3: Context $_{OriginedIn}$ (r) = {t / t ε LEL, i ε Behavioral Responses, part-of (t,i) AND optionally modeling (i,r) }

Figure 18 shows two instances corresponding to this context. The first one justifies the appearance of the responsibility, r = "to pay installment" in Subscriber class, by the application of the HC2 since the responsibility was created starting from a behavioral response of the LEL term, Subscriber. The other instance justifies the creation of the responsibility r = tochangeCar of the class SavingPlan by applying HC4.1.

Figure 18: Instances of trace view created by HC2 and HC4

Trace:	*Trace:*
Name: optionally modeling Justification: HC2 Source: to **pay monthly installment ε Subscriber class** Destination: subscriber **ε LEL** **(behavioral response: to pay monthly installment)** Cardinality: 1	Name: optionally modeling Justification: HC4.1 Source: tochangeCar ε **SavingPlan class** Destination: SavingPlan **ε LEL (** **behavioral response: to change car type)** Cardinality: 1

- Trace 14: Context $_{\text{OriginedIn}}$ (at) = {rnfm/ cl ε Class , part-of(cl,at) AND to create to(rnf,at) }

This context retrieves the non-functional rules that affect the attributes of the classes. Figure 19 shows an example that relates the attribute AllowedRejectionAmount of Administration with the non-functional rules that created it, "A subscriber can reject the car up to three times."

Figure 19: Instances of trace view created by HC9

> ***Trace:***
> Name: to create
> Justification: HM5.2
> Source: **Administration (attribute:** AllowedRejectionAmount = **3)**
> Source Cardinality : 1
> Destination: **"A** subscriber can reject the car up to three times" ε **Rule**
> Cardinality: 1

Automated Support of Traceability

As it can be observed, trace relationships generated by the application of the heuristics represent a great and detailed volume of information. Due to the volume of information that is generated during the process of software development, it is generally expensive, in terms of time and resources, to entirely store the information (Kotonya & Sommerville, 1998). For this reason, it is necessary to define a traceability model that structures the information in such a way to facilitate access to it through search mechanisms that are adaptable to the specific necessities of each project and organization (Domges & Pohl, 1998; Ramesh, 1998). Although the strategy defines all the trace relationships, a tool that implements it should necessarily allow the project administrator to select the type of traces that each particular project needs. At present, we have constructed two prototypes. MenDor is a prototype (Petersen et al., 2000) that allows engineers to define their navigational contexts. The other prototype, BaselineMentor (Antonelli et al., 1999), defines relationships at a high level of granularity between scenarios, LEL terms, and candidate classes.

CONCLUSIONS AND FUTURE WORKS

In this work, we present a strategy based on natural language-oriented requirements to define the RUP business model through the business use cases and the business objects models. This strategy is compatible with the aims of RUP for enhancing the interaction with the customer by the use of easily read and understood models (Jacobson et al., 1999). As use cases model is the key model of RUP, our strategy has incorporated use cases by means of scenario representation. However, it has also added complementary models to enhance the knowledge of the business organization for which a software system will be constructed. The LEL and the business rules models increase the abstraction degree of modeling. At the same time, they reduce the problems caused by the exclusive use of use cases for the definition of classes (Meyer, 1997). The heuristics are guides to help in the manipulation of the great quantity of information generated by the requirements models. A trace mechanism is defined in order to enhance pre- and post-traceability between the models.

There are some works that incorporate requirements strategies to RUP in its first development stage. In Oberg et al. (1998), a requirements management framework based on use cases is presented. The strategy is based mainly on UML use cases, starting with business use cases. Traceability plays an important role in this strategy and a glossary is used for the definition of the stakeholder vocabulary. Since it is a framework, a general workflow of activities is presented during which the glossary and the use cases are discovered, developed, and maintained without any concrete strategy. As such, we consider that our strategy may fit within this framework, giving concrete assistance in the development of the glossary through the LEL and the business use cases and related object models through the heuristics. In this way, our heuristics are included in the context of a well-defined workflow of activities in order to manage requirements through RUP software development. In Santander and Castro (2002) a strategy that allows the definition of uses cases, starting from the organizational model i*, is presented. This strategy captures organizational requirements to define how the system fulfills the organization goals, why this is necessary, what the possible alternatives are, and what the implications to the involved parts are. All of these are represented by the two models proposed by i*. This approach presents some guidelines to assist requirements' engineers in developing UML use cases from the organizational models in i*. This approach is a goal-based methodology that is useful in the RUP requirements definition phase because the uses cases generated are uses cases for the software system. Finally, in Barros et al. (2000), an interesting proposal is presented extending UML in order to define the organizational enterprise model for systems that will be implemented using distributed objects technology. This model is described in terms of processes, entities, lists, and events of the business. In this sense, we want to investigate if the *requirements baseline* models, in particular the business rules, can help enhance this proposal.

As future works, we aim to study the integration of the requirements *baseline* models with the RUP requirements definition stage. In this phase, starting from the business model obtained in the previous stage, use cases of the software system are defined taking into account functional and non-functional requirements and the users' interfaces. A set of use cases is selected in order to be implemented for each particular release. Although in each iteration RUP determines the priority of use cases according to the risk, it considers the importance of choosing the use cases group that defines the most significant behavior for the system (i.e., why is the system built?). In this sense, the functional rule model may be helpful for prioritizing. This model defines the policies of the organization in a natural and client-oriented way; therefore, the client can determine which policies are the highest priority and what rules he or she is interested in implementing. For each rule selected, the set of related use cases is automated. Analyzing the deficiencies presented for UML (Glinz, 2000) as a requirements specification language, we believe that new strategies and models must be incorporated during the requirements definition stage (once the business model has been defined), into the *requirements baseline*.

REFERENCES

Antonelli, L., Rossi, G., & Oliveros, A. (1999). Baseline mentor, an application that derives CRC cards from lexicon and scenarios. *Anais de WER'99: Workshop en Requerimientos. 28 JAIOO, SADIO* (pp. 5-16).

Barros, A., Duddy, K., Lawley, M., Milosevic, Z., Raymond, K., & Wood, A. (2000). Processes, roles and events: UML concepts for enterprise architecture. *Proceedings UML 2000: The Unified Modeling Language. Third International Conference. UK, October 2000.* Springer (pp. 62-77).

Beck, K., & Cunningham, W. (1989). A laboratory for teaching object-oriented thinking. *From the OOPSLA'89 Conference Proceedings, October 1-6* (pp. 1-6).

Cockburn, A. (1999). Responsibility-based modeling. *Technical Memo HaT TR-99.02.* On the World Wide Web: http://members/aol.com/humansandt/techniques/responsabilities.htm

Davis A (1993). Software requirements: objects, functions and states. Englowood Cliffs, New Jersey: Prentice-Hall.

Diaz, O., Iturrioz, J., & Piattine, M., (1997). Promoting business policies in object-oriented methods. *Actas de II Jornadas de Ingeniería de Software, JIS97, Dpto. de Informática*, Universidad del país Vasco, San Sebastián, España (pp. 384-400).

Dömges R., & Pohl K. (1998). Adapting traceability environments to project-specific needs. *Communications of the ACM, December. Vol. 41, No.12* (pp. 54-62).

Fiorini, S., Leite, J.C.S.P., & Macedo-Soares, T., (1997). Integrando processos de negocio a elicitacao de requisitos. *Revista de Informática Teorica e Aplicada, Instituto de Informática da Universidade Federal do Rio Grande do Sul, Vol. IV, N. I* (pp. 7-48).

Glinz M., (2000). Problems and deficiencies of UML as a requirements specification language. *Proceeding of the IEEE 10th International Workshop on software Specification ad Design (IWSSD-10)* (pp. 11-22).

Gotel, O., & Finkelstein, A. (1994). An analysis of the requirements traceability problem. *International Conference on Requirements Engineering* (pp. 94-101).

Henderson-Sellers, B., & Barbier, F. (1999). What is this thing called aggregation. *Proceedings of Technology of Object-Oriented Languages and Systems Europe'99, June 7-10*, Nancy, France: IEEE Computer Society Press (pp. 236-250).

Jackson, M (1983). Systems development. Prentice-Hall.

Jacobson, I., Booch, G., & Rumbaugh, J. (1999). The unified software development process. Addison-Wesley.

Juristo, N., Morant, J., & Moreno, A. (1998). A formal approach for generating OO specifications from natural language. *The Journal of Systems and Software. 48* Elsevier (pp. 139-153).

Kotonya, G., & Sommerville, I. (1998). Requirements engineering. J. Wiley and Sons, 1998.

Leite, J.C.S.P., & Franco, A.P.M. (1993). A strategy for conceptual model acquisition. *IEEE International Symposium on Requirements Engineering*, IEEE Computer Society Press (pp. 243-246).

Leite, J.C.S.P. & Leonardi, C. (1998). Business rules as organizational policies. *IEEE IWSSD9: Ninth International Workshop on Software Specification and Design*, IEEE Computer Society Press, 1998 (pp. 68-76).

Leite, J.C.S.P., & Oliveira, A. (1995). A client oriented requirements baseline. *Proceedings of the Second IEEE International Symposium on Requirements Engineering*, IEEE Computer Society Press (pp. 108-115).

Leite, J.C.S.P, Hadad, G., Doorn, J., & Kaplan, G. (2000). A scenario construction process requirements. *Engineering Journal*, Springer-Verlag, Vol.5, N1 (pp. 38-61).

Leite, J.C.S.P., Rossi, G., Balaguer, F., Maironana, V., Kaplan, G., Hadad, G., & Oliveros, A. et al. (1997). Enhancing a requirements baseline with scenarios. *Proceedings of RE 97': IEEE Third International Requirements Engineering Symposium*, IEEE Computer Society Press, 1997 (pp. 44-53).

Leonardi, C. (2001). Una estrategia de modelado conceptual de objetos basada en modelos de requisitos en lenguaje natural. *Tesis de Magister en Ingeniería de Software,* Dpto. de Informática de la Universidad Nacional de La Plata, Noviembre de 2001.

Leonardi, C., Leite, J.C.S.P., & Rossi, G., (1998). Estrategias para la identificación de reglas de negocio. *Proceeding de Sbes98, Simposio Brasilero de Engenharia de Software*, Sociedad Brasilera de Computacao, Maringa, Brasil, 14-16 de Octubre de (pp. 53-67.)

Meyer, B. (1997). Object oriented construction. Prentice Hall.

Oberg, R., Probasco, L., & Ericsson, M. (1998). Applying requirements management with use cases. *Technical Paper Tp505,* Rational Software Corporation.

Petersen, L. and Tornabene, S., Leonardi, C., & Doorn (2000). HeaR: Una herramienta de adquisición de requisitos. *Anais III Workshop en Engenharia de Requisitos, Rio de Janeiro, Julio del 2000* (pp. 38-53).

Ramesh, B. (1998). Factors influencing requirements traceability practice. *Communications of the ACM, Dec.1998, Vol.41, No.12* (pp. 37-44).

Rossi, G., (1996). An object oriented method for designing hypermedia applications. *Ph.D. Thesis*, Departamento de Informative, PUC-Rio, Brasil.

Rumbaugh, J., Jacobson, I., & Booch, G. (1999). The Unified Modeling Language reference manual. Addison-Wesley.

Santander, V. & Castro, C. Deriving use cases from organizational modeling. *Proceedings of IEEE Joint International Requirements Engineering, Germany, 9-13, September 2002.*

Schmauch, Ch. (1995). ISO 9000 for software developers, revised edition. ASQC, Quality Press.

Warner, J., & Kleppe (1999). The object constraint language: Precise modeling with UML. Addison-Wesley.

Wirfs-Brock, R. (1995). Designing objects and their interactions: Scenarios based design. In Carrol, J. (Ed.), John Wiley & Sons, Inc. (pp. 337-359).

Yu, E. (1995). Models for supporting the redesign of organizational work. *Proceedings Conference on Organizational Computing Systems, August 13-16, Milipitas, California.* On the World Wide Web: ftp://ftp.cs.toronto.edu/pub/eric.

Chapter VII

Introducing Non-functional Requirements in UML

Guadalupe Salazar-Zárate
Technical University of Catalonia, Spain

Pere Botella
Technical University of Catalonia, Spain

Ajantha Dahanayake
Delft University of Technology, The Netherlands

ABSTRACT

This chapter introduces an approach concerned with the non-functional features of software systems. The specific objectives of the research focus on the possibility of developing mechanisms to capture non-functional information in the development of software systems in a similar manner to its counterpart, the functional information. Particularly, the research described in this chapter focuses on the possible extension of the Unified Modeling Language (UML) (Booch et al., 1998). In order to get an initial specification of some non-functional requirements, the Software Quality Standard ISO/IEC 9126 (International Standard, 1991) is used. The language NoFun (Botella et al., 2001) is the basis used to achieve some organization about the non-functional concepts used in this approach.

INTRODUCTION

Requirements Engineering (RE) has been progressively recognized during the last decade as an important discipline within its own research community (Filkenstein, 1994; Lamsweerde, 2000; Nuseibeh & Easterbrook, 2000). In Zave (1997, p.315), RE has been defined as "a branch of software engineering concerned with the real-world goals for functions of and constraints on software systems. It is also concerned with the relationship of these factors to precise specifications of software behavior, and to their evolution over time and across software families."

Industry is also clamoring for importance to be placed on this discipline. A European industry survey points out "Requirements specification" and "Managing customer requirements" as the two main problems in software and system development (50% have marked both as a "major problem," 35% as a "minor problem," and less than 12% as "no problem"). This survey was performed by the European Software Institute (European Software Institute – ESI, 1996) in 17 different countries. The survey analyzed the data obtained from about 4,000 questionnaires distributed among product and services companies in the IT sector.

The interest, relevance, and vitality of the RE emerging discipline is clearly reflected in specific conferences (such as the IEEE Joint Conference on Requirements Engineering), specific Journals (e.g., the *Springer Requirements Engineering Journal*), as well as in more general conferences, workshops, and journals that consider this topic.

In the RE processes (e.g., elicitation, modeling, validation, etc.), it is common to distinguish between functional and non-functional requirements. The functional requirements describe the functions and services of the system in terms of the users' goals. Non-functional requirements are a broad term covering both qualities and constraints. Qualities (e.g., usability, scalability) can be negotiated, but constraints (as time constraints or the operating system to be used) are not subject to negotiation and must be satisfied. Therefore, both functional and non-functional requirements are relevant to software systems development.

The relevance of functional requirements has been traditionally well-covered by the modeling techniques, where a lot of research has been done. The model captures the functions and services to be provided by the system that can then be converted into design, and finally, into code. This research has resulted in techniques and tools, especially for modeling or specification languages, either formal or semi-formal. However, non-functional requirements, quality, and constraint properties are not usually covered by these modeling techniques. Quality requirements, when considered, are usually expressed in natural language as a note (an "anchor" note in the case of UML). Constraints are often expressed by means of logic expressions (using OCL in the case of UML class diagrams), inside brackets, or also in natural language rather than as part of the model. This happens despite the fact that many researchers have pointed out the convenience of non-functional features appearing in those languages (Cohen et al., 1994; Mylopoulos et al., 1992; Sitaraman, 1994; Wing, 1990; Franch, 1998). As another example, Cysneiros and Leite (2001c) states that, *"During 2001 edition of ICSE, Mantis Chen, from ACD System, presented the three most important aspects for a software in the stakeholders' point of view and the three most important ones in the developers' point of view. All the six were non-functional requirements."*

This chapter focuses on the possibility of developing mechanisms to capture non-functional information in the development of software systems. It is concerned with the possible extension of the UML (Booch et al., 1998) in order to include non-functionality. The language NoFun (Botella et al., 2001) is taken as the basis to achieve some organization for the non-functional concepts used in this approach. Special attention is given to a standard that defines the quality characteristics of software. The Software Quality Standard ISO/IEC 9126 (International Standard, 1991) is used to obtain the framework for quality measurement and the identification of some important key concepts (characteristics, subcharacteristics, attributes, metrics, etc.).

NON-FUNCTIONAL ISSUES

Functional and non-functional (NF for short) aspects regarding the external system behavior involve two different ways of evaluating and/or developing a given software system. On the one hand, functional aspects are directly connected to *what the system does*, i.e., the basic functions that a system (or a system component) must provide. On the other hand, non-functional aspects are related to *how the system behaves* with respect to some observable attributes such as performance, reliability, efficiency, reusability, portability and maintainability (i.e., some software qualities). In Chung et al. (2000, p.160), a list of non-functional requirements is shown that illustrate the wide variety of issues for software quality.

There are two basic approaches to characterize non-functional requirements (Mylopoulos et al., 1992; Chung et al., 2000):

- Product-oriented approach.
- Process-oriented approach.

The *product-oriented approach* basically focuses on the development of a formal framework so that a software product can be evaluated in relation to the highest degree it meets for non-functional requirements (constraints over non-functional properties). The measurement is based on the quantitative approach. In order to objectively determine whether a given software product is satisfactory, one needs to define precisely the specific attributes that it should hold and express them in more than general qualitative terms (reliability, portability, efficiency, etc.). *Software quality metrics* allows developers to quantify up to what degree a software system meets non-functional requirements. An excellent example on this topic is given in Keller et al. (1990). Herein the many overlapping, and sometimes apparently contradictory terms, used in the area of software quality metrics are defined. Direct and indirect metrics as a means of measuring quality are also described. Keller et al. (1990) includes an appendix of the RADC (U.S. Air Force Rome Air Development Center) methodology that illustrates the considerations and decisions involved in defining and measuring software quality. For example, he recommends that the entire set of requirements be decomposed into subsections, and each subsection in turn, be further decomposed for measurement at a detail level.

The *process-oriented approach* uses non-functional information to guide the development of software systems. Among the works dealing with this perspective of non-functionality, those of Chung et al. (1995, 2000) are without any doubt the most complete ones. The approach presents a framework that enables developers to deal with the diverse, non-functional requirements of a system in a systematic way. These requirements are used to drive the design by justifying decisions during the software development process. The framework also offers structured, graphical facilities for stating, managing, and inter-relating non-functional requirements while justifying decisions and determining their impact throughout the development process.

Mylopoulos et al. (1992) and Chung et al. (2000) make the observation that product-oriented and process-oriented approaches should not be seen as alternative, but as something complementary with each contributing to a comprehensive framework for dealing with non-functional requirements.

There are other recent works that are also concerned with non-functional require-ments. In Cysneiros and Leite (2001a) an approach that complements the work reported in Chung et al. (2000) is introduced. In this work, a strategy to drive elicited non-functional requirements in use cases and scenarios is presented. In other related work (Cysneiros et al., 2001), a framework for integrating non-functional requirements into conceptual models is described. Strategies concerned with how to identify and represent process-oriented, non-functional requirements can be found in Cysneiros and Leite (2001b, 2001c).

DEALING WITH NON-FUNCTIONALITY

In order to design a software system, we start by eliciting a set of functional requirements and a set of non-functional requirements that describe what behaviors and what characteristics must be exhibited by the implemented system.

Usually natural language text is used for non-functional requirements because of its flexibility and adaptability. However, drawbacks such as ambiguity, inconsistency, and contradictions make this kind of information more difficult to analyze. There is a strong need to deal comprehensively with such requirements in order to improve the development process and to avoid errors that often lead to greater expense in software products.

In our project, the International Standard ISO/EC 9126 (1991) will be used as a starting point to identify non-functional attributes of products that are potentially relevant to be modeled in a software development process. In a later phase, more non-functional attributes will be included. The standard is primarily concerned with the definition of quality characteristics, which are expressed in terms of some high-level features of the software such as efficiency, reliability, and others. This standard collects quality needs with the main idea of defining a *quality model* and using it as a framework for software evaluation. A *quality model* is defined by means of general *characteristics of software*, which are further refined into *subcharacteristics* in a multilevel hierarchy. Measurable *software attributes* appear at the bottom of the hierarchy.

The ISO 9126 standard defines the characteristics of functionality, reliability, usability, efficiency, maintainability, and portability are being placed at the top of the hierarchy. An informative annex of this standard provides an illustrative quality model that refines these characteristics.

Software quality metrics allows developers to quantify up to what degree a software system meets non-functional requirements. Metrics, in the ISO 9126, typically give rise to quantifiable measures that are mapped onto scales. The rating levels definition determines what ranges of values on those scales count as satisfactory or unsatisfactory. Since quality refers to given needs, which vary from one evaluation to another, then there are no general rating levels possible: they must be defined for each specific evaluation. To determine objectively whether a given software product is satisfactory or not, one needs to define precisely the specific attributes (basic attributes) rather than express them in general qualitative terms (e.g., reliability, maintainability, portability, efficiency, etc.).

A language called *NoFun* (acronym for "NOn-FUNctional") is a notation defined within our research group (Botella et al., 2001; Burgués & Franch, 2000; Franch, 1998) that focuses on representing non-functional aspects of software systems, at the product level within the component-programming framework. It is a formal language for description of software quality requirements using ISO/IEC 9126 framework (see Figure 1) to summarize quality characteristics. NoFun has also been used to represent quality models for particular software domains.

NoFun Overview

To achieve the goal of formalization within NoFun, we basically provide three different kinds of capabilities. First, there are modules for defining the different kind of concepts in the standard. Second, values for these attributes may be given and bound to particular software components, (i.e., the ones under evaluation). Third, additional constructs for representing quality requirements and assessment criteria are included.

Concerning the first category, there are three main modules: characteristic, subcharacteristic, and attribute modules. Modules may import others, and nesting is allowed also. Nesting of modules enables stating of auxiliary definitions, although visibility rules must always be taken into account (symbols defined in nested modules are not exported). Following the standard, characteristic modules may not be defined as one in terms of another one. No such restrictions appear on the other types of modules; therefore, hierarchies of subcharacteristics and attributes may (and will) arise.

The upper part of Figure 1 shows an example of distribution of a quality model into modules. There are two characteristics defined in terms of four subcharacteristics. Following the ISO/IEC appendix, sharing of subcharacteristics between characteristics does not take place (although the language does not explicitly check this situation).

Subcharacteristics do indeed form a hierarchy; they may depend on zero or one or more subcharacteristics and attributes and a subcharacteristic may influence more than one subcharacteristic. Finally, attributes are defined at the bottom of the model, although attribute hierarchies may also be defined. Attributes depending on others are named *derived attributes*, as opposed to *basic* ones, whose values must be explicitly stated.

Quality characteristics, subcharacteristics, and attributes (hereafter, *quality entities*) are declared for a particular type. In addition to pre-defined types (called domains), mechanisms to define new ones are introduced. New domains may also be defined; encapsulated in yet another kind of module. Type constructs are rich enough to allow modeling of the usual quality entities. There are sets, functions, and tuples (for more details see Botella et al., 2001).

Assignment of basic attribute values are encapsulated in new modules (*behavior modules*), which are bound to the corresponding software components that are being evaluated. Behavioral modules are abstractions of software components in the sense that they contain all of the relevant information for quality evaluation.

Finally, quality requirements may be defined as restricting the values of the quality entities. Assessment criteria can be seen as a set of quality requirements; therefore, we do not distinguish between them. Quality requirements are stated using operators over the quality entities and these requirements may be categorized according to their importance. Requirements normally refer to characteristics and subcharacteristics, and rarely to attributes, due to their lower-level nature.

The rest of Figure 1 adds the behavior and requirement modules. The three software components under evaluation include a behavior module measuring the basic attributes.

Figure 1: Layout of a quality model under ISO/IEC framework

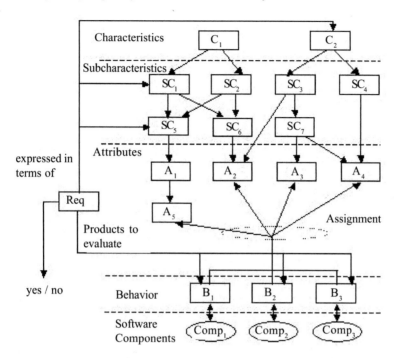

Values of the attributes propagate up to the other quality entities (following the arrows in reverse direction). The requirement module containing assessment criteria for the evaluation refers in this case to one characteristic and two subcharacteristics. Here the result is simplified to only express success or failure; but, in Botella et al. (2001) it is shown that things are a bit more sophisticated because of the categorization of requirements.

In addition to these elements, an orthogonal concept is the one of refinement. Refinement allows definition of quality models in an incremental manner, by specializing the more general ones. This kind of inheritance-like relationship yields to a structured representation of quality: models can be formulated first in a general way, later refined in particular domains (OO classes, ERP products, bespoke software, etc.), and further specialized for companies, projects, etc.

NoFun can be used to formally represent all the previously mentioned non-functional information. To illustrate what NoFun looks like, we present here an attribute module that shows basic and derived attributes:

> **attribute module** DELIVERING_ISSUES
>   **explanation** date of delivery of components
>   **attribute** Month **declared as** Integer [1..12]
>   **attribute** Year **declared as** Integer [1970..]
>   **attribute** Date **derived**
>   **declared as Tuple**(Integer[1..12], Integer[1970..])
>   **defined as** (Month, Year)

explanation name of company delivering the product.
"Own" states for software produced in the
company; use it instead of the name
attribute supplier **declared as** string
end DELIVERING_ISSUES

and a requirement module:

requirement module DATE_FACTS **on** DELIVERING_ISSUES **for**
ACME
explanation requirement on the date of creation of ACME
delivered software
definition
ACME-delivery-date: **advisable**
explanation Software made by ACME must not be dated
before April 1998, which is the date the company
started to use OO methodologies
defined as
Supplier = 'ACME' **implies**
(Date.Year > 1998) **or** (Date.Year = 1998 **and**
Date.Month >= 4)
end DATE_FACTS

Both examples have been extracted from Botella et al. (2001). In this reference, as in Franch (1998) and Burgués and Franch (2000) a description of NoFun and some detailed examples can be found.

Using the formalizing ideas of the NoFun language and following a product-oriented approach, we aim to extend the UML language (Booch et al., 1998) in order to capture non-functional information.

PORTING NON-FUNCTIONALITY TO UML

UML has today become a standard modeling language for software systems development (Object Management Group, 2000). UML is a general-purpose, visual modeling language for specifying, visualizing, constructing, and documenting the artifacts of software systems (Booch et al., 1998). UML offers a graphical notation with semantics to create models (diagrammatic representations of programs) (Rational Software Corporation, 1999). However, UML is mainly focused on functional aspects of the software development. We would like to have the same visual possibilities to cope with the non-functional aspects of the software systems.

According to UML-notation (Booch et al., 1998), *notes* are used to incorporate those aspects regarding non-functional information. UML notes may contain any information including plain text, fragments of code, or references to other documents. Because of the different domains, types, and nature of the NF-information listed within the note, specifying NF-attributes in this way may be insufficient if we want a systematic representation of the NF-information. Therefore, it is necessary to put this information in a more ordered form.

One way to identify those kinds of attributes for visualizing non-functionality in UML diagrams is through the use of the layout described above with the "NoFun" language (Botella et al., 2001). In this layout, the software quality characteristics of a quality model are broken down into subcharacteristics, as shown in Figure 1 until some basic attributes are placed at the bottom of the hierarchy, which is where *quality requirements* may be defined as restrictions over the quality model.

The following has been considered for achieving the appropriate UML extensions in order to include non-functional requirements. First, we propose to make use of stereotypes to represent the non-functionality. The UML concept of stereotype is the extensibility mechanism that UML offers to extend its modeling vocabulary, thus allowing us to create new kinds of building blocks that can be adapted to the specific problem. Second, those software quality characteristics and attributes defined in the layout (see Figure 1) can be identified, and some ad hoc stereotypes can also be defined. The models can also be refined by applying different abstraction levels during ulterior stages of the development process.

The UML concept of stereotype can be used to include non-functionality in several ways:

- *In a class diagram.* At a conceptual level, one can create sterotyped classes <<NF-Entity>> to represent a specific quality characteristic. New stereotypes can be formulated then further refined into more specialized ones. In a more detailed level, the Object Constraint Language (OCL) (Warmer & Kleppe, 1999), or an adaptation of the NoFun language can be used to establish requirements in the form of constraints.

- *In UML package diagrams.* One can group software elements under a stereotyped package, for example, to represent a collection of non-functional, stereotyped classes. In this way, a framework for further design specifications is provided that includes the required non-functional attributes.

- *In use cases.* The non-functionalities can be seen as transformation rules causing new use cases to be added and/or the structure of the use case description to be changed or replaced so that the non-functional requirements are satisfied. New actors may also be identified in the transformation process. By adding stereotypes such as <<NF-uses>> or <<NF-extends>>, one can identify the use cases that involve non-functionalities. Constraints can be attached in a special script using OCL or NoFun.

Following the analysis model proposed by Larman (1998), our work has been initially focused on the conceptual model (using UML class diagrams). At a later stage, it will continue considering the definition of other models (essential use cases, system sequence diagrams (behavior), and state diagrams.

An Example

In this example, the main idea is to use software components in an object-oriented approach. To identify the non-functional concepts, we will concentrate on the conceptual model from the analysis model (Larman, 1998). Hereafter, the software components can be seen as entities consisting of the definition of a class diagram that states both functional and non-functional characteristics. In a UML context, the functional requirements of the system are *partially* captured in a c*lass diagram* containing the classes and relationships that represent the key abstractions of the system under development.

There are various levels of granularity and the non-functionality can be applied to a whole system, package, component or class in particular. In this approach, it is not intended to model with fine granularity because we will not be able to manage the complexity of those kinds of models. Instead, we can assign software components to represent whole subsystems and to avoid an explosion in the number of the classes we need to model.

An example that includes the use of the features mentioned in the previous sections is given in Figure 2. Figure 2 shows a particular case where non-functionality is applied to a whole system as represented with a single class. The example shows a class called "ErpACME" that represents a particular conceptual model. While this is a very simple case study, it is good enough to explain the differences among the functional part of the system and the non-functional part that is modeled by the use of stereotyped classes and dependency relationships. In this example, we have a set of possible NF-attributes for the class ErpACME (their names being self-explanatory). In the attributes, the numerical and by-enumeration properties declare what valid values can be taken.

Following the organization described by Franch (1997), the functional *specification* part of a software system can be distinguished from its *implementation* part. In this way, it is possible to describe that a specification module may have several different implementations. It is also possible to select the best implementation for a given specification according to the non-functional information. Thus, both parts are described in two separate modules, while non-functional information can be bound to them by means of two further *ad hoc* modules: a NF-requirements module for the functional *specification* and a NF-behavioral module for the implementation.

In the example, a UML class diagram is created that holds different stereotyped classes to deal with some non-functional entities. We also applied the UML facility where classes can be stereotyped as *types* or *implementation classes* (Rumbaugh, 1998, p. 484). A *<<type>>* is used to specify a domain of objects, together with operations that are applied to the objects without defining the physical implementation of the objects or operations. An *<<implementationClass>>* defines the physical data structure and methods of objects. This class is said to realize a type if the implementation class includes all of the operations as the type includes with the same behavior. An *<<implementationClass>>* may realize multiple types and multiple implementation classes may realize the same type.

The following stereotypes are produced:

- Stereotyped classes <<QualityEntity >> that represent modules with *non-functional entities* can be declared. A *QualityEntity* can be used to represent characteristic, subcharacteristic, and attribute modules. As a result, non-functional attributes are defined in this stereotyped class. In this way, one can create all of the stereotyped classes needed to describe the non-functionality. A kind of hierarchy between these attributes can be simulated with dependency relationships between the classes. The stereotyped dependency <<imports>> is also created to indicate that the dependent class may import one or more modules of non-functional properties. In order to state constraints over the non-functional attributes, an extra compartment (titled <<OCL-exp>>) is added to show any constraint that has been referred to a subset of the <<QualityEntities>>. Expres-

Figure 2: Example showing non-functional stereotypes

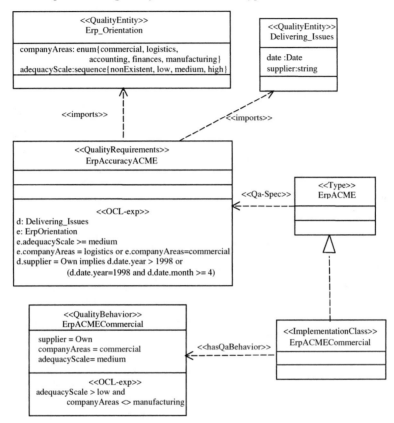

sions in this compartment obey rules expressed in OCL. This compartment is later described. In the upper part of Figure 2, we show two examples of <<QualityEntity>> classes.

- A stereotyped class called <<QualityRequirements>> for restricting the values of the quality entities can be declared. Within this stereotype, we set the non-functional requirements that are directly associated to the *specification module* (the functional part of the system) represented in Figure 2 with the <<Type>> stereotype. By using the stereotyped dependency relationship <<Qa-Spec>>, these two modules are bound. This stereotyped class also has an extra compartment <<OCL-exp>> to show the corresponding constraints over the non-functional attributes.

- The *non-functional behavior* of a component implementation is defined with the stereotype <<QualityBehavior>>, where assignment of basic attribute values is declared and bound to the corresponding software components. In UML-class diagrams, we can represent this quality behavior in dependency association to an <<implementationClass>> stereotype, which could be later encapsulated in a component. The <<QualityBehavior>> stereotype also has a compartment, <<OCL-exp>> to show the corresponding constraints on the implementations of the imported components. In addition, a stereotyped dependency relationship, <<hasQaBehavior>>, is also created to bind <<implementationClass>> and its <<QualityBehavior>>.

NF-requirements are the means to state conditions on implementations of software components. NoFun allows stating the values of non-functional attributes in component implementations. It also allows formulation of non-functional requirements over such implementations in order to state properties that each implementation must fulfill. In order to state restrictions over the non-functional attributes, the (OCL) Object Constraint Language (Warmer & Kleppe, 1999) is used. The compartment <<OCL-exp>> contains expressions written in OCL language. The result is that we can define the required non-functional attributes in the appropriate stereotyped class and then use them in the OCL compartment to state constraints over those attributes. In Salazar-Zárate and Botella (2000), another example can be found showing UML diagrams and its use of OCL.

CONCLUSIONS AND FURTHER WORK

The use of UML stereotypes as a mechanism to incorporate non-functional elements has been introduced. The possibility of developing other mechanisms to incorporate non-functional elements that can be added to the UML language as new elements is still in progress. The attempt being made is to identify the non-functional elements in order to provide a more general extension of the UML vocabulary — first at a model level, and at a later stage, at a metamodel level.

Currently, we are exploring the possibility for achieving this through the creation of a framework where basic, non-functional attributes can be defined, selected, and presented in terms of elements that can be modeled within UML diagrams.

The diagrams (classes, use cases, and package diagrams) considered in this chapter, model static aspects of software systems. UML also provides mechanisms for modeling the dynamic aspects of the system (state, sequence, and activity diagrams) that could possibly incorporate non-functional information. However, this has not been done yet, and a detailed study should be done in the future.

Our proposal can be viewed as a product-oriented approach (Chung et al., 2000). Once we have completed the analysis model, in Larman's (1998) sense, and we use the idea that process-oriented and product-oriented approaches can be complementary (again, in Chung et al., 2000), we plan to explore the possibility of complementing the method proposed by Cysneiros and Leite (2001a, 2001b) and Cysneiros et al. (2001) with our NoFun-based extension of UML.

REFERENCES

Barbacci, M.R., Klein, M.H., Longstaff, T., & Weinstock, C.B. (1995). Quality attributes. *Technical Report CMU/SEI-95-TR-021, ADA307888*. Pittsburgh, PA: Software Engineering Institute, Carnegie Mellon University.

Booch, G., Jacobson, I., & Rumbaugh, J. (1998). The Unified Modeling Language users guide. (Addison-Wesley object technology series), Addison Wesley Longman, Inc.

Botella, P., Burgués, X., Franch, X., Huerta, M., & Salazar, G. (2001). Modeling non-functional requirements. In Jornadas de Ingeniería de Requisitos Aplicada. Sevilla (Spain), June 11-12. On the World Wide Web: http://www.lsi.us.es/~amador/JIRA/JIRA.html

Burgués, X., & Franch, X. (2000). A language for stating component quality. *In Proceedings of 14ᵗʰ Brazilian Symposium on Software Engineering (SBES). Joao Pressoa (Brasil), October* (pp. 69-84).

Chung, L., & Nixon, B. A. (1995). Dealing with non-functional requirements: Three experimental studies of a process-oriented approach. *In Proceedings, 17th International Conference on Software Engineering (ICSE 95), Seattle, WA., April 24-28* (pp. 25-36).

Chung, L., Nixon, B.A., Yu, E., & Mylopoulos, J. (2000). Non-functional requirements in software engineering. Kluwer Academic Publishers.

Cohen, D., Goldman, N., & Narayanaswamy, K (1994). Adding performance information to ADT interfaces. *In Proceedings of the Interface Definition Languages Workshop, ACM SIGPLAN Notices 29(8)*.

Cysneiros, L.M., & Leite, J.C.S.P. (1999). Integrating non-functional requirements into data modeling. *In Proceedings of 4°. IEEE Requirements Engineering Simposium, Ireland, June* (pp.162-171).

Cysneiros, L.M., & Leite, J.C.S.P. (2001a). Driving non-functional requirements to use cases and scenarios. In *XV Simposio Brasileiro de Engenharia de Software. Brazil October* (pp. 7-20).

Cysneiros, L.M., & Leite, J.C.S.P. (2001b). Using UML to reflect non-functional requirements. *In Proceedings of the CASCON 2001, Toronto, Canada*.

Cysneiros, L.M., & Leite, J.C.S.P. (2001c). Using the language extended lexicon to support non-functional requirements elicitation. *In Proceedings 5ᵗʰ workshop on Requirements Engineering, Buenos Aires, Argentina*.

Cysneiros, L.M., Leite, J.C.S.P., & Neto, J.S.M. (2001). A framework for integrating non-functional requirements into conceptual models. *Requirements Engineering Journal. 6(2), April* (pp. 97-115).

European Software Institute – ESI (1996). Espiti: European user survey analysis. *Technical Report ESI-1996-TR95104, European Software Institute. On the World Wide Web:* http://www.esi.es/

Finkelstein, A. (1994). Requirements engineering: a review and research agenda. *In Proceedings of 1st Asian & Pacific Software Engineering Conference, IEEE CS Press* (pp. 10-19).

Franch, X. (1998). Systematic formulation of non-functional characteristics of software. *In Proceedings of 3ʳᵈ International Conference on Requirements Engineering (ICRE). Colorado Springs, Colorado*, IEEE Computer Society.

Franch, X., Botella, P., Burgués, X., & Ribó, J.M. (1997). ComProLab: A component programming laboratory. *In Proceedings of 9ᵗʰ Software Engineering and Knowledge Engineering Conference (SEKE), Madrid, (Spain), June* (pp. 397-406).

International Standard (1991). ISO/IEC 9126 Information technology — software product evaluation—quality characteristics and guidelines for their use. International Organization for Standardization, Geneva.

Keller, S. E., Kahn, L. G. & Panara, R. B. (1990). Specifying software quality requirements with metrics. In H.R. Thayer and M. Dorfman (Eds.) *System and Software Requirements Engineering* (pp.145-163). IEEE Computer Society Press.

Lamsweerde van, A. (2000). Requirements engineering in the year 00: A research perspective. *In Proceedings of 22nd International Conference on Software Engineering. Limerick (Ireland). June.* ACM Press.

Larman C. (1998). Applying UML and patterns. An introduction to object-oriented analysis and design. New York: Prentice Hall, Inc.

Mylopoulos, J., Chung, L., & Nixon, B.A. (1992). Representing and using nonfunctional requirements; A process-oriented approach. *In IEEE Transactions on Software Engineering, 18(6), June* (pp. 483-497).

Nuseibeh, B., & Easterbrook, S. (2000). Requirements engineering: A roadmap. *Proceedings of the 2000 International Conference on Software Engineering (ICSE 2000 the New Millenium). June 4-11, Limerick, (Ireland).* ACM Press.

Object Management Group (2000). Unified Modeling Language specification, Version 1.3. March 2000. Technical Report, Object Management Group. On the World Wide Web: http://www.omg.org/technology/documents/modeling_spec_catalog.htm.

Rational Software Corporation. (1999). UML semantics, version 1.3. June 1999. On the World Wide Web: http://www.rational.com/uml/resources/documentation/index.jsp

Rumbaugh, J., Jacobson, I., & Booch, G. (1998). The Unified Modeling Language reference manual. Reading, MA: Addison Wesley Longman, Inc.

Salazar-Zárate, G. & Botella, P. (2000). Use of UML for non-functionals aspects. *In 13th International Conference Software & Systems Engineering and their Applications. (ICSSEA 2000).* Paris, France.

Sitaraman, M. (1994). *On tight performance specification of object-oriented components. In Proceedings 3rd International Conference on Software Reuse (ICSR),* IEEE Computer Society Press (pp. 149-156).

Warmer, J. B. & Kleppe A. G. (1999). The object constraint language: Precise modeling with UML. Reading, MA: Addison Wesley Longman, Inc.

Wing, J.M. (1990). A specifier's introduction to formal methods. IEEE Computer 23(9).

Zave, P. (1997). *Classification of Research Efforts in Requirements Engineering. ACM Computing Surveys 29(4)* (pp. 315-321).

ENDNOTES

[1]   M.G. Salazar-Zárate holds a scholarship from CONACyT/México under contract 122464. The work presented in the chapter is part of her ongoing Ph.D. project.

Chapter VIII

Formalizing UML Class Diagrams

Ana María Funes
Universidad Nacional de San Luis, Argentina

Chris George
UNU/IIST, Macau

ABSTRACT

Graphical notations have demonstrated usefulness when interacting with end users, making system validation easier. However, while they can be easily communicated, they lack precision, which consequently can be ambiguous and lead to misunderstanding. It is here where formal specifications can play an important role in overcoming this drawback. In this chapter, we use the RAISE Specification Language (RSL), which is the language of the formal method RAISE (i.e., Rigorous Approach to Industrial Software), as a syntactic and semantic reference for UML. We present the semantics for UML class diagrams by using RSL as a formal basis. An automated tool that implements the translation and the abstract syntax in RSL for the RSL-translatable class diagrams are also presented.

INTRODUCTION

A common practice among software engineers is the use of diagrams for building their system models. Graphical notations become useful for interacting with the end users. They can be more intuitive and easier to grasp than textual descriptions as, according to folk wisdom, a picture is worth a thousand words.

Different forms of more or less formal diagrams have been used in software engineering for a long time. Many practitioners have adopted the use of graphical notations such as data flow diagrams (DeMarco, 1979), entity-relationship diagrams (Chen 1976), state charts (Harel, 1987) and process-oriented approaches like Jackson System Development (Jackson, 1982; Sutcliffe, 1988). Lately, object-oriented approaches seem to be the most popular. Object orientation has evolved from a programming paradigm to methods that cover the complete life cycle. There are many variations of these methods such as OMT, i.e., Object Modeling Technique, (Rumbaugh et al., 1991); OOSE (Object-Oriented Software Engineering) (Jacobson et al., 1992), Booch methods (Booch, 1991; Booch 1994), and the Unified Software Development Process (Jacobson et al., 1999). The latter has unified the notation used by the previous methodologies through the use of the Unified Modeling Language (UML) (Booch et al., 1999).

Today, UML has become the de facto standard for object-oriented modeling, and there are a wide variety of graphical tools that support it. UML is a graphical language for modeling and specifying software systems. It consists of a set of constructs common to most object-oriented languages. However, while UML notations are easily communicated, their semantics are informal, which can consequently make them ambiguous, leading to misunderstandings. Here, formal specifications can play an important role as they can be used as formal foundations for expressing the semantics of the semi-formal language. By formal specifications, we refer to the representation of software by means of formal notations (i.e., a language with a precise syntax, precise semantics, and a proof system). The use of formal specifications has benefits ranging from the possibility of building unambiguous specifications, to the possibility of proving system properties, to automatic code generation. As a result, they are an important technique for increasing the reliability of software. However, it is not used frequently in the industry as it requires a high level of expertise in algebra and mathematical logic, making communication with the end users for validating requirements difficult.

As a consequence, a combination of the advantages of both approaches has been proposed; namely, that the use of graphical and formal notations can be achieved in order to overcome the inherent problems without loss of the respective benefits, i.e., the understandability of graphical notations and the lack of ambiguity of formal specifications. Another important consequence of having a formal representation of an informal or semi-formal model is the possibility of reasoning about their properties. Since models are the result of a creative activity, they tend to contain errors and inconsistencies. This makes model verification a very important activity.

There are several studies in the literature using formal techniques for expressing the semantics of object-oriented models such as those carried out by France (1999), DeLoach and Hartrum (2000), Meyer and Souquieres (1999), and Kim and Carrington (2000). In this work, we explore the use of RSL (George et al., 1992), which is the language of the RAISE development method (George et al., 1995), to give the formal foundations for UML class diagrams. We give the semantics for UML class diagrams in RSL. An automated tool that implements the translation and the abstract syntax in RSL for the RSL-translatable class diagrams is also presented.

The general structure of the chapter is as follows: Section "Class Diagrams and UML" introduces class diagrams in UML and their use in different stages of the software development process. The next section introduces the concepts of semantic and syntactic reference and gives a concise description of RSL and the RAISE method. In the section "Formal Syntax", the abstract syntax in RSL for the considered subset of UML class diagrams is given. Section "Formal Semantics" presents the formal semantics in RSL for class diagrams. Section "RSL Templates" contains a set of RSL templates resulting from the analysis carried out when giving the semantics of UML class diagrams.

Finally, Section "Concluding Remarks" concludes with a brief description of the tool that has been developed to achieve the translation. It also discusses future work.

CLASS DIAGRAMS AND UML

UML is a graphical language that was developed to build different kinds of diagrams that can be used in different phases of the software development process. Since it is only a language, it is merely a development tool. This means that it is process independent. Consequently, it provides only tools to build diagrams rather than telling you what models should be created and when they should be created.

Several kinds of diagrams can be created using UML in order to cover different views of a system. In this work, we are only concerned with class diagrams.

Class diagrams provide a static view of the modeled system. Sometimes they are used for modeling the vocabulary of the system. This implies a decision that is based on which concepts or entities are part of the system and which concepts or entities are outside its boundaries. Class diagrams are also used to build domain models, where all of the concepts that are present in the application domain are shown in the diagram, including the relationships among them. They can also be used to model collaborations among a set of classes, which work together to provide a collaborative behavior, or even to represent a database schema, among others.

It is possible to build class diagrams at different abstraction levels and with different degrees of detail. For instance, conceptual models, which are typically used in the first phase of the development, have no implementation details, while design class diagrams would have implementation details.

A domain model, often referred to as a conceptual model, might be represented by a particular kind of UML class diagram. This model explains the structure of the application domain rather than the application structure itself. It focuses on the domain concepts, rather than on the software entities. While most of the elements will be present in the design model later on, some of them will not, and new ones could even appear.

UML class diagrams that commonly consist only of classes and their relationships can represent this kind of model. The classes, which represent the identified concepts in the domain, have only some attributes. Operations should not be present. Here, the most frequent relationship among classes is the association, which may have several adornments attached to its ends. An adornment may be a role name, a multiplicity, an aggregation, and/or a composition.

Another possible relationship among classes that is sometimes used in this kind of model is generalization. Generalization is an inheritance relation among two or more classes, sometimes called "is-a-kind-of."

In Figure 1, we give an example of a UML conceptual model that has been built for a simple library system.

In the section, Formal Semantics, we present the semantics for all of the basic constructors used in a class diagram as well as the semantics for some other language features used mainly in design class diagrams. According to these semantics, an RSL specification for the conceptual model can be derived. The resultant RSL specification is modular. For each class present in the class diagram, two RSL modules are created. One has the specification for an object of the class; the other, which uses the former, has the

Figure 1: Domain model for a library system

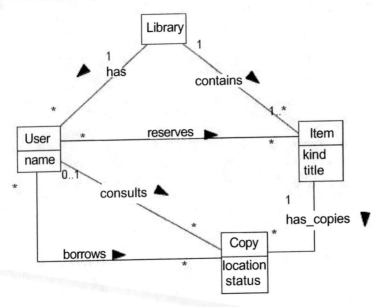

Figure 2: RSL module dependency graph

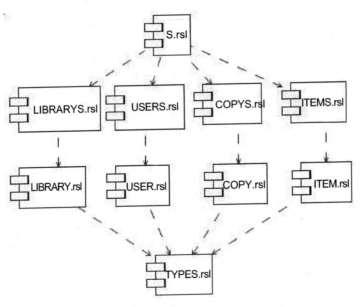

specification for the class. Those modules that have the specification for an object of the class, in turn, use an RSL module named "TYPES" which has all the definitions for the abstract types in the model. The entire specification consists of a top-level module "S" which uses the modules containing each class's specification. For the previous example, we have "S" using "LIBRARYS", "USERS", "COPYS", and "ITEMS". Each of these corresponds to a class in the class diagram, which respectively use, "LIBRARY", "USER", "COPY", and "ITEM". Finally, the last use is, in turn, the module "TYPES". Figure 2 shows the dependency module graph for the specification obtained from the class diagram.

Domain models usually have properties that must hold. These properties may be expressed as UML constraints in the class diagram. UML has no restriction for expressing constraints, which means that constraints can be written in either natural language or using any other language. Therefore, we have the possibility of expressing all of these properties in RSL without any ambiguity on the basis of the specification obtained from the class diagram.

The corresponding RSL specification for the class diagram shown in Figure 1 can be found in the section, "From a Class Diagram to the RSL Specification – An Example," which appears at the end of this chapter.

While conceptual models are problem-oriented, design class diagrams reflect a solution-oriented structure. That is, design class diagrams are concerned with the way in which the solution is given while conceptual models are concerned with the entities and the relationships that are present in the problem domain.

A design class diagram can be obtained following an analysis of interaction and collaboration between objects. Besides the structural elements present in domain models, design class diagrams have other details that can be expressed in UML (such as all of the methods identified in the collaboration diagrams, navigation in the association ends, scope and type of the attributes and operations, and even new associations discovered during the design phase). Not all of the classes present in the conceptual model will be part of the design diagram of the system. Only those that participate in the object interactions in order to achieve the functionality required for the software system are included.

From both domain models and design models, we can derive RSL specifications. These specifications can be used to carry out a rigorous analysis of the properties of the model that are represented by the class diagram or to analyze new properties that are expressed in RSL based on the obtained specification. These specifications can also be used as initial specifications that can be further refined for translated finally to executable code.

USING RSL AS SYNTACTIC AND SEMANTIC REFERENCE FOR UML

When a language is used as a reference for another language, the first language can be used to express the syntax and/or semantics of the second one. That is, the allowed elements and their formation rules (abstract syntax) of a given language, and the properties of the syntactical elements, are described in the other language using a more abstract representation.

UML is a graphical language that contains a set of elements and formation rules for building diagrams. By using UML, it is possible to build different models for each phase of the software development process, either following a particular development method, or solely for drawing diagrams used as documentation.

Although many graphical tools are available to build syntactically-correct UML diagrams, we are interested, in this case, in the use of UML for building a particular kind of class diagram. Therefore, whether an ad hoc graphical tool is built or an existing tool is adopted, the syntax for the class diagrams should be given. In the first case, the tool for building syntactically correct class diagrams uses the syntax. In the second case, when an available working UML tool is used, the syntax guides the parsing process for the outputs generated by the tool.

In the present work, both abstract syntax and semantics of the class diagrams are given in terms of RSL, i.e., RSL becomes a meta-language in which the semantics and abstract syntax of UML class diagrams are defined.

RSL is a formal specification language, which receives its name from the RAISE method. The RAISE (**R**igorous **A**pproach to **I**ndustrial **S**oftware **E**ngineering) method was the result of a European, collaborative project carried out between the years 1985 and 1990 in the context of the CEC ESPRIT program. The method consists of a number of techniques and strategies for formal development and proving. Its language, RSL, is a wide spectrum specification language. It allows the use of different styles of specifications: applicative or imperative; sequential or concurrent; direct (explicit) or axiomatic (implicit); algebraic (with abstract data types); or model-oriented (with concrete data types).

In the present work, the RSL specifications are written using an applicative and sequential style.

FORMAL SYNTAX

In this section, we present the well-formedness rules for class diagrams; but, we do not detail the meaning of each syntactic element or when it is used. This is done in section "Formal Semantics", where in first place (for each syntactic element), we explain its meaning based on UML documents (Booch et al., 1999; OMG, 2001), we show some examples, and then we give the corresponding semantics in RSL.

Note: Since a tool has been implemented to perform the translation, we have formalized the syntax for a subset of class diagram syntactic elements (i.e., those whose semantics are given in section "Formal Semantics").

We give the syntax in a top-down fashion, starting with the class diagram. As discussed in section "Class Diagrams and UML," class diagrams can be used for modeling the concepts and interactions in the application domain as well as can be used to create software system models (e.g., as in the case of design class diagrams). A class diagram in UML is formed by classes and the relationships among them. In order to build a well-formed class diagram, a set of rules must be observed for the classes, the relationships, and the entire class diagram. Therefore, we say that a well-formed class diagram is just a well-formed pair of well-formed classes and well-formed relationships.

type
    ClassDiagram =
        {| cd : ClassDiagram1 • well_formed(cd) |},
    ClassDiagram1 ::
        classes : Class-**set**
        rels: Rel-**set**

Before specifying what a well-formed class means, we give its structure. A class consists of a name, a set of attributes, a set of operations, and a multiplicity. It can be abstract, root, or leaf and can even have parameters as in the case of the template classes.

type

Class = {| c : Class1 • well_formed(c) |},

Class1 ::
    name : Name
    attributes : Attribute-**set**
    operations : Operation-**set**
    multiplicity : Multiplicity
    is_abstract : **Bool**
    is_root : **Bool**
    is_leaf : **Bool**
    parameters : FormalParameter*,

Name = **Text**,

Multiplicity :: lower : Bound upper : Bound,

Bound = = a_Nat(n : **Nat**) | asterisk,

Each attribute has a name, an optional type, a multiplicity, a scope (classifier or instance), and a changeability (frozen, add only, or changeable).

type

Attribute ::
    name : Name
    at_type : Op_Type
    multiplicity : At_multiplicity
    scope : Scope
    changeability : Changeability,

Op_Type = = null | a_Type(typ : Type),

Type = **Text**,

At_multiplicity ::
    lower : At_bound
    upper : At_bound,

At_bound = =
    a_Nat(n : Nat) | asterisk | a_parameter(name : Name),

Scope = = classifier | instance,

Changeability = = frozen | addonly | changeable

An operation consists of a name and a list of formal parameters, where each parameter has a name and an optional type. Furthermore, an operation has an optional, result-type called a scope and can be abstract.

type
   Operation ::
     name : Name
     parameters : FormalParameter*
     result : Op_Type
     is_abstract : Bool
     scope : Scope,

   FormalParameter ::
     name : Name
     par_type : Op_Type

A well-formed class "c" must satisfy a set of properties that we express as predicates in the function, "well_formed", which is used to define the type "Class". Following, we give all of these properties:

- A well-formed class must not have duplicate attribute names.

$\forall$at1, at2 : Attribute •
  (at1 $\in$ attributes(c) $\wedge$
    at2 $\in$ attributes(c) $\wedge$ at1 $\neq$ at2) $\Rightarrow$
      name(at1) $\neq$ name(at2)

- The multiplicity of each attribute must be well-formed.

$\forall$at : Attribute •
  at $\in$ attributes(c) $\Rightarrow$
    wf_AttMultiplicity(
      lower(multiplicity(at)),
      upper(multiplicity(at)), c)

- Changeability "addOnly" can be used only in attributes whose multiplicities are not a fixed number (Rumbaugh et al., 1999, p. 185) and are greater than that one (Booch et al., 1999).

$\forall$ at: Attribute •
  changeability(at) = addonly $\Rightarrow$
    case lower(multiplicity(at)) **of**
      a_Nat(l) $\rightarrow$
        case upper(multiplicity(at)) of
          a_Nat(u) $\rightarrow$ l $\neq$ u $\wedge$ u > 1,
          _ $\rightarrow$ true
        end,
      _ $\rightarrow$ true
    end

- Duplicate operation names are accepted only when they differ in scope, in types of parameters, or resultant values.

$\forall$ o1, o2 : Operation •
  (o1 $\in$ operations(c) $\wedge$
  o2 $\in$ operations(c) $\wedge$ name(o1) = name(o2) $\wedge$
  o1 $\neq$ o2) $\Rightarrow$
    (scope(o1) $\neq$ scope(o2) $\vee$
    result(o1) $\neq$ result(o2) $\vee$
    different_types(parameters(o1), parameters(o2)))

- If a class has an abstract operation, it must be abstract.

($\exists$ o : Operation •
  o $\in$ operations(c) $\wedge$ is_abstract(o)) $\Rightarrow$ is_abstract(c)

- Abstract classes have at least one abstract operation.

is_abstract(c) $\Rightarrow$
  ($\exists$ o : Operation •
    o $\in$ operations(c) $\wedge$ is_abstract(o))

- The multiplicity of the class must be valid, i.e., an order between the lower-bound and the upper-bound must be observed.

lower(multiplicity(c)) $\leq$ upper(multiplicity(c))

- There are no duplicate parameter names in a template class.

$\forall$ p1, p2: FormalParameter •
  (p1 $\in$ parameters(c) $\wedge$ p2 $\in$ parameters(c) $\wedge$ p1 $\neq$ p2)
    $\Rightarrow$ name(p1) $\neq$ name(p2)

- Since an abstract class is an incomplete class because it has abstract methods, i.e., methods without an implementation, it must be extended (inherited) in the class diagram by at least one concrete subclass. Therefore it cannot be a leaf.

is_abstract(c) $\Rightarrow$ ~is_leaf(c)

Some auxiliary functions must be defined in order to complete the specification for the syntax of a class.

```
/* Checks if multiplicity bounds are well-formed */
≤ : Bound × Bound → Bool
lo ≤ up ≡
    case lo of
        a_Nat(l) →
            case up of
                a_Nat(u) → l ≤ u,
                asterisk → true
            end,
        asterisk →
            case up of
```

```
                a_Nat(u) → false,
                asterisk → true
            end
    end,
```

/* Checks if an attribute multiplicity is well-formed */

```
wf_AttMultiplicity : At_bound × At_bound × Class → Bool
wf_AttMultiplicity(lo, up, c) ≡
    case lo of
        a_Nat(l) →
            case up of
                a_Nat(u) → l ≤ u,
                asterisk → true,
                a_parameter(name) → isin_formalPars(name, c)
            end,
        asterisk →
            case up of
                asterisk → true,
                _ → false
            end,
        a_parameter(name) →
            if ~(isin_formalPars(name, c)) then false
            else
                case up of
                    a_Nat(u) → true,
                    asterisk → true,
                    a_parameter(name) →
                        isin_formalPars(name, c)
                end
            end
    end,
```

/* Informs if a given name is a formal parameter of a given class c */

```
isin_formalPars : Name × Class → Bool
isin_formalPars(name, c) ≡
    (∃ i : Int •
        i ∈ inds parameters(c) ∧
        name(parameters(c)(i)) = name),
```

/* Informs if an attribute multiplicity bound is a parameter */

```
is_parameterized : At_bound → Bool
is_parameterized(b) ≡
    case b of
        a_parameter(p) → true,
        _ → false

    end,
```

/* Informs if two parameter lists have different types */

```
different_types :
    FormalParameter* × FormalParameter* → Bool
```

different_types(pl1, pl2) ≡
  len pl1 = **len** pl2 ⇒
    (∃ i : **Int** •
      i ∈ **inds** pl1 ∧
        par_type(pl1(i)) ≠ par_type(pl2(i)))

In a class diagram, the classes can be related through different kind of relationships. Basically, they are classified into three types: associations, generalizations, and dependencies. Instantiations are viewed in UML as stereotyped dependencies. However, as each stereotyped element has a particular meaning and we are interested specifically in instantiation, we separate it from general dependencies.

type
  Rel = {| r : Rel1 • well_formed(r) |},

  Rel1 =
    Association | Generalization | Dependency | Instantiation

Each relationship in a class diagram must be well-formed. Therefore, we define the structure for each type of relationship and we give the well-formedness rules, as we did for a class. An association is a relationship among "n" classes. The end of each association holds information, not only about the class, but it also can have several adornments: a multiplicity, a navigability, composition or aggregation and, like attributes, it has a given changeability. Furthermore, each association in the diagram has an assigned name.

type
  Association ::
    name : Name
    ends : End-**set**,

  End ::
    end_class : Class
    multiplicity : Multiplicity
    navigable : **Bool**
    kind : EKind
    changeability : Changeability,

  EKind == composite | aggregate | none

Generalizations, dependencies, and instantiations are all binary relationships. In the case of instantiations, besides the data for the involved classes, it is necessary to hold all of the information about the actual parameters.

type
  Generalization ::
    subclass : Class
    superclass : Class,

Dependency ::
    source : Class
    target : Class,

Instantiation ::
    template : Class
    instantiated : Class
    actualparameters : Value*,

Value

Below, we give the boolean function "well_formed" used to define well-formed relationships. Each kind of relationship has different properties.

value
    well_formed : Rel1 → **Bool**
    well_formed(r) ≡
        case r **of**
            mk_Association(_, ends) → well_formedAsso(ends),
            mk_Generalization(subclass, superclass) →
                well_formedGen(subclass, superclass),
            mk_Instantiation(
                template, instantiated, actualParameters) →
                well_formedIns(
                    template, instantiated, actualParameters),
            _ → **true**
        end

When the relationship is an association, a series of constraints on the association ends are imposed. All of them are defined in the function "well_formedAsso" used by "well_formed".

- An association is an N-ary relationship with N ≥ 2.

card ends ≥ 2

- The multiplicities of the association ends must be well-formed; that is, the multiplicity lower-bound must be less, or equal to, multiplicity upper-bound.

∀e: End •
    (e ∈ ends ⇒
        lower(multiplicity(e)) ≤
            upper(multiplicity(e)))

- The changeability "addOnly" can be used only in association ends where multiplicities are not fixed numbers (Rumbaugh et al., 1999, p. 185) and are greater than one (Booch et al., 1999).

∀e: End •
    changeability(e) = addonly ⇒

case lower(multiplicity(e)) **of**
  a_Nat(l) →
     case upper(multiplicity(e)) **of**
        a_Nat(u) → l ≠ u ∧ u > 1,
        _ → **true**
     end,
     _ → **true**
end

- When the association has one aggregate or composite end, the association must be binary.

∀e: End •
  ((e ∈ ends ∧
    (kind(e) = composite ∨ kind(e) = aggregate)) ⇒
       card ends = 2)

- In a composite association (or composition only), the parts of a composition must be navigable.

∀e1, e2: End •
  ((e1 ∈ ends ∧ kind(e1) = composite ∧
    e2 ∈ ends ∧ e2 ≠ e1) ⇒ navigable(e2))

- Only one end can be aggregated or composite, i.e., only one can play the role of "whole".

∀e: End •
  ((e ∈ ends ∧
    (kind(e) = composite ∨ kind(e) = aggregate)) ⇒
  ~(∃ e1 : End •
    (e1 ∈ ends ∧ e1 ≠ e ∧
       (kind(e1) = composite ∨
          kind(e1) = aggregate))))

- In a composition, the end corresponding to the "whole" cannot have a multiplicity greater than one.

∀e: End •
  ((e ∈ ends ∧ kind(e) = composite) ⇒
     upper(multiplicity(e)) ≤ a_Nat(1))

- In an association, at least one of the ends must be navigable.

∃ e : End • (e ∈ ends ∧ navigable(e))

When there is inheritance between two classes, the generalization must satisfy three constraints: a subclass cannot be root, the superclasses cannot be leaf, and the subclasses cannot redefine the attributes of their superclasses.

well_formedGen : Class $\times$ Class $\rightarrow$ **Bool**
well_formedGen(subclass, superclass) $\equiv$

/* A subclass cannot be a root class.*/
  ~is_root(subclass) $\wedge$

/* A superclass cannot be a leaf class.*/
  ~is_leaf(superclass) $\wedge$

/* A subclass cannot redefine the attributes of the superclass */
  ($\forall$at1, at2 : Attribute $\bullet$
    (at1 $\in$ attributes(subclass) $\wedge$
      at2 $\in$ attributes(superclass)) $\Rightarrow$
        name(at1) $\neq$ name(at2))

When the relationship is an instantiation, the instantiated class cannot extend nor redefine the structure and behavior of the template class, which means that the instantiated class is fully specified by the template. Moreover, the class that acts as the template in the relationship must have at least one formal parameter. Additionally, and the actual parameters of the instantiation must match the formal parameters of the template class.

well_formedIns : Class $\times$ Class $\times$ Value* $\rightarrow$ Bool
well_formedIns(
  template, instantiated, actualParameters) $\equiv$

  /* An instantiated class is fully specified by its template. */
  (**card** attributes(instantiated) = 0 $\wedge$
  card operations(instantiated) = 0 $\wedge$
  multiplicity(instantiated) = multiplicity(template) $\wedge$
  is_abstract(instantiated) = is_abstract(template) $\wedge$
  is_leaf(instantiated) = is_leaf(template) $\wedge$
  is_root(instantiated) = is_root(template) $\wedge$

  /* A template class must have at least one formal parameter */
  (**len** parameters(template) > 0) $\wedge$

  /* The actual parameters must match with the formal
  parameters in the template */
  match_ps(parameters(template), actualParameters))

Having specified what well-formed classes and well-formed relations are, we can now give the properties that must hold when a well-formed class diagram is being built.

- In a class diagram, all of the classes that are involved in a relationship must belong to the set of classes in the class diagram.

$\forall$rel : Rel $\bullet$ (rel $\in$ rels(cd) $\Rightarrow$
  case rel **of**
    mk_Instantiation(template, instantiated, _) $\rightarrow$

```
        template ∈ classes(cd) ∧
        instantiated ∈ classes(cd),
    mk_Dependency(source, target) →
        source ∈ classes(cd) ∧
        target ∈ classes(cd),
    mk_Generalization(subclass, superclass) →
        subclass ∈ classes(cd) ∧
        superclass ∈ classes(cd),
    mk_Association(_, ends) →
        (∀e: End • (e ∈ ends ⇒
            end_class(e) ∈ classes(cd)))
end)
```

- Each class must have a unique name, i.e., there are no duplicate class names.

∀c1, c2 : Class •
   ((c1 ∈ classes(cd) ∧ c2 ∈ classes(cd) ∧
   c1 ≠ c2) ⇒ name(c1) ≠ name(c2))

- UML allows the use of "rolenames" at the association ends. This allows for different associations with the same name relating to a common class should they differ in the "rolenames". However, as we do not use "rolenames" in our class diagrams, a well-formed class diagram cannot have two different associations with the same name relating to a common class.

∀a1, a2 : Association •
   ((a1 ∈ rels(cd) ∧ a2 ∈ rels(cd) ∧
   a1 ≠ a2 ∧ name(a1) = name(a2)) ⇒
       end_classes(a1) ∩ end_classes(a2) = {})

- When there is an abstract class in a class diagram, it must be the superclass of at least one class in the class diagram in order to assure the existence of a concrete subclass in the inheritance hierarchy to make it useful.

∀c: Class •
   ((c1 ∈ classes(cd) ∧ is_abstract(c1)) ⇒
       (∃ g : Generalization •
       g ∈ rels(cd) ∧ superclass(g) = c1))

- Since a template class cannot be used directly because of its unbound parameters, it cannot be a superclass or the target of an association (OMG, 2001, section 3, p. 52).

(∀ i: Instantiation, a: Association, e: End •
   ((i ∈ rels(cd) ∧ a ∈ rels(cd) ∧
       e ∈ ends(a) ∧
       end_class(e) = template(i)) ⇒ ~navigable(e))) ∧
(∀ i: Instantiation, g: Generalization •

$$((i \in rels(cd) \wedge g \in rels(cd)) \Rightarrow$$
$$\quad template(i) \neq superclass(g)))$$

- As an instantiated class is fully specified by its template; it cannot be the source of an association, rather, it can only be a target in an association.

$(\forall$ i: Instantiation, a: Association, e: End •
$\quad ((i \in rels(cd) \wedge a \in rels(cd) \wedge$
$\qquad e \in ends(a) \wedge$
$\qquad end\_class(e) = instantiated(i)) \Rightarrow$
$\quad (\forall$ e2 : End •
$\qquad (e2 \in ends(a) \wedge e2 \neq e) \Rightarrow$
$\qquad \sim navigable(e2))))$

- Although an instantiated class is fully specified by its template, it can be a subclass (OMG, 2001, section 3, p. 55); however, we do not allow the use of instantiated classes that are also subclasses due the semantics given for inheritance (see section "Generalization").

$(\forall$ i: Instantiation, g: Generalization •
$\quad ((i \in rels(cd) \wedge g \in rels(cd)) \Rightarrow$
$\qquad subclass(g) \neq instantiated(i)))$

- An instantiated class is the result of the instantiation of only one template. This means that the same class cannot appear as instantiated in two different instantiation relationships.

$\forall$ i1, i2: Instantiation •
$\quad ((i1 \in rels(cd) \wedge i2 \in rels(cd) \wedge i1 \neq i2) \Rightarrow$
$\qquad instantiated(i1) \neq instantiated(i2))$

- When two classes are related by an instantiation, no other relationship between them is possible. This means that there can be no association, generalization, or different instantiation between the involved classes. In the predicate below, we do not check the existence of another instantiation between the classes because it is given by the two previous properties. These establish that a class cannot be instantiated by more than one template; and, a template cannot be an instantiated class.

$\forall$ i: Instantiation, a: Association, e: End ,
$\quad$ g: Generalization, at: Attribute •
$\qquad (i \in rels(cd) \Rightarrow$
$\qquad\quad ((a \in rels(cd) \Rightarrow$
$\qquad\qquad \sim there\_is\_association($
$\qquad\qquad template(i), instantiated(i), a)) \wedge$
$\qquad\quad ((g \in rels(cd) \wedge subclass(g) = template(i)) \Rightarrow$
$\qquad\qquad superclass(g) \neq instantiated(i)) \wedge$
$\qquad\quad (at \in attributes(template(i)) \Rightarrow$

```
        at_type(at) ≠
        a_Type(name(instantiated(i)))))))
```

- When two classes are related by a generalization, the only relationships allowed between them are associations. It is not necessary to check for absence of instantiation because it is given by the previous predicates. It is also not necessary to check for absence of generalization on the same classes in the inverse order because it is given by the next property that establishes that generalization has no loops. We do not give the property that establishes that it is not possible to inherit more than one time from the same class, because it can be inferred from the property that establishes that multiple inheritance is not allowed.
- In a class diagram there are no loops among generalizations.

let
```
    gs = gens(cd) ∪ inss(cd),
    trans = closure(gs)
```
in
```
    ~existsRefSymmPairs(gs)
```
end

- Although UML allows for the use of multiple inheritance, we have restricted the well-formed diagrams to prevent multiple inheritance. Note that the predicate below prevents inheriting more than once.

```
∀ g1, g2: Generalization •
    ((g1 ∈ rels(cd) ∧ g2 ∈ rels(cd) ∧
    g1 ≠ g2) ⇒ subclass(g1) ≠ subclass(g2))
```

In order to complete the specification for a well-formed class diagram, we give the following auxiliary functions used before.

value
```
    /* Return the set of classes obtained from the set
    of ends of a given association */
    end_classes : Association → Class-set
    end_classes(a) ≡ {end_class(e) | e : End • e ∈ ends(a)},

    /* Return the set of pairs (subclass, superclass) related by a
    generalization of degree one in a class diagram */
    gens : ClassDiagram → (Class × Class)-set
    gens(cd) ≡
        {(c1, c2) |
        c1, c2 : Class •
            (∃ g : Generalization •
            g ∈ rels(cd) ∧
            (c1, c2) = (subclass(g), superclass(g)))},
```

/* Return the set of pairs (instantiated, template) related by an instantiation in the class diagram */
inss : ClassDiagram → (Class × Class)-**set**
inss(cd) ≡
   {(c1, c2) |
   c1, c2 : Class •
      (∃ i : Instantiation •
        i ∈ rels(cd) ∧
         (c1, c2) = (instantiated(i), template(i)))},

/* Inform if two classes c1 and c2 are involved in the association a */
there_is_association :
   Class × Class × Association → **Bool**
there_is_association(c1, c2, a) ≡
   (∃ e1, e2 : End •
      e1 ∈ ends(a) ∧ e2 ∈ ends(a) ∧ e1 ≠ e2 ∧
      c1 = end_class(e1) ∧ c2 = end_class(e2)),

/* Returns the transitive closure of a relation r */
closure : (Class × Class)-**set** → (Class × Class)-**set**
closure(r) ≡
   {(c1, c2) |
   (c1, c2) : Class × Class •
      (c1, c2) ∈ r ∨
      (∃ c : Class •
        (c1, c) ∈ r ∧ (c, c2) ∈ closure(r))},

/* Inform if c1 is a subclass of c2 because of a direct or transitive generalization in cd */
there_is_generalization :
   Class × Class × ClassDiagram → **Bool**
there_is_generalization(c1, c2, cd) ≡
   let gs = gens(cd) ∪ inss(cd), g = closure(gs) **in**
      (c1, c2) ∈ g
   end,

/* Inform if a given relation r has symmetric or reflexive pairs */
existsRefSymmPairs : (Class × Class)-**set** → **Bool**
existsRefSymmPairs(r) ≡
   (∃ (c1, c2) : Class × Class •
      (c1, c2) ∈ r ∧ (c2, c1) ∈ r)

FORMAL SEMANTICS

To give the semantics of a language in terms of another, it is necessary to define a mapping from the source language to the language that is being used as the reference. A mechanism that implements the translation should also be provided. In our case, this mechanism should be able to take an abstract representation built from a syntactically correct UML class diagram and produce an RSL specification as the output.

The process applied to explore the semantic foundations of UML class diagrams has provided a set of RSL templates, which are described in the section "RSL Templates," as the results. These templates form the basis for the proposed automatic translation mechanism, in which notations in UML are translated directly into an RSL specification without explicit reference to UML notations (e.g., class, association, etc.) but with project-specific instances defined.

We proceed first by informally analyzing the semantics of a given element using examples in UML. We then formally provide these semantics in RSL. The templates are then abstracted from the RSL semantics.

The Class

We start by formalizing the semantics of a class, which is the building block of class diagrams. In UML, a class is a description of a set of objects or class instances that share the same structure and behavior. The structure is captured by the attributes; the behavior is captured by the operations. When considering an instance or object of a class, we can capture its structure and behavior in an RSL module, where we give the corresponding specification. We define an RSL abstract type in order to specify the class sort. This RSL abstract type denotes the set of all possible class instances or objects.

During our first semantic analysis, we considered specifying it as an RSL record, whose destructors corresponded to the attributes of the class. However, when we later analyzed the semantics of generalization, we found that this class sort specification was incompatible with the use of the RSL sub-types that were used for specifying the class sort of a subclass. The section "Generalization" provides information on the semantics of a generalization relationship.

As we said earlier, the attributes correspond to the structural part of the class. Therefore, the attribute should be obtained with the corresponding observer defined on the class sort. Consequently, we must define an observer on the class sort for each attribute. Every one of these observers takes an instance of the class and returns a value belonging to the corresponding attribute type.

The class operations correspond to the behavioral part of the class. Each operation achieves a particular behavior based on the class structure and, possibly, on other parameters. Therefore, they can be specified as RSL functions, which have their domain in the Cartesian product of the class sort and the corresponding operation parameters.

Figure 3: Example of a class in UML

Person
birth
name
age(CurrentDate)

The range of an operation corresponds to the operation result type. When an operation in the class diagram does not return a value, it means that it has performed some behavior based on the class structure and the parameters, and possibly, has changed the class structure. In this situation, the RSL function will return the class sort.

The class "Person" as given in Figure 3, has two attributes: one for the name and the other for the date of birth (plus one operation that, given a date, computes the person's age). According to our interpretation, one instance of the class might be specified in RSL as follows:

```
TYPES
object PERSON :
    with TYPES in
    class
        type
            Person
        value
            birth: Person → birth,
            name: Person → name,
            age: CurrentDate × Person → Person
    end
```

Besides the typical operation related to obtaining the value of an attribute in a class, it is common to have an operation to modify it. As frequently, the update of a given attribute occurs under a given pre-condition, we generated RSL functions for this purpose. After the RSL specification is generated, the user should complete his or her pre-conditions. If this is not necessary, then pre-conditions may be removed. Accordingly, we give the following RSL specification for an instance of "Person":

```
TYPES
object PERSON :
    with TYPES in
    class
        type
            Person
        value
            birth: Person → birth,
            name: Person → name,

            update_birth: birth × Person ~→ Person
            update_birth(at, o) as o′ post birth(o′) = at
            pre preupdate_birth(at, o),

            preupdate_birth: birth × Person → Bool,

            update_name: name × Person ~→ Person
            update_name(at, o) as o′ post name(o′) = at
            pre preupdate_name(at, o),

            preupdate_name: name × Person → Bool,
```

      age: CurrentDate × Person → Person
end

    In UML, it is possible to produce class diagrams at different levels of abstraction. For instance, when we are building a conceptual model, we are concerned with showing some attributes without any information about their types. Therefore, when the type of an attribute or operation parameter is not given in the diagram, we interpret it as an abstract type and define a sort in the module "TYPES" which will hold the specification for all of the model types. However, as discussed before, when the resultant type of an operation is not present in the diagram (and, since the operations act on the object state), we specify the type returned by the RSL function corresponding to this operation as the class sort.

    We have given the semantics for an instance of a class. Now we need to give an interpretation for the class itself. As has been said before, a class defines a set of instances. If we consider that a class diagram describes all of the possible valid states in which a system can be found (i.e., all of the possible valid states of its objects, links, and association instances, at a given time), and if we consider a class in the context of a class diagram, we need to define a type that describes the set of all possible observable states in which the class can be found (i.e., a set of sets of objects or, in other words, all of the possible sets of objects that can be observed at a given moment). In order to describe this fact in RSL, we define a type for specifying all of the possible instances or objects of the class. We refer to this as the class container type.

    A characteristic of objects is that each object is distinguishable from other objects of the class, even if they have exactly the same property values. For example, two different instances of a "Person" can have the same name and age. But, they are different instances because they each have an identity. Consequently, we define the class container type as a RSL map that is defined from a set of object identifiers to the class sort. For example, if we consider the class "Person" again, we define in RSL the type "Persons" that represents all of the possible instances of the class "Person" as follows:

type
    Persons = Person_Id $\underset{m}{\to}$ Person

    The specification for a class is given in a new RSL module (in this example, "PERSONS"), which uses the module that has the specification for an object (in this example, "PERSON"). The entire class specification could be contained in only one module; however, we have decided to split it into two modules in order to gain clarity and maintainability.

PERSON
object PERSONS :
    with TYPES **in**
      class
        type
          Person = PERSON.Person,

$$Persons = Person\_Id \xrightarrow{m} Person$$

end

For each class in the class diagram, and in the context of the system described by a class diagram, new objects can be created and existing objects can be destroyed or modified. Therefore, some typical functions that operate on the set of instances of each class are defined.

PERSON
object PERSONS :
   with TYPES **in**
   class
     type
       Person = PERSON.Person,
       $Persons = Person\_Id \xrightarrow{m} Person$

     value
       empty_Person : Persons = [ ],

       add_Person : Person_Id × Person × Persons $\xrightarrow{\sim}$ Persons
       add_Person(id, o, c) ≡ c † [id ↦ o]
       pre ~ isin_Person(id, c),

       del_Person : Person_Id × Persons $\xrightarrow{\sim}$ Persons
       del_Person(id, c) ≡ c \ {id}
       pre isin_Person(id, c),

       isin_Person : Person_Id × Persons → **Bool**
       isin_Person(id, c) ≡ id ∈ **dom** c,

       get_Person : Person_Id × Persons $\xrightarrow{\sim}$ Person
       get_Person(id, c) ≡ c(id) **pre** isin_Person(id, c),

       update_Person : Person_Id × Person × Persons $\xrightarrow{\sim}$ Persons
       update_Person(id, o, c) ≡ c † [id ↦ o]
       pre isin_Person(id, c)
  end

Relationships

When we build a class diagram, we identify a number of classes that collaborate and interact among them. This fact might be modeled in UML by using different kinds of relationships. In the next subsections, we discuss each of them.

Association

The association is the most common relationship among classes. Although it is possible to find associations among any number of classes (usually referred to as "N-ary" associations), the more frequently used association is the binary association. In Figure 1 we can see, for instance, a binary association between the class "Item" and class

"Copy" named "has_copies." This means that instances of the class "Item" might be related to instances of the class "Copy" through "has_copies," and vice versa.

The interpretation for an association among "n" classes is a mathematical relationship among the sets of instances corresponding to each class. An association describes a set of association instances, called links, in UML. Therefore, an association can be viewed as a set of links, where each link is an "n-tuple" that represents an instance of "n" objects related by this association.

Regardless of its "arity", there are two possibilities for specifying an association in RSL. One possibility consists of specifying the association as a class that has "n" object-valued attributes. An object-valued attribute is an attribute whose type corresponds to the type being used to identify an object among all the instances of a class. The other possibility consists of splitting the relationship among the involved classes, i.e., each class contains only one object-valued attribute for recording the "n-1" remaining elements of the "n-tuple" (i.e., the relationship is divided into "n" functions).

Because in UML, an attribute whose type is a class that is viewed as a shorthand for a composite association (i.e., a particular kind of association as discussed in the section, "Composition and Aggregation") then technically, there is no difference between attributes and associations. Therefore, we adopt the second approach to specify all kinds of associations as object-valued attributes. Note that the first approach presents the following problem: the association is separated from the classes. As a result, if we want to reuse one of the classes involved, we have to know, or be reminded that in order to carry this information into the new system, the association has to be external to the classes. Since this coupling of information is not part of the class, it is also possible that it could be lost.

According to the adopted approach for the binary association "has_copies" as shown in Figure 1, we define two observers: One is in the class "Item" for retrieving all the existing copies for a given item, and the other is in the class "Copy" for obtaining the corresponding item for a given copy.

TYPES
object ITEM :
   with TYPES **in**
   class
      type Item

      value
         title : Item $\rightarrow$ title,
         kind : Item $\rightarrow$ kind,
         ...

         has_copies : Item $\rightarrow$ Copy_Id-**set**,

         update_has_copies : Copy_Id-**set** $\times$ Item $\overset{\sim}{\rightarrow}$ Item
         update_has_copies(a, o) **as** o' **post** has_copies(o') = a
         pre preupdate_has_copies(a, o),

         preupdate_has_copies : Copy_Id-**set** $\times$ Item $\rightarrow$ **Bool**,
         ...
     end

TYPES
object COPY :
  with TYPES **in**
  class
    type Copy

    value
      status: Copy → status,
      location: Copy → location,

      ...

      has_copies: Copy → Item_Id,

      update_has_copies: Item_Id × Copy $\overset{\sim}{\to}$ Copy
      update_has_copies(a, o) **as** o' **post** has_copies(o') = a
      pre preupdate_has_copies(a, o),

      preupdate_has_copies: Item_Id × Copy → **Bool**,
      ...

  end

Similar to defining the functions for updating the attributes, we also define all of the functions for updating the links. Therefore, the corresponding RSL functions are also included in the specifications for an item and for a copy.

Note that in the case of the class "Item" the returned type for "has_copies" is a set of object identifiers of the class "Copy". On the other hand, in "Copy", "has_copies" only returns an object identifier of the class "Item". A structural distinction is made here as the multiplicities at the association ends are different. Association multiplicities are treated separately in a later section, "Multiplicities".

The association class

In UML, associations that have attributes and/or relationships are represented by association classes (i.e., associations with the properties of a class). Figure 4 shows the association class "Job" between "Employee" and "Company". In this example, "Job" could have its own attributes and operations.

Following the semantics expressed in the OMG Unified Modeling Language Specification (OMG, 2001), in general, an association class relating "n" classes could be decomposed into an association among the "n" involved classes, plus a new class

Figure 4: An association class

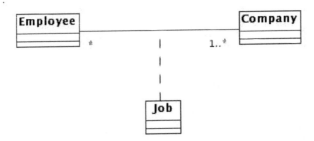

Figure 5: Decomposition of an association class

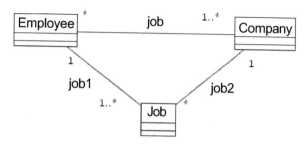

representing the association class, which is related to the "n" classes through new associations (see Figure 5).

However, it is necessary to constrain the association "job" and the two new associations "job1" and "job2" in order to satisfy the job = job1 $\circ$ job2, where $\circ$ denotes the composition operation of relations.

($\forall$ id1 : Employee_Id •
  (id1 $\in$ **dom** employees(s) $\Rightarrow$
    ($\forall$ id2 : Job_Id •
      id2 $\in$ EMPLOYEE.job1(employees(s)(id1)) $\Rightarrow$
      JOB.job2(jobs(s)(id2)) $\in$
        EMPLOYEE.job(employees(s)(id1))))) $\wedge$
($\forall$ id1 : Company_Id •
  (id1 $\in$ **dom** companys(s) $\Rightarrow$
    ($\forall$ id2 : Job_Id •
      id2 $\in$ COMPANY.job2(companys(s)(id1)) $\Rightarrow$
      JOB.job1(jobs(s)(id2)) $\in$
        COMPANY.job(companys(s)(id1)))))

The diagram shown in Figure 6 can model the same association class. Other authors express the semantics for association classes in this way (Liu et al., 2001).

However, in following Rumbaugh, et al. (1999, pp. 157), this is not enough. To comply with these semantics, we have to constrain the associations shown in Figure 5 to avoid two different instances of the association class relating the same "tuple" of objects.

($\forall$ id1, id2 : Job_Id •
  (id1 $\in$ **dom** jobs(s) $\wedge$
    id2 $\in$ **dom** jobs(s) $\wedge$ id1 $\neq$ id2) $\Rightarrow$
      (JOB.job1(jobs(s)(id1)), JOB.job2(jobs(s)(id1))) $\neq$
        (JOB.job1(jobs(s)(id2)), JOB.job2(jobs(s)(id2)))))

Figure 6: Decomposition of an association class

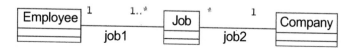

Figure 7: Example of "n-ary" association

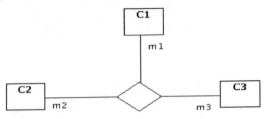

Figure 8: Decomposition of "n-ary" association

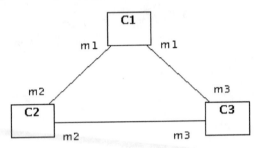

This decomposition process could be also used to deal with associations with "arity" that is greater than two. For example, the "3-ary" association depicted in Figure 7 could be transformed into three associations among the three classes involved, as Figure 8 shows.

Generalization

It is possible in UML to express inheritance among classes by using generalization. With inheritance in UML, a child class inherits the structure and behavior of the parent. Furthermore, the child may add a new structure and behavior or it may even modify the behavior.

Figure 9 shows an example of the use of generalization between the classes "Person" and "User."

"User" inherits all of the structure and behavior of the "Person" and adds a new structure through the addition of the attribute "level."

We analyzed two different approaches for representing inheritance by using RSL. Since RSL does not provide dynamic binding (i.e., the object capability to change type at run time), only sub-type polymorphism could be supported (i.e., the possibility of applying a function that has been defined for a type to a value of a sub-type of that type). We first considered the possibility of specifying the class sort (corresponding to the subclass) as a record, which holds the structure of the "superclass," plus the newly-added structure.

type
    User ::
        person : PERSON.Person ↔ replace_person
        level : TYPES.level ↔ replace_level

Figure 9: Example of generalization in UML

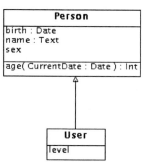

The type "user" incorporates all of the structure of a "Person." However, in order to "inherit" the superclass behavior in RSL, it is necessary to redefine all of the superclass methods in the subclass.

PERSON
object USER :
   with TYPES **in**
   class
     type
       User ::
          person : PERSON.Person $\leftrightarrow$ replace_person
         level : level $\leftrightarrow$ replace_level

    value
      name : User $\rightarrow$ Name
      name(user) $\equiv$ PERSON.name(person(user)),

      birth : User $\rightarrow$ Birth
      birth(user) $\equiv$ PERSON.birth(person(user)),

      update_name : Name $\times$ User $\rightarrow$ User
      update_name(name, user) $\equiv$
        mk_User(PERSON.update_name(name, person(user)),
             level(user)),

      update_birth : Birth $\times$ User $\rightarrow$ User
      update_birth(birth, user) $\equiv$
        mk_User(PERSON.update_birth(birth, person(user)), level(user)),

      age : Date $\times$ User $\rightarrow$ Age
      age(date, user) $\equiv$ PERSON.age(date, person(user)),

      update_level : level $\times$ User $\xrightarrow{\sim}$ User
      update_level(level, user) $\equiv$
      replace_level(level, user)
      pre preupdate_level(level, user),

      preupdate_level : level $\times$ User $\rightarrow$ **Bool**
   end

UML also allows for multiple inheritance among classes. In multiple inheritance, the subclass inherits all of the properties of the superclasses (i.e., all of the attributes and operations that have been defined for the superclasses). The subclass can even add a new structure and behavior or redefine the behavior.

The same approach that has been explained above for single inheritance could be applied to a multiple inheritance (i.e., in the subclass we define a record in RSL where the structure of the superclasses plus all of the subclass' attributes are incorporated and, all of the superclass' methods, plus the subclass' methods, are generated as well). In our approach, if in multiple inheritance we found two superclasses with common attribute names and the same maximal types, then in the subclass we get only one attribute, whose type is the minimal type among the types of the common attributes of the superclass. When the maximum types are different, there is a typical problem of multiple inheritance, i.e., clash of names. The same problems can arise as a result of overlapping behavior.

This approach presents further problems as there is no way of guaranteeing that when a developer works on the RSL specification in future development, some inconsistencies can occur between the superclass and the subclass. For instance, new behavior could be added in the superclass and omitted in the subclass, making each reference to the new method undefined when applied to an object of the subclass. Since the class sorts that have been defined for each class in the class hierarchy are disjoint, each class has its own class container. Consequently, the constraints for a superclass must be repeated for each subclass in the hierarchy, leading to more possible inconsistencies.

To solve this problem, we use sub-types instead. The sub-type that denotes the set of all the instances of the subclass is defined as an RSL sub-type of the class sort, corresponding with its superclass. Therefore, all of the functions that operate on the type that has been defined for the superclass are available for the sub-type. New attributes and operations may be added to the subclass by defining the corresponding functions on the subclass type. Also, the superclass' methods can be redefined in the subclass by redefining the corresponding names of functions. This is possible because each class has its own module, eliminating any problem of redefinition of functions that might occur in RSL.

```
PERSON
object USER :
   with TYPES in
   class
      type
         Person = PERSON.Person,
         User = {| o : Person • is_a_User(o) |}

      value
         level : User → level,

         update_level : level × User →̃ User
         update_level(at, o) as o' post level(o') = at
          pre preupdate_level(at, o),

         preupdate_level : level × User → Bool,
         is_a_User : Person → Bool
   end
```

The type corresponding to the type container of the subclass is defined as a sub-type as well. In this case, it is defined as a sub-type of the type used to specify the class container of the superclass.

type
Users =
   {| super : PERSONS.Persons •
     ($\forall$ id : Person_Id •
       id $\in$ **dom** super $\Rightarrow$ USER.is_a_User(super(id))) |}

The functions that operate on the class container are defined as usual.

USER, PERSONS
object USERS :
  with TYPES **in**
  class
    type
      User = USER.User,
      Users =
        {| super : PERSONS.Persons •
          ($\forall$ id : Person_Id •
            id $\in$ **dom** super $\Rightarrow$ USER.is_a_User(super(id))) |}

    value
      empty_User : Users = [],

      add_User : User_Id $\times$ User $\times$ Users $\overset{\sim}{\to}$ Users
      add_User(id, o, c) $\equiv$ c † [id $\mapsto$ o]
      pre $\sim$ isin_User(id, c),

      del_User : User_Id $\times$ Users $\overset{\sim}{\to}$ Users
      del_User(id, c) $\equiv$ c \ {id}
      pre isin_User(id, c),

      isin_User : User_Id $\times$ Users $\to$ **Bool**
      isin_User(id, c) $\equiv$ id $\in$ **dom** c,

      get_User : User_Id $\times$ Users $\overset{\sim}{\to}$ User
      get_User(id, c) $\equiv$ c(id) **pre** isin_User(id, c),

      update_User : User_Id $\times$ User $\times$ Users $\overset{\sim}{\to}$ Users
      update_User(id, o, c) $\equiv$ c † [id | $\to$ o]
      pre isin_User(id, c),

      consistent : Users $\to$ **Bool**
      consistent(c) $\equiv$
        ($\forall$ id : User_Id •
          id $\in$ **dom** c $\Rightarrow$ USER.consistent(c(id)))
  end

Figure 10: RSL module dependency graph

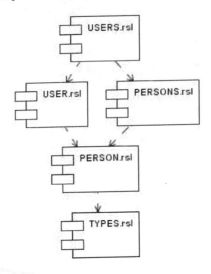

Figure 10 shows a dependency graph among the modules that have the specification for the superclass "Person" and the subclass "User".

Since we interpret the class sort of a subclass as an RSL sub-type of the superclass sort, it is not possible to represent multiple inheritance. However, in general, multiple inheritance must be used carefully because of problems that could arise from having multiple parents with overlapping behaviors or structures. There is also the issue of loss of maintainability: the more superclasses that there are, then the harder it is to know what comes from where and how the changes affect the lattice. Multiple inheritance may be replaced by delegation, where the subclass inherits from only one of the candidate superclasses and incorporates other superclasses into its structure in order to obtain their structures and behaviors. In Figures 11 and 12, we provide an example of multiple inheritance and the transformation into a delegation.

Figure 11: Multiple inheritance

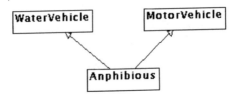

Figure 12: Delegation

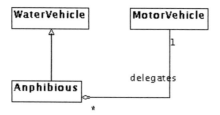

Root classes

UML allows one to constrain a class with the property {root}. This means that such a class may not have a superclass. This does not seem to be very useful, except when there is a multiple inheritance lattice and one wants to designate the head of each hierarchy.

This is a constraint that is captured in the syntax; therefore, there is no reason to give its dynamic semantics.

Leaf classes

Property {leaf} is used in UML to point out that a given class does not have children. When we give the semantics of a class having this attached property, we can fix the final structure of the sort class because there is no inheritance possible from this class (i.e., the type corresponding to its class is no longer specified as a sort, but as a more concrete RSL type or a record). For instance, if the class "Person" in Figure 3 is a leaf class, we specify it in RSL as follows:

TYPES
object PERSON :
   with TYPES **in**
   class
      type
         Person ::
            birth : birth ↔ replace_birth
            name : name ↔ replace_name

      value
         update_birth : Date × Person $\xrightarrow{\sim}$ Person
         update_birth(at, o) ≡ replace_birth(at, o)
         pre preupdate_birth(at, o),
         ...
         age : CurrentDate × Person → Person
   end

Dependency

Dependency is a binary relationship. When used between two classes, dependency expresses that one class uses the other in some way. It is possible to use a dependency between two classes when, for example, there exists the knowledge that one class is going to use another class as the parameter type in one of its operations (even if the operation has not yet been given in the class), or for expressing, e.g., that the class is locally used in an operation. Therefore, this kind of relationship can have a variety of meanings that are indirectly rather than directly derived from a class diagram.

The Class Diagram

A class diagram is useful for building static system models that are expressed in terms of classes and the relationships among them. When we use class diagrams for building conceptual models, the diagrams reflect the concepts and relationships that are present in the application domain. When class diagrams are used at the design level, they reflect a solution-oriented structure.

A class diagram represents the set of all possible object diagrams. An object diagram models instances of elements that are contained in the corresponding class diagram, i.e., objects and links. An object diagram is like a snapshot that shows one of the possible configurations for a given class diagram. As a result, an object diagram is essentially an instance of a class diagram.

We say that a class diagram describes the set of all its object diagrams or the state space of the system and that an object diagram corresponds to one system state. Therefore, we define a type in RSL to specify the state space of the system as a record whose fields are all of the present classes in the class diagram that can have instances associated with them. For example, for the class diagram given in Figure 1 we have:

ITEMS, USERS, LIBRARYS, COPYS
object S :
   with TYPES **in**
   class
     type
       Sys ::
         items : ITEMS.Items $\leftrightarrow$ replace_Items
         users : USERS.Users $\leftrightarrow$ replace_Users
         librarys : LIBRARYS.Librarys $\leftrightarrow$ replace_Librarys
         copys : COPYS.Copys $\leftrightarrow$ replace_Copys

    value
      update_Items : ITEMS.Items $\times$ Sys $\xrightarrow{\sim}$ Sys
      update_Items(c, s) $\equiv$ replace_Items(c, s)
      pre preupdate_Items(c, s),

      preupdate_Items : ITEMS.Items $\times$ Sys $\rightarrow$ **Bool**,
      ...

      update_Copys : COPYS.Copys $\times$ Sys $\xrightarrow{\sim}$ Sys
      update_Copys(c, s) $\equiv$ replace_Copys(c, s)
      pre preupdate_Copys(c, s),

      preupdate_Copys : COPYS.Copys $\times$ Sys $\rightarrow$ **Bool**
  end

In this example, all of the classes have a corresponding field in the record "Sys" to hold their class containers. It should be noted that this is not always the case. Since a subclass is a specialization of a superclass, it shares the class container with its superclass. If it is a subclass, then it in turn, does the same with its corresponding superclass (and so on). A class having several subclasses shares the container with all of them. That is, the class containers corresponding to the subclasses are subsets of the superclass container. In this way, we guarantee that each desirable property for the superclass, expressed by means of constraints on the class container, is inherited by the subclasses. For example, the type "Sys" as defined for the class diagram shown in Figure 9 has only the class container for the superclass, "Person". The class container for "User" is obtained as a result of applying a function on the superclass container:

USERS, PERSONS
object S :
   with TYPES **in**
   class
     type
       Sys :: persons : PERSONS.Persons ↔ replace_Persons

     value
      users : Sys → USERS.Users
      users(s) ≡
        persons(s) /
          {id | id : User_Id •
            id ∈ **dom** persons(s) ∧
            USER.is_a_User(persons(s)(id))},
   ...

  end

The type "Sys" describes all of the possible instances of the system being modeled by the class diagram. Since we are only interested in consistent systems, it is necessary to express consistency. This is achieved by giving a collection of axioms to express the property that all top-level, state-changing functions maintain the system in a consistent state. We capture all of the model invariants in a "Boolean" function named "consistent," which is defined as the conjunction among all of the necessary predicates that expresses all of the model constraints. All consistency constraints that can be directly derived from the diagram are therefore expressed in this function. OCL constraints (Warmer and Kleppe, 1999), as given by the user explicitly in the UML class diagram, could also be expressed as invariants in RSL through a translation mechanism. Among those derived from the class diagram, are multiplicity constraints, identifiers of objects stored as part of the attributes of a class, and bi-directional navigations. Other kinds of consistency constraints (e.g., more than one access path to the same information or potentially circular relations) cannot be automatically derived from the diagram because they depend on the semantics of the relationship. The user should express this last kind of constraints explicitly. Class diagram consistency is treated in more detail in the section "Constraints."

Beyond the semantics for a class diagram and its associations, an important issue must be pointed out:

    RSL is a structured language, while object-oriented designs might not be structured. Dependencies between classes may be circular in a class diagram while in RSL, the modular structure must be hierarchical. When we build design class diagrams, one important element is the methods. A method not only allows one to operate on the object attributes, but also makes possible interaction with other objects. In our RSL specification for a class diagram, the top-level module is the only module that could possibly perform this kind of responsibility. Therefore, all of the signatures of functions that correspond to the methods must be given in the top-level module (besides being given inside the corresponding module). Each top-level function that operates only on the attributes of the class should be defined by the only reference to that function defined inside the class module. However, when it depends in some way on other classes, it has to be defined in the top-level module.

Initial Value of an Attribute

In UML, it is possible to assign an initial value to an attribute. This initial value is assigned to the attribute each time that an instance of the class is created. Initial values in UML are optional. As an explicit constructor can modify them, it is not mandatory to check each time a new object is created to verify that its attributes have been assigned with their corresponding initial values (as is not always the intention). Therefore, when initial values are given in a UML class diagram, they are ignored in RSL.

Association Navigation

When no navigation adornment is given , then associations between two classes are assumed to be bi-directional (i.e., they can be used to navigate from objects of one class to objects of the other class and vice versa). However, there are situations in which the designer wants to restrict navigation to only one direction. This can be expressed in UML by using a navigation adornment at the corresponding association end.

When a navigation adornment is present in only one of the association ends of a binary association, rather than defining one function in each class to retrieve the related objects (as shown in all of the previous examples), only one is defined in our interpretation of class diagrams.

UML is not clear about the meaning of navigation in "N-ary" associations. For example, Figure 13 shows a general "3-ary" association with a navigation adornment at the end that corresponds to class C2.

One possible interpretation might be that all of the ends are departure and arrival ends except those having one arrow, which are considered as "only-arrive" ends. In the

Figure 13: Association navigation in "n-ary" associations

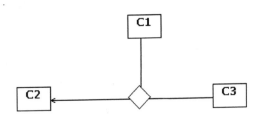

example with this interpretation, it is possible to navigate from the objects in C1 to the objects in C3 and C2; also, from the objects in C3 to the objects in C1 and C2. However, it is not possible to navigate from C2 to anywhere.

Another interpretation is that only the ends having a navigation adornment are the "arrive" and "departure ends," while the others are considered as "only-departure." According to the last interpretation, it is only possible to navigate from the objects in C1 and from the objects in C3 to the objects in C2.

If we add an arrow at the end that corresponds to class C3, according to the first interpretation it is only possible to navigate from C1 to C2 and C3. In the second interpretation, it is possible to navigate from C1 to C3 and C2, from C2 to C3, and from C3 to C2.

We have adopted the second interpretation because when the adornment is present in all of the ends, according to the first interpretation, it is impossible to navigate at all; however, in the second interpretation, it is possible to navigate from any end to any other end.

The adopted interpretation works for relations of any "arity." For example, in the case of binary associations: When the arrows are present in both ends, both are considered to be "arrive" and "departure" ends and therefore, it is possible to navigate in both directions. When the navigability is only in one direction (i.e., only one arrow is present, since the end without an arrow is considered to be "only-departure" and the other end to be "arrive and departure"), it is possible to navigate from the first one to the second one, but it is not possible to navigate in the opposite direction. This is because while the second one is a departure end, the first one is an only-departure (and not arrive).

Composition and Aggregation

Other association end adornments that are possible to use in UML are composition and aggregations. Both are used for modeling a "whole/part" relationship in which one class represents the "whole" that consists of smaller things (the "parts").

As Booch et al. (1999) establish, aggregation is purely conceptual, and does no more than to distinguish the whole from its parts. Aggregation does not change the meaning of association. Therefore, in our interpretation, aggregation between a component class and an aggregate class is equivalent to a general association among the involved classes.

On the other hand, composition has a stronger meaning. Composition is a form of aggregation where the lifetime of the partsdepends on the lifetime of the whole (i.e. the parts may be created after the whole, and can also be explicitly removed before the whole, however, if the whole is destroyed, then the parts die with it). Because of that, the multiplicity of a composite end, (unlike an aggregate end), must always be at the most one (i.e., it cannot be shared by different instances of the owner class). UML does not allow aggregation and composition in associations with an "arity" of greater than two.

In Figure 14, an example of a composition between the classes "Company" and "Department" and a recursive composition on "Department" are shown.

Structurally, a composition is equivalent to a general association that has at least one end with its multiplicity at the most equal to one. Therefore, the structure here is not a distinctive characteristic. However, when we formalize the dynamic aspects of a composition, we distinguish between a general association and a composition based on the property of coincident lifetimes of the whole and the parts. We express this property

Figure 14: Composition

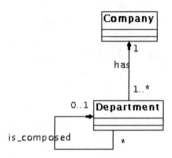

by means of a post-condition in the "remove" function of the whole. This assures that whenever a whole is deleted, all of the parts that are currently associated with the whole are also deleted.

Given the composition "has" between the part "Department" and the whole "Company" as shown in Figure 14, we specify the coincident lifetime property as follows:

del_Department : Department_Id × Sys $\widetilde{\rightarrow}$ Sys
del_Department(id, s) **as** s″**post**
   (∃
       s′ : Sys, new_whole : DEPARTMENTS.Departments,
       new_parts : DEPARTMENTS.Departments,
       parts : Department_Id-**set**
   •
       parts =
          DEPARTMENT.is_composed1(departments(s)(id)) ∧
       new_parts = departments(s) \ parts ∧
       s′ = update_Departments(new_parts, s) ∧
       new_whole =
          DEPARTMENTS.del_Department(id, departments(s′)) ∧
       s″ = update_Departments(new_whole, s))
pre can_del_Department(id, s),

can_del_Department : Department_Id × Sys → **Bool**
can_del_Department(id, s) ≡
   DEPARTMENTS. isin_Department(id, departments(s)) ∧
   (∃
       s' : Sys, new_whole : DEPARTMENTS.Departments,
       new_parts : DEPARTMENTS.Departments,
       parts : Department_Id-**set**
   •
       parts =
       DEPARTMENT.is_composed1(departments(s)(id)) ∧
       new_parts = departments(s) \ parts ∧
       preupdate_Departments(new_parts, s) ∧
       s′ = update_Departments(new_parts, s) ∧

new_whole =
   DEPARTMENTS.del_Department(id, departments(s')) ∧
   preupdate_Departments(new_whole, s))

In UML, when the type of an attribute corresponds to a class sort, this attribute is, in effect, a composition between the class and the class of the attribute. In other words, the attribute is shorthand for composition. Consequently, the semantics in RSL for this kind of attribute are given in the same way as for a composition relationship, which is navigable only from the "whole" to the parts.

Parameterized Classes

Templates or parameterized classes (i.e., classes that describe a family of classes) can be used with UML. A template class cannot be used directly; it must be instantiated first so that template classes do not contain objects. Attributes and operations within a template may be defined in terms of formal parameters so that they become bound when the template itself is bound to actual values.

Since a template instance is fully specified by its template, its content may not be extended (i.e., declaration of new attributes or operations are not permitted). Consequently, it may only be the target of an association or it can be a superclass. Since template classes cannot have instances, there can be only one-directional associations from a template class to another class. A template class can also be a subclass of another class, but it cannot be a superclass as only its instances can be a superclass. An example of a template class and two different instantiations are shown in Figure 15.

This figure shows a template class for one array of "k" elements, the instantiation of one array of three integers, and another instantiation of 24 persons.

When only the name is given (as Element) in a parameter expression, it is assumed to be a type expression that resolves to a valid data type (as Person or **Int**). Otherwise, it must resolve to a valid value expression (like three or 24 for **Int**).

Figure 15: Template and instantiated classes

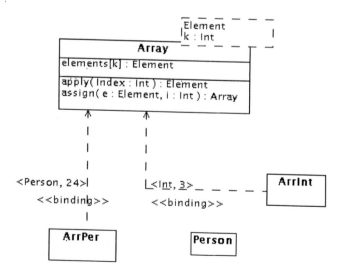

A template class may be specified in RSL in the same way as a concrete class but would use a parameterized scheme whose parameters correspond to the class's parameters.

```
TYPES
scheme ARRAY_(
    FPAR :
        with TYPES in
        class
            type Element

            value
                k : Int
        end) =
    with TYPES in
    class
        type
            Array,
            Elements = FPAR.Element-set

        value
            elements : Array → Elements,

            update_elements : Elements × Array →̃ Array
            update_elements(at, o) as o′ post elements(o′) = at
            pre preupdate_elements(at, o),

            preupdate_elements : Elements × Array →̃ Bool,

            apply : Int × Array → FPAR.Element,

            assign : FPAR.Element × Int × Array → Array_Id,

            consistent : Array → Bool
            consistent(o) ≡ card elements(o) = FPAR.k
    end
```

The parameter "k" is used for expressing a property on the multiplicity of the attribute. This becomes clearer in the section "Constraints," where consistency checks are treated separately.

Since a template class can be used only through its instantiations and cannot be used directly, the specification for its class container is not defined. However, this should be done for each instantiated class that is present in the class diagram since those present may have direct instances associated to them; and consequently, they can change the system state.

The semantics in RSL for the instantiation of a parameterized class is given by the instantiation of the corresponding parameterized scheme with its corresponding types and values. Therefore, to instantiate the array of three integers, we instantiate the scheme ARRAY_ with "Element" equal to "Int" and "k" equal to three as follows:

ARRAY_
scheme ARRINT_ =
 with TYPES **in**
 extend
  class
   object
    APAR_ArrInt :
     class
      type Element = **Int**

      value
       k : **Int** = 3
     end
  end
 with
 extend ARRAY_(APAR_ArrInt) **with class type** ArrInt = Array **end**

As usual, we create an RSL object to represent the model that corresponds to the specification of one object of the class "ArrInt".

ARRINT_
object ARRINT : ARRINT_

To instantiate the array of persons (assuming that "Person" is a class), "Element" is replaced by the object identifier of the class "Person".

ARRAY_
scheme ARRPER_ =
 with TYPES **in**
 extend
  class
   object
    APAR_ArrPer :
     class
      type Element = Person_Id

      value
       k : **Int** = 24
     end
  end
 with
 extend ARRAY_(APAR_ArrPer) **with class type** ArrPer = Array **end**

If the class "Person" does not exist, then an abstract type "Person" is defined in "TYPES". This means that we would have instead the type "Element" defined as the abstract type "Person":

ARRAY_
scheme ARRPER_ =
...

type Element = Person

...

Like concrete classes, instantiated classes can have objects; therefore, the module that holds the specification for the class container for each instantiated class is specified as usual. For example, the class container for the class "ArrInt" is given by the following RSL code:

```
ARRINT
object ARRINTS :
    with TYPES in
    class
        type
            ArrInt = ARRINT.ArrInt,
            ArrInts = ArrInt_Id ⇀ ArrInt
                                  m

        value
            empty_ArrInt : ArrInts = [ ]
    ...
    end
```

When the template class is a subclass, its corresponding instantiated classes share the container with the superclass; otherwise they have their own corresponding containers. For example, according to the new class diagram shown in Figure 16, the

Figure 16: Inheritance plus template classes

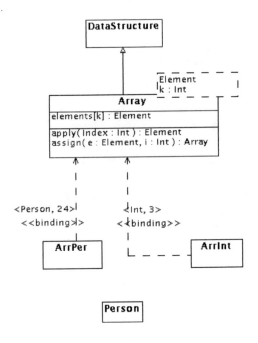

classes "ArrInt" and "ArrPer" share their class containers with the class "DataStructure." We need to define a function to obtain all of the objects corresponding to the subclass by selecting those that belongs to the subclass from the set of objects in the superclass container.

```
PERSONS, DATASTRUCTURES, ARRINTS, ARRPERS
object S :
    with TYPES in
    class
        type
            Sys ::
            persons : PERSONS.Persons ↔ replace_Persons
            datastructures :
                DATASTRUCTURES.DataStructures ↔
                replace_DataStructures

        value
            ...
            arrints : Sys → ARRINTS.ArrInts
            arrints(s) ≡
                datastructures(s) /
                {id | id : ArrInt_Id •
                    id ∈ dom datastructures(s) ∧
                    ARRINT.is_an_ArrInt(datastructures(s)(id))},
            ...
            arrpers : Sys → ARRPERS.ArrPers
            arrpers(s) ≡
                datastructures(s) /
                {id | id : ArrPer_Id •
                    id ∈ dom datastructures(s) ∧
                    ARRPER.is_an_ArrPer(datastructures(s)(id))},
            ...
            consistent : Sys → Bool
            consistent(s) ≡
                PERSONS.consistent(persons(s)) ∧
                DATASTRUCTURES.consistent(datastructures(s)) ∧
                ARRINTS.consistent(arrints(s)) ∧
                ARRPERS.consistent(arrpers(s))
            ...
    end
```

Constraints

Class diagrams, as well as their composing elements, may have different constraints associated with them. As we want to check consistency on the whole system (i.e., check that all the constraints hold), we define a series of axioms at the top-level module in order to check that the system is in a consistent state before and after any state change occurs. For this reason, we define a series of "Boolean" functions that express each different constraint of the class diagram. Inside each module that has been defined to specify either an object or a class, we define one of these "Boolean" functions with the name "consistent." These functions allow for checking the consistency of one object and the consistency of all of the instances of the class, respectively. The latter makes use of the lower-level ones (i.e., those defined for one instance of the class). We also define one function "consistent" in the top-level module in order to check the consistency of the whole class diagram. This function uses, in turn, all of the lower-level functions "consistent" that have been defined for each one of the classes. In this way, we guarantee the consistency of the whole system.

The top-level axioms use the top-level function "consistent" in combination with all of those top-level functions that change the system state. We define one axiom for each top-level changing system state function.

In which one of the several defined functions "consistent" we put the predicate for expressing a given property depends on what kind of restriction we are checking and on what we want to check it with.

In the next sections, we present the different constraints derived from a class diagram and give the corresponding predicates in RSL as well as their locations in the entire specification. In the section "RSL Templates," we give the different templates that have been abstracted from the previous analysis and those corresponding to the constraints.

Multiplicities

When a UML class diagram is built, it is possible to assign multiplicities to its classes, attributes, and/or to its association ends. A multiplicity is a specification of the range of allowable cardinalities that an entity may assume.

A class multiplicity constrains the number of instances that a class may hold. In absence of an indicator, the class may hold any number of instances, that is, its multiplicity is "*", which means precisely "any number".

A multiplicity indicator in an attribute specifies the cardinality of the set of values that the attribute may hold. In the absence of a multiplicity indicator, an attribute holds exactly one value.

When a multiplicity indicator is present in an association end, it constrains the number of instances associated to the class in the other association end to satisfy the multiplicity. In absence of a multiplicity indicator at the end, a multiplicity equal to one is assumed.

Figure 17 shows an example of the different kinds of multiplicities. The class "Player" has multiplicity equals to "*" and the class "Team" has a multiplicity of "2..*". These are shown in the top right corner of the class.

In the example, the class "Team" is constrained to always have at least two instances. The class "Player" has no restriction, therefore there is no constraint applied to its number of instances.

Since a constraint on the class multiplicity refers to the number of instances the class can hold, it is convenient to specify this property within the function "consistent,"

Figure 17: Multiplicities

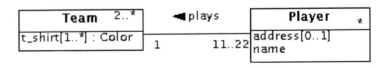

which is defined in the RSL module holding the specification for the class. This predicate will be in conjunction with other constraints on the class if it corresponds.

According to the way in which we have specified a class, the number of instances of a class is given by the domain cardinality of the map that holds all of the instances of the class. Consequently, we express the multiplicity constraint for the class "Team" as follows:

consistent : Teams → **Bool**
consistent(c) ≡
   ... ∧
  card dom c ≥ 2

Since the class "Player" has an assigned multiplicity of "*", no predicate is generated.

The interpretation for the multiplicities at the association ends is expressed in RSL by means of predicates on the cardinality of the set of instances that are reached when we navigate from one association end to another. Since associations are defined as functions in the module that holds the specification of one object of the class, the predicate used for expressing this constraint is placed in the function "consistent" of that module. In the previous example, for the association "plays," we could generate one predicate for "Player" and another predicate for "Team."

consistent: Player → **Bool**
consistent(o) ≡ ... ∧ **card** plays(o) = 1

consistent : Team → **Bool**
consistent(o) ≡ ... ∧
   card plays(o) ≥ 11 ∧ **card** plays(o) ≤ 22

In order to avoid some predicates, it is sometimes possible to constrain the association multiplicity by construction. Therefore, if we take into account their multiplicities, the association ends do not need to be always sets of object identifiers. For example, let us suppose two classes C1 and C2 that are related by a given association, and the multiplicity of this association at the end corresponding to C2 is 1. In this case, we simply use a type identifier of class C2 (C2_Id) as the type of the association rather than using both a set of identifiers (C2_Id-**set**) and a predicate. If the multiplicity is "0..1," then we specify the association type as an RSL variant type without generating a predicate for checking the set cardinality. In this way, only multiplicities specified as sets generate consistency predicates in the function "consistent" (except the unrestricted "*").

The same approach has been applied for attributes. For example, the attribute "name" in the class "Player" has a multiplicity of one; therefore, there is no multiplicity constraint generated in this case. However, the attribute "address" that has a multiplicity equal to "0..1" is specified using a type that allows for optional values. Optional values in RSL can be specified using RSL variant types.

type
   Optional_address = =
     no_address | an_address(id : address),
   address

Additionally, in the module "PLAYER" (among other definitions) we must have the definition of the function "address" to get the attribute value. The predicate for checking the multiplicity is not generated since it is given by construction.

type Player
   ...
value
   address : Player → TYPES.Optional_Address
   ...

On the other hand, the attribute "t_shirt" of the class "Team" has a multiplicity greater than one. Because of this, the function used to obtain the value of this attribute is specified as a function that returns a set.

type Team
   ...
value
   t_shirt : Team → Color-**set**
   ...

Therefore, when we add the multiplicity constraint in the function "consistent" as defined for the class "Team" we have:

consistent : Team → **Bool**
consistent(o) ≡
   card plays(o) ≥ 11 ∧ **card** plays(o) ≤ 22 ∧
   card t_shirt(o) ≥ 1

In the section "Templates for Constraints," we present the RSL templates corresponding to predicates generated for class and attribute multiplicities. The templates for association end multiplicities are also given.

Attribute and operation scope

Attributes in UML may have as their scope either the instance or the class. When the scope of an attribute is its class, it means that all of the instances of the class must always share the same value. On the contrary, if the specified scope for an attribute is given by the property "{instance}", it means that each instance in the class holds its own value for the attribute. The default is instance-scope.

Like attributes, operations may have a scope, too. Operations with class as the scope are known as class operations (e.g., class constructors and destructors). Like attributes, the default for an operation scope is instance-scope.

For example, let us suppose we want to model a class "Window" in UML. An instance of a window has a size and might be visible or invisible at a given time, while all of the windows have a default and maximal size. The last two attributes have a class-scope while the first attributes have an instance-scope. If we want to have an operation "number_of_windows" to determine how many windows have been created, we must acknowldege that an instance of the class cannot provide an answer to this message. Only the class may do this. As a result, "number_of_windows" should be a class-scope

Figure 18: Scopes for attributes and operations

Window
size : Size default size : Size max size : Size visible : boolean @title : Text
.number of windows () : Int

operation. In Figure 18, the class "Window" is shown. Class-scope attributes are shown by underlining the name and type expression string. Underlining the operation shows class-scope operations.

When an attribute has a class-scope, in RSL we have to check that all of the instances of the class hold the same value (i.e., for any pair of instances of the class, their attribute values must be equal). So, we place the corresponding predicate in the function "consistent" of the module that holds the specification for the class that owns the class-scope attribute.

consistent : Windows → **Bool**
consistent(c) ≡
    ... ∧
    ($\forall$ id1, id2 : Window_Id •
      (id1 ∈ **dom** c ∧ id2 ∈ **dom** c) ⇒
        WINDOW.default_size(c(id1)) =
          WINDOW.default_size(c(id2))) ∧
    ($\forall$ id1, id2 : Window_Id •
      (id1 ∈ **dom** c ∧ id2 ∈ **dom** c) ⇒
        WINDOW.max_size(c(id1)) =
          WINDOW.max_size(c(id2)))

When the scope of an operation is the class, we do not generate the corresponding function on an instance of the class, rather on the type that has been defined for the class container, since the operation acts on the class container. Therefore, the value used to specify the operation is placed in the module that holds the specification of the class. In the example, "number_of_windows" has been placed in the module "WINDOWS."

WINDOW
object WINDOWS :
    with TYPES **in**
    class
        type
            Window = WINDOW.Window,
            Windows = Window_Id $_m$→ Window

        value
            empty_Window : Windows = [],

add_Window : Window_Id × Window × Windows $\tilde{\rightarrow}$ Windows
add_Window(id, o, c) ≡ c † [id ↦ o]
pre ~ isin_Window(id, c),
...
number_of_windows : Windows → **Int**,

consistent : Windows → **Bool**
consistent(c) ≡
    (∀ id : Window_Id •
        id ∈ **dom** c ⇒ WINDOW.consistent(c(id))) ∧
    (∀ id1, id2 : Window_Id •
        (id1 ∈ **dom** c ∧ id2 ∈ **dom** c) ⇒
            WINDOW.default_size(c(id1)) =
                WINDOW.default_size(c(id2))) ∧
    (∀ id1, id2 : Window_Id •
        (id1 ∈ **dom** c ∧ id2 ∈ **dom** c) ⇒
            WINDOW.max_size(c(id1)) =
                WINDOW.max_size(c(id2)))

end

Attribute and association end properties

Attributes and association ends in UML have any of three different properties associated to them. The default property is "{changeable}" (i.e., there are no restrictions for modifying the attribute or the association end value), unless the properties "{addonly}" or "{frozen}" are specified. The property "{addonly}" can be used only with attributes and association ends having multiplicities not fixed and greater than one (e.g., "1..5", "2..*" are valid; "5..5" is invalid). This means that additional values may be added; but, once created, a value may not be removed or changed. The property "{frozen}" is used with attributes whose values may not be changed once an instance of the object owning the attribute has been created. The same happens with the association ends having the property "{frozen}".

Our default semantics in RSL for attributes and association ends allows attributes and association ends to be updated at any time. Therefore, when an "{addonly}" or "{frozen}" property is associated to an attribute (or association end), we must check that the attribute (or association end) has added only new values or has not been changed at all, respectively. Since this checking involves the system state before and after a function has changed it, this property must be checked at those points. Consequently, the axioms for checking consistency before and after a top-level system state changing function takes place should also check that the property holds for all of the class' instances.

For example, let us suppose that we have the axiom below for checking that the top-level function "update_windows", which can be used to change the class container of "Window", preserves consistency:

axiom
    ∀ s : Sys, c : WINDOWS.Windows •
        update_Windows(c, s) **as** s′ **post**
            consistent(s′)
    pre consistent(s) ∧ preupdate_Windows(c, s)

If we want to also check the property "{frozen}" for the window attribute "title" of the class "Window" as given in Figure 18, we need to add a predicate to the axiom for checking that the value of attribute "title" for each object of class "Window" remains unchanged after the system state has changed. Therefore, the axiom now becomes:

axiom
    ∀ s : Sys, c : WINDOWS.Windows •
        update_Windows(c, s) **as s′ post**
            consistent(s′) ∧ frozenAtts_in_Window(s′, s)
    pre consistent(s) ∧ preupdate_Windows(c, s)

Where "frozenAtts_in_Window" is defined as a "Boolean" function on the previous system state "s" and the later "s′".

value
    frozenAtts_in_Window : Sys × Sys → **Bool**
    frozenAtts_in_Window(s′, s) ≡
      (∀ id : Window_Id •
        (id ∈ **dom** windows(s) ∧
        id ∈ **dom** windows(s')) ⇒
           WINDOW.title(windows(s)(id)) =
              WINDOW.title(windows(s')(id)))

Since a frozen attribute may not be changed, the corresponding function for updating the attribute, in this example "update_title", is not generated.

Note that a frozen attribute is not equivalent to a constant. Constants in UML may be modeled by means of attributes that not only have associated the property "{frozen}", but have also designated the class as scope.

Abstract classes and abstract operations

In UML it is possible to specify in a class hierarchy that a class is abstract (i.e., it is a class that cannot have direct instances associated with it because its behavior is not completely defined). It can be used only as a base for other subclasses. Abstract classes in UML are shown with their names in italics.

Figure 19: Example of abstract class

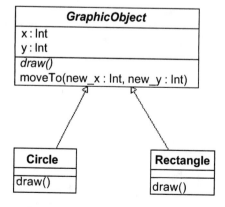

Our interpretation of an abstract class in RSL is the same as interpreted for a concrete class. The only difference is that as objects will never be created, all of the functions that operate on the class container do not need to be specified. However, we need to express a constraint on the system s in order to assure that no instances of the abstract class have been created. This means that all instances that can be in the class container correspond to one of the concrete subclasses of the abstract class. This property can be expressed as: the union of the subclass containers is equal to the abstract class container.

consistent : Sys → **Bool**
consistent(s) ≡ ... ∧
   dom graphicobjects(s) =
     dom circles(s) ∪ **dom** rectangles(s)

Abstract classes are classes that have at least one abstract operation. This means that the operation is incomplete and cannot be used; therefore, an implementation must be given by a subclass. In RSL, the semantics of an abstract operation are given by hiding the operation name outside of the module. Therefore, only references to the implementations given in the subclasses can occur outside of the class module. In the previous example, the operation "draw" is abstract. To avoid the use of "draw", we hide its name.

TYPES
object GRAPHICOBJECT :
   with TYPES **in**
   hide draw **in**
   class
     type GraphicObject

    value
      x : GraphicObject → **Int**,
      y : GraphicObject → **Int**,
      ...
      draw : GraphicObject → GraphicObject,
      ...
   end

Existence and bi-navigation constraints

In the section, "Association Navigation," we discussed the way in which the navigation of associations is treated. As we have seen, each time that it is possible to navigate from a class C1 to another class C2 through a given association, an observer for the association is generated in the specification given for an object of the class C1. However, since these observers return object identifier(s), a predicate for checking whether such object identifiers actually exist in the class container is needed.

For example, if we consider the association "has_copies" between the classes "Copy" and "Item" in Figure 1, we want to make sure that given a copy, the item identifier returned by the function "has_copies" (which is defined in the module that holds the specification of an instance of "Copy") actually exists in the container of the class "Item". Since this checking involves references to the containers of both classes, it must be placed in a module that has access to both containers (i.e., the top-level module). Therefore, in the function "consistent" of the top-level module, we add the following predicate:

($\forall$ id1 : User_Id, id2 : Copy_Id •
  (id1 ∈ dom users(s) ∧
    id2 ∈ USER.consults(users(s)(id1))) ⇒
      id2 ∈ copys(s))

Predicates for checking existence take slightly different forms depending on what the association end multiplicities are and where the class containers are.

When the association is bi-directional, it is necessary to check bi-navigability besides checking existence as done previously. By bi-navigability we mean: When we get –through the association– a set of objects of class C2 from an object of class C1; and, and if we navigate again through the association in the opposite direction from all of the objects of class C2 to C1, then we get again the same starting object in C1. The same control must be achieved when we navigate from C2 to C1. Therefore, two predicates must be generated.

For instance, the association "consults" between classes "Copy" and "User" is bi-directional as shown in Figure 1. If we want to check bi-navigability (i.e., to check for all of the copies consulted by a given user to ascertain whether each copy has been actually consulted by the user)we might include in our specification the following two predicates:

($\forall$ id1 : User_Id, id2 : Copy_Id •
  (id1 ∈ **dom** users(s) ∧
    id2 ∈ USER.consults(users(s)(id1))) ⇒
      (id2 ∈ copys(s) ∧
      an_User(id1) = COPY.consults(copys(s)(id2))))

($\forall$ id1 : Copy_Id, id2 : User_Id •
  (id1 ∈ **dom** copys(s) ∧
    an_User(id2) = COPY.consults(copys(s)(id1))) ⇒
      (id2 ∈ users(s) ∧
      id1 ∈ USER.consults(users(s)(id2))))

Note that in general, a predicate for checking existence has the form:

$\forall$ x: X, y: Y • (P(x) ∧ Q(x,y)) ⇒ R(y)

The corresponding predicate for checking bi-navigability has the form:

$\forall$ x: X, y: Y • (P(x) ∧ Q(x,y)) ⇒ R(y) ∧ S(x,y))

It can be shown that bi-navigability implies existence. Therefore, when we have a bi-directional association, the two corresponding predicates for existence are not given since they are implied from the bi-navigability predicates.

In the section, "Templates for Constraints," the variations for building existence and bi-navigability predicates are given.

When we have an association class, the corresponding predicates for existence or bi-navigability must be generated for the associations that resulted from the transformations proposed in the section "The Association Class."

RSL TEMPLATES

In this section we present a set of RSL templates, which were obtained during the analysis that was carried out when formalizing the semantics of UML class diagrams.

The text that is fixed in the template appears in either a **bold** style (RSL keywords) or in a normal style, while text in *italic* must be replaced using the corresponding names in the UML diagram. The indices are used to reference a particular element between a set of elements. The references between braces appearing on the right margin indicate conditions that must be satisfied to generate the preceding text.

Templates for a Class

In order to give the templates for a class, let us assume that the class has "m" instance-scope attributes ($0 \le m$), "b" class-scope attributes ($0 \le b$), "r" instance-scope operations ($0 \le r$), "s" class-scope operations $(0 \le s,)$ and "a" navigable associations ($0 \le a$).

CLASSNAME
object *CLASSNAMES* :
   with TYPES **in**
   class
   type
     Classname = *CLASSNAME.Classname*,

     *Classname*s = *Classname*_Id $\underset{m}{\rightarrow}$ *Classname*
   value
      empty_*Classname*: *Classname*s = [],

      add_*Classname*: *Classname*_Id × *Classname* × *Classname*s $\widetilde{\rightarrow}$ *Classname*s
      add_*Classname*(id, o, c) ≡ c † [id ↦ o]
      pre ~ isin_*Classname*(id, c),

      del_*Classname*: *Classname*_Id × *Classname*s $\widetilde{\rightarrow}$ *Classname*s
      del_*Classname*(id, c) ≡ c \ {id}
      pre isin_*Classname*(id, c),

      isin_*Classname*: *Classname*_Id × *Classname*s → **Bool**
      isin_*Classname*(id, c) ≡ id ∈ **dom** c,

      get_*Classname*: *Classname*_Id × *Classname*s $\widetilde{\rightarrow}$ *Classname*
      get_*Classname*(id, c) ≡ c(id)
      pre isin_*Classname*(id, c),

      update_*Classname*: *Classname*_Id × *Classname* × *Classname*s $\widetilde{\rightarrow}$ *Classname*s
      update_*Classname*(id, o, c) ≡ c † [id ↦ o]
      pre isin_*Classname*(id, c),

      operationName$_i$: *ParameterType*$_{i1}$ × ... ×
         ParameterType$_{it}$ × *Classname*s → *ResulType*$_i$,   {1}

consistent: *Classname*s → **Bool**
consistent(c) ≡
    (∀ id: *Classname*_Id •
    id ∈ **dom** c ⇒ CLASSNAME.consistent(c(id)))
    ∧ *multiplicity_checking*(c)   {2}
    ∧ *class_scoped_attribute_checking*$_i$(c)   {3}
end

{1} : *$0 < i \leq s$ ∧ numberOfParameters(Operation$_j$) = t*
{2} : *multiplicity(c) > 1 ∧ multiplicity(c) ≠ **
{3} : *$0 < i \leq b$*

Multiplicity_checking(c) is the predicate for checking the multiplicity of the class. *Class-scoped_attribute_checking*$_i$(c) are the predicates generated for each class-scoped attribute in order to check that all of the instances currently in the class have the same attribute value. The templates for these predicates are given in the section, "Templates for Constraints."

TYPES
object *CLASSNAME* :
  with TYPES **in**
  hide *operationName*$_i$ **in**   {4}
  class
    type
      Classname
    value
      attributeName$_i$: *Classname* → *AttributeType*$_i$,   {5}

      update_*attributeName*$_i$: *AttributeType*$_i$ × *Classname* $\overset{\sim}{\to}$ *Classname*
      update_*attributeName*$_i$(at, o) **as** o′ **post** *attributeName*$_i$(o′) = at
     pre preupdate_*attributeName*$_i$(at, o),

      preupdate_*attributeName*$_i$: *AttributeType*$_i$ × *Classname* → **Bool**, {5}

      asociationName$_i$: *Classname* → *AssociationType*$_i$,   {6}

      update_*associationName*$_i$: *AssociationType*$_i$ × *Classname* $\overset{\sim}{\to}$ *Classname*
      update_*associationName*$_i$(a, o) **as** o′ **post** *associationName*$_i$(o′) = a
     pre preupdate_*associationName*$_i$(a, o),

      preupdate_*associationName*$_i$: *AssociationType*$_i$ × *Classname* → **Bool**, {6}

      operationName$_i$: *ParameterType*$_{i1}$ × ... ×
        ParameterType$_{it}$ × *Classname* → *ResulType*$_i$, {7}

      consistent: *Classname* → **Bool**
      consistent(o) ≡
        attribute_multiplicity_checking(Attribute$_j$)   {8}
        ∧ *association_multiplicity_checking(Association$_j$)* {9}
  end

{4} : $0 < i \leq r \wedge Operation_i$ is an abstract operation.
{5} : $0 < i \leq m + b$
{6} : $0 < i \leq a$
{7} : $0 < i \leq r \wedge numberOfParameters(Operation_i) = t$
{8} : $0 < i \leq m \wedge multiplicity(Attribute_i) > 1 \wedge multiplicity(Attribute_i) \neq *$
{9} : $0 < i \leq \wedge multiplicity(Association_i) > 1 \wedge multiplicity(Association_i) \neq *$

Templates for a Subclass

Let us assume that the subclass has "m" instance-scope attributes ($0 \leq m$), "b" class-scope attributes ($0 \leq b$), "r" instance-scope operations ($0 \leq r$), "s" class-scope operations ($0 \leq s$), and "a" navigable associations ($0 \leq a$).

$SUPERCLASSNAMES, CLASSNAME$
object $CLASSNAMES$:
  with TYPES **in**
  class
    type
      $Classname = CLASSNAME.Classname,$
      $Classnames =$
        $\{| \text{ super} : SUPERCLASSNAMES.Superclassnames\bullet$
          $(\forall \text{ id} : Superclassname\_Id \bullet$
            $\text{id} \in \textbf{dom} \text{ super} \Rightarrow$
              $CLASSNAME.is\_a\_Classname(\text{super(id)})) |\}$

    value
      $empty\_Classname: Classnames = [],$

      $add\_Classname: Classname\_Id \times Classname \times Classnames \xrightarrow{\sim} Classnames$
      $add\_Classname(\text{id, o, c}) \equiv \text{c} \dagger [\text{id} \mapsto \text{o}]$
      pre $\sim isin\_Classname(\text{id, c}),$

      $del\_Classname: Classname\_Id \times Classnames \xrightarrow{\sim} Classnames$
      $del\_Classname(\text{id, c}) \equiv \text{c} \setminus \{\text{id}\}$
      pre $isin\_Classname(\text{id, c}),$

      $isin\_Classname: Classname\_Id \times Classnames \rightarrow \textbf{Bool}$
      $isin\_Classname(\text{id, c}) \equiv \text{id} \in \textbf{dom} \text{ c},$

      $get\_Classname: Classname\_Id \times Classnames \xrightarrow{\sim} Classname$
      $get\_Classname(\text{id, c}) \equiv \text{c(id)}$
      pre $isin\_Classname(\text{id, c}),$

      $update\_Classname: Classname\_Id \times Classname \times Classnames \xrightarrow{\sim} Classnames$
      $update\_Classname(\text{id, o, c}) \equiv \text{c} \dagger [\text{id} \mapsto \text{o}]$
      pre $isin\_Classname(\text{id, c}),$

      $operationName_i: ParameterType_{i1} \times ... \times$
        $ParameterType_{it} \times Classnames \rightarrow ResulType_i,$ {1}

consistent: $Classnames \rightarrow$ **Bool**
consistent(c) $\equiv$
   ($\forall$ id: $Classname\_Id \bullet$
     dom c $\Rightarrow$ CLASSNAME.consistent(c(id)))
    $\wedge$ *multiplicity_checking*(c)   {2}
    $\wedge$ *class_scoped_attribute_checking*$_i$(c)   {3}
end

{1} : $0 < i \leq s \wedge numberOfParameters(Operation_j) = t$
{2} : $multiplicity(c) > 1 \wedge multiplicity(c) \neq *$
{3} : $0 < i \leq b$

Multiplicity_checking(c) is the predicate for checking the multiplicity of the class. *Class_scoped_attribute_checking*$_i$(c) are the predicates generated for each class-scoped attribute in order to check that all of the instances currently in the class have the same attribute value. The templates for these predicates are given in the section, "Templates for Constraints."

SUPERCLASSNAME
object *CLASSNAME* :
  with TYPES **in**
  hide *operationName$_i$* **in**   {4}
  class
    type
      Superclassname = SUPERCLASSNAME.Superclassname,
      Classname = {|o: Superclassname $\bullet$ is_a_Classname(o)|}

    value
      attributeName$_i$: Classname $\rightarrow$ AttributeType$_i$ {5}

      update_*attributeName$_i$*: *AttributeType$_i$ $\times$ Classname $\xrightarrow{\sim}$ Classname*
      update_*attributeName$_i$*(at, o) **as** o' **post** *attributeName$_i$(o') = at*
      pre preupdate_*attributeName$_i$*

      preupdate_*attributeName$_i$*: *AttributeType$_i$ $\times$ Classname $\rightarrow$* **Bool,**   {5}

      asociationName$_i$: Classname $\rightarrow$ AssociationType$_i$,   {6}

      update_*associationName$_i$*: *AssociationType$_i$ $\times$ Classname $\xrightarrow{\sim}$ Classname*
      update_*associationName$_i$*(a, o) **as** o' **post** *associationName$_i$(o') = a*
      pre preupdate_*associationName$_i$*(a, o),

      preupdate_*associationName$_i$*: *AssociationType$_i$ $\times$ Classname $\rightarrow$* **Bool,**   {6}

      operationName$_i$: ParameterType$_{i1}$ $\times$ ... $\times$
         ParameterType$_{it}$ $\times$ Classname $\rightarrow$ Resultype$_i$,   {7}

      is_a_Classname: Superclassname $\rightarrow$ **Bool,**

      consistent: *Classname $\rightarrow$* **Bool**
      consistent(o) $\equiv$

$$SUPERCLASSNAME.\text{consistent}(o)$$
$$\wedge \ attribute\_multiplicity\_checking(Attribute_i) \qquad \{8\}$$
$$\wedge \ association\_multiplicity\_checking(Association_i) \qquad \{9\}$$

end

$\{4\}: 0 < i \leq r \wedge Operation_i$ is an abstract operation.

$\{5\}: 0 < i \leq m + b$

$\{6\}: 0 < i \leq a$

$\{7\}: 0 < i \leq r \wedge numberOfParameters(Operation_i) = t$

$\{8\}: 0 < i \leq m \wedge multiplicity(Attribute_i) > 1 \wedge multiplicity(Attribute_i) \neq *$

$\{9\}: 0 < i \leq a \wedge multiplicity(Association_i) > 1 \wedge multiplicity(Association_i) \neq *$

Templates for Leaf Classes

The only difference between the templates for leaf classes and those given in the section "Templates for a Class," is the specification for an object of the leaf class.

Let us assume that the class has "m" instance-scope attributes ($0 \leq m$), "b" class-scope attributes ($0 \leq b$), "r" instance-scope operations ($0 \leq r$), "s" class-scope operations ($0 \leq s$), and "a" navigable associations ($0 \leq a$). Note that when $m+a$ is equal to 0, the corresponding template used is as given in the section, "Templates for a Class."

TYPES
object CLASSNAME :
   with TYPES **in**
   hide $operationName_i$ **in** $\{1\}$
   class
      type
         $Classname ::$
            $attributeName_i: AttributeType_i \leftrightarrow replace\_attributeName_i$ $\{2\}$
            $asociationName_i: AssociationType_i \leftrightarrow replace\_associationName_i$ $\{3\}$

     value
        $update\_attributeName_i: AttributeType_i \times Classname \xrightarrow{\sim} Classname$
        $update\_attributeName_i(at, o) \equiv replace\_attributeName_i(at, o)$
        pre $preupdate\_attributeName_i(at, o),$ $\{2\}$

        $preupdate\_attributeName_i: AttributeType_i \times Classname \to \textbf{Bool},$ $\{2\}$

        $update\_associationName_i: AssociationType_i \times Classname \xrightarrow{\sim} Classname$
        $update\_associationName_i(a, o) \equiv replace\_associationName_i(a, o)$
        pre $preupdate\_associationName_i(a, o),$ $\{3\}$

        $preupdate\_associationName_i: AssociationType_i \times Classname \to \textbf{Bool},$ $\{3\}$

        $operationName_i: ParameterType_{i1} \times ... \times$
           $ParameterType_{it} \times Classname \to ResulType_i,$ $\{4\}$

        $consistent: Classname \to \textbf{Bool}$
        $consistent(c) \equiv$
          $attribute\_multiplicity\_checking(Attribute_i)$ $\{5\}$

$\wedge$ *association_multiplicity_checking(Association)*   {6}
end

{1}: $0 < i \leq r \wedge$ *Operation$_i$* is an abstract operation.
{2}: $0 < i \leq m + b$
{3}: $0 < i \leq a$
{4}: $0 < i \leq r \wedge$ *numberOfParameters(Operation$_i$) = t*
{5}: $0 < i \leq m \wedge$ *multiplicity(Attribute$_i$) > 1 $\wedge$ multiplicity(Attribute$_i$) $\neq$ ***
{6}: $0 < i \leq a \wedge$ *multiplicity(Association$_i$) > 1 $\wedge$ multiplicity(Association$_i$) $\neq$ ***

Template for a Class Diagram

Let us assume that the class diagram has "*n*" classes with ($n > 0$), excluding template classes.

CLASSNAME$_i$S
object S :   {1}
    with TYPES **in**
    class
        type
            Sys ::
                *classname$_i$*s: *CLASSNAME$_i$S.Classname$_i$*s $\leftrightarrow$ replace_*Classname$_i$*s   {2}
        value
            *classname$_i$*s: Sys $\rightarrow$ *CLASSNAME$_i$S.Classname$_i$*s
            *classname$_i$*s(s) $\equiv$
                *superclassname$_i$*s(s) /
                {id | id : *Classname*_Id •
                    id $\in$ **dom** *superclassnames*(s) $\wedge$
                    CLASSNAME.is_a_*Classname*(*superclassnames*(s)(id)),

            update_*classname$_i$*s: *CLASSNAME$_i$S.Classname$_i$*s $\times$ Sys $\overset{\sim}{\rightarrow}$ Sys
            update_*classname$_i$*s(c, s) $\equiv$ update_*superclassname$_i$*s(c, s)
            pre preupdate_*classname$_i$*s(c, s),

            preupdate_*classname$_i$*s: *CLASSNAME$_i$S.Classname$_i$*s $\times$ Sys $\rightarrow$ **Bool**,   {3}

            update_*classname$_i$*s: *CLASSNAME$_i$S.Classname$_i$*s $\times$ Sys $\overset{\sim}{\rightarrow}$ Sys
            update_*classname$_i$*s(c, s) $\equiv$ replace_*Classname$_i$*s(c, s)
            pre preupdate_*classname$_i$*s(c, s),

            preupdate_*classname$_i$*s: *CLASSNAME$_i$S.Classname$_i$*s $\times$ Sys $\rightarrow$ **Bool**,   {4}

            del_*Classname$_i$*: *Classname*_Id $\times$ Sys $\overset{\sim}{\rightarrow}$ Sys
            del_*Classname$_i$*(id, s) **as** s'' **post**
                ($\exists$
                    s' : Sys, new_whole : *CLASSNAME$_i$S.Classname$_i$*s;
                    new_parts: *PARTCLASSNAME$_j$S.PartClassnames*,
                    parts: *PartClassname*_Id-**set**
                •
                    parts =
                        *CLASSNAME$_i$.composition$_j$(classname$_i$*s(s)(id)) $\wedge$ {1.1}

new_parts = $partClassnames$ (s) \ parts $\wedge$
s' = update_$partClassnames$(new_parts, s) $\wedge$
new_whole =
$CLASSNAME_i$S.del_$Classname_i$(id, $classname_i$s(s')) $\wedge$
s'' = update_$Classname_i$s(new_whole, s))
pre can_del_$Classname_i$(id, s),   {1}

can_del_$Classname_i$: Classname_Id $\times$ Sys $\to$ **Bool**
can_del_$Classname_i$(id, s) $\equiv$
$CLASSNAME_i$S.isin_$Classname_i$(id, $classname_i$s(s)) $\wedge$
($\exists$
  s' : Sys, new_whole : $CLASSNAME_i$S.$Classname_i$s;
  new_parts: $PARTCLASSNAME_j$S.$PartClassnames$,
  parts: $PartClassname$_Id-**set**
  $\bullet$
  parts =
  $CLASSNAME_i.composition_j$($classname_i$s(s)(id)) $\wedge$ {1.1}
  new_parts = $partClassnames$(s) \ parts $\wedge$
  preupdate_$partClassnames$(new_parts, s) $\wedge$
  s' = update_$partClassnames$(new_parts, s) $\wedge$
  new_whole =
  $CLASSNAME_i$S.del_$Classname_i$s(id, $classname_i$s(s')) $\wedge$
  preupdate_$Classname_i$s(new_whole, s)),

$operationName_{ij\_}$in_$Classname_i$: $ParameterType_{ij1} \times ... \times$
$ParameterType_{ijt} \times Classname_i \times$ Sys $\to ResulType_{ij}$,   {5}

consistent: Sys $\to$ **Bool**
consistent(s) $\equiv$
$CLASSNAME_i$S.consistent($classname_i$s(s))   {1}
$\wedge$ binavegability_checkings
$\wedge$ existence_checkings
$\wedge$ abstract_class_checkings

axiom
$\forall$ s: Sys, c: $CLASSNAME_i$S.$Classname_i$s$\bullet$ update_$classname_i$s(c,s) **as** s'
  post consistent(s') $\wedge$
    frozenCheckings$_i$ $\wedge$
    addOnlyCheckings$_i$
  pre consistent(s) $\wedge$
    preupdate_$classname_i$s(c, s)   {1}

end

{1}: $0 < i \leq n$
{1.1}: $0 < j \leq numberOfParts(Class_i)$
{2}: $0 < i \leq n \wedge Class_i$ is not a subclass.
{3}: $Class_i$ is a subclass.
{4}: $Class_i$ is not a subclass.
{5}: $0 < i \leq n \wedge 0 < j \leq numberOfOperations(Class_i) \wedge Operation_{ij}$ is not abstract.

The existence and bi-navigability checkings used in the function "consistent" correspond to all of the associations in the class diagram. The *abstract_class_checkings* are generated when there are abstract classes in the class diagram.

The checkings in the post-conditions of the axioms are generated only when the class has attributes and/or associations having the "{frozen}" or "{addonly}" property as explained in the section, "Constraints."

Templates for Parameterized Classes

In order to give the templates for both a template class and an instantiated class, let us assume that the template class has "m" instance-scope attributes $(0 \le m)$, "b" class-scope attributes $(0 \le b)$, "r" instance-scope operations $(0 \le r)$, "s" class-scope operations $(0 \le s)$, "a" navigable associations $(0 \le a)$, "$p1$" typed formal parameters $(0 \le p1)$, and "$p2$" untyped formal parameters $(0 \le p2)$ with $p1+p2 \ne 0$.

Parameterized classes cannot have instances; therefore, there is no template for the module that has the definition of the type corresponding to the class container. Only instantiated classes can have instances. The template for the class container of an instantiated class is the same template as used for any other concrete class.

Template for template classes

TYPES,
scheme *TEMPLATECLASSNAME_(*
    FPAR :
      with TYPES **in**
      class
        type
          FormalParameterName$_1$...FormalParameterName$_{p2}$

        value
          formalParameterName$_i$: FormalParameterType$_i$,   {1}
      end) =
    with TYPES **in**
    class
      type *TemplateClassname*

      type *FormalParameterName$_i$s = FormalParameterName$_i$-***set**   {2}

      type Optional_*FormalParameterName$_i$s =*
        no_*FormalParameterName$_i$* |
        a_*FormalParameterName$_i$(Id:FormalParameterName$_i$)*   {3}
      value
      attributeName$_i$: TemplateClassname $\rightarrow$ AttributeType$_i$,   {4}

      update_*attributeName$_i$:*

        AttributeType$_i$ × TemplateClassname $\overset{\sim}{\rightarrow}$ TemplateClassname
      update_*attributeName$_i$(at, o)* **as** o' **post** *attributeName$_i$(o')* = at
      pre preupdate_*attributeName$_i$(at, o),*

      preupdate_*attributeName$_i$: AttributeType$_i$ × TemplateClassname $\rightarrow$* **Bool**,   {4}

      associationName$_i$: TemplateClassname $\rightarrow$ AssociationType$_i$,   {5}

        update_*associationName$_i$:*

$AssociationType_i \times TemplateClassname \;\tilde{\rightarrow}\; TemplateClassname$
update_$associationName_i$(a, o) **as** o' **post** $associationName_i$(o') = a
pre preupdate_$associationName_i$(a, o),

preupdate_$associationName_i$:
   $AssociationType_i \times TemplateClassname \rightarrow$ **Bool**, $\hspace{3cm}$ {5}

$operationName_j$: $ParameterType_{j1} \times ... \times$
   $ParameterType_{jt} \times TemplateClassname \rightarrow ResulType_j$, $\hspace{2cm}$ {6}

consistent: $TemplateClassname \rightarrow$ **Bool**
consistent(o) ≡
   $attribute\_multiplicity\_cheking(Attribute_i)$ $\hspace{4cm}$ {7}
   $\wedge\ association\_multiplicity\_cheking(Association_i)$ $\hspace{3cm}$ {8}

end

{1}: $1 \le i \le p1$
{2}: $0 < i \le p2 \wedge (\exists j:Nat \bullet 0 < j < m \wedge type(Attribute_j) = FormalParameterName_i \wedge Multiplicity(Attribute_j) > 1)$
{3}: $0 < i \le p2 \wedge (\exists j:Nat \bullet 0 < j < m \wedge type(Attribute_j) = FormalParameterName_i \wedge (Multiplicity(Attribute_j) = 0 \vee Multiplicity(Attribute_j) = 1))$
{4}: $0 < i \le m + b$
{5}: $0 < i \le a$
{6}: $0 < i \le r \wedge numberOfParameters(Operation_i) = t$
{7}: $0 < i \le m \wedge multiplicity(Attribute_i) > 1 \wedge multiplicity(Attribute_i) \neq *)$
{8}: $0 < i \le a \wedge multiplicity(Association_i) > 1 \wedge multiplicity(Association_i) \neq *$

Templates for instantiated classes

$TEMPLATECLASSNAME\_$
scheme $INSTANTIATEDCLASSNAME\_$ =
   with TYPES **in**
   use is_a_$InstantiatedClassname$ **for** is_a_$TemplateClassname$ **in** $\hspace{2cm}$ {9}
   extend
      class
         object APAR :
            class
               type
                  $FormalParameterName_i = ActualParameter_i$, $\hspace{2cm}$ {10}
               value
                  $formalParameterName_i$:
                     $FormalParameterType_i = ActualParameter_i$, $\hspace{1.5cm}$ {11}
            end
      end
   with extend $TEMPLATECLASSNAME\_$(APAR) **with class**
      type $InstantiatedClass = TemplateClassname$ **end**

{9}: $TemplateClassname$ is the name of the template class that is also a subclass.
{10}: $1 \le i \le p2$
{11}: $1 \le i \le p1$

*INSTANTIATEDCLASSNAME_*
object *INSTANTIATEDCLASSNAME*: *INSTANTIATEDCLASSNAME_*

Templates for Constraints

Class multiplicities

Class multiplicity checkings are placed into the function "consistent" that corresponds to the module that has the specification for the class. When the class multiplicity is "$N..*$," for a given $N > 0$, the template takes the following form:

consistent: *Classname*s $\rightarrow$ **Bool**
consistent(c) $\equiv$ .... $\wedge$ **card dom** c $\geq N$

For multiplicity "$N..M$," with $M > N \geq 0$, the predicate will be generated from the template:

card dom c $\geq N \wedge$ **card dom** c $\leq M$

If multiplicity is a given, fixed number "N", $N \geq 0$, then the corresponding predicate is:

card dom c $= N$

Any other class multiplicity does not generate a constraint in "consistent."

Association end multiplicities

Before giving the templates corresponding to the end multiplicities, we need to present the templates for translating associations.

Let us suppose that we have an association which is navigable from a given class c_i to a given class c_j. As we've seen before, in the module that has the specification for the class c_j, we have:

associationName: *Classname*$_i \rightarrow$ *AssociationType*

Depending on the association end multiplicity at c_j, the type of the association (denoted *AsociationType*) must be replaced by either the type corresponding to an object identifier of class c_j, by a set of object identifiers of class c_j, or by an RSL variant type.

In the former case, when the multiplicity is "1," we have that *AsociationType* must be replaced by type "*Classname*$_j$_Id," which is defined in "TYPES".

For a multiplicity of "0..1," *AsociationType* must be replaced by Optional_*Classname*$_j$, which is a variant type defined in the module "TYPES".

Optional_*Classname*$_j$ = =
  no_*Classname*$_j$ | a_*Classname*$_j$(id : *Classname*$_j$_Id)

For any other multiplicity, *AsociationType* must be replaced by:
"*Classname*$_j$_Id-**set**."

Now we can give the templates corresponding to the association end multiplicities.

For each navigable association end in which a multiplicity greater than one and different to "*" is attached to the end, a multiplicity constraint is generated. Consequently, given an association between class c_i and class c_j, one of three different predicates may be generated according to the association end multiplicity. The analysis is done for the association end at c_j.

When the multiplicity at the association end corresponding to c_j is "$N..$ *" for a given $N > 0$, a predicate in the function "consistent" of the module that holds the specification of the class c_i is generated. Assuming that o (an object of the class c_j) is the parameter of the function "consistent," then the predicate is given by the following template:

card $associationName(o) \geq N$

For multiplicity "$N..M$", with N and M given and $M \geq N > 0$, the template for the corresponding predicate is:

card $associationName(o) \geq N \wedge$ **card** $associationName(o) \leq M$

Finally, when the multiplicity is given by a fixed number N, with $N > 1$, the corresponding predicate template is:

card $asociationName(o) = N$

Attribute multiplicities

In order to give the templates for attribute multiplicities, let us assume that the RSL observer to obtain a given attribute is:

value
   $attributeName : Classname \rightarrow AttributeType$

When a parameterized class is translated and the attribute type corresponds to a formal parameter, *AttributeType* must be replaced by the formal parameter if the multiplicity is equal to one. When the multiplicity is equal to "0..1," then it must be replaced by an optional type, which is defined in the module that has the specification for the template class:

type
   Optional_*FormalParametername* = =
      no_*FormalParametername* |
      a_*FormalParametername*(Id: FPAR.*FormalParametername*)

For any other multiplicity, *AttributeType* is replaced by the type *FormalParameternames*, which is also defined locally:

type
   FormalParameternames = FPAR.*FormalParametername*-**set**

When *AttributeType* is not a formal parameter, it receives the same treatment as an attribute that belongs to a concrete class. That is, all of those attributes with class sorts types are interpreted as one-directional composition relationships (see sections "Composition and Aggregation" and "Multiplicities"). In any other case, they are specified as an object identifier, a variant type of object identifier type, or a set of object identifiers.

When the attribute has a multiplicity greater than one and different to "*", the attribute is specified as a set whose cardinality is restricted by its multiplicity. Consequently, a predicate in the function "consistent" (defined for an object o of the class) is generated accordingly to the attribute multiplicity.

If the attribute multiplicity is "$N..*$", for a given $N > 0$, we have in consistent(o) the predicate:

card $attributeName(o) \geq N$

For a multiplicity "$N..M$", with N and M given and $M > N > 0$, the template for the corresponding predicate is:

card $attributeName(o) \geq N \wedge$ **card** $attributeName(o) \leq M$

If the multiplicity is a given fixed number "N", with $N > 1$, the corresponding predicate template is:

card $attributeName(o) = N$

Any other attribute multiplicity does not generate a constraint in the function "consistent".

Class-scoped attributes

The templates used for generating the predicates for checking that an attribute is class-scoped are always placed in the templates corresponding to the specification of the class (*class_scoped_attribute_checking$_i$(c)*).

If c is the class container (i.e., parameter of the function "consistent") then, for each class-scoped attribute in the class, *class_scoped_attribute_checking(c)* must be replaced by:

$(\forall$ id1, id2 : TYPES.Classname_Id •
  (id1 $\in$ dom c $\wedge$ id2 $\in$ dom c) $\Rightarrow$
    (CLASSNAME.attributeName(c(id1)) =
      CLASSNAME.attributeName(c(id2)))))

Attribute and association-end properties

To check that the attribute properties "{frozen}" and "{addonly}" hold in the system, it is necessary to consider the system state before and after a change has taken place. For this reason, the predicates used for checking these properties are not used inside a function "consistent," but they are used in the post-conditions of the top-level axioms.

When a given class "Classname" has one or more frozen attributes, we define a "boolean" function "frozenAtts_in_Classname" according to the template given below. This function is used inside the post-condition of the top-level axioms used for checking system consistency. For instance, if "attributeName" is the name of one frozen attribute in the class "Classname", we have:

frozenAtts_in_$Classname$: Sys × Sys → Bool
frozenAtts_in_$Classname$(s', s)≡
   ($\forall$ id : TYPES.$Classname$_Id •
     (id ∈ **dom** classnames(s) ∧
       id ∈ **dom** classnames(s')) ⇒
        CLASSNAME.attributeName(classNames(s)(id)) =
         CLASSNAME.attributeName(classnames(s')(id)))

Similar templates are used for the property "{addonly}". On the basis of the previous one, the function name is changed from "frozenAtts_in_$Classname$" to "addOnlyAtts_in_$Classname$" and the equality (=) between sets is changed to inclusion (⊆). The same templates are used for association-end properties by just changing "*attributeName*" to "*associationName*".

Abstract classes

Given an abstract class "*Classname*" with "*n*" subclasses "*Subclassname$_1$*, ...,*Subclassname$_n$*," a constraint based in the template given below is generated in the function "consistent" of the top-level module.

consistent: Sys → **Bool**
consistent(s) ≡ ...∧
  dom classname =
    dom subclassname$_1$ ∪ ... ∪**dom** subclassname$_n$

Existence constraints

Existence constraints are used for checking the existence in the class container of those objects that are obtained from the functions used to specify a given association. Let us assume that the existence of a one-direction association from a class "*Classname$_i$*," to another class "*Classname$_j$*". The templates for checking existence are based on:

($\forall$ id1: TYPES.$Classname_i$_Id,
  id2: TYPES.$Classname_j$_Id •
  (id1 ∈ **dom** classname$_i$s(s) ∧
    id2 ∈ CLASSNAME$_i$.associationName(classname$_i$s(id1))) ⇒
    id2 ∈ **dom** classname$_j$s(s))

"s" denotes an instance of the system.
When the multiplicity is "0..1", the predicate

id2 ∈ CLASSNAME$_i$.associationName(classname$_i$s(id1))

in the antecedent, is changed to:

TYPES.a_$Classname$(id2) = CLASSNAME$_i$.associationName(classname$_i$s(id1))

For multiplicity equal to "1..1", we have:

id2 = $CLASSNAME_i.associationName(classname_is(id1))$

Bi-navigability constraints

When an association is bi-directional (i.e., it is possible to navigate in both directions), it is necessary to generate two predicates for checking bi-navigability. Below we present the templates for checking bi-navigability for a given association "*associationName*" between classes "*Classname_i*" and "*Classname_j*".

Only one of them is given. The other is equal to the first one, but with $_i$ and $_j$ interchanged.

($\forall$ id1 : TYPES.*Classname_i*_Id,
   id2 : TYPES.*Classname_j*_Id •
   (id1 $\in$ **dom** *classname_i*s(s) $\wedge$
   id2 $\in$ $CLASSNAME_i.associationName(classname_is(id1))) \Rightarrow$
      id2 $\in$ **dom** *classname_j*s(s) $\wedge$
      id1 $\in$ $CLASSNAME_j.associationName(classname_js(id2)))$

As existence constraints, the predicates for bi-navigability must be adapted to the association multiplicity in each case.

CONCLUDING REMARKS

Summary

We have explored the use of RSL to formalize several elements present in UML class diagrams. Some of these constructs are typically used during the creation of conceptual models, while others appear more commonly during the design phase. We have given the semantics for all of the basic constructs used for building problem-oriented class diagrams as well as for several of those used during the design. Also, a discussion and specification of class diagram well-formedness rules have been presented.

The definition of a mechanism to give the formal foundations of UML class diagrams has enhanced the precision of UML as a specification language. It has opened the possibility of carrying out rigorous analysis on the model and has allowed the creation of initial RSL specifications feasibility for further refinements.

The analysis of the semantics of UML class diagrams and its formal specification in RSL have allowed us to abstract a series of templates, which have guided the implementation of a translator tool.

The tool

Currently, there are several commercial or freely-available UML-based graphical tools. On the other hand, XMI is the more commonly used format in which these tools store the information about the models.

Based on these facts, the developed application uses a class diagram produced by a tool as input, which saves its diagrams in the XMI format. XMI is an acronym for "**XML M**etadata **I**nterchange" and XML stands for "e**X**tensible **M**arkup **L**anguage". Although XMI is a technology from the OMG (**O**bject **M**anagement Group, http://www.omg.org), it is based on the XML standard from the W3C® (the World Wide Web Consortium, http:/

Figure 20: Component diagram

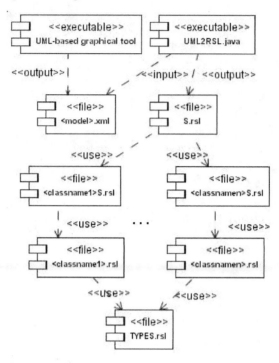

/www.w3c.org). XMI is a family of XML. Unfortunately, there are several versions for the UML XMI DTD (**D**ocument **T**ype **D**efinition). Our tool is compatible with the XML files that are compliant to the XMI DTD version 1.0.

As it is shown in the Figure 20, our tool takes an XML file produced by a UML-based graphical tool as input, which is where the information of a class diagram has been stored. It parses the XML file. If the input is syntactically correct, it produces an RSL specification based on our previously proposed semantics.

The whole RSL specification produced consists of several RSL files. The top-level module "S.rsl" that corresponds to the specification of the model represented by the class diagram uses a set of modules produced for the specification of each class in the class diagram (these modules receive as name the corresponding class name using upper case, followed by "S"). Each one, in turn, uses a lower-level module where the specification for one object of the corresponding class is given. Additionally, each one of the lower-level modules uses, in turn, the module "TYPES.rsl" where all the abstract types present in the diagram are defined.

The tool has been developed in Java™, making use of a commonly-used Application Program Interface (API) for XML processors: the **D**ocument **O**bject **M**odel (DOM) API (Maruyama et al., 2000; Holzner, 2001). In DOM, when an XML document is parsed, it is represented as a tree. DOM provides a set of API's to access and manipulate these nodes in the DOM tree. We used the DOM API contained in the org.apache.xerces. parsers.DOMParser package, which can be downloaded from http://www.alphaworks. ibm.com/tech/xml4j.

From a class diagram to the RSL specification - An example

In this section, the main parts of the RSL specifications generated by the tool from the class diagram shown in Figure 1 are given.

The whole specification consists of a top-level module "S", which uses the modules "LIBRARYS", "USERS", "COPYS", and "ITEMS" defined for each one of the classes that are present in the class diagram. Each one of these modules has the RSL specification for the corresponding class. The type "Sys" defined in "S" denotes the set of all of the possible configurations for the system (in this case for the modeled domain). Each destructor in "Sys" returns a class container. Also, a set of functions that operate on the class containers are defined in order to produce changes on the domain state. A particular function that is named "consistent" is defined to express all of the desirable properties of the model. This function is used, in turn, to write a set of axioms where consistency must be provided before and after any state-changing function is applied.

```
COPYS, USERS, LIBRARYS, ITEMS
object S :
    with TYPES in
    class
        type
            Sys ::
                copys : COPYS.Copys ↔ replace_copys
                users : USERS.Users ↔ replace_users
                librarys : LIBRARYS.Librarys ↔ replace_librarys
                items : ITEMS.Items ↔ replace_items

        value
            update_copys : COPYS.Copys × Sys →̃ Sys
            update_copys(c, s) ≡ replace_copys(c, s)
            pre preupdate_copys(c, s),

            preupdate_copys : COPYS.Copys × Sys → Bool,
            ...
            /* Here the remaining functions defined for
            each class container */
            ...

            consistent : Sys → Bool
            consistent(s) ≡
                COPYS.consistent(copys(s)) ∧
                USERS.consistent(users(s)) ∧
                LIBRARYS.consistent(librarys(s)) ∧
                ITEMS.consistent(items(s)) ∧
                (∀ id1 : Library_Id, id2 : Item_Id •
                    (id1 ∈ dom librarys(s) ∧
                    id2 ∈ LIBRARY.contains(librarys(s)(id1))) ⇒
                        (id2 ∈ items(s) ∧
                        id1 = ITEM.contains(items(s)(id2)))) ∧
                (∀ id1 : Item_Id, id2 : Library_Id •
                    (id1 ∈ dom items(s) ∧
```

id2 = ITEM.contains(items(s)(id1))) ⟹

(id2 ∈ librarys(s) ∧

id1 ∈ LIBRARY.contains(librarys(s)(id2)))) ∧

. . .

/* Here the remaining predicates for checking
binavigabily on the associations */

. . .

axiom

∀ s : Sys, c : COPYS.Copys :-

update_copys(c, s) **as** s′ **post** consistent(s′)

pre consistent(s) ∧ preupdate_copys(c, s)

. . .

/* Here the axioms for the other defined functions */

. . .

end

For each class present in the class diagram, two RSL modules are created. One has the specification for an object of the class. The other, which uses the former, has the specification for the class itself. To illustrate, we present only the RSL specifications produced for the class "User". The module "USERS", which has the specification for the class "User", uses the module "USER", which has the specification for an instance of the class "User". This uses, in turn, the module "TYPES", which has the definition of all the abstract types in the model. The general structure of the specifications for the remaining classes is similar in this example.

USER
object USERS :

with TYPES **in**

class

type User = USER.User, Users = User_Id $\overrightarrow{m}$ User

value

empty_User : Users = [],

add_User : User_Id × User × Users $\xrightarrow{\sim}$ Users

add_User(id, o, c) ≡ c † [id ↦ o] **pre** ~isin_User(id, c),

del_User : User_Id × Users $\xrightarrow{\sim}$ Users

del_User(id, c) ≡ c \ {id} **pre** isin_User(id, c),

isin_User : User_Id × Users → **Bool**

isin_User(id, c) ≡ id ∈ **dom** c,

get_User : User_Id × Users $\xrightarrow{\sim}$ User

get_User(id, c) ≡ c(id) **pre** isin_User(id, c),

update_User : User_Id × User × Users $\xrightarrow{\sim}$ Users

update_User(id, o, c) ≡ c † [id ↦ o] **pre** isin_User(id, c),

consistent : Users → **Bool**
consistent(c) ≡
    (∀ id : User_Id •
    id ∈ **dom** c ⇒ USER.consistent(c(id)))
  end

TYPES
object USER :
  with TYPES **in**
  class
    type
      User ::
        name : name ↔ replace_name
        has : Library_Id ↔ replace_has
        consults : Copy_Id-set ↔ replace_consults
        reserves : Item_Id-set ↔ replace_reserves
        borrows : Copy_Id-set ↔ replace_borrows

    value

      update_name : name × User $\xrightarrow{m}$ User
      update_name(at, o) ≡ replace_name(at, o)
      pre preupdate_name(at, o),

      preupdate_name : name × User → **Bool**,

      update_has : Library_Id × User $\xrightarrow{m}$ User
      update_has(a, o) ≡ replace_has(a, o)
      pre preupdate_has(a, o),

      preupdate_has : Library_Id × User → **Bool**,

      update_consults : Copy_Id-set × User $\xrightarrow{m}$ User
      update_consults(a, o) ≡ replace_consults(a, o)
      pre preupdate_consults(a, o),

      preupdate_consults : Copy_Id-set × User → **Bool**,

      update_reserves : Item_Id-set × User $\xrightarrow{m}$ User
      update_reserves(a, o) ≡ replace_reserves(a, o)
      pre preupdate_reserves(a, o),

      preupdate_reserves : Item_Id-set × User → **Bool**,

      update_borrows : Copy_Id-set × User $\xrightarrow{m}$ User
      update_borrows(a, o) ≡ replace_borrows(a, o)
      pre preupdate_borrows(a, o),

      preupdate_borrows : Copy_Id-set × User → **Bool**,
      consistent : User → **Bool**
  end

object TYPES :
  class
    type
        status,
      location,
      Optional_User = = no_User | a_User(id : User_Id),
      User,
      Item_Id,
      User_Id,
      Copy_Id,
      name,
      Library_Id,
      title,
      kind
  end

RELATED WORK

Kim and Carrington (2000) present a formal mapping between UML class diagrams and Object-Z as achieved at a meta-level. France (1999) also presents the semantics for some UML class diagram constructs, but using Z. The work is mainly centered on the discussion of alternative interpretations of the UML, and on examples of its use for rigorous analysis. In the work of DeLoach and Hartrum (2000), an algebraic model for object-orientation concepts is presented. This model is based on the use of Rumbaugh's Object Modeling Technique (OMT) and the specification language O-SLANG. Olderog and Ravn (2000) propose the use of a subset of UML class diagrams to define a particular domain of refinement relations, which is formalized using Z. Mayer and Souquieres (1999) present an approach to transform OMT class diagrams and state diagrams into B specifications. The approach is based (as in our work) on the use of templates; however, no automated tool is reported. No one considers scope of methods and attributes, attribute changeability, and template classes.

FUTURE WORK

As we have seen, in general, our semantics for a class diagram results in a four-layer RSL modular structure, where the top-level module has many responsibilities assigned. This drawback is due to the fact that UML allows for the creation of loops between associations. RSL encourages the structured design and consequently, does not allow for circular dependencies of modules.

UML class diagrams built for modeling the domain of the problem typically present this shape. Since a domain model is not a software model, module dependency and delegations are unimportant. However, when we build a design class diagram, they should be considered. Therefore, whenever we have a good UML design model, we should obtain a good one in RSL, too.

In general, a good design model should avoid the use of bi-directional associations. Additonally the dependencies between modules should form directed, acyclic graphs.

Bi-directional associations make maintenance more complex and lead to interdependency between the classes and consequently to highly coupled systems.

In order to improve the RSL structure, initial efforts will focus on finding a way to obtain a better RSL system architecture based on interdependencies between the classes.

Future work also includes the creation of mappings between RSL and other UML diagrams. These are mainly focused on the formalization of behavioral diagrams and pay attention to the methodological aspects concerned with the integration of both notations.

REFERENCES

Booch, G. (1991). Object-oriented design with applications. Benjamin/Cummings, Redwood City, CA.

Booch, G. (1994). Object-oriented analysis and design with applications. Benjamin/Cummings, Redwood City, CA, 2nd edition.

Booch, G., Rumbaugh, J., and Jacobson, I. (1999). The Unified Modeling Language user guide. Addison-Wesley.

Chen, P. (1976). The entity-relationship model - towards a unified view of data. *ACM Transactions on Database Systems 1.*

DeLoach, S. and Hartrum, T. (2000). A theory-based representation for object-oriented domain models. *IEEE Transactions on Software Engineering,* 26(6) (pp. 500–517).

DeMarco, T. (1979). Structured analysis and system specification. Prentice-Hall.

France, R. (1999). A problem-oriented analysis of basic UML static requirements modeling concepts. In *Proceedings of OOPSLA '99, Denver, CO.*

George, C. et al. (1992). The RAISE specification language. Prentice-Hall International (UK) Limited.

George, C. et al. (1995). The RAISE development method. Prentice-Hall International (UK) Limited.

Harel, D. (1987). Statecharts: a visual formalism for complex systems. *Science of Computer Programming 8* (pp. 231–274).

Holzner, S. (2001). Inside XML. New Riders.

Jackson, M. (1982). System development. Prentice-Hall.

Jacobson, I., Booch, G., and Rumbaugh, J. (1999). The Unified Software development process. Object technology series. Addison-Wesley.

Jacobson, I. et al. (1992). Object oriented software engineering: A use case driven approach. Addison-Wesley, Reading, MA.

Kim, S.-K., and Carrington, D. (2000). A formal specification mapping between UML models and object-Z specifications. In LNCS, no. 1878 (pp. 2–21). Springer-Verlag.

Liu, Z., He, J., and Li, X. (2001).Formalizing the use of UML in requirement analysis. *Technical Report 228*, UNU/IIST.

Maruyama, H., Tamura, K., and Uramoto, N. (2000). XML and Java, Developing Web applications. Addison-Wesley.

Meyer, E. and Souquieres, J. (1999). A systematic approach to transform OMT diagrams to a B specification. *In Proceedings of FM '99, vol. I of LNCS* (pp. 875–895).

Olderog, E. and Ravn, A. (2000). Documenting design refinement. *In Proceedings of FMSP'00, Portland, OR* (pp. 89–100).

OMG (2001). OMG-unified modeling language v1.4, chapter UML notation guide. On the World Wide Web: http: //www.omg.org/technology/documents/formal/uml.htm

Rumbaugh, J., Blaha, M., Premerlani, W., Eddy, F., and Lorensen, W. (1991). Object oriented modeling and design. Englewood Cliffs, NJ: Prentice Hall, Inc.

Rumbaugh, J., Jacobson, I., and Booch, G. (1999). The Unified Modeling Language reference manual. Object technology series. Addison-Wesley.

Sutcliffe, A. (1988). Jackson system development. Prentice-Hall.

Warmer, J. and Kleppe, A. (1999). *The object constraint language*. Object technology Series. Addison-Wesley.

Chapter IX

Forward Engineering and UML: From UML Static Models to Eiffel Code

Liliana Favre
INTIA, Universidad Nacional del Centro de la Pcia. de Buenos Aires, Argentina

Liliana Martínez
INTIA, Universidad Nacional del Centro de la Pcia. de Buenos Aires, Argentina

Claudia Pereira
INTIA, Universidad Nacional del Centro de la Pcia. de Buenos Aires, Argentina

ABSTRACT

This chapter describes a reuse-based rigorous process to transform UML static models to object-oriented code. The bases of this approach are the GSBL^{oo} algebraic language to cope with concepts of UML static models and the SpReIm model for defining structured collections of reusable components. We have defined a mapping between UML static models and GSBL^{oo}. The emphasis in this chapter is given to the last steps in the road from UML to code. Eiffel™ is the language of choice in which we chose to demonstrate the feasibility of our approach. We analyze how to transform GSBL^{oo} specifications into code. In particular, we show how to translate different kinds of UML associations to Eiffel. Also, we describe how to construct assertions from GSBL^{oo} specifications. All of the proposed transformations can be automated; they allow traceability and can be integrated into the iterative and incremental software development processes supported by the existing UML CASE tools.

INTRODUCTION

Unified Modeling Language (UML) has emerged as a standard modeling language in the object-oriented analysis and design world. It is a set of graphical and textual notations for specifying, visualizing, and documenting object-oriented systems (OMG, 2001; Booch, Rumbaugh & Jacobson, 1999).

There exists a great number of UML case tools that facilitate code generation and reverse engineering of existing software systems. Unfortunately, techniques currently available in these tools provide little support for validating models in the design stages. Additionally, they are not sufficient for the complete automated code generation. Probably, this is mostly due to the lack of a precise semantics of UML and OCL (OMG, 2001). Another source of problems in these processes is that, on the one hand, UML models contain information that cannot be explicited in object-oriented languages while on the other hand, the object-oriented languages express implementation characteristics that have no counterpart in the UML models. For example, languages like C++, Java, and Eiffel do not allow us to explicit associations, their cardinality, and their OCL constraints. It is the designer's responsibility to make good use of this information, by either selecting an appropriate implementation from a limited repertory or by personally implementing associations.

A variety of advantages has been attributed to using formal software specifications to solve these problems. A formal specification can reveal gaps, ambiguities, and inconsistencies. Any verification of UML models could take place on their corresponding specification using reasoning techniques provided by formalism. However, formal specifications alone do not address the need of industrial practitioners, who require an understandable and scalable semantics that can be integrated by using tools.

Favre and Clérici (2001) propose a rigorous process to forward engineering, UML static models using the algebraic language GSBL^{oo}. Our contribution was towards an embedding of the code generation within a rigorous process that facilitates reuse. The GSBL^{oo} language was designed to cope with concepts of the UML models. This language is relational-centric: it expresses different kinds of relations as primitives to develop specifications. The transformation of UML static models specified in OCL into GSBL^{oo} and a system of transformation rules have been described (Favre, 2001). The formal model *SpReIm* for defining structured collections of reusable components that integrate algebraic specifications and object-oriented code was defined. The manipulation of *SpReIm* components by means of reuse operators is the basis for the reusability.

The primary objective of this integration is to simplify the analysis, evolution, and maintenance of the software. Rather than requiring that developers manipulate formal specifications, we want to provide formal semantics for graphical modeling notations and develop rigorous tools that permit developers to directly manipulate models they have created.

In this chapter, the emphasis is given to the last steps in the road from UML to code. Eiffel was chosen to prove the feasibility of our approach (Meyer, 1997). Our approach is based on the "Design by Contract" principle. Contracts imply obligations and benefits for clients and contractors, and are made explicit by the use of Eiffel assertions. These features facilitate the integration of axioms of specifications with object-oriented code. We describe how to transform GSBL^{oo} specifications into Eiffel and analyze the transformation of different kinds of UML relations. We also describe how to construct Eiffel assertions from GSBL^{oo} specifications.

The chapter has the following structure: We first take a look at related work and then we describe the formalization of UML class diagrams in the GSBL$^{\infty}$ language. Next we outline a rigorous process to transform UML static models into Eiffel. We show how to integrate GSBL$^{\infty}$ specifications with Eiffel code. This is followed by conclusions.

BACKGROUND

UML Case Tools

There are a great number of UML CASE tools in existence that facilitates code generation and reverse engineering of existing software systems. As examples of commercial CASE tools we can mention *Rational Rose*®, *Together, Objecteering, GDPro*®, *StP/UML, Argo/UML* and *MagicDraw UML*. Unfortunately, the current techniques available in these tools provide little automation for forward and reverse engineering processes.

As an example, *Rational Rose* will be analyzed (Quatrani, 1998). *Rational Rose* allows generating databases definitions, class interfaces, and relations in which the class participates. The current modeling languages available in *Rational Rose* do not have precisely defined semantics. This hinders the code generation processes. Another source of problems in these processes is that, on the one hand, the UML models contain information that cannot be expressed in object-oriented languages while on the other hand, the object-oriented languages express implementation characteristics that have no counterparts in the UML models. For instance, languages like C++, Java, and Eiffel do not allow explicit associations, cardinality, nor constraints. Reverse engineering processes in *Rational Rose* are facilitated by inserting annotations in the generated code. These annotations are the link between the model elements and the language. As such, they should be kept intact and not be changed. It is the programmer's responsibility to know what he or she can modify and what he or she cannot modify.

To solve implementation problems, the programme can modify the code by adding or removing classes, modifying class attributes or operations, changing operation signatures, etc. These code modifications require the programmer's ability to maintain integration between the model and the language.

Moreover, the existing tools do not exploit all of the information contained in the UML models. For instance, cardinality and constraints of associations, pre-conditions, post-conditions, and class invariants in OCL are only translated as annotations. Assertions in OCL could be translated to assertions in an object-oriented language that supports them, like Eiffel. Furthermore, reuse is based on object-oriented language libraries rather than on specifications that describe relationships between classes and their operations free from implementation details.

The formalization of UML can help to overcome these problems. UML CASE tools could be enhanced with functionality for formal specification, deductive verification, and semi-automatic forward and reverse engineering.

Formalization of UML

A lot of work has been carried out dealing with the semantics for UML models. The Precise UML Group, *pUML*, was created in 1997 with the goal of giving precision to UML (Evans, France, Lano & Rumpe, 1998). It is difficult to compare the existing results and to see how to integrate them in order to define a standard semantics since they specify different UML subsets and they are based on different formalisms. Siau and Halpin (2001) and JDM (2000) identify some problematic aspects of UML and propose possible solutions.

Bruel and France (1998) describe how to formalize UML models using Z, Lano (1995) describes this using Z++, and Breu et al. (1997) do a similar job using stream-oriented algebraic specifications. Additionally, Gogolla and Ritchers (1997) do this by transforming TROLL to UML, Overgaard (1998) achieves it by using operational semantics, and Kim and Carrington (1999) do it by using OBJECT-Z. Firesmith and Henderson-Sellers (1998) describe advanced meta-modeling and notation techniques that allow the enhancement of UML. Barbier, Henderson-Sellers, Opdahl, and Gogolla (2001) analyze the semantics of UML's aggregation and composition.

Currently, there are few development methods that include OCL. The most important is catalysis (D'Souza & Wills, 1999). Bidoit, Hennicker, Tort, and Wirsing (1999) present an approach for specifying UML interface constraints and proving the correctness of implementation relationships between interfaces and classes. Their approach includes a proposal for an interface constraint language that is similar to OCL. Mandel and Cengarle (1999) have examined the expressive power of OCL in terms of navigability and computability. Varizi and Jackson (1999) argue that OCL is too implementation-oriented and therefore, not well-suited for conceptual modeling. They propose a tool, Alcoa (Alloy Constraint Analyzer), for analyzing object models that uses its own language, Alloy, which is based on Z. Ritchers and Gogolla (2000) propose an approach for validation of UML models and OCL constraints that is based on animation.

Hussmann, Cerioli, Reggio, and Tort (1999) analyze the integration of UML models, OCL constraints, and CASL. Padawitz (2000) proposes the first steps towards a translation of class diagrams, OCL constraints, and state machines into "Swinging Types". Ahrendt et al. (2002) propose the *Key System* that enhances the UML/Java-based CASE tool.

Forward Engineering and UML: Our Approach

In previous work we propose a rigorous process to transform UML static models to object-oriented code (Favre & Clérici, 2001). Starting from UML class diagrams, an incomplete algebraic specification can be built by instantiating reusable schemes and classes that already exist in a GSBL$^{\infty}$'s pre-defined library. On the other hand, preconditions, post-conditions, and invariants in OCL can be translated to pre-conditions and axioms in GSBL$^{\infty}$. This translation requires the definition of a transformation rules system (Favre, 2001). Thus, an incomplete algebraic specification containing the highest information that can be extracted from UML models can be built semi-automatically. It allows us to carry out a rigorous analysis of the modeled behavior as well as to create more informative and precise UML models. The refinement of the GSBL$^{\infty}$ incomplete specification to the complete algebraic specifications and code is based on a library of reusable components defined by the *SpReIm* model. This model allows defining structured collections of reusable components that integrate algebraic specifications and object-oriented code. It takes advantage of the algebraic formalism power to describe behavior in an abstract way while integrating it with concrete implementations. It consists of three abstraction levels:

- *specialization* (hierarchies of incomplete specifications related by specialization relations),
- *realization* (hierarchies of complete specifications linked by realization relations), and
- *implementation* (hierarchies of object-oriented class schemes related by implementation relations).

The component reuse is based on the application of operators (*Rename, Hide, Extend*, and *Combine*) that were defined on the three levels of the *SpReIm* model.

The following differences between our approach and some of the existing ones are worth mentioning. In the first place, the GSBL^{oo} language was defined taking into account the structuring mechanisms of UML. The central innovation of this language with regards to other languages is that it is relation- centric. GSBL^{oo} allows us to keep a trace of the structure of UML models in the specification structure that will make easier to maintain consistency between the various levels when the system evolves. On the other hand, a transformational approach is introduced for the integration of the static diagrams that UML specified in OCL with algebraic languages and object-oriented code. Transformations are supported by a library of reusable schemes and by a system of transformation rules that allow translating UML constructs to GSBL^{oo} and Eiffel — step by step. All of the proposed transformations can be automated; they allow traceability and can be integrated into the iterative and incremental software development processes.

The emphasis in this chapter is given to the transformation of complete algebraic specifications in GSBL^{oo} to Eiffel. In particular, we present a systematic way to transform UML relationships into Eiffel code and the generation of Eiffel assertions.

FORMALIZING UML STATIC MODELS IN THE GSBL^{OO} LANGUAGE

The existing algebraic specification languages do not provide an explicit syntax for expressing UML relationships (dependency, association, generalization, and realization). These are generally buried in client and inheritance relationships. However, associations are semantic constructions of equal weight to the classes and generalizations in the UML models, and should not be treated as only implementation constructions. In fact, the associations allow abstracting the interaction between classes in the design on large systems. They also affect the partition of the systems in modules. Since an integrated method requires common structuring mechanisms for object-oriented models and algebraic specifications, the GSBL^{oo} language has been defined. GSBL^{oo} extends GSBL (Clérici & Orejas, 1988) with constructions that allow the expression of different kinds of UML relationships. "Object class" and "association class" specify classes and associations (ordinary, qualified, and association-class) respectively.

In Figure 1 we show the syntax of a GSBL^{oo} class specification.

In GSBL^{oo} strictly generic components can be distinguished by means of explicit parameterization. The elements of *<parameterList>* are pairs C1: C2, where C1 is the formal generic parameter constrained by an existing class C2 (only subclasses of C2 will be a valid actual parameter).

Figure 1: GSBL°° class syntax

```
OBJECT CLASS className[<parameterList>]
USES <usesList>
REFINES <refinestList>
BASIC CONSTRUCTORS <constructorList>
DEFERRED
SORTS <sortList>
OPS <opsList>
EQS <varList> <equationList>
EFFECTIVE
SORTS <sortList>
OPS <opsList>
EQS <varList> <equationList>
END-CLASS
```

The "USES" clause expresses dependency relations. The specification of the new class is based on the imported specifications declared in *<usesList>* and their public operations may be used in the new specification.

In the "REFINES" clause, the specification of the class is built from the union of the specifications of the classes appearing in the *<refinesList>*. The components of each of these specifications become components of the new class. Additionally, its own sorts and operations become own sorts and operations of the new class.

GSBL°° allows us to define local instances of a class in the "USES" and "REFINES" clauses by the following syntax:

ClassName [<bindingList>],

where the elements of *<bindingList>* can be pairs of class names *C1:C2*, being *C2* is a component of ClassName; pairs of sorts *s1:s2*, and/or pairs of operations *o1: o2* with *o2* and *s2* belonging to their own part of *ClassName*.

The sort of interest of a class (if any) is also implicitly renamed each time the class is substituted or renamed. Instances of parameterized classes can be defined with the usual syntax, i.e., *ClassName[<actual-parameter-list>]* when no additional renaming or substitution are needed.

The syntax of a complete class can include the "BASIC CONSTRUCTORS" clause that refers to generator operations.

GSBL°° distinguishes incomplete and complete parts. The "DEFERRED" clause declares new sorts, operations, or equations that are incompletely defined. The "EFFEC-TIVE" clause either declares new sorts, operations, or equations that are completely defined, or completes the definition of some inherited sort or operation.

Sorts and operations are declared in the "SORTS" and "OPS" clauses. In GSBL°° it is possible to specify any of the three levels of visibility for operations: public, protected, and private. These are expressed by prefixing the symbols: +(public), #(protected), and -(private). If we don't decorate an operation with a symbol of visibility, it can be assumed that it is public.

Generic relations can be used in the definition of concrete relations by instantiation. New associations and whole-part relations (aggregation and composition) can be defined by means of the following syntax:

ASSOCIATION <relationName>
IS <constuctorTypeName>[...:Class1;..:Class2;...:Role1;...:Role2;...: mult1; ...:mult2...:visibility1;...:visibility2]
CONSTRAINED BY <constraintList>
END

WHOLE-PART <relationName>
IS <constructorTypeName> [...: Whole;...: Part; ;...:Role1;...:Role2;...: mult1; ...:mult2;...:visibility1;...:visibility2]
CONSTRAINED BY <constraintList>
END

The "IS" clause expresses the instantiation of *<constructorTypeName>* with classes, roles, visibility, and multiplicity. The "CONSTRAINED-BY" clause allows the specification of static constraints in first order logic. Relations are defined in an "OBJECT CLASS" by means of the following syntax:

OBJECT CLASS C...
"<relationName>" **ASSOCIATES** <className>
"<relationName>" **HAS-A SHARED** <className>
"<relationName>" **HAS-A NON-SHARED** <className>
...
END-CLASS

The keywords "ASSOCIATES" and "HAS-A" identify ordinary association or aggregation, respectively. The keywords "SHARED" and "NON-SHARED" refer to simple aggregation and composition, respectively. An association may be refined to have its own set of operations and properties. Such an association is called an "Association Class".

The "PACKAGE" is the mechanism provided by GSBL°° for grouping classes. It also controls its visibility and matches the UML semantics. Taking classes and their relations from a system design into a series of packages might be separated using the GSBL°° import dependencies to control access among these packages.

Figure 2 exemplifies a UML class diagram for a company's information system. There is an association between *"Staff"* and *"Company"* specifying that managers

Figure 2: UML class diagram "company information system"

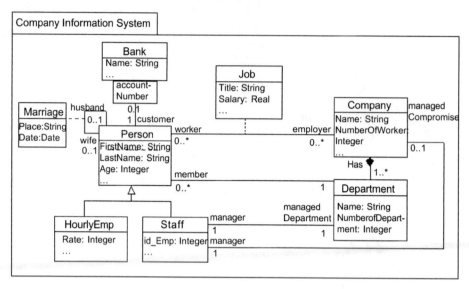

(instances of *Staff*) manage companies. Every manager may manage only one department and every company may have only one manager. There is a qualified association between "*Person*" and "*Bank*". In the context of "*Bank*", an "*accountNumber*" (qualifier) identifies a particular customer. In an "employer/worker" relationship between "*Company*" and "*Person*", there is a "*Job*" that represents the properties of that relationship, which applies to exactly one pairing of "*Person*" and "*Company*". Figure 3 partially shows the object class, "*Company*". Figure 4 depicts a reusable scheme "*Bidirectional-3*" for a Bi-directional, "many to many" association. Finally, Figure 5 partially show the GSBL°° specification of Figure 2.

Figure 3: OBJECT CLASS company

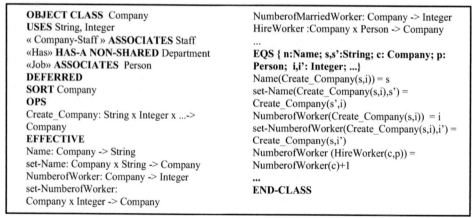

TRANSFORMING GSBL^{oo} SPECIFICATIONS TO EIFFEL CODE

Starting from UML static diagrams, an algebraic specification can be automatically built. It is obtained by translating the UML/OCL constructions to GSBL^{oo}. This specification allows one to detect inconsistencies in the class diagrams and simulate the behavior of the system before coding starts. Then GSBL^{oo} specifications need to be converted into object-oriented code. This section discusses a process for transforming GSBL^{oo} constructs to Eiffel.

Mapping Classes

The algebraic specifications must be integrated with Eiffel code. For each object class in GSBL^{oo} an Eiffel class is built. To achieve this, every clause and relationship present in a GSBL^{oo} specification was analyzed.

GSBL^{oo} and Eiffel have the same syntax for declaring class parameters. Then, this transformation is reduced to a trivial translation.

The relationship introduced in GSBL^{oo} using the clause "USES" will be translated into a client relationship in Eiffel. The relationship expressed through the keyword "REFINES" in GSBL^{oo} will become an inheritance relationship in Eiffel. This provides the mechanism to carry out modifications on the inherited classes that will allow adaptation.

Figure 4: Reusable scheme bidirectional-3

```
RELATION CLASS Bidirectional-3
USES Collection-C1 :Collection [Class1]
Collection-C2: Collection[Class2]
REFINES BinaryAssociation
BASIC CONSTRUCTORS create, addLink
EFFECTIVE
name, frozen , changeable , addOnly , getRole1,
getRole2, getMult1,
getMult2, getVisibility1, getVisibility2
create: Typename-> Bidirectional-3
addLink: Bidirectional-3(a) x Class1(c1) x
Class2(c2) -> Bidirectional-3
pre:  not isRelated(a,c1,c2)
isEmpty: Bidirectional-3-> Boolean
isRightLinked: Bidirectional-3 x Class1 ->
Boolean
isLeftLinked: Bidirectional-3 x Class2 -> Boolean
rightCardinality: Bidirectional-3 x Class1-> Nat
leftCardinality: Bidirectional-3  x Class2 ->Nat
getClass2: Bidirectional-3(a) x Class1(c1) ->
Collection-C2
pre: isRightLinked(a,c1)
getClass1: Bidirectional-3(a) x Class2(c2) ->
Collection-C1
pre: isLeftLinked(a,c2)
remove: Bidirectional-3 (a)  x Class1 (c1)  x
Class2 (c2) -> Bidirectional-3
pre: isRelated(a,c1,c2)
isRelated:
Bidirectional-3 x Class1 x Class2 ->Boolean
```

```
EQS{ a:Bidirectional-3; c1,cc1: Class1;
c2,cc2:Class2; t:TypeName}
name(create(t))= t
name(add(a,c1,c2)) = name(a)
isEmpty( create(t))= True
isEmpty(addLink(a,c1,c2))= False
frozen  (a)= <True or False>
changeable  (a)= <True or False>
addOnly  (a) = <True or False>
getRole1(a) = <role name>
getRole2 (a)  = <role name>
getMult1(a) = <multiplicity>
getMult2(a) = <multiplicity>
getVisibility1(a) = <visibility>
getVisibility2(a) = <visibility>
isRelated (create(t),c1,c2) = False
isRelated(addLink(a,c1,c2),cc1,cc2) =
(c1=cc1 and c2=cc2) or isRelated(a,cc1,cc2)
isRightLinked(create(t),c1)= False
isRightLinked(addLink(a,c1,c2),cc1) =
if c1=cc1 then True else isRightLinked(a,cc1)
rightCardinality(create(t),c1) = 0
rightCardinality(addLink(a,c1,c2),cc1) =
if c1=cc1 then 1 + rightCardinality(a,cc1)
else rightCardinality(a,cc1)
leftCardinality(create(t),c2) = 0
leftCardinality(addLink(a,c1,c2),cc2)=
 if c2=cc2 then 1 + leftCardinality(a,cc2)
else leftCardinality(a,cc2)...
END-RELATION
```

Figure 5: Package company information system

```
PACKAGE Information-System                OBJECT CLASS Bank
                                          «Person-Bank» ASSOCIATES Person
OBJECT CLASS Person                       ...
USES Integer, String, Boolean, Date,...   END-CLASS
«Member-Department» ASSOCIATES            OBJECT CLASS Department
Department                                ...
«Person-Bank» ASSOCIATES Bank             «Manager-Department» ASSOCIATES Staff
«Job» ASSOCIATES Company                  «Member-Department» ASSOCIATES Person
«Marriage» ASSOCIATES Person              «Has» HAS-A NON-SHARED Company
...                                       ...
END-CLASS                                 END-CLASS
OBJECT CLASS HourlyEmp                    ASSOCIATION CLASS Job
USES Integer                              IS Bidirectional-3 [Person: class1; Company:
REFINES Person                            class2; worker: role1; employer: role2; 0..* :
OPS                                       mult1; 0..* : mult2; + : visibility1;+ : visibility2]
Rate: HourlyEmp -> Integer                EFFECTIVE
set-Rate: HourlyEmp x Integer -> HourlyEmp  Title: Bidirectional-3  -> String
...                                       StartDate: Bidirectional-3 -> Date
END-CLASS                                 Salary: Bidirectional-3 -> Integer
OBJECT CLASS Staff                        END
USES Integer                              ASSOCIATION Company-Staff
«Company-Staff» ASSOCIATES  Company       IS Bidirectional-2 [Company: class1; Staff:
«Manager-Department» ASSOCIATES           class2; managedCompanies: role1;manager: role2
Department                                 0..1: mult1; 1: mult2;+:visibility1;+:visibility2]
REFINES Person                            END
OPS                                       ASSOCIATION CLASS Marriage
Id-Emp: Staff -> Integer                  IS Bidirectional-1 ...
EQS {p1,p2: SalaryEmp;...}                END
...                                       ASSOCIATION Manager-Department
END-CLASS                                 ...
OBJECT CLASS Company                      END
USES String, Integer                      ASSOCIATION Person-Bank
« Company-Staff » ASSOCIATES Staff        IS Q-Association [Person:class1; Bank:class2;
«Has» HAS-A NON-SHARED Department         AccountNumber:qualifier; client:role1; Bank:
«Job» ASSOCIATES Person                   role2; 1:mult1; 0..1:mult2;
DEFERRED                                  +: visibility1; +:visibility2]
SORT Company                              END
OPS                                       ASSOCIATION Member-Department
Create_Company:                           ...
String x Integer x ... -> Company         END
EFFECTIVE                                 WHOLE-PART Has
Name: Company -> String                   IS Composition-2 [Company: Whole;
set-Name: Company x String -> Company     Department: Part; Company: role1; depart: role2;
NumberofWorker: Company -> Integer        1: mult1; 1..*: mult2; + : visibility1; + :visibility2]
set-NumberofWorker:                       END
Company x Integer -> Company
...                                       END-PACKAGE
END-CLASS
```

The "DEFERRED" and "EFFECTIVE" clauses in GSBL^{oo} declare sorts and operations of the class with the equations that define their behavior. If an object class is incomplete, i.e., it contains sorts and operations in the clause "DEFERRED," the keyword "class" in Eiffel is preceded by the keyword "deferred." Sorts do not require explicit translation.

From the signature of the operations, the interfaces for the methods of the Eiffel class are generated (i.e., feature in Eiffel). The translation of each operation has a different

Figure 6: Translating GSBL°° classes to Eiffel

OBJECT CLASS Person
USES Date, Integer, String, Sex, Boolean
DEFERRED
SORT Person
OPS
create:Boolean x Boolean x Date x Integer x String
x String x Sex x Integer x ...→ Person
EFFECTIVE
OPS
get_Age: Person → Integer
get_FirstName: Person → String
get_LastName: Person → String
...
EQS   {p:Person;   d:Date;   b,b1:Boolean;s1,s2:
String; i,j:Integer; t-sex:Sex}
...
get_Age(create (b1,b ,d,i,s1,s2,t-sex,j)) = i
get_FirstName(create (b1,b ,d,i,s1,s2,t-sex,j)) = s1
get_LastName(create (b1,b ,d,i,s1,s2,t-sex,j)) = s2
...
END-CLASS
OBJECT CLASS Staff_Emp
REFINES Person
...
EFFECTIVE
SORT Staff_Emp
OPS
get_idFile: Staff_Emp → Integer
...
END-CLASS
	class PERSON creation
	        make
	feature -- data members for class attributes
	FirstName, LastName: STRING;
	Age: INTEGER; ....
	feature -- operations for class attributes
	get_Age: INTEGER is
	do Result:= Age
	end; --get_Age
	set_Age(e: INTEGER) is
	do Age:=e
	end; --set_Age
	get_FirstName: STRING is...
	get_LastName: STRING is...
	feature {NONE}
	 make (first, last: STRING...) is
	do FirstName:= first;
	             LastName:= last; ...
	end -- class PERSON
	
	class STAFF_EMP inherit PERSON
	feature
	-- data members for class attributes
	idFile: INTEGER;
	-- operations for class attributes
	get_idFile: INTEGER is
	do Result:= idFile
	end; -- get_idFile
	set_idFile (number:INTEGER) is
	do idFile:=number
	end; -- set_idFile
	...
	end -- class STAFF_EMP

treatment according to the type of feature to which it makes reference (functions, procedures, variables, or constants). It should also be considered that of all the domains of an operation, the first one that coincides with the sort of the specified class is the object "Current" in the object-oriented language and it should be eliminated from the list of parameters of the resultant feature.

Functions and procedures can present arguments. Once each name is obtained either by an explicit requirement to the user or by extracting it from the specification, the list of arguments of each feature is built. Functions and procedures require a body defined by the keywords "do end", which will be completed by the user. Figure 6 shows the classes "Person" and "Staff" in GSBL°° and Eiffel.

Eiffel provides an assertion language. Assertions are "Boolean" expressions of semantic properties of the classes. They "serve to express the specification of software components: indications of what a component does rather than how it does it" (Meyer 97).

They can play the following roles:

• Pre-condition: expresses the requirements that the client must satisfy to call a routine.

- Post-condition: expresses the conditions that the routine guarantees on return.
- Class invariant: expresses the requirements that every object of the class must satisfy after its creation.

Pre-conditions and axioms of a function written in GSBL$^{\infty}$ are used to generate pre-conditions and post-conditions for routines and invariants for Eiffel classes.

It is worth clarifying for the assertion generation that a basic functionality f: s x $a1$ x $a2$ x ......an, where "s" is the sort of interest, is translated into Eiffel syntax as $f(a1,a2,....an)$. The sort of interest is associated to the keyword "*Current*" in Eiffel. In like manner, the axiom terms must be translated in respect to the Eiffel syntax.

A GSBL$^{\infty}$ pre-condition, which is a well-formed term defined over functions and constants of the global environment classes, is automatically translated to Eiffel method pre-condition. In Figure 7, we show how to translate a GSBL$^{\infty}$ pre-condition of the operation "*remove_department*" in the "WHOLE-PART Has" to an Eiffel pre-condition in the Eiffel class "Company" (the Whole).

Axioms in a formal specification language represent the constraints the class introduces on the operations. Axioms are translated to Eiffel post-conditions and invariants.

The system can automatically derive an invariant if it can establish a correspondence between the functions in the axiom and the class features that only depend on the state of the object.

A post-condition can automatically be generated from one axiom if a term *e(<list-of-arguments>)* which is associated to an operation, can be distinguished within itself in such a way that any other term of the axiom depends upon the *<list-of-arguments>* or constants. Then, the post-condition will associate itself with the method that reflects the term and will obviously depend only upon the previous state of the method execution,

Figure 7. Constructing Eiffel pre-conditions

WHOLE-PART Has
...
remove_department:
Has(a) X Company(c) x Department(d) -> Has
  pre: is_related (a, c, d) and not addOnly (a)
  and not frozen (a)
	remove_department(d: DEPARTMENT) is
	
	require is_related_department(d) and
	not add_only_department and
	not get_frozen_department

Figure 8: Constructing Eiffel post-condition

OBJECT CLASS Company
 	
NumberofWorker: Company -> Integer
HireWorker: Company x Person ->
Company
...
EQS {c: Company; p: Person; ...}
NumberofWorker (HireWorker (c,p))=
NumberofWorker(c)+1
	HireWorker (p: PERSON) is
	do
	  -- write code here
	
	ensure
	NumberOfWorkers= old NumberOfWorkers
	+ 1
	  end; --HireWorker

upon the state after its execution and upon the method arguments. The axiom in Figure 8 is translated to a post-condition of the "*HireWorker*" method in Eiffel.

If the selected term is linked with a value belonging to the sort of interest, it is associated to "*Current*" and the sort of interest then it is associated to "*Result*".

Another type of situation cannot be automatically derived.

The programmer can also incorporate assertions that reflect purely implementation aspects.

Mapping Associations

Associations are transformed by instantiating reusable schemes that exist in the *SpReIm* library. The *SpReIm* model allows us to describe object hierarchies at three different abstraction levels: specialization, realization, and implementation (Favre & Clérici, 2001; Favre, 1998).

The specialization level describes a hierarchy of incomplete algebraic specifications as an acyclic graph G=(V,E), where V is a non-empty set of incomplete algebraic specifications and E-> V x V defines a specialization relationship between specifications. In order to integrate the *SpReIm* model with UML diagrams, the specialization level has two views. One view is based on GSBL$^{\infty}$ specifications and the other view is in OCL. Every leaf in the specialization level is associated with a sub-component at the realization level. A realization sub-component is a tree of algebraic specifications: the root is the most abstract definition, the internal nodes correspond to different realizations of the root, and the leaves correspond to sub-components at the implementation level. Every specification at the realization level corresponds to a sub-component at the implementation level, which groups a set of implementation schemes associated with a class in an object-oriented language.

There is a relationship between the other two levels and the implementation level. Every incomplete algebraic specification in the specialization level is associated with a deferred class in an object-oriented language that matches the specified incomplete behavior. Internal nodes of the realization level components, including the root, correspond to an abstract class that defers implementation in the object-oriented level and leaves in the realization level correspond to concrete classes in an object-oriented language.

Figure 9 depicts the "*Association*" component. The specialization level describes the different associations through incomplete specifications classified according to kind, degree, and connectivity.

The realization level describes a hierarchy of specifications associated to different realizations. For example, for a "binary, bi-directional and many-to-many" association, different realizations through hashing, sequences, or trees could be associated. The implementation level associates each leaf of the realization level with different implementations in an object-oriented language.

Implementation sub-components express how to implement associations and aggregations. For example, a bi-directional binary association with the multiplicity "one to one" will be implemented as an attribute in each associated class containing a reference to the related object. On the contrary, if the association is "many to many," then the best approach is to implement the association as a different class in which each instance represents one link and its attributes.

For each "HAS-A" clause, an implementation scheme will be selected and the "aggregate" and the "part" will be instantiated. For example, if the aggregation is "one-to-many" for an attribute in the "aggregate", a reference to a sequence of pointers to the "part" will be generated.

Analogously, for every "ASSOCIATES" clause, a scheme in the implementation level of the association component will be selected and instantiated. In these cases, the implementation level schemes suggest including "reference" attributes in the classes or introducing an intermediate class or container. Notice that the transformation of an association does not necessarily imply the existence of an associated class in the generated code as an efficient implementation can suggest including "reference" attributes in the involved classes.

Figure 10 partially shows the Eiffel resulting code of transforming the GSBL$^{\circ\circ}$ relations of the classes "*Company*" and "*Person*".

Figure 9: The "Association" component

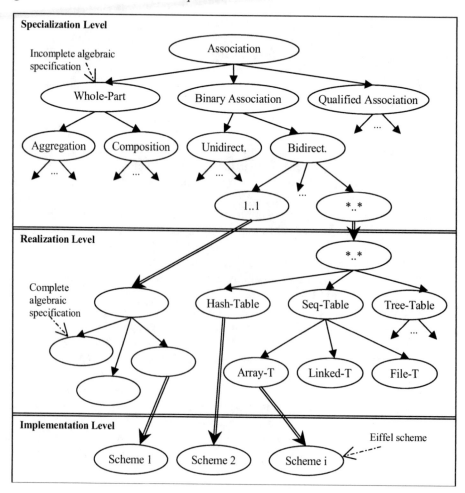

Figure 10: Transforming associations to Eiffel

```
class COMPANY creation
make
feature {NONE}
-- data members for association Has
        department: LINKED_LIST
[DEPARTMENT];
        mult_department: MULTIPLICITY;
-- data members for association Company-StaffEmp
        manager: STAFF_EMP;
        mult_manager: MULTIPLICITY;
-- data members for association class Job
        worker: LINKED_LIST[JOB];
-- data members for class attributes
        Name: STRING;
        NumberOfWorkers: INTEGER;
feature
-- operations for class attributes
        get_Name: STRING is
        do
                Result:= Name
        end;
        get_NumberOfWorkers: INTEGER is
        do
                Result:=NumberOfWorkers
        end;
        HireWorker (p: PERSON) is
        do
        -- write code here
        ensure
        NumberOfWorkers=
        old NumberOfWorkers + 1
        end; --HireWorker
        DropWorker (p: PERSON) is
        do
        -- write code here
        ensure
        NumberOfWorkers=
        old NumberOfWorkers + 1
        end; --DropWorker
        ...
-- operations for association Company-StaffEmp
        get_mult_manager : MULTIPLICITY is
        do
                Result:= mult_manager
        end;
        get_frozen_manager : BOOLEAN is
        do
                Result:= false
        end;
        add_only_manager : BOOLEAN is
        do
                Result:= false
        end;
        changeable_manager : BOOLEAN is
        do
                Result:= true
        end;

invariant
worker.count >= 0
--invariants for association Company-StaffEmp
mult_manager.get_lower_bound = 1;
mult_manager.get_upper_bound = 1;
--invariants for association Has
mult_department.get_lower_bound = 1;
mult_department.get_upper_bound >= 1;
department.count >= 1
end -- class COMPANY

class PERSON creation
make
feature
-- data members for association Member_Department
        department: DEPARTMENT;
        mult_department: MULTIPLICITY;
-- data members for association Person_Bank
        bank: BANK;
        mult_bank: MULTIPLICITY;
-- data members for association class JOB
        employer: LINKED_LIST[JOB];
-- data members for association class Marriage
        wife: MARRIAGE;
        husband: MARRIAGE;
-- data members for class attributes
        Birthdate: INTEGER;
        IsUnEmployed: BOOLEAN;
        IsMarried: BOOLEAN;
        FirstName, LastName: STRING;
        Age, NumberOfSon: INTEGER;
        Gender: STRING;
feature
-- operations for association Member-Department
        get_mult_department : MULTIPLICITY is
        do
                Result:= mult_department
        end;
        get_frozen_department : BOOLEAN is
        do
                Result:= false
        end;
....
invariant
Age>=18;
--invariants for association Member-Department
mult_department.get_lower_bound = 0;
mult_department.get_upper_bound = 1;
--invariants for association Person-Bank
mult_bank.get_lower_bound = 1 OR
mult_bank.get_lower_bound = 0;
mult_bank.get_upper_bound = 1 OR
mult_bank.get_upper_bound = 0;
--invariants for association class JOB
employer.count >= 0
end -- class PERSON
```

CONCLUSIONS AND FUTURE TRENDS

In this research work, the bases of a rigorous process for the systematic code generation starting from UML models were described. One of the stages of this process, the Eiffel code generation starting from algebraic specifications, was analyzed in detail. In particular, the automatic transformation of different types of UML associations was described. All of the UML model information (classes, associations, and OCL constrains) are overturned in specifications having implementation implications.

Our approach is directly connected with the goal of reusability. The aim is to construct specifications by combining standard, prefabricated elements. If a class diagram is specified starting from the "*SpReIm*" component, then the implementations will also be built reusing *SpReIm* sub-components of the implementation level.

The proposed transformations preserve the integrity between specifications and code. Software developers could perform maintenance and evolution on the system specification, but not on the implementations. Modifications at specification levels must be applied again to produce a new and efficient implementation. Most of the transformations can be undone, which provides great flexibility in software development.

The transformation of algebraic specifications to Eiffel code was prototyped. Later works introduced an integration of the proposed method with UML. To allow the automatic generation of algebraic specifications from UML models that are specified in OCL, we have developed a transformation system prototype. The obtained results show the feasibility of our approach; however, we cannot make an analysis of its pragmatic implications. We foresee the integration of our results in the existing case-tools environments.

REFERENCES

Ahrendt, W., Baar, T., Beckert, B., Giese, M., Hähnle, R., Menzel, W., Mostowski, W., & Schmitt, P. (2002). The KeY system: Integrating object-oriented design and formal methods. In Proc. of FASE at ETAPS 02. Grenoble, France.

Barbier, F., Henderson-Sellers, B., Opdahl, A., & Gogolla, M. (2001). The whole part relationship in the Unified Modeling Language: A new approach. *In Unified Modeling Language: System Analysis, Design and Development Issues (K.Siau and T. Halpin eds.). Chapter 12.* USA. Idea Group Publishing.

Bidoit, M., Hennicker, R., Tort, F., & Wirsing, M. (1999). Correct realizations of interface constraints with OCL. *In Proc. 2nd Int. Conf.. UML'99-The Unified Modeling Language-Beyond the Standard. Lecture Notes in Computer Science 1723.* Springer Verlag (pp. 399-415).

Booch, G., Rumbaugh, J., & Jacobson, I. (1999). The Unified Modeling Language user guide. Addison-Wesley.

Breu, R., Hinkel, U., Hofmann, C., Klein, C., Paech, B., Rumpe, B., & Thurner, V. (1997). Towards a formalization of the Unified Modeling Language. TUM-I9726 Technische, Universitat Munchen.

Bruel, J., & France, R. (1998). Transforming UML models to formal specifications. *In Proc. of UML'98-Beyond the Notation. Lecture Notes in Computer Science 1618,* Springer-Verlag (pp. 78-92).

Clérici, S., & Orejas, F. (1988). GSBL: An algebraic specification language based on inheritance. *In Proc. of the European Conference on Object-oriented Programming ECOOP 88.* Springer (pp. 78-92).

D'Souza, D., & Wills, A. (1999). Objects, components, and frameworks with UML. Addison-Wesley.

Evans, A., France, R., Lano, K., & Rumpe, B. (1998). The UML as a formal modeling notation. *In Proc. of UML'98-Beyond the Notation, Lecture Notes in Computer Science 1618.* Springer-Verlag.

Favre, L. (1998). Object-oriented reuse through algebraic specifications. *In Proc. Technology of Object-oriented Languages and Systems, TOOLS 28. IEEE Computer Society* (pp. 101-112).

Favre, L. (2001). A formal mapping between UML static models and algebraic specifications. *Lecture Notes in Informatics (p. 7) SEW Practical UML-Based Rigorous Development Methods-Countering or Integrating the eXtremist* (A. Evans, R. France, A. Moreira, B. Rumpe, eds.). GI Edition, Konner Kollen-Verlag (pp. 113-127).

Favre, L, & Clérici, S. (2001). A systematic approach to transform UML static models to code. In *Unified Modeling Language: System Analysis, Design and Development Issues* (K.Siau and T. Halpin, eds.). Chapter II , USA. Idea Group Publishing.

Firesmith, D.G., & Henderson-Sellers, B. (1998). Clarifying specialized forms of association in UML and OML. JOOP, 11(2) (pp. 47-50).

Gogolla, M., & Ritchers, M. (1997). On combining semi-formal and formal object specification techniques. *In Proc. WADT97, Lecture Notes in Computer Science 1376.* Springer-Verlag (pp. 238-252).

Hussmann, H., Cerioli, M., Reggio, G. & Tort, R. (1999). Abstract data types and UML models. *Report DISI-TR-99-15.* University of Genova.

JDM (2000). *Journal of Database Management.* Idea-Group Publishing, 11(4).

Kim, S. K., & Carrington, D. (1999). Formalizing the UML class diagram using object-Z. *In Proc. UML 99, Lecture Notes in Computer Science 1723* (pp. 83-98).

Lano, K. (1995). Formal object-oriented development. Springer-Verlag.

Mandel, L., & Cengarle, V. (1999). On the expressive power of the object constraint language OCL. Available on the World Wide Web: http://www.fast.de/projeckte/forsoft/ocl

Meyer, B. (1997). Object-oriented software construction. Prentice Hall.

OMG (2001). Unified Modeling Language specification, v. 1.3. document ad/99-06-08. Object Management Group.

Overgaard, G. (1998). A formal approach to relationships in the Unified Modeling Language. *In Proc. of Workshop on Precise Semantic of Modeling Notations, International Conference on Software Engineering.* ICSE'98, Japan.

Padawitz, P. (2000). Swinging UML: How to make class diagrams and state machines amenable to constraint solving and proving. In A. Evans & S. Kent (Eds.), *Proc. of <<UML>> 2000-The Unified Modeling Language. Lecture Notes in Computer Science 1939.* Springer (pp. 162-177).

Ritchers, M., & Gogolla, M. (2000). Validating UML models and OCL constraints. In Proc. of <<UML>> 2000. The Unified Modeling Language (Evans, A., Kent, S. eds.). *Lecture Notes in Computer Science 1939.* Springer (pp. 265-277).

Siau, K., & Halpin, T. (2001). Unified Modeling Language: System analysis, design and development issues. K. Siau; T. Halpin (eds.). USA, Idea-Group Publishing.

Quatrani, T. (1998). Visual modeling with Rational Rose and UML. Addison-Wesley.

Varizi, M., & Jackson, D. (1999). Some shortcomings of OCL, The object constraint language of UML. Available on the World Wide Web: http://sdg.lcs.mit.edu/~dnj/publications.htm

ENDNOTE

This work is partially supported by CIC (Comisión de Investigaciones Científicas de la Pcia. de Buenos Aires) in Argentina.

Chapter X

Transforming UML Class Diagrams into Relational Data Models

Devang Shah
eXcelon Corporation, USA

Sandra Slaughter
Carnegie Mellon University, USA

ABSTRACT

*The **Entity-Relationship (ER)** method is the most popular method for relational database design. On the other hand, the **Unified Modeling Language (UML)** is widely used in object- oriented analysis and design. Despite the increasing use of object-oriented techniques for software design and development, there is a large installed base of relational databases, Additionally, object-oriented databases are still not in widespread use. Thus, software designers and developers often turn to the relational databases to make their application objects persistent. Considering the fundamental differences between the two methods, the transformation from UML to a relational data model could be a non-trivial task, The purpose of this chapter is to describe a process that can be used to map a UML class diagram into an ER diagram, and to discuss the potential of using the UML notation to draw ER diagrams. An example of an actual systems design is used throughout to illustrate the mapping process, the associated problems encountered, and how they could be resolved.*

INTRODUCTION

The Entity–Relationship (ER) model is the most widely used data model for the conceptual design of relational databases. It focuses solely on data, representing a "data network" that exists for a given system. It has emerged as the leading formal structure for conceptual data representation and has become an industry standard. The ER model is based on only a few modeling concepts and has a very effective graphical representation in which each element of the model is mapped to a distinct graphical symbol (Batini, Ceri, & Navathe, 1992).

In the past few years, the Unified Modeling Language (UML) has emerged as a prominent modeling language for object-oriented analysis and design (see Oestereich, 2002; Fowler & Scott, 2000; Booch, Rumbaugh, & Jacobson, 1999; Rumbaugh, Jacobson & Booch, 1999). The class diagram is an important part of the UML, as it captures the static view of the system. The class diagram models classes in the real world and specifies the relationships between them. The underlying concept of class diagrams may seem to be similar to that of ER diagrams; however, there are a few fundamental differences between the two modeling languages. Usually, the ER model is used with the method Structured System Analysis and Design, which is primarily process-centric (see Pressman, 1997; Meilir Page-Jones, 1988; Yourdon, 1988). On the other hand, object modeling is a part of the method (Object Oriented Analysis and Design), which is primarily functional / data-centric (see Muller, 1999; Bahrami, 1999; Dewitz, 1995). Having said that, if we ignore the method / operation property of objects, we can say that object modeling, in concept, is very similar to data modeling. As Rumbaugh et al. (Rumbaugh, Blaha, Premerlani, Eddy & Lorensen, 1991) have observed, the Object Modeling Technique (OMT) is an enhanced form of ER that includes some new concepts (such as qualification). Thus, UML is an enhanced form of OMT and an enhanced form of the ER model[1] (Ou, 1997).

Although object-oriented methods enjoy some success in the software development field, software engineers often turn to ER diagrams and relational databases to implement the objects, i.e., to make them persistent (Muller, 1999). This raises a number of important issues. If the class diagram is a superset of the ER diagram, then why do we need a separate notation to draw the ER diagrams? Can the UML class diagram notation be used to draw the ER diagrams? What is the advantage of that? How would the UML class diagram handle different constructs of the ER diagrams such as primary key constraint, referential integrity constraint, or unique key constraint? What about normalization?

Translating a class diagram into an ER diagram could be a non-trivial task, as several symbols and notations used in the class diagram (e.g., n-ary relationships[2], aggregation, composition) do not have direct mappings to the ER diagram. A logical and a physical relational database design will require a systematic, step-by-step process to translate a class diagram into the ER diagram. This chapter discusses a process that can be used to simplify the database design task of making an object persistent. It explains how to transform UML class diagrams into relational data models. Some have argued that object modeling is the same as relational modeling. Others have confronted this view; however, we do not delve into that issue in this chapter. Our intent is to examine the efficacy of the UML class diagram as a vehicle to draw the ER diagram. We illustrate data modeling in UML using a real example from an extranet-based retail pharmacy drug dispensing system that was designed for a regional health care network of hospitals, pharmacies, pharmacy brokers, patients, and drug manufacturers. We also discuss some of the challenges faced by application developers in implementing object-oriented relational database applications and several tools and application programming interfaces that address these challenges.

The rest of this chapter is organized as follows: we first review related work and provide some background information. We then discuss the notational differences between UML and the ER diagram; this following section describes the mapping steps that can be followed to convert the conceptual view into the logical schema. We then present the result of the work on the complete class diagram and discuss programming challenges, industry tools, and programming language enhancements available to alleviate the problem. Finally, we draw a number of conclusions and implications,

BACKGROUND

The topic of making objects persistent and the relationship between class diagrams and ER diagrams is not novel (e.g., see Bahrami, 1999; Banerjee, 1987; Dewitz, 1995; and Muller, 1999). Ever since the emergence of object-oriented technologies, system designers have struggled with how to resolve the mismatch that exists between the two different methodologies while making objects persistent. A number of recent articles have explored various dimensions of this dilemma. For example, Tong, Li and Ma (2002) have developed a methodology to synthesize object-oriented and relational data models called "MDMS" (model object data management system) in which the object manager controls data access to the relational database and the data access function is separated from the area data object. Rahayu, Chang, Dillon, and Taniar (2001) have developed and evaluated the performance of an object-relational transformation methodology that allows the use of object-oriented methodologies for data modeling and then transforms the model into a relational logical model for implementation in relational database management systems. Maciaszek and Kin-Shing (2000) have defined a number of extensions to UML needed to map from object-oriented design models to an object-relational implementation. Ou (1997) defines a mapping from UML to the ER model. Ou's work addresses many of the UML constructs; however, it provides a mapping at the conceptual schema level rather than at the logical schema level. Other significant work on this topic has also been done by Muller (1999). On the other hand, using the class diagram notation to draw the ER diagrams can be complex. In order to understand the relationship between the two models, one must consider the underlying principles from which both notations have evolved.

As noted by Ling and Teo (1994), even though the object-oriented approach is very popular, it has a number of inadequacies, e.g., lack of a formal foundation, lack of a standard query language, etc. Over the past couple of years, significant research has been done to address the formality issue. As a result, the Object Constraint Language (OCL) has been introduced by IBM to formally represent the constructs in the UML diagrams. Gogolla discusses the notation differences and the work-around solution (Gogolla & Richters, 1998). Today, some computer-supported software engineering (CASE) tools provide support for forward and reverse engineering between UML class diagrams and the relational database schema. Such tools include the Rational® Rose data modeler from Rational Software Corporation, ObjectF® developed by MicroTOOL, Inc., the PowerDesigner™ tool by Sybase Inc., SILVERRUN ModelSphere by Magna Solutions, and QDesigner™ by Quest Software. However, the effectiveness of many of these tools in the CASE tool market is yet to be determined.

As mentioned earlier, our purpose in this chapter is two-fold: to describe how to make objects persistent, i.e., how to convert the class diagram into the relational database schema, and to assess the effectiveness of using the class diagram notation to draw the ER diagram. Throughout the chapter, we use a real example of a systems design for an extranet-based retail pharmacy drug dispensing system. We briefly describe this system in the next section, and then continue with our discussion of mapping from class diagrams to relational database schemas.

EXAMPLE – RETAIL PHARMACY (DRUG DISPENSING) SYSTEM

There are a number of actors in the retail pharmacy (drug dispensing) system. A central actor is the Pharmacy Broker Manager (PBM). The PBM sets up a contract with a retail pharmacist. The employer buys health care benefits plans from the PBM. The PBM issues a health care insurance card to the employer's employee. The employee becomes ill (patient) and goes to the doctor. The doctor diagnoses the patient's condition. The doctor asks the patient about prior health conditions, existing prescriptions, and any preferred formularies. Based upon this information and the diagnosis, the doctor writes out a prescription for the patient.

The patient goes to a retail pharmacy and gives the prescription to the pharmacist. The pharmacist gives the patient the prescribed brand drug or makes a generic substi-

Figure 1: UML class diagram of retail pharmacy system

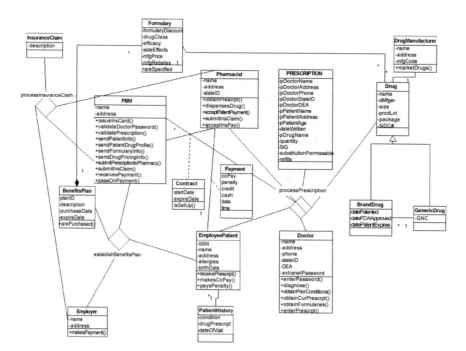

Drug Dispensing System: Extranet-Based

tution. The patient can pay a co-payment and may also incur a penalty for brand drugs that are not on the preferred formulary. The pharmacist and PBM submit the insurance claim. The PBM receives payment from the employer for the patient's prescription costs and passes the payment on to the pharmacist.

Drug manufacturers market and sell their brand drugs to the pharmacists. They also "detail" (advertise) the benefits of their drugs to doctors in the hopes of getting their brand drugs prescribed. Figure 1 illustrates the class diagram representing the design of the retail pharmacy system.

EXTENDING THE UML META-MODEL[3]

The UML meta-model specifies constructs for the classes (also includes attributes and operations) and for the relationships between classes (includes binary and "n-ary" associations, inheritance, dependency, and instanceOf). In addition to this, various adornments can be specified at the class, attribute, operations, and association levels. On the other hand, the UML meta-model is not semantically rich when it comes to specifying constraints. It offers some mechanisms for specifying integrity constraints. For example, the properties of an "AssociationEnd" such as aggregation, isNavigable, multiplicity, and qualifier, can be used to specify integrity constraints. However, the core UML meta-model does not include specification of integrity constraints. For example, the uniqueness constraint, or primary key field constraint is not included (Ou, 1998).

The OCL can be used to specify the constraints at the model level; however it is semi-formal. The Rational Rose Data Modeler uses new stereotypes and tag values to extend the meta-model and achieve the goal of specifying integrity constraints during UML modeling; however, it may be argued that this is not the best way to denote the constraints as it violates the standard UML constraint notation (i.e., specifying constraints within braces). On the other hand, some authors (e.g., Ou, 1998) have added compartments in the class diagram and have introduced new model elements and some attributes to the core package of the UML meta-model. In this chapter, we show the primary key and foreign key constraints using {PK} and {FK} notations, respectively. We now describe the steps for converting class diagrams into logical database schemas using our example of the retail pharmacy system to illustrate the process.

STEPS FOR CONVERTING THE CLASS DIAGRAM INTO A LOGICAL SCHEMA

The UML class diagram forms the conceptual view of the system that needs to be converted into the logical view to design the relational database schema. This section reviews different UML class diagram constructs and discusses a process that can be used for translating these constructs into the logical view.

Mapping Classes

A class is a descriptor for a set of objects with similar structures, behaviors, and relationships. It represents a concept within the system being modeled. Classes have data structure and behavior as well as relationships to other elements. Graphically, a class is outlined as a solid rectangle containing three compartments separated by horizontal lines. The top compartment holds the class name.

One table can be created for each persistent class of the conceptual view. However, things can become complicated when considering generalization and associations with other classes of the schema. Generalization and associations (binary and n-ary associations along with different types of association adornments) are discussed in more detail later in this section.

Mapping Attributes

An attribute displays the various properties or characteristics of the class. It is shown as a text string within the second compartment of the class. When mapping attributes into columns, an attribute can be mapped to zero or more columns. Attributes that can be derived from other attributes can be left unconverted. In the UML diagram, one can also specify different attribute properties at the attribute level.

Visibility: At the database level, all of the columns of a table are public. Hence, while mapping an attribute into columns, this property can be ignored.

Multiplicity: Multiplicity is of the form: "lower-bound... upper-bound." For example, a multiplicity of 0..1 denotes an attribute as not-mandatory, single-valued; whereas, a multiplicity of 1..* denotes an attribute as mandatory, multi-valued. A mandatory / non-mandatory property of an attribute could be translated as a null / not-null property at the database level. However, translating a multi-valued attribute is not a straight-forward task. This is because in relational databases, it is not possible to store multiple values in one column. If the number of values that a multi-valued attribute can take is fixed (for example, days of the week), then a column can be created for each value of an attribute (i.e., one column for each day of the week). However, if the number of values that an attribute can take is not fixed, then the best way will be to create a separate table to store the values and link this table with the original table using a foreign key reference.

Property-string: The UML syntax uses property-string to denote a type (domain) of an attribute. Translating an attribute type into a corresponding column type at the database level will depend on the set of types supported by a particular database management system (DBMS). There could be some differences. For example, an attribute of type 'String' in C++ can occupy "n" number of characters, whereas a corresponding "VARCHAR2" column at the Oracle® database level restricts column size to only 255 characters. This problem could be alleviated by identifying such differences beforehand and implementing constraints at the code level.

Mapping Associations

Mapping Binary Associations: An association is a relation between two or more classifiers. Binary associations are shown as lines connecting two classifier symbols. Note that a binary association includes the possibility of an association from a classifier to itself. Ternary and higher-order associations are shown as diamonds connected to class symbols by lines. A binary association is drawn as a solid path connecting two classifier symbols.

A multiplicity item specifies the range of allowable cardinalities that a set may assume. It may be given for roles within associations, parts within composition, repetitions, and other purposes. Multiplicity is often shown in the format: "lower-bound

... upper-bound," where lower-bound and upper-bound are literal integer values that specify the closed range of integers from the lower-bound to the upper-bound. The symbol '*' is used to denote the unlimited non-negative integer range. Note that UML combines the concepts of multiplicity and modality whereas in the ER diagrams both of these concepts are orthogonal.

Mapping One-to-One Associations: Either separate tables can be created for each class involved in the association or classes can be combined to form one table. The decision usually depends on the application domain and the degree of coupling that exists between the two tables. To illustrate this point further, consider the scenario where the designer has created two classes to represent patient information: the first one includes the patient's name, age, and other personal information whereas, the second class contains address information. However, at the database level, it may be inefficient to store this information in two separate tables. Hence information can be combined and stored into one table.

Mapping One-to-Many Associations: A separate table can be created for each class involved in the association. An association is realized by storing the primary key of the class (the class whose one instance participates in the relationship) as a foreign key into the second class (the class whose 'n' instance participates in the relationship). For example, Figure 2 shows the mapping where a patient can have a history of multiple visits. This diagram can be converted into a logical schema as shown in Figure 2. The relationship between the two classes is stored in the 'Patient History' table as a foreign key.

Mapping Many-to-Many Associations: A separate table can be allocated for each class involved in the association. In addition, one table can be created to store the association itself. This table will also maintain the primary key of both the associated tables and the associated attributes. For example, Figure 3 shows the mapping where drugs can be included on many formularies, and formularies include many drugs.

Mapping "N-Ary" Associations: An n-ary notation is an association among three or more classifiers (a single classifier may appear more than once). Each instance of an

Figure 2: Mapping one-to-many associations

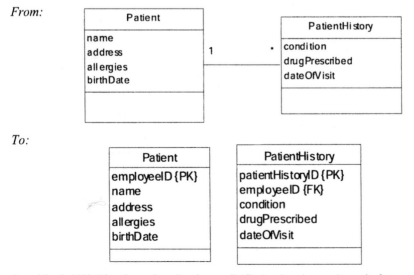

Figure 3: Mapping many-to-many associations

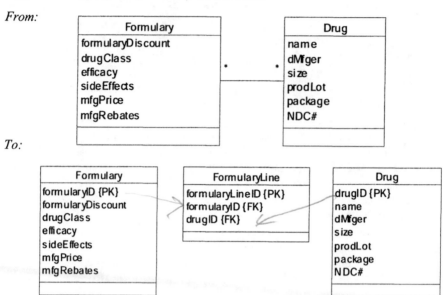

association is an "n-tuple" of values from the respective classifier. A binary association is a special case having its own notation. The multiplicity of a role represents the potential number of instance "tuples" in the association when the other n-1 values are fixed. An association can also have an association class. An association class may be attached to the diamond by a dashed line. This indicates an n-ary association that has attributes, operations, and/or associations. While converting the class diagram into the logical schema, n-ary relationships can be broken down into a series of binary relationships. Moreover, depending on the cardinality of the relationship, each relationship can be further divided as per the rules mentioned later in this section. For example, the pharmacist and the PBM submit the insurance claim. The PBM receives payment from the employer for the patient's prescription costs and passes on the payment to the pharmacists. In the class diagram, this is modeled as an n-ary association between 'Insurance Claim,' 'Employer,' 'Pharmacist,' and 'PBM'. While converting the class diagram into the logical schema, this n-ary relationship can be broken down into following sets of binary relationships: (1) relationship between 'Pharmacist' and 'Insurance Claim' (one-to-many), (2) relationship between 'PBM' and 'Insurance Claim' (one-to-many), and (3) relationship between 'Employer' and 'Insurance Claim' (one-to-many). The logical schema is shown in Figure 4 and labeled "first approach." Another approach to map an n-ary association is to create a separate table to store the relationship. In the above example, such a conversion will create the following tables as shown in Figure 4 under "second approach."

However, it is not always possible to break down n-ary associations into a series of binary associations without adding additional implementation concerns (Jones & Song, 1995). Whether or not an n-ary association can be decomposed without loss into binary forms depends on the association's application domain. Also, loss-less decomposition does not always provide a complete basis on which to judge equivalent

Figure 4: Mapping n-ary associations

First approach:

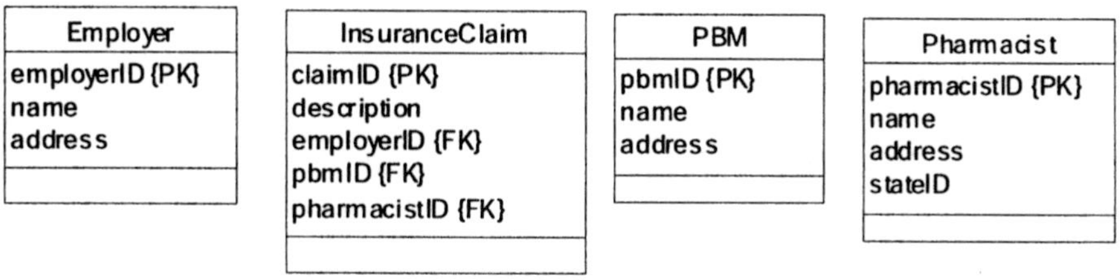

Employer
employerID {PK}
name
address

InsuranceClaim
claimID {PK}
description
employerID {FK}
pbmID {FK}
pharmacistID {FK}

PBM
pbmID {PK}
name
address

Pharmacist
pharmacistID {PK}
name
address
stateID

Second approach:

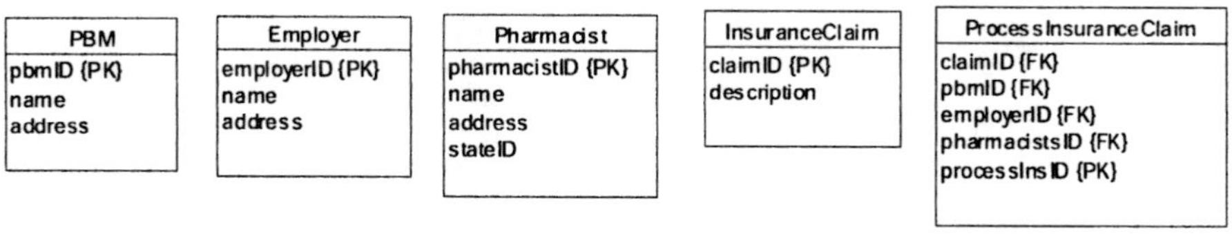

PBM
pbmID {PK}
name
address

Employer
employerID {PK}
name
address

Pharmacist
pharmacistID {PK}
name
address
stateID

InsuranceClaim
claimID {PK}
description

ProcessInsuranceClaim
claimID {FK}
pbmID {FK}
employerID {FK}
pharmacistsID {FK}
processInsID {PK}

modeling capabilities. N-ary associations are usually difficult to implement, and the resultant schema should always be verified against database normalization principles.

Mapping Aggregation and Composition

When placed on the target end, the relationship specifies whether the target end is an aggregation with respect to the source end. Only one end can be an aggregation. If the end is an aggregate, the other end is a part and must have an aggregation value of none. The part may be contained in other aggregates. If the end is a composite, the other end is a part and must have the aggregation value of none. The part is strongly owned by the composite and may not be part of any other composite. Composition is a form of aggregation with strong ownership and coincidental lifetime of part with the whole. The multiplicity of the aggregate end may not exceed one (it is unshared). Composition may be shown by a solid, filled diamond as an association end adornment. Alternatively, UML provides a graphically-nested form that is more convenient for showing composition in many cases.

Depending on the multiplicity of the association, classes can be converted into tables. For example, if there is a 1:M relationship between aggregate and part, then two tables can be allocated: one for aggregate and one for part. Additionally, the relationship can be stored in the part table as a foreign key. If there is an M:N relationship between aggregate and part (note that this case is not possible for composition because with the composition, one instance of a part cannot be shared by more than one instance of the aggregate), then three tables can be allocated: one for each class and one to the store the relationship. However, care must be taken while designing the physical schema, as usually with the composition and aggregation relationship, one would prefer to retrieve part along with the aggregate and similarly for the insert, delete, and update operations. To illustrate, Figure 5 shows the mapping of an aggregate into a logical schema for the example where benefit plans are composed of one or more drug formularies.

Figure 5: Mapping aggregates

From:

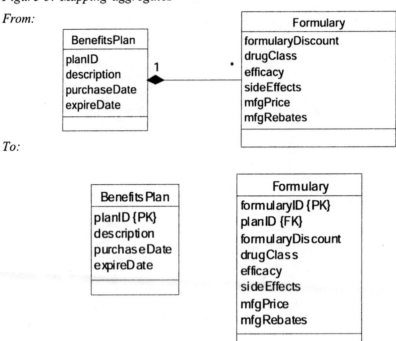

To:

Association End – Adornments: Different adornments can be specified at the "Association End," such as multiplicity, ordering, qualifier, navigability, aggregation indicator, role name, and changeability.

   Ordering: If the multiplicity is greater than zero, then the set of related elements can be ordered or unordered. While translating such associations, one solution could be to write triggers at the database level.

   Navigability: UML supports the concept of either one-directional or bi-directional relationships. However, at the database level, the relationship is stored in the tables and it does not support the concept of a uni-directional relationship.

   Role name: UML indicates the role played by the class attached to the end of the path near the role name. It does not have any impact on an implementation and it is used to enhance readability. Some versions of ER diagrams (for example, the Oracle version) provide support for specifying relationship names in both directions. For these versions, translating the role name in the class diagram to the database-level ER diagram should not be a problem.

   Qualifier: A qualifier is an attribute or list of attributes whose values serve to partition the set of instances associated with an instance across an association. The qualifiers are attributes of the association. A qualified association can be mapped to a relationship just like any other association. However, depending on the multiplicity, the multiplicity and primary key of the resultant relationship can differ (Ou, 1997).

   Changeability: This adornment denotes whether the links are changeable or not. The property "{frozen}" indicates that no links may be added, deleted, or moved from an object after the object is created and initialized. The property "{addOnly}" indicates that additional links may be added; however, links may not be modified or deleted. One way to map these two "({frozen}" and "{addOnly})" constraints, is to control insert, update, and delete operations via a trigger at the database level.

Mapping Generalizations

Generalization refers to the relationship between a more general element (the parent) and a more specific element (the child) that is fully consistent with the first element and that adds additional information. In UML, it is shown as a solid-line path from the child (the more specific element, such as a sub-class) to the parent (the more general element, such as a super-class), with a large hollow triangle at the end of the path where it meets the more general element. Implementing the generalization hierarchy is one of the more difficult tasks when converting the conceptual view into the logical view. Usually there are three possible alternatives: the first alternative is to allocate a table for each class, including the parent class; whereas, the second alternative is to copy the attributes of the parent class into the child classes while converting concrete classes into tables. A third alternative is to allocate a single composite table, containing attributes of the parent class as well as attributes of all the child classes. Note that none of the above three options is perfect; however, each option offers some advantages as well as disadvantages over other options. As a result, the choice will be governed by the application domain. To illustrate, Figure 6 shows the UML class diagram for the generalization example where there are two types of drugs: branded drug and generic drug. Branded drugs are developed by drug manufacturers, whereas generic drugs are copies of the original drug.

Solution 1: Allocate a separate table for each class. One solution would be to create one table for each class, including the abstract class. For the generalization example, as shown in Figure 7, three tables can be created: one for the 'Drug' class, one for the 'Brand' class and one for the 'Generic' class. Advantages of this approach would be the ease of modification. If in the future, there is a need to add some more attributes into the abstract class, then changes will be relatively easy to accommodate. Also, this

Figure 6: Generalization example

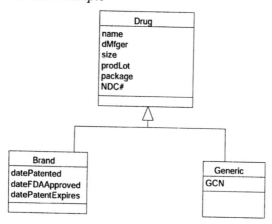

Figure 7: Mapping generalization: Solution one

Brand
drugID {PK}
datePatented
dateFDAApproved
datePatentExpires
genericDrugID {FK}

Drug
drugID {PK}
name
dMfger
size
prodLot
package
NDC#
drugMfgerID {FK}
type

Generic
drugID {PK}
GCN

approach is preferable when there exists a relationship between an abstract class and some other class. If there exists a relationship between a 'Drug' and a 'Formulary,' then it will be beneficial to have a separate class for 'Drug' rather than copying down its attributes into its child classes. An apparent disadvantage of this approach is in terms of performance. Now every access to the child class will result in two accesses: one for the child class itself and another one for the parent class. The same would be true for the insert and delete operations.

   Solution 2: Create one table for each child class. A second solution is to create a table for each child class, duplicating the parent class attributes into the child class (Figure 8). An apparent advantage of this approach would be a performance gain. Since there will no access overhead for getting the information from the super-class, better performance can be realized. A disadvantage of this approach is that the solution is not flexible enough to accommodate future changes with respect to the parent class.

   Solution 3: Create one table for entire hierarchy. A third solution is to create one single table for the entire hierarchy as shown in Figure 9. The table would contain the attributes of the parent class as well as attributes of child classes. An advantage of this approach would be the performance gain. Only one access to the table would be needed to access any type of drug information. However, this approach would offer less

Figure 8: Mapping generalization: Solution two

Brand
drugID {PK}
datePatented
dateFDAApproved
datePatentExpire
genericDrugId {FK}
drugMfgerID {FK}
type
name
size
prodLot
package
NDC#

Generic
drugID {PK}
GCN
drugMfgerID {FK}
type
name
size
prodLot
package
NDC#

Figure 9: Mapping generalization: Solution three

Drug
drugID {PK}
drugMfgerID {FK}
type
name
size
prodLot
package
NDC#
datePatented
dateFDAApproved
datePatentExpire
genericDrugID {FK}
GCN

flexibility, as any modifications such as the addition of an extra child would be difficult to achieve. Another disadvantage would be the data redundancy, as in the "Brand table," fields like 'GCN' and brand 'drugID' would be null for the branded drugs and the fields 'datePatented,' 'datePatentExpire,' and 'dateFDAApproved' would be null for the generic drugs.

Selecting Primary Keys

In a relational database, a unique identifier is needed in order to identify each distinct row in the table, as well as to store the relationships. An identifier should be assigned to each object (or to each 'row' in relational database terminology) in order to uniquely identify it. There are several options for selecting primary keys:

Selecting an attribute that has a functional meaning as a primary key: One of the attributes having a business or functional meaning can be selected as a primary key, for example, the 'Order Number' attribute in the 'Order' class, or the 'Invoice Number' attribute for the 'Invoice' class. An advantage of this approach would be that the users of the system are familiar with the key. A disadvantage would be that if a business domain changes, then the key having a functional meaning changes its definition as well. For example, consider the case where "Invoice Number" is used as a primary key in the table 'Invoice' and is used as a foreign key in the tables 'Invoice Line' and 'Payment'. Changing the size of the 'Invoice Number' field will require changes in the base table, as well as in all the dependent tables.

Assigning a separate attribute to store the object identifier: A separate attribute can be added in the class definition to store unique key identifiers, for example, the 'Order Id' attribute for the 'Order' class or the 'Invoice Id' attribute for the 'Invoice' class. These separate attributes can be automatically generated by the system. A disadvantage of this approach would be that since the primary key will not have a functional meaning, a table will still need one more field to serve as a unique key. For example, in the "Invoice" table, apart from "Invoice Id," the "Invoice Number" column will still be necessary. "Invoice Id" can be assigned as a primary key field and can be used in joining other tables, whereas "Invoice Number" will serve as a unique functional key on the table.

An Example of the Mapping Process

We applied the different methods mentioned in this section to the conceptual view (i.e., the UML class diagram as shown in Figure 1) of the drug dispensing system. We encountered some additional considerations and issues in mapping the class diagram to a logical schema.

Selecting a Primary Key: We decided to assign a separate attribute, i.e., to create separate fields in the table to store object identifiers of the class diagram. The key selected as a primary key does not have any functional meaning associated with it. A separate 'Id' column has been added in all the tables.

Mapping Classes into Tables: In this step, we considered only those classes that are related via one-to-one relationships. In later steps, we mapped generalizations and associations.

Mapping Attributes Into Columns: This was a straight-forward task as none of the columns were multi-valued; however, some of the attributes that we could have computed from the other attributes were left unconverted.

Realizing Generalization: In this step, we considered the generalization between the classes 'Brand,' 'Generic,' and 'Drug.' 'Brand' and 'Generic' are inherited from 'Drug'. We decided to assign a separate persistent table to each class ('Brand' and 'Generic') as well as to the parent class ('Drug'), because of the association between the 'Drug' class and other three classes (i.e., 'Formulary,' 'Doctor,' and 'Drug Manufacturer.'

Mapping Binary Associations: In this step, we considered "1:M" and "M:N" associations present in the class diagram. In all cases, the 1:M association was replaced by storing the primary key of the class (whose one instance participates in the association) as a foreign key into the second class (whose multiple instances participate in the association), and "M:N" association was replaced by a separate table to store the relationship.

Mapping n-ary Associations: This was a particularly interesting problem, and the solution was driven by domain knowledge. The n-ary relationship between 'Doctor,' 'Prescription,' 'Pharmacist,' 'Drug,' 'Employee/Patient,' and 'PBM' was broken into the following multiple binary associations: (1) relationship between 'Prescription' and 'Doctor' (M:1 relationship), (2) relationship between 'Prescription' and 'Employee/Patient' (M:1 relationship), (3) relationship between 'Prescription' and 'Drug' (M:1 relationship), and (4) relationship between 'Prescription' and 'Pharmacist' (M:1 relationship). Binary association mapping rules, discussed earlier in this section, were applied to each of these relationships.

The n-ary relationship between the classes 'Employer,' 'Benefits Plan,' 'PBM,' and 'Employee/Patient' was broken down further into following binary relationships: (1) the relationship between 'PBM' and 'Benefits Plan', and (2) the relationship between 'PBM,' 'Employee/Patient,' and 'Employer' was broken down further by adding one more table 'Insurance Card' ('PBM' issues an insurance card to an employer and the card eventually gets assigned to the employee).

Mapping Aggregation and Composition: The relationship between 'Benefits Plan' and 'Formulary' was converted by considering the relationship as a 1:M relationship.

Figure 10 shows the resultant logical schema of the retail pharmacy drug dispensing system. The logical schema does not show the relationship between different tables

Figure 10: Logical schema for retail pharmacy system

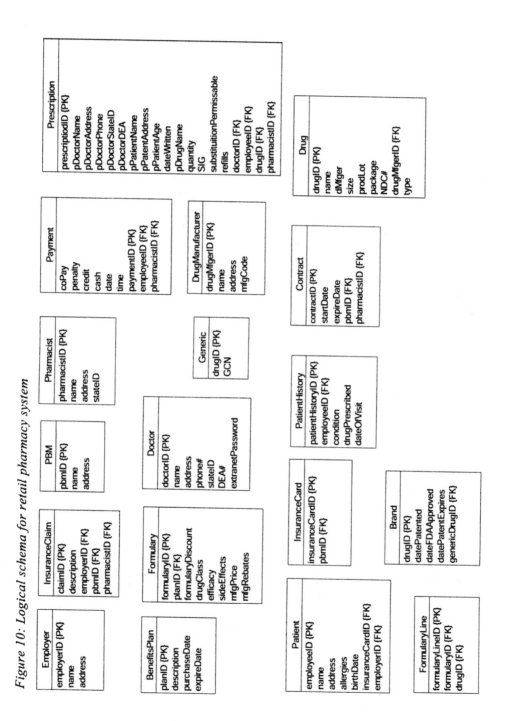

explicitly because in the relational database, the relationship between two tables is defined implicitly via foreign key constraints.

In the next section, we discuss some of the challenges faced by application developers in implementing object-oriented relational database applications and discuss several tools and application programming interfaces that address these challenges.

PROGRAMMING CHALLENGES

Mapping class diagrams to object diagrams is not the only issue application that developers face when trying to implement an object-oriented relational database application. Other challenges include: how to access database tables and records, how to maintain relationships between various tables, how to manage database transactions and ACID (Atomicity, Consistency, Isolation and Durability) properties of these transactions, how to read a large set of records from the database without incurring a performance penalty, how to design and develop a robust application that is relatively immune to the underlying database schema changes or even which is database platform independent, and how to write the database access code that conforms with object-oriented principles and fits well with the rest of the application code.

There are number of tools and application programming interfaces (APIs) in the market that attempt to address these problems. Some of the solutions are offered as a part of programming languages or even as an API extension of a programming language, while others are third party tools providing proprietary APIs and mapping support. Below is a brief summary of some of the solutions.

Application Programming Interfaces

APIs like ODBC (Open Database Connectivity) and JDBC™ (Java Database Connectivity) simplify the task of sending Structured Query Language (SQL) statements to relational systems and, by supporting all dialects of SQL, shield developers from the differences between databases. These APIs are used to invoke SQL calls directly, so applications can send queries or update statements to the database. However, the onus of implementing the mapping, maintaining relationships between database tables and managing transactions is on the developers. These solutions do not provide transparency between objects and persistence store.

Enterprise JavaBeans™

The Enterprise JavaBeans (EJB) architecture (which is the core component of the Sun™ J2EE™ specification) is a server-side technology for developing and deploying distributed components that contain the business logic of an enterprise application. There are two types of EJBs: Session Beans, which carry out operations on behalf of a client, or Entity Beans, which are persistent objects representing data held in a database. Entity Beans can either manage their own persistence or can delegate this to their container. In case of container-managed persistence, the container's provider tools are used to generate the code that moves data between the enterprise bean's instance variables and a database or an existing application. The developers are responsible for providing mapping information between objects and its instance fields, and the corresponding database table and fields.

With Container Managed Persistence (CMP) Entity Beans, the application server is responsible for maintaining mappings, relationships and transactions. Another advantage of using CMP Entity Beans is that entity beans are largely independent from the data store in which the entity is stored. However, this solution is a part of the J2EE architecture and not of the Java language itself.

Java Data Objects

The Java™ Data Objects (JDO) specification is a high level Java API that defines a standard way for applications to store Java objects in transactional data stores. It allows users to query their application program logic and conduct queries in Java. Mappings to the database are specified using an implementation-specific mechanism, but the application's Java interface is identical across all implementations. The interface allows developers to use the Java programming language model to model the application domain and transparently store and retrieve data. The JDO does a much better job in terms of transparently accessing enterprise data stores than does the JDBC API. JDO technology appears promising; however, its specification version 1.0 has only been released recently, and major vendor implementations are still at an early stage.

Object / Relational Mapping Tools

Object / relational mapping tools simplify the process of creating relational models from object models. In many cases, this is by providing graphical interfaces that can display a visual representation of the mapping. The code that performs the translation is generated automatically. Some of these tools additionally offer functionality like generating a database schema from the class diagram and even generating class diagrams from the database schema. Tools like Oracle's TopLink and Oracle's Business Component for Java (BC4J) framework fall into this category. However, is it important to note that, in general, these tools have proprietary interfaces and may use patented mapping technology. Applications generated using such tools are not generally portable. The tools may well use JDBC as the interface to the underlying relational database, thus providing a degree of database independence.

FUTURE DIRECTIONS

In this chapter, we have described a step-by-step process for transforming a UML class diagram into an ER diagram, which can be used to make objects persistent. We have also shown the possibility of using the UML notation to draw the ER diagrams. We admit that the chapter does not address all conversion issues. We have concentrated only on the static behavior of the class diagram, and during the process, we have ignored the dynamic aspect of the UML class diagrams. Also, some of the qualifiers such as "Dependency" and "instanceOf" are not addressed in this chapter.

One potential area where further study can be conducted is how to implement the class operations at the database level. Muller has discussed this issue in some detail in his book (Muller, 1999). The work could be enhanced to draw similarities and differences between dynamic aspects of the UML (sequence diagrams, activity diagrams, etc.) and the Structured Systems Analysis and Design Data Flow Diagrams and their other notations.

Another interesting topic for future research could be how to map access information to the ER model level. For example, one can mark the attribute "private / public / protected" at the class model level; however, at the relational database level, all of the columns are public. Class diagrams are also often decomposed into packages (or a hierarchy of packages), whereas this concept does not exist at the relational database level. Mapping access information and other constraints from class diagrams to ER diagrams could also be an interesting topic for further research.

We also briefly discussed programming challenges in making objects persistent. Some of the tools and APIs available in the market to alleviate this problem were also mentioned. A wider comparison of these tools and measurements of their effectiveness could be useful research topics as well.

Finally, formalizing the base of the UML model could also be a very challenging research topic.

CONCLUSION

Making objects persistent is one of the most challenging tasks facing the developer of an object-oriented system today. Although application development using object-oriented methodologies is widespread, the relational database is still the norm for storing the persistent objects. In this chapter, we have tried to bridge the gap between the two methods. We have specified the steps that can be followed to convert the conceptual schema; designed using the UML class diagram notation into a logical schema. Relational database normalization principles can be applied to the logical schema to ensure that the schema is in the intended normal form before converting it into the physical schema. Converting the class diagram into the logical schema is a difficult task. Although both of them share some of the same concepts, their underlying principles can be very different. While the class diagram enjoys success for being more realistic and closer to the user, ER diagrams are based on sound formal notations and design rules such as normalization.

Another purpose of this chapter was to show that the syntax of the class diagram can also be used to draw the ER diagrams. The logical schema represented in this chapter has been drawn using the UML class diagram notation. Based on our experience, we believe that if the syntax of the UML class diagram can be extended, it can also be used as a basis to draw the logical schema. Systems built using object-oriented programming languages and databases like Oracle, and Microsoft® SQL*Server™ as a backend (for example) are ubiquitous. Having two different sets of tools (i.e., one to maintain the schema and another to maintain the use cases, class diagrams, etc.) results in two different sets of documentation that are independent of each other, and that can often be out of sync. UML has the potential to become a standard modeling notation that can be used across applications. However, to achieve this, the underlying syntax and semantics of UML need to be enhanced to incorporate ER diagram notations such as "Primary Key," "Foreign Key," and "Uniqueness."

REFERENCES

Ambler, Scott (2000). Mapping objects to relational databases. On the World Wide Web: http://www.AmbySoft.com

Bahrami, A. (1999). *Object* oriented system design using the Unified Modeling Language. New York: Irwin/McGraw-Hill.

Banerjee, J. (1987). Data model issues for object-oriented applications. *ACM Transactions on Office Information System, 5*(1) (pp. 3-26).

Batini, C., Ceri, S., & Navathe, S. (1992). Conceptual database design: An entity-relationship approach. New York: The Benjamin/Cummings Publishing Company, Inc.

Booch, G., Rumbaugh, J., & Jacobson, I. (1999). The Unified Modeling Language user guide. New York: Addison-Wesley.

Chen, P. (1976). The entity-relationship model – toward a unified view of data. *ACM Transactions on Database Systems, 1*(1) (pp. 9-36).

Chen, P. (1977). The entity-relationship approach to logical data base design. New York: Q.E.D. Information Sciences, Inc.

Date, C. J. (2000). An introduction to database systems. New York: Addison-Wesley.

Dewitz, S. (1995). Systems analysis and design and the transition to objects. New York: McGraw-Hill.

Elmasri, R. & Navathe, S. (1994). Fundamentals of database systems (2nd ed.). New York: The Benjamin/Cummings Publishing, Inc.

Fowler, M. & Scott, K. (2000). UML distilled: A brief guide to the standard object modeling language (2nd ed.). Boston, MA: Addison-Wesley.

Gogolla, M. & Richters, M. (1998). Transformation rules for UML class diagram. *The Unified Modeling Language <<UML>> '98: Beyond the Notation.*

Jones, T. & Song, I. (1995). Binary representation of ternary relationships in ER conceptual modeling. *OOER '95 – Object-Oriented and Entity-Relationship Modeling, 14th International Conference.*

Ling, T. & Teo, P. (1994). A normal form object-oriented entity relationship diagram. *Technical Report, Department of Information Systems and Computer Science, National University of Singapore.*

Maciaszek, L. & Kin-Shing, W. (2000). UML dialect for designing object-relational databases. In *Challenges of Information Technology Management in the 21st Century.* 2000 Information Resources Management Association International Conference, Hershey, PA: Idea Group Publishing (pp. 473-477).

Muller, R. (1999). Database design for smarties – using UML for data modeling. New York: Morgan Kaufman Publishers.

Oestereich, B. (2002). Developing software with UML: Object-oriented analysis and design in practice (2nd ed.). Boston, MA: Addison-Wesley.

Open Fusion (2002). Java data objects: A white paper. On the World Wide Web: http://www.prismtechnologies.com

Ou, Y. (1997). On mapping between UML and entity-relationship model.

Ou, Y. (1998). On using UML class diagrams for object-oriented database design – specification of integrity constraints. *The Unified Modeling Language <<UML>> '98: Beyond the Notation.*

Page-Jones, M. (1988). The practical guide to structured systems design. Englewood Cliffs, NJ: Prentice-Hall.

Pressman, R. (1997). Software engineering – A practitioner's approach. New York: McGraw-Hill.

Rahayu, J., Chang, E., Dillon, T., & Taniar, D. (2001.) Performance evaluation of the object-relational transformation methodology. *Data & Knowledge Engineering*, 38, 3 (pp. 265-3000).

Rational Software White Paper, *Mapping Objects to Data Models with the UML*.

Rumbaugh, J., Blaha, M., Premerlani, W., Eddy, F., & Lorensen, W. (1991). Object-oriented modeling and design. Englewood Cliffs, New Jersey: Prentice Hall.

Rumbaugh, J., Jacobson, I., & Booch, G. (1999). The Unified Modeling Language reference manual. New York: John Wiley & Sons.

Sun Microsystems (2001). Enterprise Java Beans specification, version 2.0. On the World Wide Web: http://www.java.sun.com

Sun Microsystems (2002). Java data objects specification, version 1.0. On the World Wide Web: http://www.java.sun.com

Tong, L., Li, X., & Ma, Y. (2002). Research of object-oriented data management methodology based on relational data model. *Mini-Micro Systems*, 23, 4 (pp. 500-504).

Yourdon, E. (1988). Modern structured analysis. Englewood Cliffs, NJ: Prentice-Hall.

ENDNOTES

[1]   Having said that, there are a few occasions where a corresponding notation does not exist in the UML model, for example, for specifying unique keys.

[2]   Some versions of the ER diagram, including Chen's original notation, (see Chen, 1976; Chen, 1977) does include support for n-ary notation; however, the concept is not supported at the logical schema level, as none of the currently-available relational databases support the concept of n-ary associations at the implementation level.

[3]   Here, our discussion is limited to the class diagrams and the static behavioral part of object modeling.

Chapter XI

Specification and Checking of Dependency Relations between UML Models

Claudia Pons
LIFIA, Universidad Nacional de La Plata, Argentina

Roxana Giandini
LIFIA, Universidad Nacional de La Plata, Argentina

Gabriel Baum
LIFIA, Universidad Nacional de La Plata, Argentina

José Luis Garbi
LIFIA, Universidad Nacional de La Plata, Argentina

Paula Mercado
LIFIA, Universidad Nacional de La Plata, Argentina

ABSTRACT

During the object-oriented software development process, a variety of models of the system is built. All of these models are not independent; they are related to each other. Elements in one model have trace dependencies to other models; they are semantically overlapping and together represent the system as a whole. It is necessary to have a precise definition of the syntax and semantics of the different models and their relationships since the lack of accuracy in definition can lead to wrong model interpretations and inconsistency between models. In this chapter, we classify relationships between models along three different dimensions and propose a formal description of them. The goal of the proposed formalization is to provide formal foundations for tools that perform intelligent analysis on models thereby assisting software engineers throughout the development process. In this direction, we discuss the construction of a tool based on the formalization and support the verification of traces between requirement and analysis models specified in the Unified Modeling Language.

INTRODUCTION

A software development process, e.g., The Unified Process (Jacobson et al., 1999) is a set of activities needed to transform users' requirements into a software system. Modern software development processes are iterative and incremental; they repeat over a series of iterations making up the life cycle of a system. Each iteration takes place over time and consists of one pass through the requirements, analysis, design, implementation, and test activities, to build a number of different artifacts (i.e., models). All of these artifacts are not independent; they are related to each other and they are semantically overlapping. Together they represent the system as a whole. Elements in one artifact have trace dependencies to other artifacts. On the other hand, due to the incremental nature of the process, each iteration results in an increment of artifacts built in previous iterations.

Different relationships existing between models can be organized along the following three dimensions:

- Internal dimension (artifact-dimension).
- Vertical dimension (activity-dimension).
- Horizontal dimension (iteration-dimension).

The *internal dimension* deals with relationships between sub-models that coexist, consistently making up a more complex model. For instance, an analysis model consists of an analysis class diagram, interaction diagrams, and collaboration diagrams. All of the artifacts within a single model are related and must be compatible with each other.

The *vertical dimension* considers relationships between models belonging to the same iteration in different activities (e.g., a design model realizing an analysis model). Two related models represent the same information, but from different abstraction level. They coexist and should be syntactically and semantically compatible with each other.

The *horizontal dimension* considers relationships between artifacts belonging to the same activity in different iterations (e.g., a use case is extended by another use case). In this dimension, new models are built or derived from previous models by adding new information that was not previously considered or by modifying previous information.

Figure 1 illustrates the three dimensions described above. It lists the classical activities (requirements, analysis, design, implementation, and test) in the vertical axis and the sequence of iterations in the horizontal axis.

Relationships between models should be formally defined since the lack of accuracy in their definitions can cause problems, for example:

- Wrong model interpretations and discussion regarding the model, i.e., the interpretation done by the user that reads the model may not coincide with the interpretation of the model's creator.
- Inconsistency among the different models, i.e., if the relationship existing among the different sub-models is not accurately specified, it is not possible to analyze whether its integration is consistent or not.

Figure 1: Dimensions in the software development process

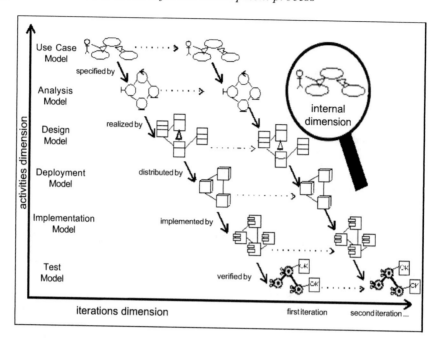

- Evolution conflicts, i.e., when a model is modified, unexpected behavior may occur in other models that depend on it.

At the present, the Unified Modeling Language (UML) is considered the standard modeling language for object-oriented software development processes. The specification (UML, 2001) of UML constructs and their relationships is semi-formal, i.e., certain parts of it are specified with well-defined languages while other parts are described informally in natural language. There is an important number of theoretical works giving a precise description of core concepts of UML and providing rules for analyzing their properties (see for instance, the works of) Evans et al. (1998; 1999), Kim and Carrington (1999), Breu et al. (1997), Knapp (1999), Övergaard (1999; 2000), and Pons and Baum (2000). These works improve the precision of syntax and semantics of isolated UML models without dealing with relationships between models.

In addition, Övergaard and Palmkvist (1998; 2000), Petriu and Sun (2000), Sendall and Strohmeier (2000), Whittle et al. (2000), Egyed (2001), Glinz (2000), Pons et al. (2000), Giandini et al. (2000), and Engels et al. (2001) between others focus on relationships between different UML models. It is useful to explicitly know these relationships. In fact, they help to perform verification activities on systems' models in order to check the correctness and consistency. They are also needed for change control, development process control, and risk control. Clearly, these relationships allow developers to verify if the requirements of one phase are correctly translated to elements in the following phase. It is essential to maintain these relationships from the system requirements to the whole development process to assure that the final product satisfies user needs.

An essential element in a software development process is support offered by case tools. Existing case tools offering support to software processes, facilitate the construction and manipulation of models; but, in general they do not provide checks of consistency between models along either horizontal or vertical dimensions. Tools neither provide automated evolution of models (i.e., propagation of changes when a model evolves to its dependent models). The weakness of tools is mainly due to the lack of a general underlying formal foundation for the software development process (particularly focused on relationships between models).

To overcome this problem, in this chapter we propose a classification of relationships between models along three different dimensions and give a formal description of them. On top of this formal framework, we then describe the construction of a case tool supporting the verification of traces between requirement and analysis UML-models built during the development process.

INTERNAL-DIMENSION RELATIONS

Every model is constructed from a number of related sub-models (or artifacts) that have to be semantically compatible and obey several constraints between them.

The UML specification document (UML, 2001) defines the abstract syntax of UML by class diagrams and well-formedness rules expressed in the Object Constraint Language (OCL) (UML, 2001). Most of the well-formedness rules in that document are examples of constraints on internal-dimension relationships.

For example:

- Well-formedness rule for "ClassifierRole" in (UML, 2001), saying that the features of the "ClassifierRole" must be a subset of the features of the base classifier:

```
∀r:ClassifierRole •(r.allAvailableFeatures ⊆
r.base.allFeatures)
```

- Well-formedness rule for "Association" in (UML, 2001), stating that the connected "Classifiers" of the "AssociationEnds" should be included in the "NameSpace" of the "Association":

```
∀a:AssociationEnds • ∀r∈a.allConnections • (r.type ⊆
a.nameSpace.allContents)
```

After a number of revisions, the UML specification document still contains ambiguities and inconsistencies. We have analyzed internal relationships between models in order to improve their specification. To see examples of improvements in UML and the inconsistencies that we detected, readers are referred to Cibrán et al. (2000).

On the other hand, within the internal-dimension we consider relationships between separated models defining different views of a system (e.g., class diagrams specifying structural aspects and state machines describing behavioral aspects). Although each one of these models has its own self-contained meaning, global compatibility rules among them should be specified. The following ones are examples of compatibility rules; more detailed examples can be read in Pons (1999).

Example 1: Pre/Post Conditions vs. State Machines

Any model element may be associated with a constraint expressing some property of it. There are problems when the constrained element also has a behavior that is precisely defined elsewhere in the model. For example, a constraint on an operation (given as a pre-post condition) may be inconsistent with the specification of the same operation given by an associated state machine. Therefore, it is necessary to integrate both views of the system to guarantee that they are consistent with each other.

Example 2: Generalizations vs. Other Elements

Generalization diagrams have a strong influence on other diagrams in the model of the system.

For example, if two classes, $c1$ and $c2$, are connected by a generalization relationship (e.g., $c1$ is a subclass of $c2$), then the behavior of instances of $c1$ should be a refinement of the behavior of instances of $c1$. This requirement is defined by the following formula:

$$\forall c1,c2:\texttt{Classifier} \bullet$$
$$(\texttt{IsA}(c1,c2)\rightarrow\texttt{refinement}(\texttt{behavior}(c1),\texttt{behavior}(c2)))$$

A similar problem occurs when constraints are linked to classes in a generalization hierarchy (e.g., if $c1$ is a subclass of $c2$ then every constraint on $c1$ should be consistent with every constraint on $c2$). This requirement is expressed by the following formula:

$$\forall c1,c2:\texttt{Classifier}\bullet$$
$$(\texttt{IsA}(c1,c2)\rightarrow\texttt{consistent}(\texttt{constraints}(c1)\cup\texttt{constraints}(c2)))$$

VERTICAL-DIMENSION RELATIONS

In this section, we analyze vertical relations, i.e., relationships between models belonging to the same iteration in different activities. As an example, we describe relationships between the requirement phase and the analysis phase.

Creating Analysis Models from Use Cases

A use case in the use-case model is realized by a "Collaboration" within the analysis model that describes how a use case is realized and performed in terms of analysis classes and their interacting analysis objects. A use case realization has class diagrams that depict its participating analysis classes and interaction diagrams that depict the realization of a particular flow or scenario of the use case in terms of analysis object interactions. Figure 2 shows the relationship between a use case and its realization.

Example: We present the model of a system to maintain a "Library". The members of the library share a collection of books. The system should allow members to borrow books, to return them, or to renovate loans. When returning or when renovating a loan

Figure 2: Use case realization

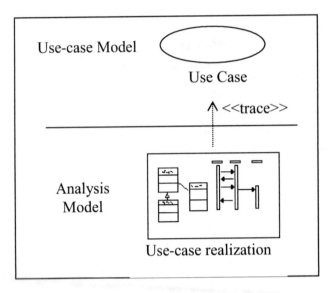

of a book, the member should pay a fee. In the event that this fee is not paid, then the member will not be able to borrow a new book or to renovate a loan. Use case "RenewLoan" specifies the functionality of the system for the renew of a loan.

Use cases can be specified in a number of ways. Generally natural language, structured as a conversation between user and system, is used (see Jacobson et al., 1993; Cockburn, 2001). The conversation shows the request of a user and the corresponding answer of the system at a high level of abstraction. The following paragraph shows a conversation between an actor (a member of the library) and the system. The conversation considers the normal action sequence as well as alternative sequences (e.g., if the book is not available) as follows:

User Actions: 1. User-asks-for-renew-loan.

System Answers: 2. Validate-member-id, 3.validate-book-availability, 4.ask-for-debt, 5.renew-loan.

Alternatives: Member-identification-is-not-valid, then reject-loan. Book-is-not-available, then reject-loan. Member-has-debt, then ask-for-payment, then renew-loan.

In the UML, a use case is a kind of classifier having a collection of operations (with their corresponding methods). Operations describe the messages that instances of the use case can receive. Methods describe the implementation of operations in terms of action sequences that are executed by the instances of the use case. In general, instead of having a set of operations, a use case has only a single operation, for example, the "RenewLoan" use case has a single operation named "ask-for-renew-loan." The method that implements the operation contains the set of action sequences; some of the sequences in this set correspond to normal execution paths, while others correspond to alternative cases.

Let "uc" be the use case defined above. The definition of uc (using the standard UML meta-model (UML, 2001) is as follows:

uc.operations = <op1>
op1.name=ask-for-renew-loan
op1.method.body= {<validate-member-id, validate-book-availability, ask-for-debt, renew-loan>, <validate-member-id, reject -loan>, <validate-member-id, validate-book-availability, reject-loan>, <validate-member-id, validate-book-availability, ask-for-debt, ask-for-payment, renew-loan>}.

In general, we abbreviate "op.method.body" by "op.actionSequence." The body of a method is a procedural expression specifying a possible implementation of an operation. The definition of procedural expressions is out of the scope of UML (here we interpret a procedure expression as a set of action sequences).

Moving forward in the development process, developers build a more detailed model (in general, collaboration diagrams) to provide a realization of the use case model. Figure 3 shows a collaboration model, including a set of classifier roles and their connections, and one of the iteration diagrams specifying the message flows between objects playing the roles in the collaboration. Figure 4 contains the textual representation of the diagrams using the standard UML meta-model. These diagrams are expected to realize the use case above; this fact will be formally proved in next section.

Figure 3: A collaboration realizing the use case

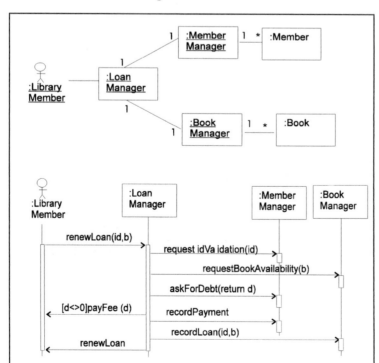

Figure 4: Textual representation of the collaboration

Let RenewLoan be the Use Case defined above, and let CRenewLoan
be the collaboration. The definition of CRenewLoan is as follows:

CRenewLoan.representedClassifier= RenewLoan
CRenewLoan.interaction={int1,int2, int3,int4}
CRenewLoan.classifierRole={R1,R2,R3,R4,R5}
R1.name=LoanManager, R2.name=Book, R3.name=Member,
R4.name=MemberManager, R5.name=BookManager
CRenewLoan.associationRole={A1,A2,A3,...}

....

int1.message={ (*Actor*, LoanManager, renewLoan(id,b)),
(LoanManager, MemberManager, requestIdValidation(id)),
(LoanManager, BookManager, requestBookAvailability(b)),
(LoanManager, MemberManager, askForDebt(d)) ,
(LoanManager, BookManager, renewLoan) }
int2.message={ (*Actor*, LoanManager, renewLoan(id,b)),
(LoanManager, MemberManager, requestIdValidation(id)),
(LoanManager, BookManager, requestBookAvailability(b)), (
LoanManager, MemberManager, askForDebt(d)),
(LoanManager , Actor,payFee(d)), (LoanManager, BookManager,
renewLoan) }

....

Where each message m is represented by a triple
(m.sender,m.receiver,m.action), where m.sender denotes the role of
the instance that invokes the communication, m.receiver is the role of
the instance that receives the communication, m.action is the action
which causes a stimulus to be sent according to the message.

Formalizing the Realization Relationship between Use Cases and Collaborations

We now define a set of concepts that are necessary for formalizing the relationships between use cases and collaborations.

Definition 1: Let (MS,≥) be the "poset" of messages in an interaction (messages are partially ordered by the predecessor/successor relation). The set of linearizations on MS is defined as the set of sequences of messages in MS, and it is denoted as lin(MS).

Definition 2: MaxLin(MS) is the set of maximal linearizations on MS. It is obtained from lin(MS) by dropping every sequence that is contained in another sequence in the set.

Definition 3: Let "S" be a set of sequences of actions. External(S) denotes the sequences of "S" that are obtained by omitting all of the actions that are not visible externally.

Definition 4: A conformance declaration is a correspondence between action names in a use case and action names in a collaboration. Each name in the use case is mapped to (a name of) an action in the collaboration. This mapping provides more flexibility in the development process, allowing analysts to modify the name of the actions as the process evolves.

For example, the following is a conformance declaration between the use case and the collaboration above:

δ: Actions in the UC ————> Actions in the Collaboration
ask-for-renew-loan ————> renewLoan(id,b)
validate-member-id ————> requestIdValidation(id)
validate-book-av. ————> requestBookAvailability(b)
ask-for-debt ————> askForDebt(d)
ask-for-payment ————> payFee(d)
renew-loan ————> renewLoan
reject-loan ————> reject.

At this point we can define the realization relationship between a collaboration "C" and a use case "UC". A use case is realized by a collaboration if the classifiers' roles in the collaboration jointly cooperate to perform the behavior specified by the use case (but not more). In the event that the collaboration includes more behavior than the one specified by the use case, the use case would be only a partial specification of the behavior described by the collaboration. On the other hand, a use case specifies actions that are visible from outside the system; but, does not specify internal actions such as creation and destruction of instances, communication between internal instances, etc. (for example, recordPayment and recordLoan are internal actions).

Definition 5: A collaboration "C" is a realization of a use case "UC" according to the conformance declaration δ, denoted C$\geq_\delta$ UC, if both of the following holds:

a. $\forall$uo$\in$ UC.operation. $\forall$ut$\in$ uo.actionSequence. $\exists$int$\in$ C.interaction. $\exists$ms$\in$ lin(int.message).
     (δ(uo.name)=act.operation.name $\wedge$ δ^+(ut)=external(ms.tail.actions))

b. $\forall$int(C.interaction. $\forall$ms(maxLin(int.message). $\exists$uo$\in$ UC.operation. $\exists$ut$\in$ uo.actionSequence.
     (δ(uo.name)= act.operation.name $\wedge$ δ^+(ut)=external(ms.tail.actions).

where:

act = (ms.head).action,
ms.head is the first element in the sequence ms,
ms.tail is the subsequence obtained from ms by dropping the first element,

ms.actions is an abbreviation for ms.collect (e.action)
$\delta^+(ut)= ut.collect (\delta (a))$.

The definition above states that every action sequence specified by the use case must have a corresponding action sequence in the collaboration, that is equal to it (except for internal actions), and vice versa.

HORIZONTAL-DIMENSION RELATIONS

In this section, we analyze horizontal relations, i.e., relationships between models belonging to the same activity in different iterations.

Evolving the Use-Case Model

A use case model may be evolved in different ways. The UML considers at least two forms of evolution: the "extends" and the generalization relationships between use cases. In this chapter, we only take into consideration the "extends" relationship.

The extends relationship represents the enrichment of a use case by the definition of additional actions (see Figure 5) . An extends relationship from use case "A" to use case "B" indicates that an instance of use case "B" may include (constrained by specific conditions specified in the extension), the behavior specified by "A".

The definition of extends includes both a condition for the extension and a reference to an extension point in the target use case, i.e., a position in the use case where additions may be made. Once an instance of a (target) use case reaches an extension point to which an extends relationship is referring, the condition of the relationship is evaluated. If the condition is fulfilled, the sequence obeyed by the use case instance is extended to include the sequence of the extending use case.

Example

The use case "RenewLoan" can be extended in order to count how many people have renovated loans of a technical book. This extension can be achieved without modifying the original use case by means of an extends relationship and a new use case specifying the increment of behavior. Figure 5 shows this relationship between use

Figure 5: Relationship between a use case in the use case model and its extension

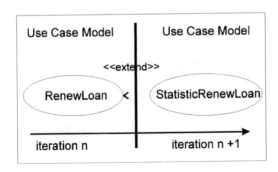

cases. In this case, the extension point specified by the extends relationships is the action of "renewing-a-loan". The condition of the extension is that the book is a technical one.

Let "Statistic" be the use case mentioned above, specifying the increment of behavior. "Statistic" has a single operation with a single action sequence, as follows:

Statistic.operation.actionSequence= {<updateRenewsCounter>}.

The extends relationship *ext* is as follows:

ext.base=RenewLoan
ext.extension=Statistic
ext.condition= the book is technical
ext.extensionPoint= { renew-loan }.

Let "StatisticRenewLoan" be the use case that developers expect to obtain from "RenewLoan" by the application of the extension above, i.e.:

StatisticRenewLoan = RenewLoan $\oplus_{ext}$ Statistic.

Operation $\oplus_{ext}$ between use cases is formally defined in next section. Textual representation of the expected use case is as follows:

StatisticRenewLoan.operation.actionSequence=
{< validate-member-id, validate-book-availability, ask-for-debt, renew-loan, updateRenewsCounter>, < validate-member-id, reject-loan>, < validate-member-id, validate-book-availability, reject-loan>, < validate-member-id, validate-book-availability, ask-for-debt, ask-for-payment, renew-loan , updateRenewsCounter >}.

Formalizing Use Case Extensions

A use case "UC" is the extension of UC1 by UC2 through an "extends" relationship *ext*, i.e., UC = UC1 $\oplus_{ext}$ UC2 if the following holds:

a.   **Applicability Conditions:** UC1 is extensible by *ext* if for each extension point of *ext*, there exists a corresponding action inside the sequences of actions of the use case:

$\forall i \in$ ext.extensionPoint$\bullet$ $\exists uo \in$ UC1.operation $\bullet$ $\exists uot \in$ uo.actionSequence $\bullet$ i.location$\in$ uot.

b.   **UC1-Completeness:** Every action sequence in UC1 is extended in every possible way:

$\forall o1 \in$ UC1.operation$\bullet$$\exists o \in$ UC.operation$\bullet$(o.name=o1.name $\wedge$ ($\forall s1 \in$ o1.actionSequence$\bullet$extensions(s1,ext,UC2) $\subseteq$ o.actionSequence)).

c.   **UC1-Correctness:** Every action sequence in UC is an extension of some action sequence in UC1.

$\forall o \in$ UC.operation $\bullet \exists o1 \in$ UC1.operation $\bullet$ (o.name=o1.name $\land$ ($\forall s \in$ o. actionSequence $\bullet \exists s1 \in$ o1.actionSequence $\bullet$ s $\in$ extensions (s1,ext,UC2))).

Definition 6: (Function definitions)
isExtensible: ActionSequence x Extend.
    The predicate is true if the action sequence contains some extension point defined by the extends relationship.

$\forall$s:ActionSequence $\bullet \forall$ext:Extend $\bullet$ isExtensible(s,ext) $\leftrightarrow \exists$ i $\in$ *ext*.extension Point $\bullet$ i.location $\in$ s.

extensions: ActionSequence x Extend x UseCase -> Set(ActionSequence).
    The function *extensions*(s,ext,uc) returns the set of all possible extensions of the sequence "s" given by the extends relation "*ext*" and the use case "uc". The function is defined by cases as follows:

Case 1: if $\neg$isExtensible(s,ext) then *extensions*(s,ext,uc)={s}
Case 2: if isExtensible(s,ext) then
extensions(s,ext,uc)= {before(s,i.location);s2;after(s,i.location) / i $\in$ ext.extension Point
    $\land$ i.location $\in$ s $\land$ s2 $\in$ uc.actionSequence }.

Definition 7: UC extends UC1 if there exists a use case UC2 such that UC is the extension of UC1 by UC2 through an "*ext*" relation:

UC extends$_{ext}$UC1 $\leftrightarrow \exists$UC2 $\bullet$ (UC=UC1 $\oplus_{ext}$ UC2).

Evolving the Collaboration Model

    The UML does not consider special dependency relationships between the collaboration. However, since collaborations realize use cases, it is important to reflect the relationships between use cases (i.e., extends relationships) on its realizing collaborations. As well as use cases being extended by adding actions (defined in other use case), collaborations can be extended with additional message sequences specified in another collaboration.
    For further details about the relationship between collaborations, based on the corresponding relationship between use cases, readers are referred to Perez et al. (2002).

TOOL SUPPORT: THE DEPENDENCY RELATIONS CHECKER

    Tracing elements between different models is not an easy task. An essential element to perform this activity is the support offered by case tools. In particular, it is useful to deal with formal mechanisms that contribute to a precise and rigorous verification of the relationship.

For this, we built a tool named DRC (Dependency Relations Checker). DRC verifies the relationship between the elements in the use case model and the analysis model. The DRC is based on the formal foundation for dependency relationships.

The main idea of the DRC is to provide a friendly approach to formal verification of the dependency relationships that exist between different UML models.

In particular, the current version of DRC is focused on verifying if a given use case realization actually corresponds to a specific use case diagram. In other words, DRC verifies if a use case realization represents the behavior established by a use case diagram.

DRC takes place in the early phases of the development process (between the requirements phase and the analysis phase). It helps developers to verify consistency among the two phases and has the benefit of the formal background.

The Main Components of the Dependency Relations Checker

DRC does not provide a complete environment for the specification of models. This functionality is provided by the support of case tools, like Rational Rose. Our tool can be extended to allow the construction of UML models. However, the current approach provides a flexible working mechanism and allows for an easy insertion of our tool in the development process because it deals with Rational Rose, which is a highly-accepted industry tool.

Clearly, we have two distinguished layers: the specification layer given by Rational Rose, which represents the DRC input, and the verification layer, which performs

Figure 6: Architecture of the tool

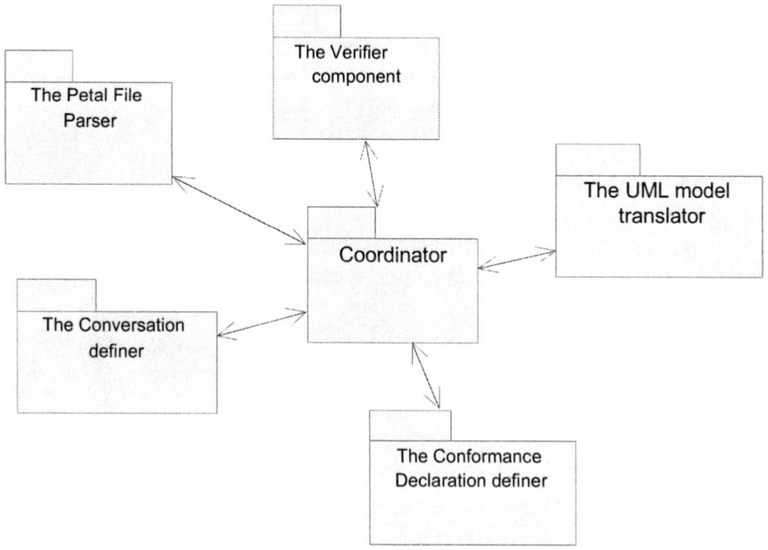

checking activities that generate the final result. In the next section, we concentrate on the verification layer.

This section describes the main components of the verification layer. DRC was thought of as a set of entities that inter-collaborate to perform the global task. Figure 6 shows this relationship.

The components are namely: the Petal File parser, the UML model translator, the conversation definer, the conformance declaration definer, and the verifier component. All of these modules are coordinated by a "coordinator" component and are implemented in the Cincom Smalltalk™ environment VisualWorks®, version 3.0.

The role of each component of the DRC is described below.

The Petal File Parser

The Dependency Relations Checker takes the UML models that have been defined with Rational Rose/C++, version 4.0.3. In order to create an internal representation of the UML model that the "Verifier" component understands, the "Petal File Parser" component parses the content of the files generated by the Rational Rose (MDL files) and generates a collection of objects that represent it.

The UML Model Translator

Once the Petal File Parser has translated the file to an object collection, it is taken by the UML model's translator component. This component translates the object representation of the petal file to a simplified instance of the UML meta-model that represents the models that have been generated in the requirement and analysis phases.

This component also has the responsibility of noticing any inconsistency among the diagrams' definitions, for example, the absence of a diagram and/or its wrong construction, and errors in the "Conversation" or "Conformance Declaration" syntax, among others.

The definition of these translation components gives great flexibility to the design of the tool. It simplifies the task of extending the DRC to support different kinds of file formats provided by the great quantity of case tools used to specify models. On the other hand, it allows for removal and substitution of these components by better ones that perform the same task faster or more precisely.

The Conversation Definer

The definition of a "Conversation" is part of the construction of a use case diagram. This task can be performed in both Rational Rose and the Dependency Relation Checker. In Rational Rose, this is achieved attaching a "Note" to the use case diagram, where you must manually write the "Conversation" using the given syntax. The DRC also provides a graphical interface that allows for creation of a conversation for a given model. Figure 7 shows the interface used to define a conversation. Defining the conversation with the tool provides a flexible working mechanism within the model.

The Conformance Declaration Definer

The conformance declaration establishes the correspondence between the actions in the use case and the actions in the collaboration. Like the conversation, the conformance declaration can be defined in Rational Rose using a "Note" and the given syntax; or, it can be created with the conformance declaration definer made available in the tool.

The main idea of providing different ways of defining a conversation and a conformance declaration is to provide users greater flexibility.

In general, conversations are informally written during the definition of a use case diagram. UML does not provide a rigorous syntax for it. In order to develop the tool, we define a precise syntax for a conversation and provide a graphical interface for defining conversations. Developers can choose to use either the given syntax or the conversation definer.

The Verifier Component

The verifier component takes as its input, the UML model translated by the UML model translator. It also takes the conversation and conformance declaration. The verifier component performs the verification task of determining if a set of analysis diagrams are the realization of a use case diagram. This module applies the mathematical formulas mentioned above on the UML model and informs the user of its conclusions.

It is important to say that the model can be easily extended to support different verifier components that perform other checking using the same model. In this way, we can consider the tool as being an initial schema that allows for different kinds of verification over UML models.

Figure 7: The conversation definer

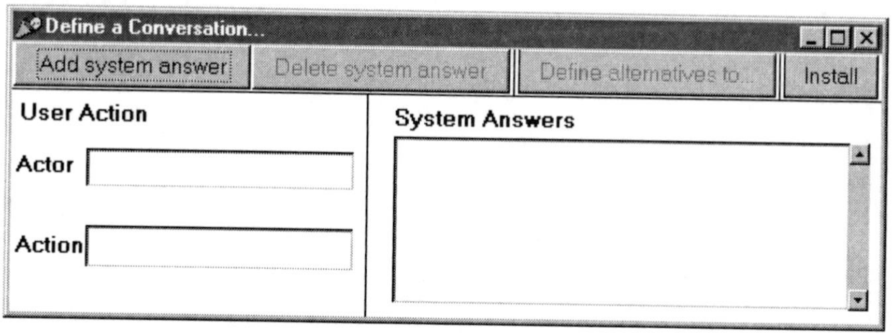

CONCLUSION

Relationships between software models should be formally defined since the lack of accuracy in their definition can lead to wrong model interpretations, inconsistency among models, inconsistent evolution of models, etc. In this chapter, we classify relationships between models along three different dimensions (i.e., artifact dimension, activity dimension, and iteration dimension) and propose a formal description of them.

The goal of the proposed formalization is to provide formal foundations for tools that perform intelligent operation on models, such as:

- Checking the consistency between models belonging to different activities, such as a requirements model and an analysis model (i.e., consistency along the activity dimension).

- Checking the consistency of models through its evolution along the process (i.e., consistency along the iteration dimension).
- Checking the internal consistency of models (i.e., consistency along the artifact dimension).
- Checking the consistency of the process as a whole (i.e., consistency among the different dimensions).

As an example applied formalization, we have described the main components of the Dependency Relations Checker (DRC), which is a case tool giving support to verifying traces between the use case and analysis models. This tool is very open, due to the clear separation between its modules. This approach allows for easy extends or changes of its characteristics. This kind of tools represents an advance over the present state of the practice for project management.

A step beyond this work will be to use this formalization to define automatic rules of evolution to assist the software engineer during the development process. For example, given an analysis model, the rules could suggest possible forms of realizing such a model in terms of design models. Additionally, given a model, the rules could suggest possible ways to refine or extend it.

REFERENCES

Breu, R., Hinkel, U., Hofmann, C., Klein, C., Paech, B., Rumpe, B., and Thurner, V. (1997). Towards a formalization of the unified modeling language. *ECOOP'97 procs., Lecture Notes in Computer Science, vol.1241.*

Cibrán, M., Mola, V., Pons, C., & Russo, W. (2000). Building a bridge between the syntax and semantics of UML collaborations. *In ECOOP'2000 Workshop on Defining Precise Semantics for UML*. France.

Cockburn, A. (2001). Writing effective use cases. Addison-Wesley.

Egyed, A. (2001). Scalable consistency checking between diagrams – The VIEWINTEGRA approach. *Proceedings of the 16th IEEE International Conference on Automated Software Engineering (ASE)*. San Diego, CA.

Engels G., Kuster J., Heckel R., & Groenewegen, L. (2001). A methodology for specifying and analyzing consistency of object oriented behavioral models. *Proceedings of the IEEE International Conference on Foundation of Software Engineering*. Vienna.

Evans, A., France, R., Lano, K., & Rumpe, B. (1998). *Developing the UML as a formal modeling notation. UML'98 Conference, Lecture Notes in Computer Science 1618.* Springer-Verlag.

Evans, A., France, R., Lano, K., & Rumpe, B. (1999). Towards a core metamodelling semantics of UML, Behavioral specifications of businesses and systems. Kluwer Academic Publishers.

Giandini, R., Pons, C., & Baum, G. (2000). An algebra for use cases in the Unified Modeling Language. *OOPSLA'00 Workshop on Behavioral Semantics*. Minneapolis, MN.

Glinz, M. (2000). A lightweight approach to consistency of scenarios and class models. *Proceedings of the Fourth International Conference on Requirements Engineering*. Schaumburg, Illinois.

Jacobson, I., Booch, G., & Rumbaugh, J. (1999). The unified software development process. Addison-Wesley.

Jacobson, I., Christerson, M., Jonsson, P., & Övergaard, G. (1993). Object-oriented software engineering: A use case driven approach. Addison-Wesley.

Kim, S. & Carrington, D. (1999). Formalizing the UML class diagrams using object-Z. *Proceedings UML '99 Conference, Lecture Notes in Computer Science 1723*.

Knapp, A. (1999). A formal semantics for UML interactions. *Proceedings of the UML '99 Conference, Colorado. Lecture Notes in Computer Science 1723*. Springer.

Övergaard, G. (1999). A formal approach to collaborations in the UML. *In UML '99 Conference, Colorado. Lecture Notes in Computer Science 1723*. Springer.

Övergaard, G. (2000). Using the boom framework for formal specification of the UML. *In Proc. ECOOP Workshop on Defining Precise Semantics for UML*. France.

Övergaard, G., & Palmkvist, K. (1998). A formal approach to use cases and their relationships. *In UML '98 Conference, Lecture Notes in Computer Science 1618*. Springer-Verlag.

Overgaard, G. & Palmkvist, K. (2000). Interacting subsystems in UML. *Proc. of the Third International Conference on the UML. LNCS*.

Perez, G., Giandini, R., & Pons, C. (2002). Model refinements in the object oriented software development process. *Argentinean Symposium on Software Engineering ASSE'2002*. Santa Fe, Argentina.

Petriu, D. & Sun, Y. (2000). Consistent behaviour representation in activity and sequence diagrams. *Proc. of the Third International Conference on the UML. LNCS*.

Pons, C. (1999). A dynamic logic theory as a formal foundation of the model-based software development process. *Thesis*, Faculty of Science, University of La Plata, Buenos Aires, Argentina.

Pons, C. & Baum, G. (2000). Formal foundations of object-oriented modeling notations. *3rd International Conference on Formal Engineering Methods, ICFEM 2000*. IEEE Computer Society Press.

Pons, C., Giandini, R., & Baum, G. (2000). Specifying relationships between models through the software development process. *10th International Workshop on Software Specification and Design, USA*. IEEE Computer Society Press.

Sendall, S. & Strohmeier, A. (2000). From use cases to system operation specifications. *Proc. of the Third International Conference on the UML, UK*. LNCS.

Unified Modeling Language (UML) Specification (2001). Version 1.3, September 2001, UML Specification, revised by the OMG on the World Wide Web: http://www.omg.org

Whittle, J., Araújo, J., Toval, A., & Fernandez Alemán, J. (2000). Rigorously automating transformations of UML behavioral models. *UML '00 Workshop on Semantics of Behavioral Models*. UK.

Chapter XII

Info-Mathics –
The Mathematical Modeling
of Information Systems

Andrew S. Targowski
Western Michigan University, USA

ABSTRACT

This chapter reviews Information Systems (IS) modeling techniques, including relational algebra, structured design, architectural design, and Unified Modeling Language. A new technique "info-mathics" (i.e.,mathematical description of the hierarchical systems architecture) is defined to secure the system reliability and quality. The classification of IS categories and its attributes such as components, structure, relationships, system level, system product, system deepness, system width, system list, system end, and other are presented. Examples of the mathematical notations are provided and their meaning for the practical implications of info-mathics in system analysis and design are indicated.

INTRODUCTION

The design of IS evolves from the art towards engineering as systems evolve from simple to more complex. The introduction of relational databases triggered the application of relational algebra (Merrett, 1984). Its application is limited to the database design. The structured design of systems, introduced in the 1980s, was a step forward after structured programming was offered in the 1970s (Kowal, 1988). However, this approach is applied mostly at the very low system level of data flow diagrams and, is used mostly in file updating or transaction processing. The architectural system design was a step beyond Data Flow Diagrams (DFD) and aimed at the large scale-system (Targowski 1990).

BACKGROUND

The recent trend in system design emphasizes a technique called Unified Modeling Language (UML) (Siau & Halpin 2001). It is aimed at the design of object-oriented software at the level of programming. To design higher-level application systems it is necessary to apply similar techniques as have been applied in mechanical or civil engineering, where the main product solution is based on a Bill of Material Processor (BOMP). BOMP lists product components and indicates their assembling sequences (Pawlak, 1969). This study presents a mathematical modeling of application information systems leading to the development of a Bill of Systems Processor (BOSP). This is a step for transforming the art of system design into information engineering.

GRAPHIC MODEL OF A HIERARCHICAL INFORMATION SYSTEM

As an example of an information system, we will analyze an Hierarchical Management Information System (MIS) which is composed of only three systems:
- Enterprise Information Portal (EIP).
- Enterprise Performance Management (EPM).
- Data Mining System (DMS).

at the following management levels (Figure 1):
- The headquarters level (ex.: General Motors Corporation):

  $HMIS^c = \{(EIP^C, EPM^C, DMS^C), R^C\}$
  Where R – structure of relationships among systems

- The group level (ex.: Buick-Oldsmobile-Cadillac):

  $GMIS^G = \{(EIP^G, EPM^G, DMS^c), R^G\}$

- The plant level (ex.: Cadillac):

  $PMIS^P = \{(EIP^P, EPM^P), R^P\}$

In the current IS practice, the graphic modeling (also called the architectural planning), is the only technique applied. However, in more complex IT environments this technique is limited. Graphical modeling in sciences is a superior technique versus the scenario technique, but is an inferior technique to mathematical modeling.
We attempt generalizing an IS definition by applying the mathematical technique.

MATHEMATICAL MODELING OF A HIERARCHICAL INFORMATION SYSTEM

A generalized model of a hierarchical information system is shown in Figure 2. We introduce a relation $B \subset R$, which we will call the direct relationship of a component of a given IS. We say that SI(x) is the direct component of SI(y) if:

1. SI(x) is a component of SI(y), which means that SI(x) and SI(y) are in the relation B, and it is noted as:

    $$B\{SI(x), SI(y)\},$$

2. There is no such SI(z), belonging to the set $U\{SI(z) \in U\}$, which is the component SI(y), [SI(z) and SI(y) are not in the relation B] and whose component is SI(x) [SI(x), and SI(z) are not in the relation B].

Figure 1: A hierarchical management information system

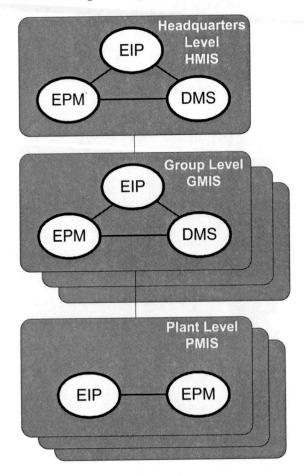

If the set of SI(x) is the direct component of the set SI(y), then we will note it as SI(x) = β{SI(y)}.

The B relation will be called the schema of a system, which can be illustrated in a diagram where circles represent subsystems (Figure 2).

If B{S(x), SI(y)}, then the circles representing subsystems x and y will be linked by a line from x to y. In such a manner, for each system, one can subordinate a tree as shown in Figure 3. This tree is a graph of all B relations. The system schema means the same as "to be a direct component."

Systems x and y will be called the same (equivalent) if their schema are equal, which means that they have the same components and linked by the same relationships.

With every system SI(x), we associate a number l {(SI(x)} (called a **system level**) in the following manner:

1.   If SI(x) is the end subsystem, then l {SI(x)} = 0.
2.   If B{SI(x), SI(y)}, then l {SI(x)} = l {SI(y)} + 1.

Figure 2 illustrates a level of each system. A level of SI is nothing more than a story in which there is a given subsystem in the system schema.

To each system SI(x), we will attribute a number χ {SI(x)} (called a **system product**), as noted in the following manner:

$$\chi \{SI(x)\} = \overline{\beta} \{SI(x)\}$$

where: $\overline{\beta}$ {SI(x)} is the number of components of a set β {SI(x)}, which is the direct components of system SI(x).

A system product is the number of direct components.

A **system depth** of SI(x) is the maximal level of its subsystems. This has been noted as ¡ {SI(x)}. A system depth is the number of system levels, reduced by one.

A **system width** of SI(x) is the maximal number of subsystems of the same system level, which will be noted as d{SI(x)}.

Figure 2: The levels of a hierarchical information system (I=0, I=1, I=2, I=3)

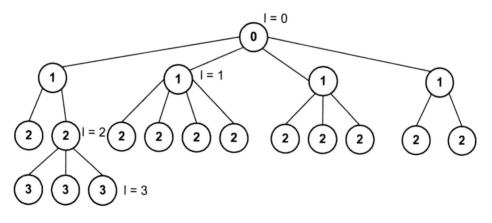

BILL OF SYSTEMS PROCESSOR (BOSP)

Following a concept of BOMP (Bill of Material Processor), we introduce a concept of BOSP, which is a list of a system's components. Different components should have different names and the same components should have the same names is the condition of defining a BOSP.

1.   If $SI(x)$ is a system then $\overline{SI}(x)$ is a name of this system and λ is the number of subsystems of $SI(x)$.
2.   If $SI(x)$ is the simple system, then $\lambda\, SI(x) = SI(x)$.
3.   If $SI(y)$ and $SI(x_1),\ldots.SI(x_k)$ are such systems that:

$$\beta\,\{SI(y) = \{SI(x_1),\ldots.SI(x_k)\},\text{ then } \lambda\,SI(y) = \overline{SI}(y)\,\{lSI(x_1),\ldots SI(x_k)\}.$$

This notation means that a BOSP of a simple system is composed of a system name and BOSP; a complex system is composed of a system name and direct components. We will now consider SI with a name CIS as shown in Figure 1. For this system:

$$\beta\,(HMIS) = \{\,EIP^c,\,EPM^c,\,DMS^c\}$$
$$\beta\,(GMIS) = \{\,EIP^G,\,EPM^G,\,DMS^G\}$$
$$\beta\,(PMIS) = \{\,EIP^P,\,EPM^P\,\}.$$

According to the provider definition, a BOSP of this system will have the following notation:

$$\mathbf{HMIS}\,[EIP^c,\,EPM^c,\,DMS^c,\,\mathbf{GMIS}\{EIP^G,\,EPM^G,\,DMS^G,\,\mathbf{PMIS}(EIP^P,\,EPM^P)\}].$$

A BOSP has been created in such a manner, which satisfies the above requirements. In this list, all subsystems appear. It is easy to recognize subsystems coming up to the upper system.

If the parentheses are eliminated and the number of components are noted in a subscript, then one can define a BOSP in the following manner:

$$\mathbf{HMIS}_3\,EIP^c_0\,EPM^c_0\,DMS^c_0\,\mathbf{GMIS}_3\,EIP^G_0\,EPM^G_0\,DMS^G_0\,\mathbf{PMIS}_2\,EIP^P_0\,EPM^P_0.$$

The PMIS' subsystems have only names because they do not have components. Very often it is necessary to find out what components belong directly to the upper system. Then the notation can be as follows:

$$\mathbf{HMIS}_3\,EIP^c_0\,EPM^c_0\,DMS^c_0\,\mathbf{GMIS}_3$$
$$EIP^c_0$$
$$EPM^c_0$$
$$DMS^c_0$$
$$\mathbf{GMIS}_3\,EIP^G_0\,EPM^G_0\,DMS^G_0\,\mathbf{PMIS}_2$$
$$EIP^G_0$$
$$EPM^G_0$$
$$DMS^G_0$$

Figure 3: A tree of a corporate information system

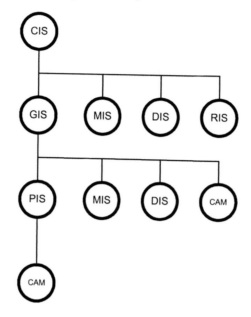

PMIS$_2$ EIP$^P_0$ EPM$^P_0$
EIP$^P_0$
EPM$^P_0$.

In the notation provided, left column determents (i.e., the notation without paren-thesis and components in a row) are direct components.

We now define a BOSP for an example in Figure 3 where:

CIS – Corporate Information Systems
GIS – Group Information System
MIS – Management Information System
DIS – Dealers Information System
RIS – Retail Information System

CIS$_4$ GIS$_4$ MIS$_0$, DIS$_0$, RIS$_0$
MIS$_0$
DIS$_0$
RIS$_0$
GIS$_4$ MIS$_0$, DIS$_0$, RIS$_0$
MIS$_0$
DIS$_0$
RIS$_0$
PIS$_1$ MIS$_0$, DIS$_0$, CAM$_0$
CAM$_0$.

The left column contains 10 subsystems, as much as it is shown in Figure 3. Applying the previously defined attributes, one can characterize the CIS as follows:

- System Level: $1(CIM)=0, 1(GIS)=1, 1(PIS)=2, 1(CAM)=3$
- System Product: $\overline{\beta}(CIM)=4, \overline{\beta}(GIS)=4, \overline{\beta}(PIS)=1, \overline{\beta}(CAM)=0$
- System Depth: $\Upsilon(CIM)=3, \Upsilon(GIS)=2, \Upsilon(PIS)=1, \Upsilon(CAM)=0$
- System Width: $\delta(CIM)=4$
- End System = CIM (it does not belong to the upper system)
- Simple System = CAM (cannot be divided into subsystems).

Figure 4 illustrates a generalized BOSP for the federated architecture of enterprise-wide systems (Targowski, 1990).

Figure 4: Bill of systems processor (BOSP)

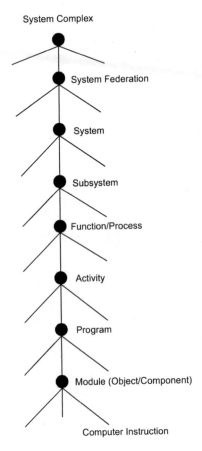

CONCLUSION

The presented theory argues that the info-mathic technique of designing large-scale application systems should introduce more order into the sets of enterprise information systems because it is similar to other engineering techniques applied in well developed industries (e.g., such as the motor or machine-tool industries).

REFERENCES

Kowal, J. A. (1988). Analyzing systems. Englewood Cliffs, NJ: Prentice Hall.

Merret, T. H. (1984). Relational information systems. Reston, VI: Reston Publishing Co.

Pawlak, Z. (1969). Matematyczne aspekty procesu produkcyjnego. Warsaw: PWN.

Siau, K. and T. Halpin (2001). Unified Modeling Language. Hershey, PA: Idea Group Publishing.

Targowski, A. (1990). The architecture and planning of enterprise-wide information management systems. Hershey, PA: Idea Group Publishing.

Chapter XIII

Use of UML Stereotypes in Business Models

Daniel Brandon, Jr.
Christian Brothers University, USA

ABSTRACT

This chapter presents some particularly useful UML stereotypes for use in business systems. Stereotypes are the core extension mechanism of UML. If you find that you need a modeling element or information extension to an element that is not in UML but it is similar to something that is, you treat your addition/extension as a stereotype. These new stereotypes are defined and the need for them is discussed. The stereotypes aid in both the design/drawing phase and in the implementation (coding) phase of the overall system construction. An example case study illustrates their usage with both design drawings and the implementation code (C++).

INTRODUCTION

The UML (Unified Modeling Language) has become a standard in software design of object-oriented computer systems. UML provides for the use of stereotypes to extend the utility of its base capabilities. In the design and construction of business systems, we have found some particularly useful stereotypes, which are defined and illustrated in this chapter.

BACKGROUND

"Stereotypes are the core extension mechanism of UML. If you find that you need a modeling construct that isn't in the UML but it is similar to something that is, you treat your construct as a stereotype" (Fowler, 2000). The stereotype is a semantic added to an existing model element and when diagrammed, it consists of the stereotype name inside of guillemots (a.k.a. chevrons) within the selected model's element. The guillemot

Figure 1

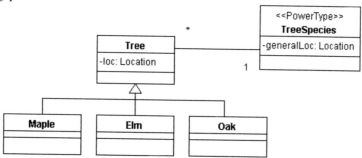

looks like a double angle bracket (<< ... >>), but it is a single character in extended font libraries (Brown, 2002). The UML defines about 40 of these stereotypes such as "<<becomes>>," "<<include>>," and "<<signal>>" (Scott, 2001). However, these 40 standard stereotypes do not add the necessary meaning for automatic code generation in a UML case tool.

One common, general use of the stereotype is for a meta-class. A meta-class is a class whose instances are classes; these are typically used in systems in which the developer needs to declare classes at run time (Eriksson, 1998). A similar general use is for powertypes. A powertype is an object type (class) whose instances are sub-types of another object type. Figure 1 shows an example of the use of stereotypes for powertypes (Martin, 1998).

USER-DEFINED STEREOTYPES FOR BUSINESS SYSTEMS

In the design of business systems, we have found some stereotypes that were useful, and two stereotypes that were extremely useful. When defining stereotypes, it is necessary to describe (Eriksson, 1998):
1. On which [UML] element the user-defined stereotype should be based.
2. The new semantics the stereotype adds or refines.
3. One or more examples of how to implement the user-defined stereotype.

A common use of stereotypes in business systems is for interfaces as found in Java or CORBA; this is shown in Figure 2. An interface typically has public functionality but not data (unless holding data for global constants). The class model element has been modified with the "<<interface>>" notation. This is commonly used for UML case products that do not have separate interface symbols or where these symbols do not allow data (i.e., global constants).

Still another common use of a stereotype in business systems is to clarify or extend a relationship. Figure 3 shows a stereotype called "history" which implies a "many" cardinality for history purposes, i.e., each person has zero or one current employer(s), but may have many employers in terms of the employee's history. It may imply some common functionality upon code generation such as (Fowler, 2000):

Company Employee::getCompany(Date);

Figure 2

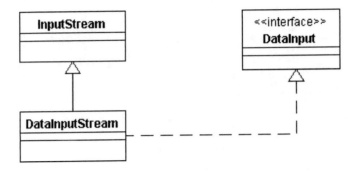

Figure 3

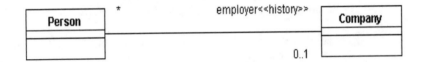

CODE WRITING AND GENERATION

Most modern UML case (computer aided software engineering) products can generate "skeleton" classes from the UML class diagrams and possibly other diagrams. For business systems design, we need to write the code for our classes (usually implemented in Java or C++) based on both the structural model (UML class diagram) and the dynamic model (UML activity diagram). This process is shown in Figure 4. It is very important that consistency between the two diagrams is achieved.

Figure 4

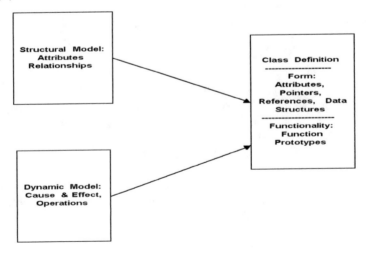

Many such case products allow the user to write his or her own "class generation scripts" in some proprietary scripting language or in a general scripting language (i.e., Python). With user-defined stereotypes, the user can modify the class generation script code to use his or her stereotypes as needed.

RELATIONSHIP OBJECT TYPES

Often simple relationships (such as basic associations) need to be modeled as object types because these relationships have data content and/or functionality. Figure 5 shows a simple association between two object types representing the relationship "current marriage." If we need to maintain an attribute on each marriage (such as rating), then we can more effectively represent the relationship as an object type as shown in Figure 6. Here we use the "relationship" stereotype to indicate that this object type is a relationship and the code generation can use a simpler class representation. Others authors have suggested other notation for relationship object types such as "placeholders" (Martin, 1998) and UML suggests using the dotted line from a standard object type (class) to the relationship line. But implementing these other diagramming techniques in code generation is difficult and has ambiguity problems.

Figure 5

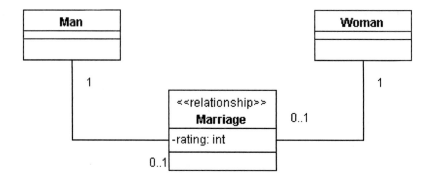

Figure 6

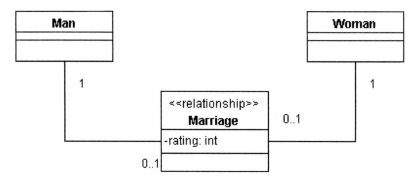

ACTIVITY DIAGRAMS

A UML activity diagram is a state diagram in which most of the states are action states and most of the transitions are triggered by the completion of these action states. This is the case in most models of business systems. Activity diagrams identify action states, which we call operations (Martin, 1998) and the cause and effect between operations. Each operation needs to belong to an object type, at least for a C++ or Java implementation. Operations may be nested, and at some point in the design, the operations need to be defined in terms of methods. The methods are the processing specifications for an operation and can be so specified in lower-lever activity diagrams, pseudo code, or language-specific code. Note that the term "methods" may cause some confusion here since in programming terminology, a method is a function defined within a class and it is invoked upon an object (unless it is a static method). At the lowest level of the design, these methods either read or change the state of an object. "Changing the state of an object" involves object creation, object destruction, changing the values of attributes, or changing relations to other objects (Martin, 1998).

Current Drawing Methodology

Figure 7 shows a typical UML activity diagram for a simple ordering process. The operations are represented in the ovals and the arrows show the cause and effect scenarios or the "triggers." In this diagram, there are two "fork/join" model elements, and the use of "conditional branch states" is also common. Each of the operations must be associated with a particular object type. The standard way to do that in this UML type diagram is to use "swimlanes." Swimlanes are the vertical lines shown in Figure 7.

Figure 7

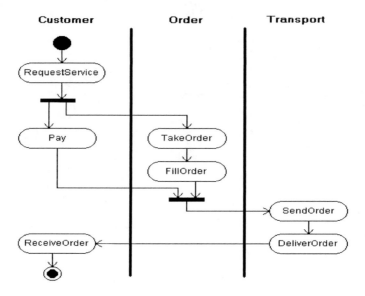

There are two problems with the standard representation as shown in Figure 7. The first problem is that as the system becomes more complex (more object types and operations), it is very difficult to draw in swimlanes. The second problem is that code generation is very difficult in UML case products since you have to scan the geometry of the drawing to find out which operations lay in which swimlanes, instead of simply reading the data file of the items in the drawing.

Stereotype Usage for Operations

Our solution to the above problems with standard UML activity diagrams is to use a stereotype for the operations element to indicate the object type (class) that owns that operation. Figure 8 shows the same systems as Figure 7, which is drawn with the "operation owner" stereotype.

Figure 8

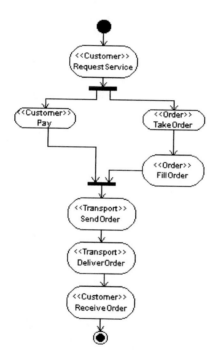

Model Consistency

A final business system design will involve several UML diagram types. For example, business systems typically have a static structural diagram (class diagram) and a dynamic diagram (UML activity diagram). These diagrams must be consistent with one another, in particular:

1. The object types (shown with the operation stereotyped notation) that contain the operations in the activity diagram must be included on the structural diagram.
2. The operations shown in the activity diagram (along with the object types identified with the stereotyped notation) must be included as operations in the same object type on the structural diagram.

EXAMPLE USAGE

This section describes an example of the use of our "operation owner" stereotype on a simple problem. The UML case product used was Object Domain (version 2.5) [Object Domain] and the example was implemented in C++.

Design

The business system being modeled is the process of registering students for classes. In this simple model, we have just two object types: student and class. The static structure diagram (UML class diagram) is shown in Figure 9. Figure 10 shows the activity diagram for the registration process, which is an operation in the student object type). Figure 11 is the breakdown of that registration operation into other operations, again using our "operation owner" stereotypes.

Figure 9

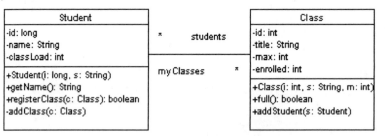

Figure 10

To express the processing specifications of each operation (the "methods"), we can use pseudo code, specific language code, or lower-level activity diagrams. Figures 12 and 13 show processing specifications represented in activity diagrams. Here our "operation owner" stereotyped notation uses the object type name and operation name (i.e., Class::addStudent) since the information within the oval is a process description and not an operation name. At code generation, the information within these ovals is just added to the code for the operation as a comment (i.e., //add student to class list).

Figure 11

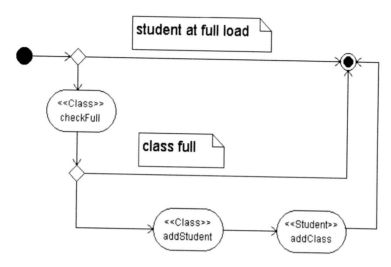

Figure 12

Figure 13

Implementation

An implementation of these diagrams (in C++) is shown in Figures 14 through 17. Figure 14 shows the class definitions. Figure 15 shows the implementation of the operations (C++ functions) of the student class. Figure 16 shows the implementation of the operations (C++ functions) of the class. Figure 17 is a sample "driver" or C++ main function.

Figure 14

```
#include <iostream.h>
#include <string.h>

#define MAXSTUD 25
#define MAXCLASS 5

enum boolean {FALSE, TRUE};
class Class;

class Student
{
  private:
      long id;
      char name [30];
      int classLoad;
      Class *myClasses[MAXCLASS];
      void addClass(Class *c);
  public:
      Student (long, char*);
      char * getName();
      boolean registerClass(Class *);
};

class Class
{
  private:
      int id;
      char title[20];
      int max;
      int enrolled;
      Student *students[MAXSTUD];
  public:
      Class (int, char *, int);
      boolean checkFull();
      void addStudent(Student *);
};
```

CONCLUSION

UML stereotypes can be very useful in designing business systems. The use of a "relationship" stereotype is helpful in static structural models (UML class diagrams) and the use of an "operation owner" stereotype is most helpful in dynamic models (UML activity diagrams). These stereotypes aid in both the design/drawing phase and in the implementation (coding) phase of the overall system construction.

REFERENCES

Bahrami, A. (1999). *Object oriented systems development*, McGraw-Hill.

Brown, D. (2002). An introduction to object-oriented analysis. John Wiley & Sons.

Coad, P. (1997). *Object models: Strategies, patterns, and applications.* Yourdon Press.

Figure 15

```
Student::Student (long i, char * s)
{
      id = i;
      strcpy(name, s);
      classLoad = 0;
      for (int j = 0; j < MAXCLASS; j++)
            myClasses[j] = NULL;
      cout << "New student created: " << s << endl;
      return;
}

char * Student::getName()
{
      return name;
}

boolean Student::registerClass(Class *c)
{
      if (classLoad == (MAXCLASS - 1))
      {
            cout << "No more classes for this student" << endl;
            return FALSE;
      }
      if (c->checkFull() == TRUE)
      {
            cout << "Class is full" << endl;
            return FALSE;
      }
      c->addStudent(this);
      addClass(c);
      return TRUE;
}

void Student::addClass(Class *c)
{
      myClasses[classLoad] = c;
      classLoad++;
      return;
}
```

Dewitz, S. (1996). *Systems analysis and design and the transition to objects.* McGraw-Hill.

Erikson, H.-E., & Penker, M. (1998). UML toolkit. John Wiley & Sons.

Fowler, M. & Kendall, S. (2000). *UML distilled.* Addison-Wesley.

Martin, J. & Odell, J. (1998). *Object oriented methods – A foundation* (UML Edition). Prentice Hall.

Object Domain, Object Domain Systems Inc. (2001). On the World Wide Web: www.objectdomain.com

Satzinger, J., & Orvik, T. (2001). The object oriented approach. *Course Technology.*

Schach, S. (2002). *Object-oriented and classical software engineering.* McGraw Hill.

Scott, K. (2001). *UML explained.* Addison-Wesley.

Figure 16

```
Class::Class(int i, char * s, int m)
{
        id = i;
        strcpy(title, s);
        max = m;
        enrolled = 0;        .
        for (int j = 0; j < MAXSTUD; j++)
                students[j] = NULL;
        cout << "New class created: " << s << endl;
        return;
}

boolean Class::checkFull()
{
        if (enrolled == max)
                return TRUE;
        else
                return FALSE;
}

void Class::addStudent(Student *s)
{
        students[enrolled] = s;
        enrolled++;
        cout << "Student: " << s->getName();
        cout << " enrolled in " << title << endl;
}
```

Figure 17

```
/* ------ Main Function ------- */
int main()
{
        // Create a student
        Student s1 (123456789, "John Doe");

        // Create a class
        Class c1 (352, "Object Oriented", 20);

        // Register the student in the class
        s1.registerClass(&c1);

        return 0;
}
```

Chapter XIV

Extension to UML Using Stereotypes

Daniel Riesco
Universidad Nacional de San Luis and Universidad Nacional de Rio Cuarto,
Argentina

Paola Martellotto
Universidad Nacional de Rio Cuarto, Argentina

German Montejano
Universidad Nacional de San Luis, Argentina

ABSTRACT

The objective of this chapter is to first present the basic extension mechanisms proposed by UML. We then propose an extension to facilitate the modeling of specific applications. UML provides three extension mechanisms to allow the modelers to make some common extensions without having to modify the language of modeling underlying "Tag Values," "Restrictions," and "Stereotypes." There are several adaptations of UML, which occasionally exceed the extension mechanisms of UML. In this chapter, we present our proposal of "Evolutionary Stereotypes." We also present a tool that incorporates evolutionary stereotypes within two modules: the model checker and the dynamic semantics. A case study about time restrictions in a real-time system is shown. The reason for this proposal is that UML provides mechanisms for doing extensions; but, UML does not assure incorporation of new elements to the meta-model with dynamic semantics.

INTRODUCTION

Unified Modeling Language (UML) provides a wide set of modeling and notational concepts to cover the needs of modeling software projects. However, users often require new notations and additional characteristics, which are not included in the standard UML. These needs are satisfied by way of different extension mechanisms, which allow new classes of modeling elements to be included. These mechanisms can be used to define the semantics, characteristics, and notations of new elements in relation to the UML meta-model.

The extension mechanisms provided by UML (Booch, Rumbaugh & Jacobson, 2000) are the tag values, the restrictions, and the stereotypes. Additionally, there are several proposals to extend UML that exceed the extension mechanisms proposed by UML. Among them, is the possibility to mention the different types of stereotypes as decorative, descriptive, and restrictive stereotypes defined by Schleicher and Westfechtel (2001). These add more semantics to the meta-model and build a base for model analysis. However, to assure consistency and code generation, external modules should be introduced.

The stereotypes have been broadly used in different domains, for example, to instance the model of Web applications, to assist in the design of real-time, object-oriented systems, to assist in the design framework, to capture the structure and behavior of communication protocols, etc. In these proposals, the stereotypes (like extensions to UML) are used. The best stereotypes are restrictive; but, they do not allow a new semantics to be associated to the elements that have been incorporated in order to assure consistency with the UML meta-model.

The evolutionary stereotypes (Riesco et al., 2002) are found in other existing proposals to extend the UML meta-model. These are incorporated into modeling tools so that developers can modify the meta-model, incorporating new elements with the corresponding semantics. This incorporation is carried throughout the definition of classes that introduce new semantics, but that also maintain consistency with the meta-model. The modules to check consistency and for code generation are incorporated in modeling tools to facilitate the developer's task when extending the UML meta-model.

The objective of this chapter is to present the basic mechanisms of the extension proposed by UML, as well as extension proposals that have arisen to facilitate the modeling of specific applications.

UML EXTENSION MECHANISMS

UML provides three extension mechanisms to allow modelers to make some common extensions without having to modify the underlying modeling language. The UML extension mechanisms (Booch, Rumbaugh & Jacobson, 2000) include:

- **Tag values**: Tag values provide a form for defining new properties of elements that already exist.
- **Restrictions**: These provide a form for imposing rules about the elements and their properties.
- **Stereotypes**: Sterotypes provide a form for defining new extensions of elements and refining the semantics of elements that already exist.

On the whole, these three extensibility mechanisms allow for configuration and extensions of UML according to the specific project requirements. These mechanisms also allow UML to adapt new software technologies, such as the probable appearance of more potent languages of distributed programming and the impact of their coalition with the hardware modeling languages for the modeling of systems. New construction blocks can also be added to modify the specification of the existent ones, and even to change the semantics.

An extension, by definition, deviates the UML standard way and it can lead to interoperability problems. The modeler should carefully consider both advantages and costs before using extensions.

Therefore, it is important that this be made in a controlled way so that it remains, through these extensions, faithful to the purpose of UML, i.e., the communication of information.

It is very probable that when complex models are built and when there is a need to visualize or to specify some concepts, that a few stereotypes, tag values, or restrictions are used repeatedly. Some extensions are used so frequently that they have already been defined as standard elements of UML.

In the following sections, each of the UML extension mechanisms previously mentioned are explained and some UML standard elements are shown.

Tag Values

The tag values extend the properties of a UML construction block, allowing for the creation of new information in the specification of that element. Tag values can be used to store any information about the elements. They are particularly useful for storing information on the administration of projects, such as the date an element was created, its development state, and the state of the test.

Any string can be used as a tag name, except attribute names that are incorporated in the meta-model.

The tag values also provide a way to add information, depending on the implementation. For example, a code generator needs the additional information about the code type to be generated from a given model. Certain tags can be used as indicators to point out to the generator what implementation to use. The tags can also be used to store information about stereotyped elements of the model.

A tag value is a pair of strings: a tag string and a value string. A tag value can unite with any individual element, including elements of the model and elements of the presentation. The tag is the name of a certain property that the modeler wants to register; and, the value is the value of that property. In most cases, a tag value is represented using the name of the tag, the equal sign, and a value for the associated element. Additionally, the tag value is contained between braces (see Figure 1).

The tags with values containing long text can be represented by separation in a compartment at the bottom of the icon of the classifier.

Some tag names that are pre-defined in UML are:

- **Documentation**: This is the comment, description, or explanation of the associated element.
- **Location**: This is applied to almost all elements of UML and it specifies the node or the component in which the element resides.
- **Semantics**: This is applied to a class or an operation and it specifies their meaning.

Figure 1: Example of tag value

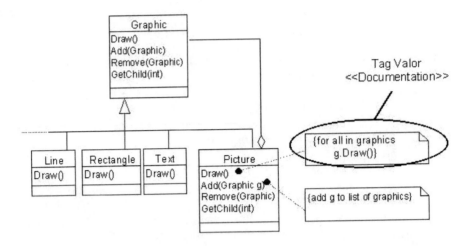

In the Figure 1, an example is shown.

The following definition is given by OMG (Object Management Group) (OMG, 2001):

Tag value according to standard of OMG

A tag value is a pair (tag, value) that allows arbitrary information to be associated to some element of the model. A tag is an arbitrary name. Some names of tags are pre-defined as standard elements.

Attributes
> *name:* This is an identifier of some property the modeler wants to record.
> *dataValue:* This specifies the value of that property for the given element.

Restrictions

Restrictions extend the semantics of a UML construction block, allowing the addition of new rules or modification of the existent ones. They express limitations and relationships that cannot be expressed using the UML notation. They are particularly useful to indicate the global conditions or the conditions that affect certain elements. The restrictions can be added to an element of a list, associated to a dependency, or included in a note.

A restriction is a semantic condition represented as a textual expression. Each expression has an implicit language of interpretation that can be a formal mathematical notation, such as a notation of a theory of groups, an on-line language of restriction such as OCL, a programming language such as C++, or an informal natural language. If the language is informal, its interpretation is also informal and a person should make it. Even if the restriction is expressed in a formal way, it does not mean that it will be automatically made complete. The maintenance techniques of truths cannot cover most of the cases but at least the semantics will be exact.

The restrictions are represented by placing them next to an element and containing them between braces as {complete}. They can also be represented by placing them in a note that is connected to their element with a dependency.

Some names of restrictions that are pre-defined in UML are:

- **Incomplete**: An incomplete restriction is applied to a set of generalizations specifying that all of the children have not been detailed and that one waits for the addition of other children.
- **New**: A new restriction (i.e., restriction of classifier role and association role), denotes that an instance of the role is created during the execution of the interaction that contains it, and that the instance continues to exist after concluding the execution.
- **Xor**: An Xor restriction (i.e., association restriction), is applied to a set of associations that share a connection with a class. It specifies that all objects of the shared class will have connections coming from only one of the associations.
- **Complete**: A complete restriction is applied to a generalization symbol. It specifies that all the children in the generalization have been specified in the model (although some can be omitted in the diagram), and that no additional child is allowed.

In Figure 2, an example is shown.

Figure 2: Example of a restriction

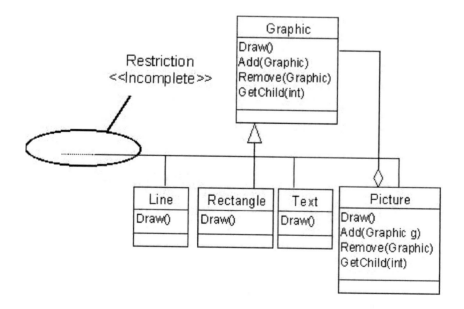

OMG defines a restriction as:

Restriction according to standard of OMG

The restriction concept allows for new semantics to be linguistically specified for an element of the model. The language can be specifically designed to write restrictions (such as OCL), a programming language, mathematical notation, or the natural language. If an editor of the model executes the restrictions, then this tool should understand the syntax and semantics of the language of restrictions. Since the election of the language is arbitrary, the restrictions are an extension mechanism.

In the meta-model, a restriction directly associated to an element of the model describes the semantic restrictions that this model's element should obey.

Attributes
  name: This is an identifier of some restriction that the modeler wants to record.
  body: This is a text expression defining the restriction. The expressions are written as strings in the design language.

Stereotypes

Stereotypes extend the vocabulary of UML, allowing the creation of new types of construction blocks that are derived from the existing ones, although they are specific to a problem. Stereotypes are the most important mechanisms of meta-model extensions. They provide a way of classifying elements of the object model and facilitate the addition of UML "virtual" meta-classes with new meta-attributes and semantics (i.e., the stereotypes are UML elements that are used to classify other UML elements in such way that they work in some aspects as if they were instances of new "virtual" classes of the meta-model based on the "base" classes that exist).

A stereotype is based on an element of the existing model. The content of information of the stereotyped element is the same as that of the element of the existing model. This allows a tool to store and manipulate the new element in the same way as done in the existing element. The stereotyped element can have its own icons. The stereotype can also have a list of the restrictions that are applied to its use. A tool of general purpose cannot automatically verify all of the restrictions, but it can be made complete manually or be verified by using an additional tool that understands the stereotype.

A stereotype can introduce additional values, additional restrictions, and a new graphical representation. All of the elements classified by a particular stereotype receive these values, restrictions, and the graphical representation. The stereotypes share the attributes, associations, and operations of their base class; however, they can also have other restrictions and different semantics. The content of the information and the form of a stereotype are the same as those of an existing class of elements of the base model, but their meaning and use are different.

A stereotype is represented by placing the name of the stereotype above the name of the element, and by containing the name of the stereotype between angles, for example, in <<trace>>. Each stereotype can have an associated icon that can be used as an alternative means to visualize the element.

Some examples of defined stereotypes as UML standard elements are:

- <<**trace**>>: This is applied to a dependency and specifies that the destination is a historical predecessor of the origin.
- <<**actor**>>: This is applied to a class and it specifies a coherent set of roles that the users of the use cases play when interacting with these use cases.
- <<**extend**>>: This is applied to a dependency and it specifies that the use case destination extends the behavior of the use case origin in a given extension point.
- <<**include**>>: This is applied to a dependency and it specifies that the use case origin incorporates, in an explicit way, the behavior of another use case in a localization specified by the origin.
- <<**utility**>>: This is also known as classifier stereotype, which is a stereotyped classifier that groups global variables and procedures in the form of a class declaration.
- <<**precondition**>>: This is also known as restriction stereotype, which should be associated to an operation. It denotes conditions that should be completed the moment the operation is invoked.
- <<**invariant**>>: This is also known as restriction stereotype, which is a restriction that should be associated to a set of classifiers or relationships. It denotes the conditions that should impose the restriction to effects of the classifiers or relationships and their instances.

In Figure 3, an example is shown.

Figure 3: Example of stereotype

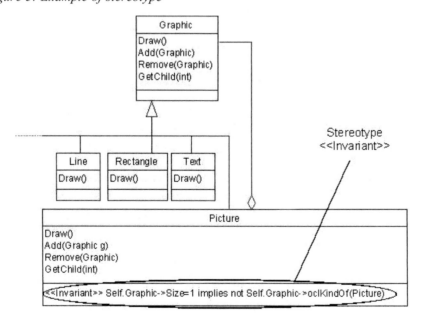

OMG defines a stereotype as:

Stereotype according to standard of OMG

A stereotype provides a form of classifying elements in such a way that they work in some aspects as if they were instances of a new constructor of the "virtual" meta-model. The instances have the same structure (attributes, associations, operations) as the "not stereotyped" instances of the same class. The stereotype can specify additional restrictions and can require tag values that are applied to the instances. A stereotype could also be used to indicate a meaning or different use between two elements with identical structure.

In the meta-model, the meta-class stereotype is a subtype of elements that can be generalized. The tag values and restrictions associated to a stereotype are applied to all the elements of the model that have been classified by that stereotype. A stereotype can also specify a geometric icon to be used to present elements with the stereotype.

Attributes
  baseClass: This specifies the names of one or more elements from UML modeling to which the stereotype is applied, such as classes, associations, refinements, and restrictions.
  icon: This is the geometric description for the icon that will be used to present an image of the element of the marked model with the stereotype.

STEREOTYPE APPLICATIONS

The mechanisms of UML extension have been broadly used for different, particular domains. They are given different applications in diverse, real domains.

Web Applications Modeling

In Hypermedia Design Model (Baresi, Garzotto & Paolini, 2001), different UML stereotypes are defined to instance the model of Web applications. The Web applications, contrary to traditional Web sites, integrate operations with hypermedia capacities that affect the content and the navigational states. These innovations are obtained by extending the UML with concepts of Web applications design taken from the Hypermedia Design Model (HDM). The hypermedia elements are described through appropriate UML stereotypes.

In Conallen (1999), extensions are presented to UML using the formal extension mechanisms of Web applications modeling. The extensions are designed in such a way that the Web component can be integrated with the rest of the system model. They are also designed to exhibit the level of abstraction and appropriate detail for the designers, implementers, and architects of Web applications.

In Bergner et al. (1999), a concept of structured interfaces to manage the incremental complexity of the class diagrams during the OO systems development is intended. It is a relationship of flexible refinement among the class diagrams and the use of templates of attributes, operations, and relationships to abstract the self form the implementation details. The utility of the introduced concept is illustrated through the development of a distributed editor that is based on Web applications.

Real Time Systems Modeling

In another completely different type of domain, i.e., object-oriented real time systems design, the application of these extensions is very interesting. In McLaughlin and Moore (1998), extensions to UML are presented that allow for solving the deficiencies of the UML in the critical areas of real time systems development, such as timing, concurrence, and hardware/software interfaces.

In De Miguel, Alonso and De la Puente (1997), different problems in real time systems design are identified and forms for solving these problems are described in an integrated framework that includes operational specification and planning analysis. The intent is to use stereotypes to allow for the analysis and evaluation of real time designs; however, to make a design model that includes information about the structure and operation of the system.

Frameworks Modeling

A more interesting integration, although not defined explicitly as stereotypes, is the one given in Ho, Pennaneac'h and Plouzeau (2000) where elements of their framework proposal are associated with elements of the UML meta-model's associating OCL restrictions.

In Ho et al. (2000), UMLAUT is described as a framework to transform UML to manipulate UML models and to solve the limitations of many OO tools for complex manipulations, such as the application of the design with patterns and the code generation for simulations and validations. These manipulations are expressed as algebraic compositions of elementary transformations, and they are open to extensions through inheritance and aggregate relationships.

In Fontoura, Pree and Rumpe, it is shown how to explicitly model variation points of a framework in UML using static and dynamic diagrams of description that capture the allowed structure and semantics of these variation points. A new member of the UML language is proposed, including extensions (through the mechanisms of extension of UML) to aid in the development and the adaptation of the framework.

Communication Protocols Modeling

GDPL (Generalized Distributed Programming Language) is a language used to capture the structure and behavior of communication protocols. This language is based on UML. In Parssinen et al. (2000), the linkage and the different necessary compilers for using a commercial tool such as Rational Rose (Rational Rose, 2000) are shown. They are defined and different stereotypes are used in which the semantics are specified externally to the Rational Rose tool through the different compilers (R2D2, TPDL2SDL, and SDT).

Workflows Modeling

The adaptations of the UML meta-model to specific domains often exceeds, the extension mechanisms' characteristic of UML. In Schleicher and Westfechtel (2001)

UML applications that are characterized by the modeling of these specific domains and the code generation are investigated. The modeling of specific domains requires extensions to the meta-model, while the code generation requires forcing some restrictions. Their intent is for different alternatives of stereotypes, such as the descriptive and restrictive stereotypes and the workflows modeling for the development of processes in software engineering, which is introduced as a study case.

Rules on Meta-model

In Hausmann, Heckel and Sauer, a dynamic meta-model is intended to specify the operational semantics of the UML behavioral diagrams based on UML collaborative diagrams that are interpreted as graphical transformation rules. It is also shown how this focus can be developed to specify the semantics of UML extensions. The specification of the semantics of sequence diagrams is studied. This specification is extended to include characteristics of multimedia applications modeling.

In Juric and Kuljis (1999), the problem of object-oriented case tools that force their own supportive methodology is discussed. An evaluation instrument is developed to analyze how the commercial OO tools support UML, based on the extraction of a set of rules that are supposedly those that are continued in order to sustain satisfaction in UML. A set of rules (checkups) is extracted for all of the UML modeling constructors. In particular, the rules are given for the different extension mechanisms in the package of "Foundation".

KINDS OF STEREOTYPES

Although UML is used as a universal technique in object-oriented application modeling and it covers a great range of domains, it is not adequate in some domains and must be adapted. Therefore, there are several adaptations of UML. In some instances, these exceed UML's own extension mechanisms.

Schleicher and Westfechtel (2001) propose the following classification:

- *Decorative Stereotypes*. These are used to adapt the UML notation to a specific domain. They lack the support in the meta-model.
- *Descriptive Stereotypes*. These introduce new elements that do not change the UML semantic. They are used to express subjacent domain elements, with which the user can create UML models using meta-model elements of a specific domain.
- *Restrictive Stereotypes*. These are new semantic elements added to UML. They do not change the UML base; rather, they only extend it. They are more powerful than descriptive stereotypes in associating declarative restrictions.
- *Redefined Stereotypes*. These provide the means to substitute any elements of the meta-model through a new element that redefines the restrictions and semantics of UML's original element.

We also present our proposal of evolutionary stereotypes in Riesco et al. (2002):

- *Evolutionary Stereotypes*. These provide the means to incorporate new elements in the UML meta-model, including the syntax and semantic extensions. Evolutionary stereotypes allow the engineer, who defines the new stereotypes, to create other classes of a UML meta-model with their respective semantics.

Decorative Stereotypes

The decorative stereotypes are used to adapt the UML notation to a specific domain. They do not restrict usage; therefore, they are regular classes of UML. Decorative stereotypes are not important because they lack support in the meta-model.

Descriptive Stereotypes

The descriptive stereotypes associate meta-model classes with descriptive stereotypes. Any class of the domain model is represented by its own stereotype, symbolized by its own icon.

The model structure maintains a hierarchy of stereotyped packages and the definitions of the new elements are modeled inside a stereotyped class diagram. However, this kind of stereotype does not allow an engineer to forbid the structures without means when using the stereotype in a particular domain. The software engineer, who uses UML to model a domain, can freely create any kind of class diagram without any validation of the extensions. Therefore, it is impossible to generate a formal and interpretative definition from a UML model without providing a model checker. The solution is to introduce external modules to check the model. The same occurs with the possibility to generate the code or simulate the model for specific domain. Other external module is necessary for this.

The tool that implements these stereotypes allows the engineer to check the consistency of the model; but, it is necessary to include the model checker and code generator as external modules. This is shown in Figure 4. For example, the Rational Rose 2000 allows the engineer to incorporate only descriptive stereotypes.

Figure 4: Architecture of a tool that supports descriptive stereotypes

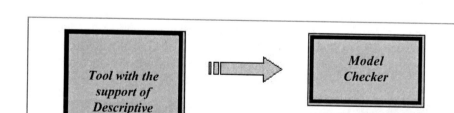

Restrictive Stereotypes

UML provides more expressive techniques for meta-modeling than the descriptive stereotypes. For each stereotype, it is possible to define a set of tagged values that can be interpreted as attributes of the meta-level. The restrictions can also be formulated as stereotypes.

With the use of restrictive stereotypes it is not necessary to code a model checker in an external module. It is possible to define the restrictions as part of the tool. A set of restrictions is defined for each stereotype so that the stereotypes are used in the correct form. The restrictions define the way that the engineer can use stereotypes.

A tool, which includes the possibility of defining restrictive stereotypes, incorporates the model checker module. However, it is necessary to separately code the code generator or simulator module. This kind of stereotype is similar to the previous stereotype in that it is not possible to define dynamic aspects for the newly created models. This is shown in Figure 5.

Figure 5: Architecture of a tool that supports restrictive stereotypes

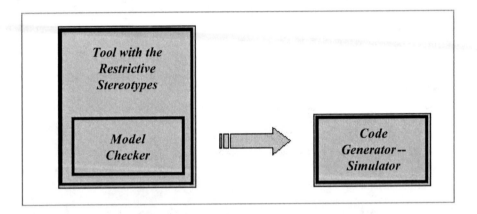

Redefined Stereotypes

The redefined stereotypes provide the means to change any meta-model element by a new element and to define a set of completely different restrictions. This produces radical change in the original language and generates a new language of modeling. The redefined stereotypes are not considered to alter the UML meta-model, creating a UML dialect.

Evolutionary Stereotypes

The evolutionary stereotypes (Riesco et al., 2002) that are incorporated in the modeling tools for engineers to modify the UML meta-model include new elements with the corresponding syntax and semantics. In this way, the tool's environment dynamically changes in appearance and functionality to allow the engineers to use the diagrams with the extensions done in the meta-model.

These stereotypes allow the engineers to access the definition of meta-model to do the extensions (syntax and semantics). As an example, if the tool uses the Delphi™

Figure 6: Architecture of a tool that supports evolutionary stereotypes

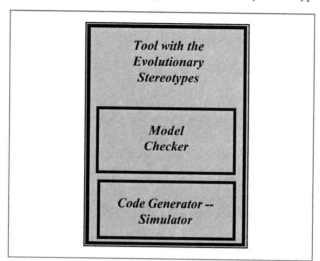

programming language, it is necessary to implement the meta-meta-model level UML architecture; this will support the concept class (meta-class in the UML meta-meta-model) and allow the meta-model to be built. In this way, it is possible to implement all of the classes and relationships that compose the UML meta-model.

The incorporation of this kind of stereotype will determine the creation of new classes in the meta-model. The stereotypes included are not only decorative, but they also introduce a new semantic to the meta-model. For this, a formal mechanism to the definition of the semantic is required. As such, the OCL rules and Delphi attributes and methods are used.

Graphically, a tool that incorporates evolutionary stereotypes has the structure of Figure 6.

It is possible to observe that the model checker, the code generator, and simulator modules are included in the tool. In this way, it is easier for the engineer to extend the UML meta-model. The simulator module includes the possibility to model the dynamic aspects of the diagrams as well.

In the next section, a case study about time restrictions in "Real Time System" is shown. Examples defining descriptive, restrictive, and evolutionary stereotypes for modeling time restrictions are presented.

STUDY CASE: INCLUSION OF STEREOTYPES TO MODEL RESTRICTIONS OF TIME IN REAL TIME SYSTEMS

UML provides a framework to model the object-oriented system. Indeed, the UML utility as a common language for defining and designing independent software of a specific implementation language, increases its success in several software development areas.

However, UML is not enough in such a critical area as real time systems, in particular, for time, concurrence, and the hardware/software interface. These deficiencies for modeling certain aspects of a system can be solved using extensions to UML.

The requirements, which lead to development of these systems, often establish specific considerations of time, i.e., these systems have by definition, time constraints.

The two main categories of time information for modeling in an object-oriented system are:

Latency: This the amount of time that two objects need to collaborate (communication by a message).

Duration: This is the amount of time required by an object to end its processing once it has received a message.

Through the combination of these two concepts, it is possible to identify the general constraints of time for a set of operations.

In the collaboration diagrams (OMG, 2001), these constraints can be associated to the messages that are sent between objects for the communication.

In the next section, a typical problem of process control (De Miguel, Alonso & De la Puente, 1997) and the proposal extensions are presented. The application of evolutionary stereotypes in the collaboration diagram is shown.

Problem

A subsystem of transport with a transportation band moves tin. A scanner detects the bad tins before they are kept in storage. Each tin is identified by a bar code, which is detected at the beginning of the process. The detector's driver is a part of the transportation system. The scanner unit (a device coordinated by the transportation system) identifies the defective tins as they travel by the band. The scanner indicates the defective tins to a robotic unit. The robot removes the defective tins from the band. The system has local buttons to start and stop the equipment. The operators can monitor and operate the system from a remote terminal. The system needs to process an average of 30 tins each minute. The operations that start and stop the system should also allow for detection of defective tins.

Collaboration Diagram

Figure 7 shows the collaboration diagram for the problem being presented.

The collaboration diagrams are interaction diagrams that show a set of objects, their relationships, and the messages that they can send one other. The collaboration diagrams are an alternative to the sequence diagram for representing the interaction among objects. Unlike the sequence diagram, they can show the operational context (which objects are attributes, which objects are temporal, etc.) and the execution cycles.

An object is an instance of a class in a class diagram. It is represented by a rectangle, which has the name of the object and its class in the format *objectName:className*. A link is an instance of an association in a class diagram. It is represented by a continuous line that joins two objects. A message specifies a communication among objects that transmits information. A directed arrow close to a link represents the messages.

The diagram of the Figure 7 illustrates the time attributes associated to the message (time constraints enclosed between braces) and the actions (time constraints inside the

Figure 7: Example of a collaboration diagram of the process control system

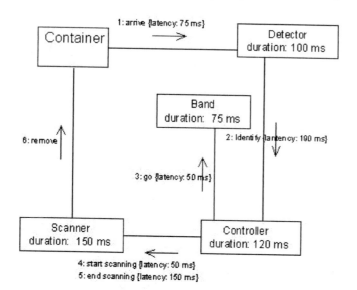

objects). For example, the process control system has a latency of 75 minutes between the message "arrive," which needs 100 minutes to process the action. In additional to the individual time attributes, it is useful to specify the total time constraint for the set of operations. Here, the total time has to be less than two seconds to assure that the requirement of processing 30 tins per minute is met.

Proposed Stereotypes to This Problem

- *ActiveObject*: This represents the active objects of the process control system.
- *Temporization*: This represents the time constraints associated to the messages.
- *Simulation*: This to represent the dynamic aspects of the collaboration diagram.

Constraints

The receptor of a message of temporization has to be an active object (restrictions on *Temporization*).

Definition of Stereotypes

The *ActiveObject* and temporization are defined according to each type of defined stereotype:

1) Descriptive Stereotype: <<ActiveObject>>

For a case having the extension *ActiveObject*, it is possible to define this as a descriptive stereotype because it is only necessary to distinguish the active object from the rest of the objects. It is not necessary to constrain it. The definition of the extension is as follows:

Name: ActiveObject.
Meta-model Class: ActiveObject inherits from the class ClassifierRole of the UML meta-model.
Description: Is used to specify an active object of a process control system.
Semantics: If a particular semantic is required, it is necessary to develop the independent and external modules of the tool for model checking and code generation.
Syntax: An active object has a special icon for active object.

---

2) Restrictive stereotype: <<Temporization>>

For a case having the extension *Temporization*, it has to be defined by a restrictive stereotype as otherwise there is a constraint that says, "The receptor of a message of temporization has to be an active object." The definition of the extension is as follows:

Name: Temporization.
Meta-model Class: The temporization class inherits from the message class of the UML meta-model.
Description: Is used to specify a time message of a process control system.
Semantics: If a particular semantic is required, it is necessary to develop an independent and external module of the tool for the code generation; but, it is possible to define the constraint required by this stereotype.
Syntax: A time message is represented with a special icon for time.

---

3) Evolutionary stereotype: <<Simulation>>

For the case having the extension *Simulation*, an evolutionary stereotype is required to define it because the purpose of this extension is to show the dynamic aspects of the model created for the problem presented. This extension allows for the engineers to simulate how the communication between the classes and associations is done. It also calculates the general results of the model by average latency and duration. The definition is as follows:

Name: Simulation.
Meta-model Class: The class simulation inherits from the class collaboration of the UML meta-model.
Description: Is used to show the dynamic aspects of a collaboration diagram and calculate the general results.
Semantics: Must show the dynamism of a collaboration diagram, how the messages are sent to the objects, and how to calculate the average latency and duration. This semantic is specified in the code generator module "simulation".
Syntax: Does not have an icon.

Note: For implementation of this stereotype, it is necessary to transform the stereotypes *ActiveObject* and *Temporization* as evolutionary stereotypes as additional methods are needed in order to stand out as the simulation occurs.

The collaborations package meta-model and the proposed extensions are shown in Figure 8.

Figure 8: Meta-model of collaborations package and proposed extensions

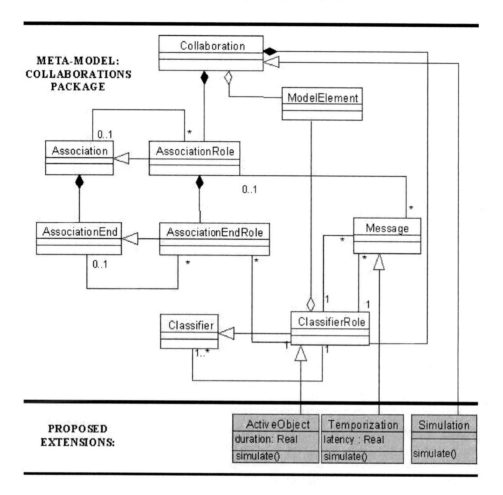

Figure 9: Definition of class ActiveObject

Type ActiveObject = **class** (ClassifierRole)
   duration: Real

{public procedures}

{private procedures}

end.

Figure 10: Definition of class temporization

```
Type Temporization = class (Message)
   latency: Integer

{public procedures}

{private procedures}

{OCL}
Self.AssociationEndRole.AssociationRole.Message.ClassifierRole →
   .forAll ( cr / cr.oclIsKindOf (ActiveObject) )

end.
```

The classes, which define the descriptive and restrictive stereotypes, will be the subjects of Figures 9 and 10.

For the case having the evolutionary stereotype *Simulation*, it is defined as:

Name: Indicates the stereotyped name, which must be different from all other elements of the meta-model (neither the class names of the UML meta-model, nor the name of the others that have been incorporated through the evolutionary stereotypes). In this case, the name is *Simulation*.

Base Class: Indicates the class of the UML meta-model from which the new stereotype inherits. In this case, the class is *collaboration*.

Graphic Representation: Indicates the graphic that represents this stereotype. In this case, the stereotype *simulation* does not have a graphical representation.

Attributes: Defines the new attributes that the stereotype will have.

Declaration of Private and Public Methods: Declares the methods for the new element. In this case, the methods for calculation will be average of the latency and duration of the model.

Implementation of Private and Public Methods: Implements the methods declared previously.

Definition of Well Formed Rules: Defines the constraints of the new class through OCL rules.

Figure 11: Definition of the class simulation

```
Type Simulation = class (Collaboration)
   baseClass: Collaboration

{public procedures}

{private procedures}
   Simulate()

end.
```

Figure 12: Definition of the procedures simulate

```
Simulation.Simulate()
    Self.AssociationRole → selectOne()
    T = AssociationRole.Temporization → selectOne()
    if T <> Null then T.Simulate()

Temporization.Simulate()
    Self.CalculateLatency()
    Self.ActiveObject.Simulate()

ActiveObject.Simulate()
    Self.CalculateDuration()
    T = Self.AssociationEndRole.AssociationRole.Message → selectOne()
    if T <> Null then T.Simulate()
```

The new class has the characteristics in Figure 11.

The definition of the procedure *Simulate* for the evolutionary stereotype *Simulation*, and the corresponding procedures for the evolutionary stereotype *ActiveObject* and *Temporization* are shown in Figure 12.

In this way, the different kinds of stereotypes presented are specified and exemplified.

CONCLUSION

UML is a universal language for modeling applications for a great range of domains; but, in several instances it is not powerful enough to express certain domains of the world. UML is, however, an open language, which allows extensions of its semantics and its syntax for modeling certain kinds of applications.

The mechanisms of extension provided by UML provides are one way to extend the meta-model. Often they are not sufficient as they do not allow a new semantic to be associated to the incorporated elements to ensure consistency with the meta-model.

The evolutionary stereotypes are kinds of extensions to the meta-model. They are integrated to the UML and incorporate static semantics to check the model through a formal language such as OCL and to complete dynamic semantics, which are not specified in OCL, through a programming language. This is done using two modules: a checking module to assure the consistency of the model with respect to the meta-model and a code generation/simulation module to automatically generate code from the definition of the new stereotype and to show the dynamic aspects of the model through the simulator.

Other works use the stereotypes as extensions of UML; but in general, they are restrictive stereotypes. Contrary to evolutionary stereotypes, the restrictive stereotypes do not allow for associating semantics to the new elements unless it is coded manually in the model checking and code generator modules. An advantage of evolutionary stereotypes is that they allow for specification of the semantics of the new elements and for automatically generating code to maintain the consistency of the UML model.

The evolutionary stereotypes are incorporated into the modeling tool in such a way that they can modify the UML meta-model, including the new elements with their corresponding semantics. In this way, the environment of a tool can dynamically change its appearance and functionality to allow software engineers to use the stereotypes previously defined in the diagrams.

Clearly, the evolutionary stereotypes are the most complete way to extend UML because they allow for the incorporation of new elements to the meta-model with a new semantics to assure the consistency of the UML meta-model.

REFERENCES

Baresi, L., Garzotto, F., & Paolini, P. (2001). Extending UML for modeling Web applications. *Proceedings of the 34th Hawaii International Conference on System Sciences*. IEEE Press.

Bergner, K., Rausch, A., Sihling, M., & Vilbig A. (1999). Structuring and refinement of class diagrams. *Proceedings of the 32nd Hawaii International Conference on System Sciences*. IEEE Press.

Booch, G., Rumbaugh, J., & Jacobson, I. (2000). El Lenguaje Unificado de Modelado. Addison-Wesley.

Booch, G., Rumbaugh, J., & Jacobson I. (2000). El proceso unificado de desarrollo de software. Addison-Wesley.

Conallen, J. (1999). Modeling Web application architectures with UML. Rational Software. A version of this material appears in the October 1999 (Vol. 42, No.10) issue of *Communications of the ACM*.

De Miguel, M., Alonso, A., & De la Puente, J. (1997). Object-oriented design of real time systems with stereotypes. *Proceedings of the 9th Euromicro Workshop on Real Time Systems*. IEEE Press.

Fontoura, M., Pree, W., & Rumpe, B. Framework development and adaptation with UML.

Hausmann, J. H., Heckel, R., &, Sauer, S. Towards dynamic meta modeling of UML extensions: An extensible semantics for UML sequence diagrams.

Ho, W. M., Jézéquel, J.M., Le Guennec, A., & Pennaneac'h, F. (2000). UMLAUT: An extendible UML transformation framework. *Proceedings of the 14th IEEE International Conference on Automated Software Engineering*.

Ho, W. M., Pennaneac'h, F., & Plouzeau, N. (2000). UMLAUT: A framework for weaving UML-based aspect-oriented designs. *Proceedings of the Technology of Object-Oriented Languages and Systems (TOOLS 33)*. IEEE Press.

Juric, R., & Kuljis, J. (1999). Building an evaluation instrument for OO CASE tool assessment for Unified Modelling Language support. *Proceedings of the 32nd Hawaii International Conference on System Sciences*. IEEE Press.

McLaughlin, M., Moore, A. (1998). Real time extensions to UML. Timing, concurrency, and hardware interfaces.

OMG (2001). OMG Unified Modeling Language specification. On the World Wide Web: http://www.omg.org

Parssinen, J., Von Knorring, N., Heinonen, J., Oy, T., & Turunen, M. (2000). UML for protocol engineering - Extensions and experiences. *Proceedings of the Technology of Object Oriented Languages and Systems (TOOLS 33)*. IEEE Press.

Rational Rose (2000). On the World Wide Web: http://www.rational.com

Riesco, D., Grumelli, A., Macció, A., & Martellotto, P. (2002). Extensions to UML meta-model: Evolutionary stereotypes. *3rd ACIS International Conference on Software Engineering, Artificial Intelligence, Networking and Parallel / Distributed Computing*. Madrid, Spain.

Schleicher, A., & Westfechtel, B. (2001). Beyond stereotyping: Metamodeling approaches for the UML. *Proceedings of the 34th Hawaii International Conference on System Sciences*. IEEE Press (p. 4).

Chapter XV

An Extension to a UML Activity Graph from Workflow

Daniel Riesco
Universidad Nacional de San Luis and Universidad Nacional de Rio Cuarto,
Argentina

Edgardo Acosta
Universidad Nacional de Rio Cuarto, Argentina

German Montejano
Universidad Nacional de San Luis, Argentina

ABSTRACT

This chapter proposes an extension to the activity graph of the Unified Modeling Language (UML) to support the Workflow Management Coalition (WfMC) standard. The definition of a business process has been standardized by the WfMC with the purpose of satisfying the need of interaction and connectivity between process definition tools and different workflow systems. Here, the WfMC meta-model is explained. The UML activity diagrams, used for the business process modeling, support less detail than the WfMC standard. In this chapter, an extension of the UML's activity graph meta-model is proposed, and its formalization using the workflow meta-model is defined. The purpose of this chapter is to obtain an extension of UML to support the workflow process definition without changing the standard with the same expressive power as the WfMC. It increments the expressive power of the activity diagrams so that the business processes modeled with the UML notation can be executed by a workflow engine.

INTRODUCTION

A workflow process is defined as the automation, in a total or partial way, of a business process during which documents, information, or tasks are passed from one participant to another for action according to a set of procedural rules (Allen, 2000). That is, there is a system that manages the execution of workflows through the use of software running on one or more workflow engines. This environment where the processes are interpreted and executed is called Workflow Management System (WMS). The environment is capable of interactions with participants of the workflow and of invoking tools or applications, when necessary.

A process involves a set of logically-related steps that are executed with the intention of obtaining a particular result (Champy, 1995). A workflow process is a coordinated (parallel and/or serial) set of business activities that are connected in order to achieve a common business goal. Such activities may be manual activities and/or computer-automated activities. There are also human as well as material resources and business procedures involved; all of them with the purpose of producing a benefit for the organization.

A workflow process is a special case of a business process, i.e., it is a business process that is automated (Allen). Therefore, there are details in the workflow process that are not necessary in the normal business process, but are essential in a workflow for their execution by the Workflow Enactment Services (WfES).

The process modeling or business modeling is a means to help in the visualization of tasks, activities, and flows of a process. It also shows the different organizational units involved in the process (Jacobson, 1996; Davenport & Young, 1990; Hammer & Champy, 1993).

In the development of every industry, it is very important to have a coherent, well-planned process. A coherent, well-planned workflow provides much better possibilities: faster adaptability, easier reengineering, and simulation of the future processes. In any case, a coherent, well-planned representation of the process is advisable, and sometimes indispensable, to ensure that an organization does the right things at the right time and in the right way.

A UML activity diagram (Rumbaugh, Jacobson & Booch, 1999) is an example of a tool that may be used to build models of organizational processes. It might as well be employed for modeling computational processes (Rumbaugh, Jacobson & Booch, 1999). However, while each of these models is created in a different application domain, both strive to put software into context. That is, both business process engineering and product engineering work to allocate a role for computer software and, at the same time, to establish the relationships that tie software to other elements of computer-based systems. Workflows are a special case of business processes that are much more intrinsically-related to software; that is, because the activity diagram would be a tool for business. Nevertheless, the activity diagram's notation supports a relatively high level of abstraction. Some details cannot be properly modeled, and this produces ambiguities and/or inconsistencies in the interpretation. Therefore, a process specification based on activity diagrams would not be correctly interpreted and executed automatically by a workflow engine.

The level of details supported by this notation is not adequate to model the major specificity that present the workflow processes. A workflow process has its own details of automation process that the activity diagrams cannot express, i.e., the definitions of process generated from an activity diagram probably need some type of external assistance to be interpreted and executed by workflow engine.

In the beginning, different workflow products had their own view of workflow processes: each used different representations of workflow processes according to their needs. Vendors had their own logical view of what a workflow was. Nevertheless, elements in common could be identified. However, even though having elements in common, it was highly unlikely that different products used the exact same format for process definitions. Thus, different products assuredly used different definitions for the same process, preventing the chances of sharing or exchanging definitions. That is because the initial growth of workflow technology ended up in numerous workflow products that were unable to interact.

It was necessary to obtain a common language due to this diversification. The Workflow Management Coalition (WfMC) arises with the objective to formulate specifications that would allow the interoperability of different workflow products.

The WfMC was created with the purpose to promote and develop the use of workflow systems through the definition of standards for the terminology, the interoperability, and the connection among workflow products. For this, the WfMC identifies the generic components contained in all workflow systems and defines the Workflow Reference Model. This model describes the structure of a workflow generic application identifying areas of common functions and the interfaces for the interoperability. In addition to the reference model, the WfMC specifies the standard format for the interchange of data among the diverse areas.

Figure 1: Interfaces of a workflow reference model

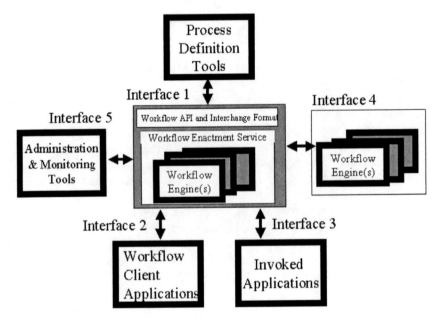

The reference model covers the common characteristics of the distinct workflow products. The different areas of common functionality and interfaces are shown. These areas and interfaces are shown in Figure 1.

Interface 1 is defined to allow for the exchange of information between the tools of process definition and the service of workflow execution (Workflow Enactment Services – WfES) (WfMC Work Group 1, 1999). By means of Interface 1, it is possible to transfer the process definitions: a vital topic for the operation of any class of workflow systems. This interface provides independence and good communications among modeling tools and the products of workflow execution.

The WfMC defines a standard for the Interface 1. It specifies a format for common interchange, which allows the transference of workflow process definitions between the modeling tools and the workflow engine without losing or modifying their semantics.

Interface 1's standard includes a common logical meta-model of workflow process definitions and specifies a standard format for workflow process definitions, i.e., the Workflow Process Definition Language (WPDL).

Different workflow process definitions could be exchanged by standardized workflow products without losing or modifying the semantics. For example, a WfES could interpret process definitions generated or modified by different heterogeneous modeling tools.

In this chapter, we show a proposal for the integration of UML with the WfMC Interface 1 standard. We neither present guidelines to create coherent, well-planned process definitions, nor methods to be applied in business process engineering.

Our main goal is to allow UML modeling tools to generate artifacts that are representations of workflow processes that can be translated to the standard WfMC format. That is, we merely extend the abstract syntax of the activity graph, including "well-formedness" rules and semantics, including specifying how an artifact generated with the extension should be translated to the corresponding WPDL text.

We do not deal with the extension of the concrete graphical syntax of the activity diagram. Such a topic can, without inconvenience, be treated separately based on the results exposed here.

We first list the limitations of UML activity diagrams in modeling automated organizational processes according to the WfMC standard, and then we explain how the UML meta-model should be extended in order to overcome such limitations.

UML ACTIVITY GRAPH META-MODEL OF THE OBJECT MANAGEMENT GROUP

The set of diagrams that conform to the UML standard notation allow complex systems to be approached through independent views: each one providing a perspective of the system under analysis or development (Booch, Rumbaugh & Jacobson, 1999). Each perspective is a model that focuses on particular aspects of the underlying system. These models are integrated so that a self-consistent system can be analyzed and built. In this document, our main concern is the modeling of processes, so our interest is focused on the activity diagram.

The UML standard is specified by a four-layer, meta-modeling structure, which consists of the following layers: user objects, model, meta-model, and meta-meta-model (OMG). In this document, we are mainly interested in the UML meta-model. The meta-model layer defines the language used in the specification of models, i.e., a model is an instance of the meta-model.

The UML meta-model is a logical model rather than a physical (or implementation) model.

A UML meta-model is described in a semi-formal manner using these views:

- Abstract syntax expressed in class diagrams.
- "Well-formedness" rules (Object Constraint Language).
- Semantics described in informal, but precise language.

The UML meta-model is organized into a structure of logical packages. For example, the package *StateMachine* groups together the metaclasses, which represent the own concepts of a state machine.

The *StateMachines* package specifies a set of concepts that can be used for modeling discrete behavior through finite state-transition systems. It provides the semantic foundation for activity graphs described in the *ActivityGraphs* package.

As a part of the UML standard, the activity diagram can be applied to a model's computational processes and used to model organizational processes. For organizational processes, the notation expresses the flow control among activities of a process.

The abstract syntax and the semantics of the notation of an activity diagram are defined in the package *ActivityGraph*, where a structure called activity graph is described.

An activity diagram is a projection of a view of an activity graph.

The concepts found in a process are described in the *ActivityGraphs* package. These concepts are defined as subtypes of the basic concepts found in the *StateMachines*

Figure 2: StateMachine package

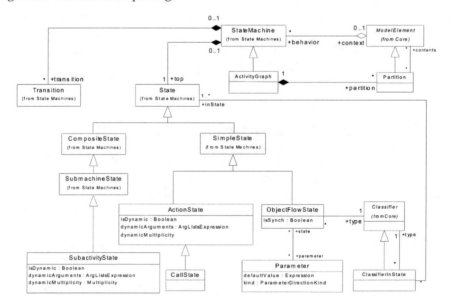

package (see Figure 2). Figure 2 shows that the semantics of the activity graph are based on the semantics of state machine.

UML defines to the activity graph as a special case of a state machine where all (or most) states are action states and each transition is fired to finish the action in the source state.

An activity graph applies all of the characteristics of state machines; therefore, an activity diagram used in process modeling can have simple and compound states (e.g., branch, join or "unbranch", fork, and merge or "unfork").

The specification of the activity diagrams also include the concrete graphical syntax and the mapping between the concrete syntax and abstract syntax that has been defined in the activity graph meta-model. The elements or symbols of the activity diagram's notation acquire means through this mapping.

Like every artifact in the OMG's UML standard, activity graph is defined by:
1. The activity graph meta-model.
2. The activity diagram graphical notation (presentation).
3. The mapping between activity graph and the graphical notation.

WORKFLOW META-MODEL OF THE WORKFLOW MANAGEMENT COALITION

WfMC defines a generic interpretation/view of what a workflow is. Such an interpretation/view is based on an analysis of numerous/different workflow products and is expressed by the Workflow Process Definition Meta-model (Workflow Meta-model). Such a meta-model is a logical model: it expresses the abstract syntax and the semantics of a workflow process definition.

The standard format for definitions exchange, as defined by the WfMC, includes the common process definition meta-model, which we call workflow meta-model, and the grammar of a Workflow Process Definition Language (WPDL). This language is used for textual definition of workflow processes according to the Workflow meta-model. That is, there is a mapping between the abstract syntax expressed in the workflow meta-model and the concrete syntax expressed by the WPDL grammar.

WfMC's standard is defined by:
1. The Workflow Process Definition Meta-model (workflow meta-model).
2. The Workflow Process Definition Language (WPDL), i.e., BNF specified.

The WfMC does not express the mapping between the meta-model and the grammar. The workflow meta-model is described by:
1. Entities described through attribute tables and informal language.
2. Entity Relation Diagrams that express the abstract syntax of the process definitions.

The class diagram of Figure 3 is equivalent to the Entity Relation Diagram provided by the WfMC to express the abstract syntax of the workflow process definitions.
The entities identified are:
• *Workflow process.*
• *Workflow activity.*

Figure 3: Class diagram defining the abstract syntax of workflow process

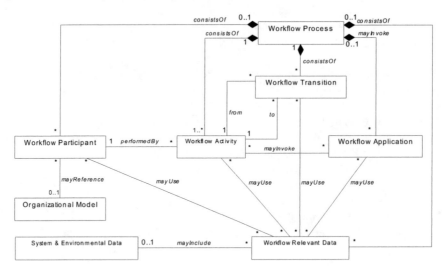

- *Workflow transition.*
- *Workflow application.*
- *Workflow relevant data.*
- *Workflow participant.*
- *System and environmental data.*
- *Organizational model.*

This model is a basic model, where only the fundamental entities commonly found in a workflow process definition are described. However, the level of detail with which each entity is described is deeper than that corresponding to an activity graph. The attributes are described by a data dictionary (attribute tables).

Each one of the entities has associated a set of attributes, which describe the characteristics of the entity. Some attributes are required and others are optional. When it is necessary to describe additional characteristics, the user can define extended attributes. The extensions can possibly be accepted by the WfMC and incorporated to the meta-model as standard attributes.

In addition to the mechanism of extending attributes to expand the meta-model, it is possible to implement extended library functions.

DESCRIPTION OF THE MAIN ENTITIES OF THE WORKFLOW META-MODEL

In this section each entity is described.

Workflow Process

The Workflow Process Entity, or simply Process, represents the workflow process in the meta-model. It has attributes for the identification and description of a process, for the administration of the process definitions, and for use during the execution.

Workflow Activity

A process activity is a logical step or description of a piece of work that contributes to the achievement of the process. Each activity corresponds to a logic working and an auto-contained unit. It represents the work to be processed by a combination of resources (assigned participants) and computational applications (assigned applications).

In the meta-model, the entity Workflow Activity, or simply Activity, represents the workflow process activities. A process definition consists of one or more Workflow Activities. The activity scope is local to a definition of specific processes.

There are several types of activities:

- Atomic Activity: This is a minimal auto-contained working unit, which is executed either automatically or manually.

- Subflow Activity: This is a container for the execution of a process definition, which is separately defined and can be executed in the local service or remote service. The process definition identified inside the sub-flow contains its own definition of activities as nested processes for transitions, resource assignments, and applications,. Input and output parameters allow for the interchange of workflow relevant data between the caller and the called process. Furthermore, the data can be returned.

- Loop Activity: This works as a control activity for the repeated execution of a set of activities inside the same process definition. This set of activities is connected to the control activity (loop activity) by special transitions (loop begin transition and loop end transition).

- Dummy Activity: This is a purely structural activity, which does no work and does not exist in execution time (and therefore it has not associated resources or applications). It simply allows for the choice of paths between the incoming and outstanding transitions.

- Inline Block: This is a group of activities that can form an inline block, which is specified by a particular construction of transitions and activities. It can be used as an alternative to the activity sub-flow to represent the explosion of an activity of higher level inside a process definition.

Workflow Transition

The activities are related to each other through flow control conditions. In a process instance, transitions define the criteria for moving from the current activity to the next activity or activities.

Entity Workflow Transition, or simply Transition in the meta-model, represents the workflow process transitions.

According to the meta-model, each transition has three elemental properties: the source activity, the destination activity, and the condition under which the transition is fired. The transition can be conditional or unconditional. In the first case, an expression has to be evaluated to allow or to inhibit the transition. The transitions of a process can result in the sequential or parallel operation of individual activities inside a process. The condition "split" and the condition "join" of the control thread are evaluated in the appropriate activity: The evaluation of condition split is a post-activity process in the source activity, and the evaluation of the condition join is a pre-activity process in the destination activity. The information related to these conditions is defined in the corresponding activity. This focus allows the control processing that is associated with the creation and synchronization of control threads in a process instance to be managed as part of an associated activity. In addition, the transitions are limited to indicate the flow path.

The scope of a particular transition is local to the process definition based on where the activity is and local to the associated activities.

Structures of arbitrary complexities can be specified to express more complex transitions using the basic transition "together" with activities "dummy."

Workflow Application

The work processing associated to a workflow activity is partially or totally supported by a software program. This software or application can be a generic commercial tool, specific services of a department or company, or procedures implemented inside the own administration system of workflow, i.e., the application IT (Information Technology) can be invoked by the WfES to do either the partial or total processing necessary to carry out the objective of an instance of workflow activity.

In the meta-model, the entity Workflow Application, or simply Application, represents the applications of workflow. The applications, which give the support to an instance of activity, are identified by the attribute application assignment of this activity.

The definition of an application, inside the process definition, reflects the interface between the workflow engine and the application, including any parameters passed among them.

Workflow Relevant Data

The workflow relevant data is created and used within each process instance during process execution.

The activities, the invoked applications, and the conditions of transitions can reference relevant data.

In the meta-model, the entity Workflow Relevant Data, or simply Relevant Data, represents the relevant data of a workflow.

The data is made available to activities or applications executed during the workflow and may be used to pass persistent information or intermediate results between activities and/or to evaluate conditional expressions such as in transitions or participant assignments. Workflow relevant data is of a particular type: WPDL includes the definition of various basic and complex data types (including date, string, etc.) Activities, invoked applications, and/or transition conditions may refer to workflow process relevant data.

Each workflow relevant data definition has a particular type: WPDL (Workflow Process Definition Language) includes the definition of several basic and complex types, e.g., date, string, etc. A relevant type of workflow is a name that identifies a type (simple or complex). Moreover, in the workflow model, there is a section that groups the set of relevant types of workflow (declared by the user). The types declared in this section can be used for all definitions of workflow entities. They can be used, for example, in the definition of workflow relevant data, of extended attributes, or recursively, in the definition of workflow relevant types.

Workflow Participant

A workflow participant is a resource that performs partially, or in full, the work represented by a workflow activity instance.

In the meta-model, the activity Workflow Participant, or simply Participant, represents the workflow participants.

The particular resources, which can be assigned to perform a specific activity, are specified as an attribute of the activity. The participant assignment indicates the set of resources that may be allocated to it. The workflow participant declaration does not necessarily refer to a single person, but it may also identify a set of people of appropriate skills or responsibility or machine resources rather than human.

System and Environment Data

The data of the system and the environment are maintained by the WfMS or the local system environment, but may be accessed by workflow activities or used by the WfMS in the evaluation of conditional expressions in the same way as workflow relevant data. In this way, it may be regarded as an extension to workflow relevant data. A small number of standardized data entities (accessed by pre-defined library functions) are defined. Others may be added through the extended library function mechanism.

Organizational Model

In more sophisticated scenarios, the participant declaration may refer to an Organizational Model, external to the workflow process definitions, which enables the evaluation of more complex expressions, including reference to business functions, organizational entities, and relationships.

INCONVENIENCE OF THE PROCESS DEFINITIONS GENERATED FROM ACTIVITY DIAGRAMS

With the UML notation, is not possible to generate a workflow process definition that carries out the standard of Interface 1. The activity diagram can be used to model business processes, but an activity diagram does not have the adequate level of detail for a workflow engine to interpret it without ambiguity. The level of detail required for the workflow definitions are due to the need of interpretation and execution by workflow automatic systems (WfES).

In particular, an activity diagram cannot model some concepts identified in the workflow generic model depicted by the WfMC (identifiers, simulation data, valid date, definition author, etc.). As a consequence, it is not possible to generate from an activity diagram, a workflow process definition that satisfies the standard of Interface 1, i.e., the UML standard does not fulfill the WfMC standard.

The problems of process definitions generated from activity diagrams are:

- The lack of details of administration (for workflow engine). The entities, which are part of workflow definition, include attributes that contain information specifically destined to administrate an instance of entities by the workflow engine. This occurs because the model has to be interpreted and executed by automated systems. For example, the workflow engine uses the attribute "identifier" to reference a particular instance. Other attributes indicate how the workflow engine has to be used in certain instances. The entity Workflow Activity has attributes that indicate how the activity has to be initiated or finished. These and other attributes are not present as meta-classes in the UML meta-model.

- The lack of parameterized processes. This concept can be found in the WPDL definition but it is not in the UML definition. According to the workflow meta-model, the invocation to a workflow process can include the input and output parameter passage. In UML, the invocation of processes lacks this mechanism.

- The lack of simulation data. The UML meta-model does not have the possibility of explicit specification of data to be used in the simulation of processes. The simulation of a process described by an activity diagram requires that estimate data be externally specified to the diagram. The workflow meta-model allows for the specification of estimate values (duration, cost, wait time, etc.) associated to processes and activities.

- The lack of determination of executors in execution time. A distinct characteristic of a WPDL definition about an activity diagram is the possibility to determine the responsibility of a process and the executor of each activity in execution time. An activity diagram allows for the static association of activities and organizational units through the mechanism called "swimlanes." A swimlane allows for organizing the diagram into groups of activities that are each associated to a part of the organization that is responsible for these activities. In the workflow meta-model, the entities "Activity" and "Process" each present an attribute that indicates what the assigned participant will do through an expression.

How to Obtain the Integration

For the integration of two standards, it is necessary to define the same generic model with the same level of detail. As the generic model defined by the WfMC is more specific and detailed than the UML model, the integration means the adaptation of the UML standard to satisfy the WfMC standard.

The adaptation of the UML notation cannot be done directly on the graphical notation of the activity diagram. It has to be adapted to the meta-model, which describes the concepts recognized by UML in a business process. In other words, the integration of both standards has to be done through an extension of the UML meta-model, which incorporates the lacking concepts to equal the expressive power of the workflow meta-model.

Workflow Meta-model Represented by Class Diagram

Before explaining the extension, it is necessary to establish what the lacking concepts are. The identification of similarities and differences between meta-models is necessary as a previous step to any extension.

A graphical mechanism is proposed to express these differences and similarities. Class diagrams represent the concepts expressed in the workflow meta-model. These diagrams have a structure similar to the UML meta-model.

Using each table of attributes, as shown in Table 1, it is possible to obtain the class diagram of Figure 4. Table 1 contains only part of the attributes. The complete table can be obtained in WfMC Work Group 1 (1999).

The diagram in Figure 4 expresses part of the abstract syntax of the workflow process definition. Concretely, it describes the logical structure that the workflow meta-model recognizes in the workflow process.

The meta-class *SimulationData* is introduced. It groups the necessary data for the simulation, and it is associated to Workflow Process by replacing the attribute Simulation Data. This association is a composition because the simulation data is exclusive of each process. The components of this attribute, duration, working time, and waiting time, are now attributes of the meta-class *SimulationData*. The attributes instantiation and cost are contained in Simulation Data. This mapping is done for each attribute in Table 1.

The other attributes of the entity Process are shown in Figure 5.

Table 1: Table of attributes of the entity workflow process

Name	O/R	Keyword in WPDL	Data type	Description
Identifier	R	WORKFLOW	IDENTIFIER	Used to identify the process.
Name	O	NAME	STRING	Text used to identify the process.
Description	O	DESCRIPTION	STRING	A brief textual description of the process.
Duration Unit	O	DURATION_UNIT	Keyword	Duration Unit.
...	...	...	...	...

Figure 4: Class diagram corresponding to a workflow process

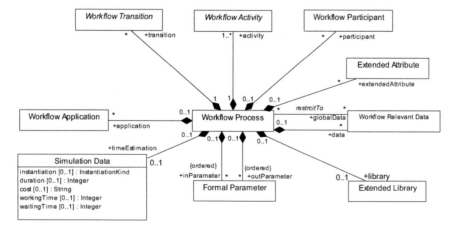

Figure 5: Class for the entity process

Workflow Process
identifier : String
name [0..1] : String
description [0..1] : String
durationUnit [0..1] : DurationKind
created [0..1] : Date
author [0..1] : String
version [0..1] : String
characterSet [0..1] : String
codepage [0..1] : String
countryKey [0..1] : String
responsible [0..1] : Expression
status [0..1] : StatusKind
validFrom [0..1] : Date
validTo [0..1] : Date
classification [0..1] : String
priority [0..1] : Integer
limit [0..1] : Integer
documentation [0..1] : String
icon [0..1] : String

Semantics and Structural Similarities and Differences

Comparing this diagram with the diagram corresponding to the abstract syntax of activity graph, it is possible to detect the differences and similarities between both structures.

Some similarities:
- Activities.
- Transitions.
- Attributes defined by the user.
- Name.
- Possibility to be referenced by the caller activity/state.

Some differences:
- Has own attributes of workflow process.
- Participants.
- Applications.
- Simulation data.
- Extend library.
- Formal parameters.

AN EXTENSION PROPOSAL

Similar to the UML activity graph, the workflow meta-model presents the processing as possible traverses using the directed graph. In the graph, the nodes represent activities and the transitions model the steps of control from one activity to another.

In UML, the activity diagrams provide more adequate notation to model processes. However, they are insufficient to model all of the details included in a standardized workflow process. It is necessary to define a new type of activity graph, which includes its own elements of the workflow process.

To preserve the package structure, we proposed the package *workflows* in the UML meta-model, as shown in Figure 6.

The abstract syntax and semantics of the extension are described in the package *workflows*. In this package, a new meta-class called *WorkflowProcess*, which inherits from *ActivityGraph*, is proposed. This specialization is adequate not only semantically, but also structurally, because a great part of the attributes and associations of the entity Process can be found in the meta-class *ActivityGraph* (possibly with another name but with the same semantics). The incorporation of this meta-class allows for the specification and modeling of business organizational processes using elements of workflow.

The basic semantics of a graph that models the control flow among the process activities is proposed in this extension. The capacities for the passage of parameters between processes, the management of resources, and the simulation are included.

The activity graph, as with the state machine, is essentially a state transition system. In the same sense, a workflow process can be shown as a state transition system.

Abstract Syntax of the Proposed Extension

Structurally, the meta-class *WorkflowProcess* inherits:

- From *ModelElement*, the attribute name, which is equivalent to the attribute name of the entity process in the workflow meta-model. The name of a workflow process is unique inside the workflow model.

- From *StateMachine*, the composition with *State*. It is possible to reference the root state through this composition. In this way, the *WorkflowProcess* is a subclass from *ActivityGraph*, and indirectly from *StateMachine*. In addition, generic Activity is a subclass from *State;* therefore, a *WorkflowProcess* inherits the composition in order to have activities.

- From *StateMachine*, the composition with Transition. It is possible to reference the transitions that compose the graph and that can be applied during execution using this composition.

- From *StateMachine*, the association context with *ModelElement*, which indicates the model element whose behavior is specified by the state machine.

- From *StateMachine*, the association with *StateSubmachine*, which allow a state submachine to specify the referenced state machine. This machine is called when the state is activated.

- From *ActivityGraph*, the composition with Partition. It is possible to reference a set of partitions through this composition.

- From *ModelElement*, the composition of multiplicity * with *TaggedValue*. This composition is associated to a workflow process with a set of zero or more attributes

Figure 6: The new package Workflows in the UML meta-model

Figure 7: The attributes of WorkflowProcess

WorkflowProcess
identifier : String
description [0..1] : String
durationUnit [0..1] : DurationKind
created [0..1] : Time
author [0..1] : String
version[0..1] : String
characterSet [0..1] : String
codepage [0..1] : String
countryKey [0..1] : String
responsible [0..1] : Expression
status [0..1] : StatusKind
validFrom [0..1] : Time
validTo [0..1] : Time
classification [0..1] : String
priority [0..1] : Integer
limit [0..1] : Integer
documentation [0..1] : String
icon [0..1] : String

defined by the user. This composition corresponds to Extended Attribute of the workflow meta-model. In the extension, an extended attribute is a special case of a tagged value.

In spite of the similarities of a workflow process with an activity graph, there are differences from a structural point of view. *WorkflowProcess* includes the following specific attributes of the workflow process:

- Identifier: An identifier of the process, which is unique inside a workflow meta-model.
- Description: Description of the process.
- DurationUnit: The duration unit used in the simulation.
- Created: Date when the process definition was created.
- Responsible: Participant who is responsible for the process. This attribute provides the capacity to determine who will be responsible for the process during execution time. The expression is written in WPDL and has to return a workflow participant.
- ValidFrom: Date of valid beginning.
- ValidTo: Date of valid expiration.

Figure 8: Abstract syntax for WorkflowProcess

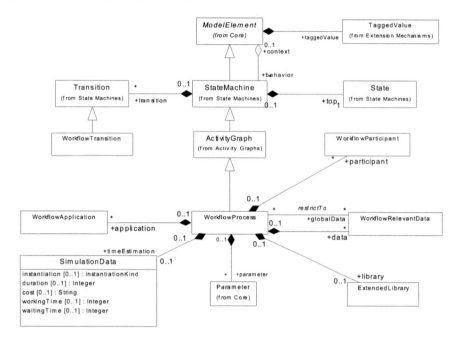

- Limit: Duration limit of the process.
- Documentation: References the documentation of the process.

Other attributes are shown in Figure 7. These attributes are included in the meta-class *WorkflowProcess* of UML with the same name and semantics that are presented in the workflow meta-model.

In addition to attributes, *WorkflowProcess* includes association and composition with the meta-classes *WorkflowApplication*, *WorkflowParticipant*, *ExtendedLibrary*, and *SimulationData*. These relationships complete the structure needed for a workflow process in UML that contains the same information of process definitions written in WPDL. These relationships are shown in Figure 8.

Well-Formedness Rules for the Proposed Extension

In this section, the static semantics of the extension are shown. The invariants presented here correspond only to constraints of the extension shown in this chapter. The OCL notation (Warmer & Kleppe, 1999) is the same one used in the original UML specification.

The following "well-formedness" rules as applied in the package *workflows* are:

Workflow Process

(1)   The root activity of a workflow process is an instance of Block.
      self.top.oclIsKindOf(Block)

(2)   All transitions of a workflow process are workflow transitions.
      self.transition → ∀ (oclIsKindOf(WorkflowTransition))

(3)   The instances of *WorkflowProcess* can be related through the association
      taggedValue, but only with instances of ExtendedAttribute.
      self.taggedValue → ∀ (oclIsTypeOf(ExtendedAttribute))

(4)   The relevant data defined in the process is not global data.
      self.data → intersection(self.globalData) → isEmpty

(5)   If the process has an access restriction, only the global data declared can be a formal
      parameter of the process.
      self.globalData → size > 0 ⇒
      self.formalParameters → ∀ (r | self.globalData → includes(r))

(6)   The parameters of a process reference relevant data of a workflow.
      self.parameter → ∀ (state → size = 1 ∧ state.oclIsTypeOf(Workflow
      RelevantData))

(7)   The responsibility of a process is determined by an expression WPDL.
      self.responsible.language = 'WPDL'

(8)   It is not possible to define two extended attributes with the same identifier in a
      workflow.
      process.self.taggedValue →
      (a1, a2|
      a1.oclAsType(ExtendedAttribute).identifier =
      a2.oclAsType(ExtendedAttribute).identifier
      ⇒ a1 = a2)

(9)   It is not possible to define two activities with the same name in a workflow process.
      self.allActivities → ∀ (a1, a2| a1.name = a2.name ⇒ a1 = a2)

Additional operations

(10) The operation *allActivities* returns the set of all activities of the process.
      allActivities: set(StateVertex);
      allActivities = self.top → union(self.top.allActivities)

Concrete Syntax of the Extension

The concrete syntax of the process definitions is described by an EBNF (Extended
Backus Naur Form), which specifies the grammar of the Workflow Process Definition

Language. This language forms the standard format to interchange the process definitions between the modeling tools and the workflow engine.

The mapping between the concrete syntax and abstract syntax is not explicit in the
workflow meta-model.

The mapping is defined using OCL through the operation "mapping()." This
operation is added in each new meta-class of a package *workflows* and specifies its own
mapping between concrete syntax and abstract syntax. Figure 9 shows part of the
specification of this mapping for *WorkflowProcess*.

Figure 9: Mapping between abstract and concrete syntax for WorkflowProcess

```
    mapping() : String;
     mapping = 'WORKFLOW ' + self.identifier + ' ' +
     attributeText('CREATED', self.created)+
     nameAttributeText('NAME', self.name)+
     attributeText('DESCRIPTION', self.description)+
     attributeText('AUTHOR', self.author)+
     attributeText('VERSION', self.version)+
     attributeText('RESPONSIBLE', self.responsible)+
     attributeText('STATUS', self.status)+
      attributeText('DURATION_UNIT', self.durationUnit)+
     attributeText('PRIORITY', self.priority)+
     attributeText('LIMIT', self.limit)+
     attributeText('VALID_FROM', self.validFrom)+
     attributeText('VALID_TO', self.validTo)+
     attributeText('CLASSIFICATION', self.classification)+
      attributeText('DOCUMENTATION', self.documentation)+
     attributeText('ICON', self.icon)+
    self.taggedValue->iterate(a: TaggedValue; result: String = ''|
          result = result + a.oclAsType(ExtendedAttribute).code + ' ') +
     self.parameter->iterate(p: Parameter; result: String = 'IN_PARAMETERS '|
          result =
              if (p.kind = #in or p.kind = #inout)
                  then result + p.state.oclAsType(WorkflowRelevantData).identifier + ' '
                  else result
              endif) +
     self.parameter->iterate(p: Parameter; result: String = 'OUT_PARAMETERS '|
          result =
              if (p.kind = #out or p.kind = #inout)
                  then result + p.state.oclAsType(WorkflowRelevantData).identifier + ' '
                  else result
              endif) +
     self.top.allWorkflowActivities->iterate(a: WorkflowActivity; result: String = ''|
          result = result + a.code + ' ') +
     self.transition->iterate(t: Transition; result: String = ''|
          result = result + t.oclAsType(WorkflowTransition).code + ' ') +
     self.participant->iterate(p: WorkflowParticipant; result: String = ''|
          result = result + p.code + ' ') +
     self.application->iterate(a: WorkflowApplication; result: String = ''|
```

Figure 9: Mapping between abstract and concrete syntax for WorkflowProcess (continued)

```
            result = result + a.code + ' ')
    +

    ....
    'END_WORKFLOW'
```

Additional Operations

```
    attributeText(tag: String, attribute: String): String;
    attributeText = if attribute = null
                    then ''
                        else tag + ' ' + attribute + ' '
                endif

    attributeText(tag: String, attribute: Integer): String;
    attributeText = if attribute = null
                    then ''
                        else tag + ' ' + integerToString(attribute) + ' '
                endif

    attributeText(tag: String, attribute: Date): String;
    attributeText = if attribute = null
                    then ''
                        else tag + ' ' + dateToString(attribute) + ' '
                endif

    nameAttributeText(tag: String, attribute: Name): String;
    nameAttributeText = if attribute = null
                        then ''
                            else tag + ' ' + attribute.body + ' '
                        endif

    attributeText(tag: String, attribute: Expression): String;
    attributeText = if attribute = null
                    then ''
                        else tag + ' ' + attribute.body + ' '
                    endif
```

CONCLUSIONS

In this chapter, an extension of the UML activity graph meta-model is shown. This extension supports the workflow standard. The basic goal of the extension is to model workflow processes using the UML activity diagram. It allows modeled processes to verify the standard defined by the WfMC, achieving interoperability and portability with other processes that are defined by means of that standard. This extension allows for adaptation of the UML to the new workflow technologies and extends its expressive power to automate business processes.

UML activity diagrams have several restrictions with respect to workflow processes. They cannot specify details of administration to indicate particular characteristics of a specific process to a workflow engine. Moreover, they lack the input and output parameter passages for a process. Another characteristic is that the tools, which define the workflow processes, have the capacity to simulate the behavior of the process. A UML activity diagram lacks this capacity. Therefore, the extension of UML activity diagrams as proposed here, resolves all of these problems.

Some entities of the workflow meta-model are defined as an example of the extension. The extension does not only aggregate elements, but also imposes restrictions to exclude situations that are allowed in the activity graph but not in workflow. These constraints have been defined using OCL. The abstract syntax is shown with the corresponding class diagram; and, the mapping between abstract syntax and concrete syntax is done using OCL.

The new UML activity diagram includes the possibility of simulation, the capacity of defining executors at run time, the possibility of invoking parameterized processes, and the option of assigning individual resources/applications for each activity.

REFERENCES

Allen, R. Workflow: An introduction. *Open Image Systems Inc.*, United Kingdom Chair, WfMC External Relations Committee.

Allen, R. (Oct. 2000). The workflow handbook 2001. *Published in association with the Workflow Management Coalition* (WfMC).

Booch, G., Rumbaugh, J., & Jacobson, I. (1999). The Unified Modeling Language user guide. Addison-Wesley Longman, Inc..

Champy, J. (1995). Reengineering management. *Harper Business*.

Davenport, T.H., & Young, J.E. (1990). The new industrial engineering: Information technology and business process redesign. *Sloan Management Review*.

Fischer, L. (2001). *Workflow hand book*.

Hammer, M., & Champy, J. (1993). Reengineering the corporation: A manifesto for business revolution. Harper Collins Publishing, Inc.

Hollingsworth, D. (1995). The workflow management coalition specification workflow management coalition. *The Workflow Reference Model. Document Number TC00-1003, Document Status - Issue 1.1*. On the World Wide Web: http://www.wfmc.org

IEEE. On the World Wide Web: http://www.ieee.org

Jacobson, I. (1996). Objectifying business process reengineering. Addison-Wesley.

Jacobson, I., Booch, G., & Rumbaugh, J. (1999). The unified software development process. Addison-Wesley.

Jacobson, I., Ericsson, M., & Jacobson, A. (1995). The object advantage: Business process reengineering with object technology. Addison-Wesley.

OMG. (March 2000). Unified Modeling Language specification (version 1.3, first edition). On the World Wide Web: http://www.omg.org

Rumbaugh, J., Jacobson, I., & Booch, G. (1999). The Unified Modeling Language reference manual. Addison-Wesley.

Warmer, J., & Kleppe, A. (1999). The object constraint language: Precise modeling with UML. Addison-Wesley Longman, Inc.

WfMC. *White Paper*. Embedded & autonomous workflow. On the World Wide Web: http://www.wfmc.org

WfMC Work Group 1, Workflow Management Coalition (1999). Interface 1: Process definition interchange process model. *Document Number WfMC TC-1016-P (Version 1.1; official release).* On the World Wide Web: http://www.wfmc.org

Chapter XVI

Business Processes in UML

Peter Rittgen
Technical University Darmstadt, Germany

ABSTRACT

Today, modeling business processes and modeling software is done using different notations that are designed to fit the special needs of the respective tasks. However, this fact results in a painful methodological gap between business models and software models, which is hard to bridge. This problem becomes even more painful if we try to build software to support certain business models because a smooth transition between the employed notations is usually not supported, or due to methodological problems, impossible. In order to allow for a smoother transition, we propose using Business Process Diagrams (BPDs), which are based on the UML activity diagrams (in both business and software worlds). We show how to derive BPDs from the well-known business process language of Event-driven Process Chains (EPCs) using Petri nets as a common process meta- model.

INTRODUCTION

When analyzing a company for possibilities of information systems support, a major task consists in identifying the relevant business processes and describing them in a suitable modeling language. Many such languages have been developed over the years: IDEF (Integrated DEFinition, (Bruce, 1992)); Role Activity Diagrams (Ould, 1995); and ARIS/EPC (ARchitecture of integrated Information Systems / Event-driven Process Chain, (Scheer, 1999)) to name but a few.

These languages share a common characteristic in that they are not equipped to support the design of software. The Unified Modeling Language (UML), cp., e.g., (Rational Software et al., 1997), on the other hand, does provide the features pertinent to software engineering although it is less qualified for use in domain-oriented models. In practice, this leads not only to a separation of concerns, but also to a heterogeneous usage of modeling languages: domain experts using business languages and software engineers using UML. This creates an undesirable gap between domain and software models and represents a source for mistakes that are hard to correct.

Hence, we suggest Business Process Diagrams (BPDs), i.e., a language closely related to UML activity diagrams, for both business and software development when taking a closer look at a typical business process language called Event-driven Process Chains (EPCs). Our main objective is to ensure that all features of EPCs are present in BPDs, too. At the same time, we want to make certain that the semantics of the corresponding EPC and BPD diagrams coincide. We achieve this by using the formal, i.e., mathematical, process language of Petri nets as a common meta-model to define the meaning of both diagram types. That will allow us to conclude that the resultant language of BPDs is suitable for designing processes for not only software, but also in the business domain. It also enables an automatic transformation from EPC to BPD and back, i.e., switching between business and software views.

In the following sections, we first introduce Event-driven Process Chains as typical models for business processes and define their semantics in the light of the common meta-model of Petri nets. We then enhance the suitability of UML activity diagrams for business modeling, which leads us to Business Process Diagrams (BPDs). Their semantics are also based on the common meta-model, which ensures the compatibility of both EPC and BPD. We conclude by showing examples of typical business processes with representations as EPCs and BPDs.

BACKGROUND: EVENT-DRIVEN PROCESS CHAINS

Event-driven Process Chains were introduced to draw a graphical representation of a business process. They consist of the following elements as shown in Figure 1.

Ever since the introduction of EPCs by Scheer, there have been many opinions on how a correct EPC should look. Proposals ranged from syntactical issues (which nodes can be linked to one another?) to semantics (what is the exact meaning of a connector?). On the syntactical level, some rules have been established that are now generally accepted, for example, (Keller & Teufel, 1997): An EPC consists of strictly alternating sequences of events and functions (i.e., processes) that are linked by logical connectors (AND, OR, XOR). There are opening connectors (splits) and closing connectors (joins). The AND stands for parallel threads, the XOR for mutually exclusive alternatives, and the OR for arbitrarily selecting many alternatives. Events are instantaneous happenings that trigger a business function or process. Events may also be the results of finishing a function or a process. A function is an elementary business activity; a process is a business activity, which is refined through another EPC. A function/process can have the organizational unit that is responsible for it and data containers from where it gets input or stores output attached to it. Among the syntactical restrictions for EPCs that are named in Keller and Teufel (1997) are:

K1:   There are no isolated nodes.
K3/4:   Functions and events have exactly one incoming and one outgoing edge (except start and end events).

Figure 1: EPC elements

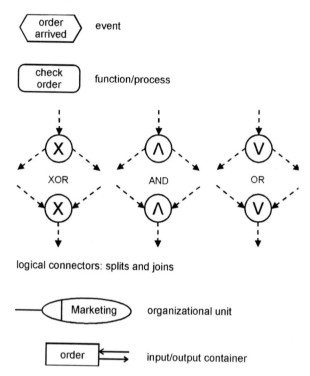

order arrived — event

check order — function/process

logical connectors: splits and joins

Marketing — organizational unit

order — input/output container

K6:   Connectors are either splits (one input, several outputs) or joins (several inputs, one output).

K8/9:   An event is always followed by a function and vice versa (modulo connectors).

It is also sometimes requested that an event should not be followed by an XOR split because an events cannot make a decision. Figure 2 shows an example of how an EPC looks. A more detailed EPC that also contains organizational units is shown in Figure 5.

The example in Figure 2 describes a simple order processing. The event *order arrived* signals that a customer order has been received, which triggers a check of this order (function *check order*). Depending on the outcome, either the left or the right path is taken (XOR) and the corresponding activity is performed. The final XOR connector rejoins both paths and raises the end event *order processed*.

Figure 2: EPC example

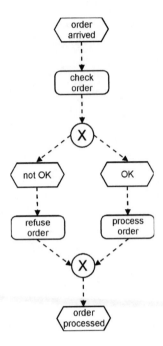

A PETRI-NET MODEL FOR EVENT-DRIVEN PROCESS CHAINS

The precise meaning of an EPC is largely subject to personal interpretation, especially where unmatched joins and timing are concerned (Rittgen, 1999). This seeming deficiency is not the result of a bad language design, but rather it is a requirement for the analysis stage where the participants typically do not yet have a deep and clear understanding of the business process. Freedom of interpretation is an advantage at this stage. Therefore, precise semantics were intentionally left unspecified by the proponents of the EPC. At later stages, we do require more precise models. Hence, the issue of a formal semantics for EPCs has been studied quite thoroughly (e.g., Chen & Scheer, 1994; Langner et al., 1997; Rump, 1997). All that the approaches have in common is that they transform the ambiguous EPC into a Petri net having a unique and precise meaning. This transformation entails that a number of possible interpretations are discarded. Only the "correct" interpretation is represented in the Petri net. But who is to say which interpretation is correct? This way, we might easily eliminate the one that was intended by the modeler or the one that would have been the result of the collective process driven by the people involved in building the information system: users, domain experts, software engineers, (project) managers, etc.

In Dehnert and Rittgen (2001), we therefore suggest that all possible interpretations be kept during the transformation into a formal language. As a consequence, we arrive at the rules displayed in Figure 3. The left side of each bar shows an EPC element; on the right side the corresponding Petri net element is found. For a detailed description of this

Figure 3: Transformation EPC ® Petri net

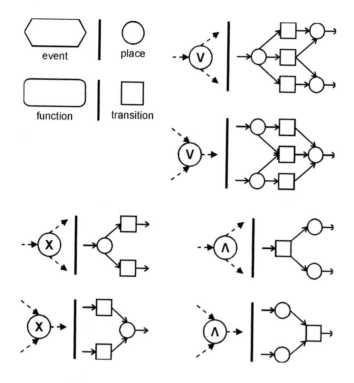

process, refer to Dehnert and Rittgen (2001). On the basis of these rules, and a Petri net semantics for BPDs (enhanced activity diagrams),we will be able to translate between EPCs and BPDs and hence, between business and software views of processes.

ACTIVITY DIAGRAMS AND BUSINESS PROCESSES

Although the proponents of UML suggest that activity diagrams can be used for business process modeling cf., OMG (2000, pp. 1-9), there is some doubt as to whether they actually cover all aspects required for modeling business processes, cf., Nüttgens et al. (1998). Simons and Graham (1999) point out that activity diagrams are better suited for this purpose than use cases and other UML diagrams. Barros et al. (2000) identify areas of improvement. Among the business process features missing in the UML (version 1.3) activity diagrams are:

- An event-control mechanism.
- Handling of errors / exceptions.
- Flexible assignment of organizational units that will be responsible for an activity.
- Assignment of data containers (here: objects) to activities.

OMG (2000, p. 3-146) defines:

"An activity diagram is a special case of a state diagram in which all (or at least most) of the states are action or subactivity states and in which all (or at least most) of the transitions are triggered by completion of the actions or subactivities in the source states. The entire activity diagram is attached (through the model) to a class, such as a use case, or to a package, or to the implementation of an operation. The purpose of this diagram is to focus on flows driven by internal processing (as opposed to external events). Use activity diagrams in situations where all or most of the events represent the completion of internally-generated actions (that is, procedural flow of control). Use ordinary state diagrams in situations where asynchronous events occur."

This means that in activity diagrams, a transition is typically not associated with an event because it is triggered by the completion of its predecessor. Nevertheless, it does no harm to allow for this because the activity diagram is formally a special case of a state chart diagram and the latter provides event-controlled transitions. We only have to define what an event-controlled transition leaving an action state means, especially in the presence of additional, event-less transitions, because this is not covered by the original definition (see Figure 4).

If the *event* takes place before the *activity* is finished, the *activity* is aborted and state *S2* is entered. Otherwise, *S1* is entered upon termination of the *activity*. This mechanism can also be used to handle errors / exceptions where the error is an event aborting the current activity and entering a state of error handling / recovery.

To assign organizational units to activities (OMG, 2000) suggests the use of the so-called swimlanes. A swimlane is a rectangular area separated by vertical lines that extend from the swimlanes to the right and to the left. Each swimlane represents an organizational unit. All activities that fall within the responsibility of this organizational unit are collected within its swimlane. While this notation is quite useful for smaller diagrams, it becomes more and more tedious as the number of activities increases. There is a trade-off between the vertical partitioning into organizational units and the horizontal ordering along the control flow that often results in a 'messy' arrangement of the transitions: activities that follow each other temporally might be in distant swimlanes and activities in adjacent swimlanes might be far removed from on another concerning the logic of execution. In such cases, the diagram cannot be arranged clearly.

Figure 4: Events in activity diagrams

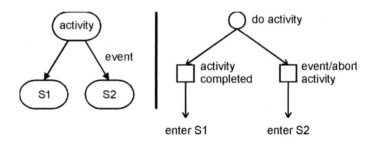

Figure 5: BPD example

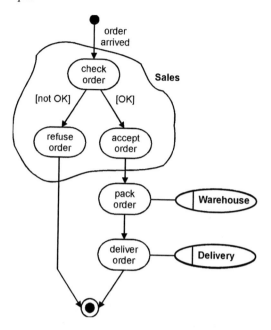

The first step toward solving this problem consists of relaxing the strict geometric shape of a swimlane from a rectangle to an arbitrary closed curve (a 'cloud'). Figure 5 shows how a cloud can be employed to group the activities for which a sales department is responsible. But even a cloud cannot group activities satisfactorily if they are scattered over a large area with many unrelated activities in between. In these cases it makes sense to attach the organizational unit directly to the activity as done in EPCs, i.e., in the form of an ellipse with a vertical bar. Such a notation is also useful when an organizational unit is responsible for only one activity in the whole BPD as the example in Figure 5 shows.

To summarize the argument, we suggest use of a mixture of notations to represent the organizational aspect of a business process, i.e.:

- Swimlanes as proposed for activity diagrams in OMG (2000) (for small diagrams).
- Clouds for grouping neighboring activities (in larger diagrams).
- EPC-style ellipses for scattered or individual activities (in larger diagrams).

A similar notation can be used for the assignment of data containers / objects.

PETRI-NET SEMANTICS OF BUSINESS PROCESS DIAGRAMS

If we intend to use business process diagrams for both business processes and the dynamics of software, we have to go into the precise meanings of these diagrams first. Activity diagrams are defined in OMG (2000) as a variation of state machines, where each state represents the performance of an activity. It is drawn as a rectangle with rounded,

Figure 6: Activity state (notation and semantics)

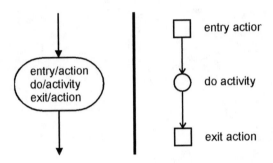

vertical lines. The state contains a "do" activity and optionally, an "entry" and/or an "exit" action. Entry and exit actions are performed upon entering or leaving the state, respectively. Their execution is considered to be instantaneous. The "do" activity is performed while it is in the state, which can take any amount of time. Upon termination of this activity, the state is left.

Figure 6 shows a generic activity state together with its semantics in Petri net notation. A Petri net is a bipartite graph of places (circles) and transitions (squares,) where a transition can fire if all incoming places are occupied by tokens. Upon firing, a token is removed from each incoming place. Thereafter, one token is put on each outgoing place. See Peterson (1981) for a detailed treatment of Petri nets. In the Petri net of Figure 6, the entry action is performed (upon entering the state) and a token is put on the place. While the activity is performed, the token remains on the place. Upon its termination, which coincides with performing the exit action, the token is removed.

Figure 7: Guarded branch (notation and semantics)

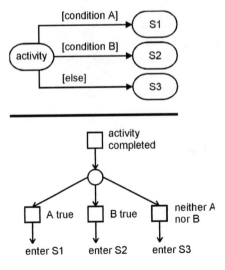

Figure 8: Cascaded branch

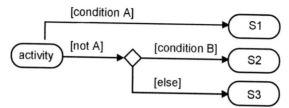

Figure 9: Guarded fork (notation and semantics)

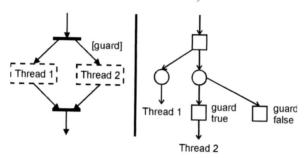

If we want to express non-sequential behavior, there are two different ways of splitting the path of execution: branching into alternative paths and forking into parallel paths. The branch is simply denoted by more than one arrow leaving a state (see Figure 7). A guard should be specified to determine which path is selected. A guard is a "Boolean" condition written in square brackets. If it evaluates to "true," then the corresponding path is chosen. An "else" guard can be specified, which holds true if all other guards are false. In fact, it should be present if such a situation should arise in order to prevent the process from blocking. Exactly one path is chosen so that the branch corresponds to the exclusive OR (XOR) connector of EPCs. If more than one guard is true, then one of the associated paths is selected arbitrarily. To avoid misinterpretation in this situation, it is recommended that the decisions be cascaded in the form of a binary tree as shown in Figure 8.

The notational element for cascading guards is the diamond shape. This shape has no semantics of its own and only serves as an anchor point for splitting a path. The design in Figure 8 ensures that condition "A" is given preference if both "A" *and* "B" are true.

The second way of splitting up the execution is by using the fork. The fork is denoted by a bar (see Figure 9). If it is unguarded, then it simply refers to the parallel, independent execution of both paths (called thread 1 and thread 2). In this case it corresponds to the "AND" connector of EPCs. The joining of the parallel paths is synchronous, i.e., it waits for the completion of both paths. If a path is guarded and the guard is false, then it is neither taken nor waited for. A fork where all paths are guarded corresponds to the (inclusive) "OR" connector of EPCs as arbitrarily, many paths can be taken. The rules governing activity diagrams demand that guarded threads be well-nested, i.e., jumping in or out of such a thread is not allowed except for synchronizing between threads. Please observe that this restriction is problematic in the case of business process modeling as it drastically limits the number of valid models. A detailed discussion of this problem in the context of EPCs can be found in Rittgen (2001).

TRANSLATING BETWEEN BPDS AND EPCS: EXAMPLES

Typical Patterns in Business Processes

In the literature on business process reengineering, recurring basic process patterns are identified (e.g., Rosemann, 1996; Becker & Schütte, 1996). In the following, we discuss the most important ones.

Pattern 1: Refinement of events

By definition, each function of an EPC is triggered by (at least) one event, e.g., the function *process order* in Figure 10 is triggered by an event called o*rder arrived*. A situation like this (i.e., business function triggered by a single event) is typical for business process models in their early stages. Later, as the underlying business processes become more transparent for the people who are in charge of the modeling, the model often becomes more detailed, e.g., by subdividing the single starting event into different starting events.

In Figure 10, we find such a pattern. In order to express that a business function may be triggered by different starting events, we join the new (detailed) starting events, which together replace the old starting event, by a logical connector, e.g., inclusive or exclusive disjunction.

After becoming more familiar with the underlying business processes, the original starting event *order arrived* became more detailed. In order to distinguish between different possible starting events, the original starting event was replaced by two refined starting events expressing the channel used to submit the customer's order. As a customer order might arrive via both channels, i.e., a phone call could be accompanied by a corresponding fax, we used an inclusive disjunction operator. However, in the given model, timing conditions remained rather fuzzy and are mostly subject to personal interpretation.

Figure 10: Refinement of events

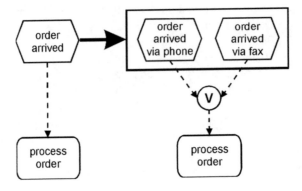

Figure 11: Sequential events

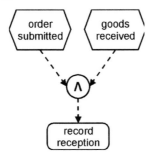

Pattern 2: Sequential events

In EPCs, events may trigger functions. With respect to the sequence of events and functions, EPCs are bipartite graphs. Because of this, there could be interpretative problems if there are some sequentially-ordered events that need to occur in conjunction with one another in order to trigger a specific business function. We give such an example in Figure 11. Figure 11 shows two events that both need to take place in order to trigger the business function *"record reception (of goods)."*

If we take a closer look at the underlying business logic, it becomes obvious that we have to submit an order first (event *order submitted*). After some time, the second event (*goods received*) would occur. The events are connected by a conjunction operator, since both events are necessary to trigger the recording of the received goods.

A possible design guideline to model relations of this type between events using EPCs is to model the main process along an assumed horizontal time line. Additional (mandatory) starting events that succeed other events (without an intervening function) are drawn to the right and connected using a conjunction operator. However, a guideline like this is not really satisfying – especially with respect to the task of designing software.

Pattern 3: Parallel tasks

In cases of parallel tasks, it is necessary to split business processes accordingly. We do this by using the conjunction or inclusive disjunction operator of the EPC, cf., Figure 12. The operator is placed after the business function, generating a starting event for each concurrent thread.

The example in Figure 12 shows a business process that is typical for industrial production. As soon as a customer order arrives, we calculate the secondary demand (e.g., the parts required to produce the ordered good or the so-called primary demand). During calculation of the secondary demand, we also decide whether to buy or produce the corresponding parts (make-or-buy decision). Here it is important to note that there may be thousands of parts that are necessary to build the ordered product, e.g., a car as the primary demand.

For each secondary demand we either initiate procurement (buy decision) or production (make decision). As we treat procurement and production differently, we split the business process at this point. Both resultant threads may be processed in parallel. A procurement decision leads to corresponding procurement activities (function *procure parts*). A production decision, on the other hand, leads to a change of the production

Figure 12: Parallel tasks

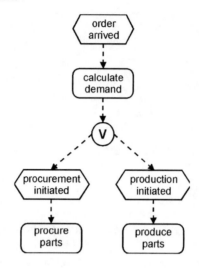

plan (function *produce parts*). Further functions describing the production process are left open.

Pattern 4: Alternative tasks

We call tasks alternative if one, and only one, thread can be chosen out of a set of possible threads. To represent the required choice, we use the exclusive disjunction operator (Figure 13). After the business function decides between the possible alternatives, we connect the exclusive disjunction operator, which in turn, is connected to the

Figure 13: Alternative tasks

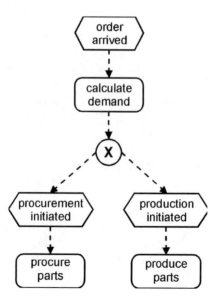

starting events triggering the alternative threads. The last function of each thread leads to a corresponding closing exclusive disjunction operator finalizing the alternative choice pattern.

Figure 13 shows a real world example of this process pattern. During the calculation of "demand," a decision is drawn whether *all* parts should be bought or *all* parts should be produced. The alternative threads are then connected via an exclusive disjunction operator to the deciding business function (*calculate demand*). Each thread has its own starting event. With this, the parts are either bought (function *buy parts*) or produced (function *make parts*). The alternative threads finally lead to a closing exclusive disjunction operator (not shown here).

BPD Equivalents of the Patterns

In the last section we identified a number of important patterns that typically arise when we model business processes. These patterns were introduced in the form of EPCs, but could have been specified in any other semi-formal language intended for business process modeling. The 'semi' in semi-formal means that only one-half of the language, namely the syntax, is given precisely: the basic elements such as events, processes, and connectors and how these can be put together. The other half, the semantics, is only described informally and often relies on the intuition of the modeler. If we put experience from process reengineering together with the precise semantics of the BPDs, then we arrive at the patterns outlined in this section. We thereby show how process patterns that frequently occur in many business scenarios and which, in most cases, are given in a semi-formal way, can be transformed into a rigorous representation that facilitates the development of software.

Figure 14 shows the BPD pattern for the refinement of events. *Process order* becomes an activity in an activity state. Events in BPDs are represented as labels on the corresponding transition. This implies that the event triggers the transition from the preceding to the succeeding state. The detailed events in the EPC pattern of Figure 10 are merged by an inclusive "OR" connector. This is equivalent to a guarded fork. Contrary to an EPC where multiple starting events are allowed, an activity diagram has always exactly one entry point (i.e., the initial state drawn as a full black circle). This means that

Figure 14: Refinement of events as BPD

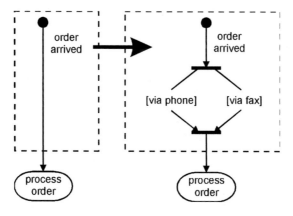

Figure 15: Sequential events as BPD

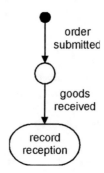

the single entry path has to be split first into two parallel threads; one thread for each channel used for transmitting an order. Parallel threads are required because we want to ensure that the same order is sent over more than one channel, e.g., as a phone call accompanied by a fax. The guards ensure that the function *process order* only waits for the channels that are actually used.

The rules of EPCs require processes and events to alternate strictly: no two events may follow each other immediately. This prevents us from expressing a situation where a process is triggered by two consecutive events in a natural way. In BPDs there is no such restriction. As a consequence, we simply insert a pseudo-state between the events (see Figure 15). In this way, we can specify that both events are required for the execution of the process and can also specify the order in which they occur.

According to the transformation rules, the "OR" connector of Figure 12 maps to a fork (see Figure 16). The outgoing arrows of the fork are labeled with the events in the form of guards. In this way procurement and production can be done in parallel; but, procurement is only performed if a corresponding procurement decision has been made for the part in question. The same applies to the production thread.

An XOR connector in an EPC diagram (see Figure 13) is transformed into a branch in BPD notation (see Figure 17). For a good design, it is imperative that the guards be mutually exclusive to avoid the arbitrary selection of a path. In our example, this means that we should not decide for both procurement and production at the same time.

Figure 16: Parallel tasks as BPD

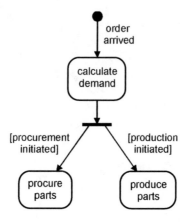

Figure 17: Alternative tasks as BPD

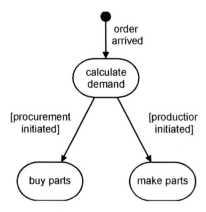

FUTURE TRENDS

The introduction of UML provided a standard, which not only influenced the modeling of software, but also that of businesses. Many methods that were thus far primarily focused on the business domain are now being equipped with interfaces to UML. On the other hand, early versions of the UML paid little attention to business applications. The use case seemed to be the only UML concept for business modeling and it was hence often stretched beyond its original scope, e.g., by employing it to model business processes. Many authors have therefore tried to make use of the powerful UML concept of stereotypes to build application-oriented languages. Contrary to this development, the ideas outlined here argue that we need more original support for business-oriented concepts in UML rather than having to specify them as add-ons. The reason for this is that the latter makes it much more difficult to establish a standard for the 'business add-ons' and to integrate the business models into the UML world. We have taken one step in this direction by adding the concept of business processes to UML. Others should follow suit to make UML a truly unified language for all aspects of developing information systems.

CONCLUSION

Building an information system is a complex, time-consuming, and costly endeavor. Its success depends largely on the amount of understanding that can be established between the major players: users, domain experts, software engineers, managers, etc. Understanding can be established through models that serve as a basis for the communication of ideas and designs by supporting the individual view of each group of players while at the same time making sure that they really talk about the same model. This requires that the views have a common semantics base (or meta-model) and can translate into one another. In the area of business processes, models have been suggested that support a business view (e.g., EPC) and others have been suggested that support a software view (e.g., activity diagrams). Instead of being only different views of one and the same model, they are actually completely different models that cover a similar area, but that do not have a common basis (semantics or meta-model). Hence, translating between the views is difficult and the resultant communication between the players is weak and subject to misunderstandings. This, in turn, leads to a poor system design.

We have therefore developed business process diagrams, which inherit the concepts of both EPCs and activity diagrams and put both on a sound common basis, i.e., the Petri net meta model. This facilitates the translation between the views and thus enables players from different groups to discuss the same model while retaining their individual views. In this way differing interpretations or expectations of the system can be identified early and can be prevented from evolving into serious mistakes in the software design or into disappointment for the users.

REFERENCES

Barros, A., Duddy, K., Lawley, M., Milosevic, Z., Raymond, K., & Wood, A. (2000). Processes, roles, and events: UML concepts for enterprise architecture. In A. Evans, S. Kent, & B. Selic (Eds.), UML 2000 - The Unified Modeling Language. Advancing the Standard. *Third International Conference, York, UK, October 2000. Proceedings. Lecture Notes in Computer Science 1939* (pp. 62-77, Berlin: Springer.

Becker, J., & Schütte, R. (1996). Handelsinformationssysteme. Landsberg.

Bruce, T. A. (1992). Designing quality databases with IDEF1X information models. New York: Dorset House.

Chen, R., & Scheer, A.-W. (1994). Modellierung von prozessketten mittels petri-netz-theorie. *Report 107, Institute of Information Systems*, University Saarbrücken.

Dehnert, J., & Rittgen, P. (2001). Relaxed soundness of business processes. In K.R.Dittrich, A. Geppert, & M.C. Norrie (Eds.). Advanced Information Systems Engineering. *13th International Conference, CAiSE 2001, Interlaken, Switzerland, June 4-8, 2001. Proceedings. Lecture Notes in Computer Science 2068* (pp. 157-170). Berlin: Springer.

Keller, G., & Teufel, T. (1997). SAP R/3 prozeßorientiert anwenden: Iteratives prozeß-prototyping zur bildung von wertschöpfungsketten, (2. ed.). Bonn: Addison-Wesley-Longman.

Langner, P., Schneider, Ch., & Wehler, J. (1997). Prozessmodellierung mit Ereignisgesteuerten Prozessketten (EPKs) und Petri-Netzen. *WIRTSCHAFTSINFORMATIK, 39(5)* (pp. 479-489).

Nüttgens, M., Feld, T., & Zimmermann, V. (1998). Business process modeling with EPC and UML: Transformation or integration? In M. Schader, & A. Korthaus (Eds.). *The Unified Modeling Language - Technical Aspects and Applications* (pp. 250-261). Heidelberg: Springer

OMG (Ed.). (2000). OMG Unified Modeling Language specification: Version 1.3, March 2000. Needham: OMG.

Ould, M. (1995). Business processes: modeling and analysis for re-engineering and improvement. Chichester: John Wiley and Sons.

Peterson, J. L. (1981). Petri net theory and the modeling of systems. Englewood Cliffs: Prentice-Hall.

Rational Software, Microsoft, Hewlett-Packard, Oracle, Sterling Software, MCI Systemhouse, Unisys, ICON Computing, IntelliCorp, i-Logix, IBM, ObjecTime, Platinum Technology, Ptech, Taskon, Reich Technologies, & Softeam (1997). *UML Notation Guide: Version 1.1, 1 September 1997*. On the World Wide Web: http://www.rational.com/uml [1999, 04-17].

Rittgen, P. (1999). Modified EPCs and their formal semantics. *Report 19, Institute of Information Systems*. University Koblenz-Landau.

Rittgen, P. (2001). E-commerce software: From analysis to design. In A. Gangopadhyay (Ed.). *Managing Business with Electronic Commerce: Issues and Trends* (pp. 17-36). Hershey, PA: Idea Group.

Rosemann, M. (1996). Komplexitätsmanagement in prozeßmodellen: Methodenspezifische gestaltungsempfehlungen für die informationsmodellierung. Wiesbaden: Gabler.

Rump, F. (1997). Erreichbarkeitsgraphbasierte analyse ereignisgesteuerter prozessketten. *Technical Report 04/97, OFFIS Institute,* University Oldenburg.

Scheer, A.-W. (1999). ARIS - Business process modeling. (2 ed.). Berlin: Springer.

Simons, A. J. H., & Graham, I. (1999). 30 things that go wrong in object modelling with UML 1.3. In H. Kilov, B. Rumpe, I. Simmonds (Eds.). *Behavioral Specifications of Businesses and Systems*, Chapter 17 (pp. 237-257). Amsterdam: Kluwer Academic Publishers.

Chapter XVII

The CORAS Methodology: Model-based Risk Assessment Using UML and UP

Folker den Braber
SINTEF Telecom and Informatics, Norway

Theo Dimitrakos
CLRC Rutherford Appleton Laboratory, UK

Bjørn Axel Gran
Institute for Energy Technology, Norway

Mass Soldal Lund
SINTEF Telecom and Informatics, Norway

Ketil Stølen
SINTEF Telecom and Informatics, Norway

Jan Øyvind Aagedal
SINTEF Telecom and Informatics, Norway

ABSTRACT

This chapter introduces the CORAS methodology in which Unified Modeling Language (UML) and Unified Process (UP) are combined to support a model-based risk assessment on security-critical systems. The hypothesis is that modeling techniques like UML contribute to increased understanding for the different stakeholders involved during a risk assessment. In the CORAS methodology, a traditional risk management process is integrated with UP, which is a well-accepted system development process. CORAS tries to show how UML can contribute to better understanding, documentation, and communicating during the different phases of the risk management process. CORAS addresses both systems under development and systems already in use.

INTRODUCTION

After the development of information technology (IT) in the last part of the previous century, it has become impossible to imagine a world without IT systems. The impact of this development has been enormous and has opened up a lot of new possibilities and challenges. One of these challenges regards risks. To make use of these new techniques in a dependable way, it is of vital importance to get an overview and understanding of the different risks connected to the use of IT systems. This chapter addresses model-based risk assessment; a methodology developed in the CORAS project. CORAS (2000) is funded by the European Union and develops a tool-supported framework for precise, unambiguous, and efficient risk assessment of security-critical systems. CORAS aims at a methodology for risk assessment that is easy to understand and that functions as a natural part of both the IT system development and the maintenance life cycle. To achieve this CORAS leans on the knowledge gained from the use of models in graphical, semi-formal languages like the Unified Modeling Language (UML) (OMG, 2001b). The main focus of this chapter lies on the part of the CORAS project that addresses the integration of risk management and system development.

The remainder of this chapter is divided into five sections. First, some background is presented. The section thereafter addresses model-based risk assessment and some of the problems connected to this. The main part of the chapter is contained in the section on the risk management process and the integrated risk management and system development process. After a section on related work, a brief conclusion is given.

BACKGROUND

The CORAS approach focuses on the tight integration of viewpoint-oriented UML modeling in the risk management process. An important aspect of the CORAS project is the practical use of UML and the Unified Process (UP) (Kruchten, 1999) in the context of security and risk assessment. This chapter concentrates on the integration of UML and UP in the risk assessment process.

CORAS addresses security-critical systems in general, emphasizing IT security. IT security includes all aspects related to defining, achieving, and maintaining confidentiality, integrity, availability, non-repudiation, accountability, authenticity, and reliability of IT systems (ISO/IEC TR 13335:2001). An IT system, in the sense of CORAS, is not just technology. It is also the humans interacting with the technology and all relevant aspects of the surrounding enterprise context.

The Rationale

Model-based risk assessment employs modeling technology for three main purposes:
1. To describe the target of assessment at the right level of abstraction.
2. To act as a medium for communication and interaction between different groups of stakeholders involved in risk assessment.
3. To document risk assessment results and the assumptions on which these results depend.

Model-based risk assessment is motivated by several factors:

- Risk assessment requires correct descriptions of the target system, its context, and all relevant security features. The modeling technology improves the precision of such descriptions. Improved precision is a prerequisite for improving the quality of risk assessment results.

- The graphical style of UML aims at improving the communication and interaction between stakeholders involved in a risk assessment. This is expected to improve the quality of results; also to speed up the risk assessment process since the danger of wasting time and resources on misconceptions is reduced.

- The modeling technology facilitates a more precise documentation of risk assessment results and the assumptions on which their validity depends. This is expected to reduce maintenance costs by increasing the possibilities for reuse.

- The modeling technology provides a solid basis for the integration of assessment methods that should improve the effectiveness of the assessment process.

- The modeling technology is supported by a rich set of tools from which the risk management may benefit. This may improve quality (as in the case of the two first bullets of this list) and reduce costs (as in the case of the second bullet). It also increases productivity and maintenance.

- The modeling technology provides a basis for tighter integration of risk management and assessment in the system development process. This may considerably reduce development costs and help ensure that the specified security level is achieved.

The main CORAS result is the CORAS framework for model-based risk assessment. As illustrated by Figure 1, the CORAS framework has four main anchor points:
1. A risk management process.
2. A risk documentation framework.
3. An integrated risk management and development process.
4. A platform for tool-inclusion based on data integration.

The risk management process provides the core for the CORAS process from a traditional risk analysis background. Combined with the risk documentation framework, this provides the basis for the development of the integrated risk management and development process. The fourth anchor point represents the CORAS platform, which is a tool that is interoperable with different tools from both the risk analysis field and the modeling world, providing a model-based risk assessment product that can be used on either existing systems or on systems under development.

Figure 1: The CORAS framework for model-based risk assessment

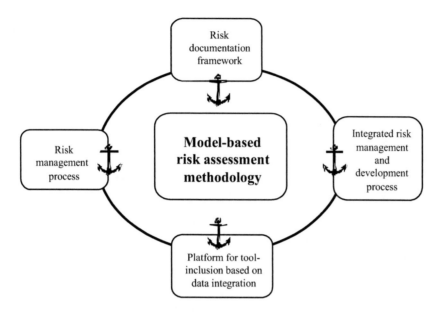

Project Background

For a project like CORAS, it is impossible to develop everything from scratch. A lot of the work is based on existing standards and techniques. To avoid mystifying this chapter by mentioning every standard or method used when it occurs, we summarize the main references here. In addition, we will also say something about the parts of the project that are not addressed in this chapter.

The CORAS risk management process is based on the following standards: AS/NZS 4360:1999 "Risk Management" (AS/NZS 4360, 1999) and ISO/IEC 17799: "Code of Practice for Information Security Management" (ISO/IEC 17799:2000), which are both well established in the field of risk assessment. These standards are complemented by ISO/IEC 13335: "Guidelines for the management of IT-Security" (ISO/IEC 13335:2001) and IEC 61508: "Functional Safety of Electrical/Electronic/Programmable Electronic Safety-Related Systems" (IEC 61508:2000).

The CORAS risk-documentation framework is a specialization of the Reference Model for Open Distributed Processing (RM-ODP) (ISO/IEC 10746, 1995).

In order to make the CORAS methodology available, the CORAS platform is developed. The CORAS platform is built around an internal data representation formalized in XML (W3C, October 6, 2000). Based on XSLT (Clark, November 1999), relevant aspects of the internal data representation may be mapped to the internal data representations of other tools (and vice versa). This allows the integration of sophisticated case tools targeting system development as well as risk assessment tools and tools for vulnerability and threat management.

The CORAS platform consists of three interfaces for XML based data exchange:
- Interface based on IDMEF (Intrusion Detection Exchange Format) (Curry, December 28, 2001). IDMEF is an XML DTD targeting tools for intrusion detection that was developed by the Intrusion Detection Working Group.
- Interface based on XMI (XML Metadata Interchange) (OMG, 1999), as standardized by the Object Management Group and targeting tools for UML modeling.
- Interface targeting risk assessment tools.

The CORAS platform contains a repository divided into two parts:
1. The assessment repository storing the concrete results from assessments already completed and assessments in progress.
2. The reusable elements' repository storing reusable models, patterns, and templates from pre-defined or already completed risk assessments.

The CORAS framework and process are being validated in extensive user trials in the areas of e-commerce and tele-medicine. These user trials began in January 2001 and run until July 2003.

The Consortium

The CORAS consortium consists of three commercial companies: Intracom (Greece), Solinet (Germany), and Telenor (Norway); seven research institutes: CLRC/RAL (UK), CTI (Greece), FORTH (Greece), IFE (Norway), NCT (Norway), NR (Norway), and SINTEF (Norway); as well as one university college: Queen Mary University of London (UK).

MODEL-BASED RISK ASSESSMENT

The CORAS risk assessment methodology incorporates a documentation framework, a number of closely integrated risk assessment techniques, and a risk management process based upon widely-accepted standards. It gives detailed recommendations for the use of UML-oriented modeling in conjunction with risk assessment in the form of guidelines and specified diagrams. Risk assessment requires a firm, but nevertheless easily understandable, basis for communication between different groups of stakeholders. Graphical, object-oriented modeling techniques have proven well suited in this respect for requirements capture and analysis. It is fair to assume that they are as equally suited as part of a language for communication in the case of risk assessment. Class diagrams, use case diagrams, sequence diagrams, activity diagrams, dataflow diagrams, and state diagrams represent mature paradigms used daily in the IT industry throughout the world. They are supported by a wide set of sophisticated case tools, are to a large extent complementary, and together support all stages of system development.

We use the term "risk assessment" to refer to the combination of the systematic processes for risk identification and determination of their consequences as well as to determine how to deal with these risks. Many risk assessment methodologies exist which focus on different types of risks or different areas of concern.

The CORAS risk assessment methodology is built on:
- HAZard and OPerability study (HazOp) (Redmill, 1999).

Figure 2: Model-based risk assessment

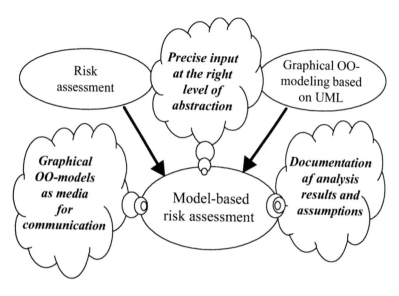

- Fault Tree Analysis (FTA) (IEC 1025, 1990).
- Failure Mode and Effect Criticality Analysis (FMECA) (Bouti, 1994).
- Markov Analysis (Littlewood, 1975).

These methods are to a large extent complementary. All types of risks associated with the target system can potentially be revealed and dealt with using these method-ologies. The methods also cover all phases of the system development and maintenance process. However, they are traditionally applied as separate methods, with each provid-ing its own results. The combination of the output and integration with a modeling language like UML is what makes CORAS unique.

Another aspect of the CORAS risk assessment methodology is the process part. The CORAS process is based on the UP. As a well understood and largely accepted process in software development, the UP is a suitable candidate to serve as a basis in developing our methodology for integrating risk management in the development process. Of course, the UP needs some adjustments in order to be able to profit from the risk management that is carried out in parallel.

For example, two aspects of risk assessment that affect the development process are system requirements and security policies.

A set of agreed-upon system requirements is one important outcome of the inception and elaboration phases. As one cannot expect that all security requirements are present from the start, these requirements have to be elicited. We anticipate that (appropriately adapted) model-based, security risk assessment can help with eliciting security requirements. However, risk assessment methods are traditionally designed to cope with unwanted incidents arising from design errors rather than specification problems related to missing requirements. For security risk assessment to play a significant role in the elaboration phase, the CORAS risk assessment methods are being adapted to properly address requirement elicitation. For this purpose, we are currently developing tailored templates to extend a scenario-driven analysis with security risk assessment throughout the development life cycle. Important sources of inspiration include the work of Cockburn (1997) and Schneider/Winters (1998).

Another consideration with respect to improving the system's security, which is being addressed by the CORAS approach, is to assess security policies and to recommend how a system should be used in order to minimize loss or damage in the presence of the identified security vulnerabilities. We expect that the CORAS framework can support incorporation of system documentation and control guidelines (about changes to the way the system is used or operated) targeting improvement of the system's security.

THE RISK MANAGEMENT PROCESS AND THE INTEGRATED RISK MANAGEMENT AND DEVELOPMENT PROCESS

Following the overview of the CORAS approach to model-based risk assessment provided in the previous sections, we now focus on the integration of the CORAS risk management methodology into a system development and maintenance process.

The left part of Figure 3 shows the risk management process divided into sub-processes for context identification, risk identification, risk analysis, risk evaluation, and

Figure 3: The CORAS risk management process and the role of UML

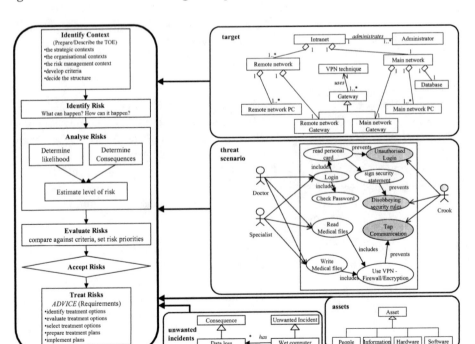

Figure 4: The CORAS documentation framework

CORAS Risk Management Process

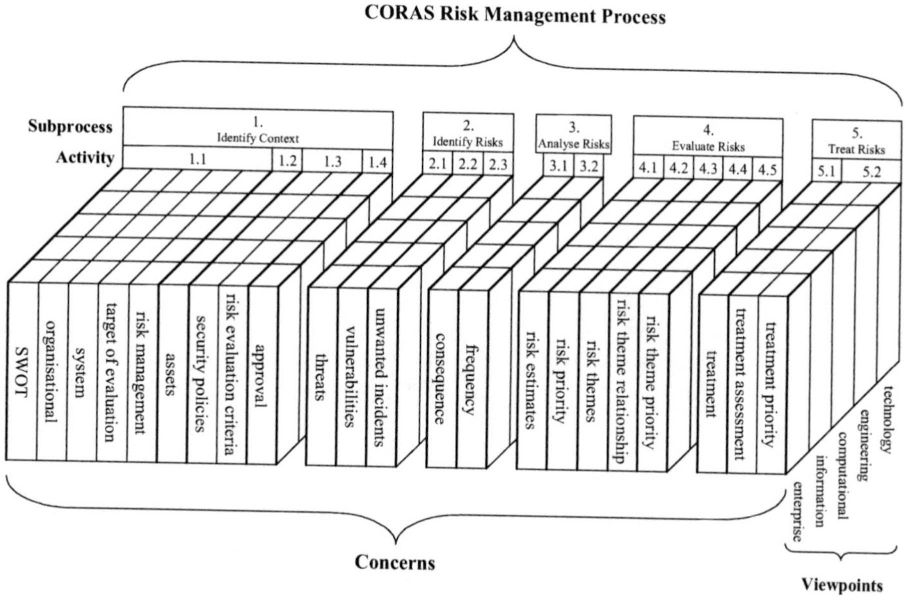

risk treatment. For each of these stages, the CORAS methodology gives detailed advice with respect to which models should be constructed, and what they should express.

The CORAS risk management process is divided into five sub-processes. These sub-processes are then divided into activities. In addition, each activity has one or more concerns connected to it.

Each concern is divided into the five RM-ODP viewpoints. One or several of its viewpoints may be empty depending on the concern in question as well as the target and rigor of evaluation. However, if not empty, each concern-viewpoint will contain a set of element instances. An element may be a model, a risk assessment table, a tree, natural language text, etc. Different instances of the same element may occur within different viewpoints of the same concern. Elements may be classified into:

- Elements containing non-CORAS specific documentation, which refers to elements that are not prepared as a part of the CORAS risk management process. Since CORAS should be applicable to a wide scope of systems, including existing systems, this kind of element is unconstrained.

- Modeling elements (constructed as part of the risk management process) expressed in UML.

- Logs from intrusion detection tools and computerized vulnerability assessment representations.

- Risk assessment tables and trees.

Using RM-ODP as the basis for our documentation framework, every concern can be observed from five different viewpoints. CORAS defines 22 concerns shown in Figure

4. This figure shows the complete CORAS documentation framework with the concerns and viewpoint divided over the different activities under their sub-processes.

The CORAS Ontology

Carrying out a risk assessment requires a clear understanding of all areas of the system to be assessed. Typically, many different stakeholders are involved in a risk assessment. It is therefore crucial that all parties involved have the same understanding of the language and concepts used during the assessment. Figure 5 provides an overview of the elements of the CORAS ontology. The concepts are drawn as classes in a simplified class diagram. The guiding words give extra explanation about the specified relations.

Starting from the bottom right corner, we see that the *Context* influences the *Target* that contains *Assets* and has its *Security requirements*. *Security requirements* lead to *Security policies,* which protect *Assets* by reducing its *Vulnerabilities*. Continuing: a *Threat* may exploit the *Vulnerability* of an *Asset,* thereby reducing the *Value* of the *Asset.* A *Risk* contains an *Unwanted incident* having a certain *Consequence* and *Frequency* of occurrence.

Figure 6 provides a pictorial overview of the integration of the model-based risk management methodology into the system development and maintenance process. In analogy to UP, the system development process is both stepwise incrementally and iterative. In each phase of the system lifecycle, sufficiently refined versions of the system (or its model) are constructed through subsequent iterations. Then the system lifecycle moves from one phase into another.

Figure 5: The CORAS ontology

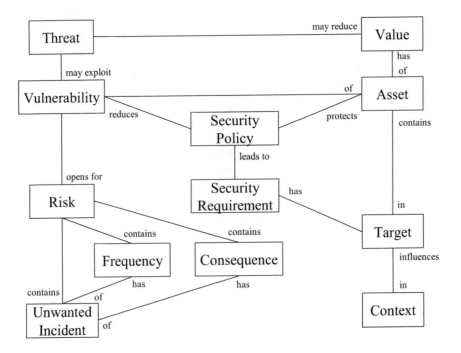

Figure 6: The integrated risk management and development process

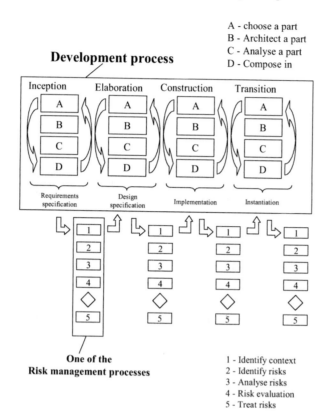

After every phase of the development process, a risk assessment is carried out with its five complete sub-processes. It should be clear that the character of the specific risk management process is different depending on the actual phase of development. Identifying, analysing, and treating risks will be done after all four phases; but, for example, treating a risk that has been identified after the inception phase would be different from treating a risk after the construction phase.

Sub-process 1: Identify Context

In this sub-process of the CORAS process, the context of the system is identified. Context identification establishes the strategic, organizational, and risk management contexts.

This means identifying everything that has to do with the system, including the system itself in addition to the people using it, maintaining it, and configuring it.

The identify context, a sub-process is divided into four activities:

- Identify areas of relevance.
- Identify and value assets.
- Identify policies and evaluation criteria.
- Approve.

Activity 1.1: Identify areas of relevance

The results from this activity are documented by five concerns:

- SWOT (Strengths, Weaknesses, Opportunities, Threats).
- Organizational.
- System.
- Target of evaluation.
- Risk management.

The SWOT Concern

The result of a SWOT analysis may be displayed in a SWOT-diagram. SWOT-diagrams are specialized UML class diagrams in the *enterprise viewpoint*, where strengths, weaknesses, opportunities, and enterprise threats are represented by easy-to-understand symbols. These are clear examples of how modeling in UML can contribute to easy understanding and communication.

The "SWOT-elements" are related to key stakeholders and key assets. This may provide additional direction to the assessment.

An example of a SWOT-diagram is shown in Figure 7.

The Organizational Concern

The organizational context concern documents the relevant aspects of the organization within which the assessment will be conducted.

The System Concern

The system documentation concern has six elements:

- System documentation in any form.

Figure 7: SWOT diagram

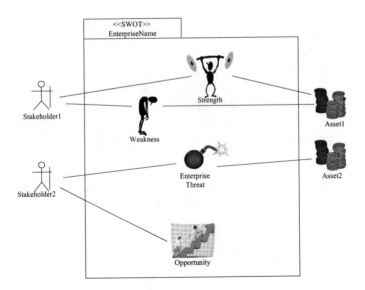

- A specification of the main components and the system boundaries using dataflow diagrams or UML component/deployment diagrams.
- A specification of the stakeholders and main services of the system using UML use-case and sequence diagrams.
- A specification of the main information structure using UML class diagrams.
- A specification of the logical infrastructure, including the main interfaces of components and their connections based on UML state diagrams.
- A specification of the physical infrastructure and the distribution of components in this infrastructure using UML deployment diagrams.

The Target of Evaluation Concern

The target of evaluation concern specifies the part of the system to be assessed with particular emphasis on characterizing the borderlines between the part that should be considered and the rest.

The Risk Management Concern

The risk management concern documents the risk management context for the assessment. The risk management concern is based on four tables: one describing the team that will perform the risk management process, one describing detailed plans for the meeting, one showing the applied methods, and one containing additional informal descriptions.

Activity 1.2: Identify and Value Assets

This activity is connected to only one concern, the asset concern.

The Asset Concern

The asset concern documents the results from the assets' identification and validation. Assets play a key role in risk assessment (talking about risks means basically talking about assets). For every system, the assets are the carriers of the value of the system. This can be anything from knowledge to physical hardware, information etc. A risk is nothing more than the change of an asset through decreasing its value. This is why the identification of assets is central in connection with risk assessment.

The assignment of assets to asset themes and stakeholders may be illustrated in a UML class diagram, in the *enterprise viewpoint,* as the one shown in Figure 8. This kind of diagram may also document important relationships between the assets.

Activity 1.3: Identify Policies and Evaluation Criteria

Two concerns are used to document the results from this activity:
- Security policies.
- Risk evaluation criteria.

The Security Policy Concern

The security policy concern documents the security policies of relevance. The security policies concern has one element: the security policy documentation. No specific requirements are given about the format of this documentation since the CORAS

Figure 8: Asset relationship diagram

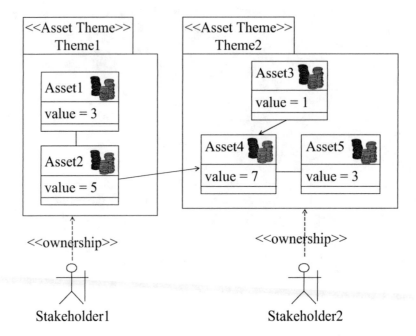

framework should be applicable to existing systems for which security policies probably already exist in a format that is most likely not CORAS-specific.

The Risk Evaluation Concern
The risk evaluation concern documents the risk evaluation criteria. It specifies the acceptable loss from the perspective of the assessment customer. The risk evaluation concern has one element that is in the form of a table.

Activity 1.4: Approval
The approval activity is covered by the approval concern.

The Approval Concern
The approval concern documents the results from a "formal walk through" through all relevant documents at the end of the "Identify context" sub-process. The approval concern contains one table listing the agreed-upon changes identified by the different stakeholders.

Sub-process 2: Identify Risks

The risk identification sub-process consists of three activities. The first two are complementary and may be carried out in any order. The third is first performed after the other two have been completed.

Activities 2.1 and 2.2 address the risk identification from two different angles. Activity 2.1 focuses on identifying "threat" scenarios that may lead to a loss in asset

Table 1: Threat, vulnerability and unwanted incident relationships

Threat	Vulnerability	Unwanted Incident
TRUE	TRUE	Unwanted incident: There exists a threat that may exploit an existing vulnerability.
FALSE	TRUE	Potentially unwanted incident: There exists a vulnerability, but (so far) no threat that may exploit this vulnerability.
TRUE	FALSE	"Blocked" unwanted incident: A threat exists, but has no known vulnerabilities to exploit.
FALSE	FALSE	Ideal/normal behavior.

value. Activity 2.2 focuses on identifying the vulnerabilities of assets (or the associated system) that may be exploited by threats. Table 1 illustrates the complementary nature of Activities 2.1 and 2.2.

Note that Activities 2.1 and 2.2 have threats and vulnerabilities as their main focus, which is where the analyst will try to identify the associated unwanted incidents each time a new threat or vulnerability is found. Hence, the combined effort of Activities 2.1 and 2.2, addressing both threats and vulnerabilities, results in the identification of unwanted incidents. The objective of Activity 2.3 is to integrate, refine, organize, and carefully document the results from the two previous activities.

Activity 2.1: Identify threats to assets

The threat concern documents results from Activity 2.1. The risk analysis methods provided for Activity 2.1 are HazOp, FMECA, and FTA. These three methods provide different approaches on how to identify threats and their unwanted incidents. They work at three different levels of details. HazOp is best suited for identifying general threats to a system, where FMECA deals separately with each component in the system. FTA, for this activity, is used to identify threats related to identifying high-level unwanted incidents, such as (e.g., unwanted incidents identified through SWOT).

The Threat Concern

Threat diagrams are inspired by the misuse cases proposed by Sindre and Opdahl (2000). Threat diagrams are specialized use case diagrams.

Figure 9 provides an example of a "Threat" diagram. Threats are specialized use cases that model possible scenarios that must be considered threats. As with use cases, threats are specified by textual descriptions. Sequence diagrams and activity diagrams may also be used to specify threats, if desired. A threat is related to the asset it is threatening, and may also be related to a user role or a mis-user role if the threat involves actions carried out by humans.

In a threat diagram, assets are defined by their vulnerabilities as well as by their attributes and operations. Vulnerabilities are the negative or undesirable properties of an asset, which are modeled by specialized attributes and operations. These are attributes that an asset (preferably) should not have, and operations that for an asset a(preferably) should not be possible. Vulnerability operations may be specified further by, e.g., state diagrams.

Figure 9: Threat diagram

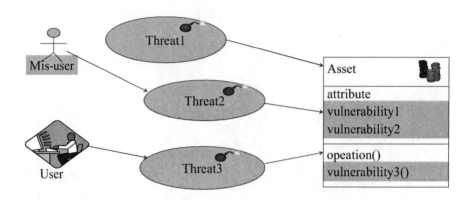

Models Supporting HazOp

HazOp analysis is basically brainstorming that has been structured. Input models to HazOp must communicate important system issues and help guide the brainstorming process. UML sequence diagrams and activity diagrams can be used to provide this information. One important feature of sequence diagrams is that they are able to capture how the functionality in a system is provided at any abstraction level. The abstraction level provided by the sequence diagram needs to reflect the knowledge of the members in the analysis group and the level of abstraction desired for the results provided.

In Figure 10, an example of a HazOp table is given showing how a message originating from a sequence diagram can be analyzed through HazOp guidewords.

Figure 10: Example of a HazOp diagram

Item	Attribute	Guideword	Unwanted Incident
Message: Advice from doctor to patient	Data content	No	Patient does not get medical advice
		Parts missing	Patient gets incorrect advice
		Faulty	Patient gets incorrect advice
		Too much	Patient may get misleading advice
	Control flow	Wrong sender	Patient may get advice concerning another patient
		No receiver	Patient does not get medical advice
		Wrong receiver	Patient does not get medical advice
			Unauthorized persons get information about patient
		Too many receivers	Unauthorized persons get information about patient
	Timing	Too early	Probably no problem
		Too late	Patient may not get medical advice
	Presentation	Difficult to read	Patient may get misleading advice
		Wrong colors	
etc.	etc.	etc.	etc.

Figure 11: Part of a FMECA diagram

Ref No.	Item	Failure modes	Failure cause	Failure mechanism	Local failure effect	System failure effect	Consequences	Failure detection	Frequency	Remarks
1	Transmission of patient data from parent to doctor	Disclosure	Transmission is being read by other actor (not parent or doctor)	Transmission can be read by other actor (not parent or doctor)	Patient data are exposed	Confidentiality of system is compromised because patient information is revealed	Critical	None	High	Encryption of transmission is a possible solution.
2		Manipulation	Transmission is written by other actor (not parent)	Transmission can be written by other actor (not parent)	Patient data are not correct	Integrity of system is compromised because other actors may produce, alter or send information	Catastrophic	None	Medium	A digital signature on the transmitted data is a possible solution
			Transmission is altered by other actor (not parent)	Transmission can be altered by other actor (not parent)						
			Transmission is sent by other actor (not parent)	Transmission can be sent by other actor (not parent)						
3		Denial	Transmission is not possible.	Transmission can not be sent	Patient data are not received	Availability of system is compromised because system is not available	Marginal	System is not available	High	

Models Supporting FMECA

The identified assets are based on the target of evaluation models. All relevant components should then be identified and refined through these two activities. A list of assets supported by a sequence diagram should be provided as input to FMECA to illustrate the functionality in the system covering the role of the assets identified and show whether it is a physical or an informational asset. Again, the abstraction level of the sequence diagram needs to reflect the abstraction level of the assets identified.

Figure 11 shows an example of a FMECA table that assesses the transmission of data in a tele-medicine application.

Models Supporting FTA

FTA is used during threat identification to relate threats to identified, unwanted incidents, either through SWOT analysis or through the help of HazOp and FMECA. The top event would be the unwanted incident identified. The input model for the levels above

Figure 12: FTA example

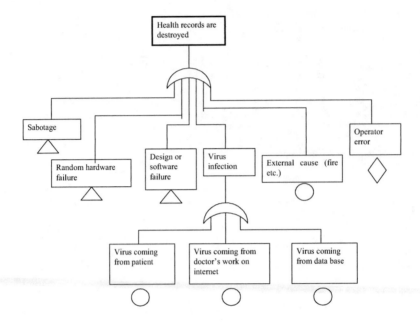

would then be a sequence diagram illustrating all of the assets involved and their relationships. This sequence diagram would need to reflect the relationships in the asset graph and for this system would include human, information, software, and physical assets. To be able to identify the threats that led to the unwanted incident, one could consider information assets first, software assets second, and finally physical assets. However, this depends on the required abstraction level.

Activity 2.2: Identify vulnerabilities of assets

Earlier we have seen that vulnerability is related to both threats and assets. It is the (negative) glue between them. A threat is only harmful to an asset if there exists a vulnerability that makes the asset vulnerable to the threat. Therefore, a vulnerability appears to be a negative quality of an asset.

The Vulnerability Concern

The vulnerabilities are documented in the threat scenario diagrams (Figure 9).

Activity 2.2: Document unwanted incidents

Unwanted incidents are generated from Activity 2.1 and 2.2 results in which threats and vulnerabilities have been identified. Unwanted incidents specify what happens if a threat becomes reality. Events are typically specified in UML through state diagrams.

The Unwanted Incident Concern

Unwanted incidents are documented in tables; however, they also appear in state diagrams such as the one shown in Figure 15.

Figure 13. Risk matrix

Consequence \ Frequency	Rare	Unlikely	Possible	Likely	Almost certain
Insignificant	No	No	Low	Low	Moderate
Minor	No	Low	Low	Moderate	Moderate
Moderate	Low	Low	Moderate	Moderate	High
Major	Low	Moderate	Moderate	High	High
Catastrophic	Moderate	Moderate	High	High	Extreme

Sub-process 3: Analyze Risks

Risk analysis is the systematic use of available information to determine how often specified, unwanted incidents might occur and the magnitude of their consequences.

Figure 13 shows the frequency and consequence values in one matrix. Note that this information is available before any risk is identified. Knowing the consequence and frequency of a certain risk makes it possible to determine the total risk value through the risk matrix.

Activity 3.1: Consequence evaluation

Consequence Concern

State diagrams can be used to specify consequences and can describe all possible behavior in the system, both "good" and "bad" (Houmb, 2002). The "good" behavior in the system is reflected through the normal behavioral states. These states illustrate normal and authorized behavior within the system. The "bad" behavior is reflected through the unwanted incident states identified in sub-process 2 as identified risks.

An example giving such a state diagram is shown in Figure 14.

Figure 14: Normal behavior

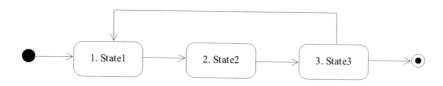

If we now add the "bad" behavior to the state diagram, we see that "bad" behaviour is represented by 'thick' states. The interesting thing is that we find already identified unwanted incidents back on transitions from good states to bad states.

Figure 15: Bad states, their unwanted incidents, and their consequences

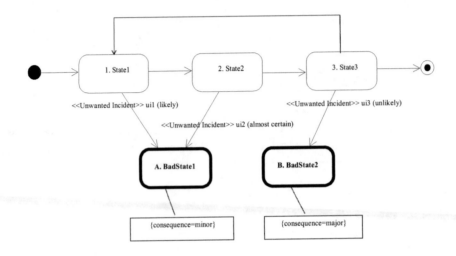

Activity 3.2: Frequency evaluation

Frequency Concern

To be able to calculate or simulate the likelihood of occurrences for the identified consequences ("bad" states), we need to extend the diagram with a state transition probability matrix. The state transition probability matrix stores probabilities related to all possible transitions within the state diagram, i.e., the probability of going from state i to state j. These probabilities will typically be obtained through empirical data, through subjective expert judgment, or both. Figure 16 provides an example of such a transition probability matrix. A transition probability matrix will be based on a state diagram such as the one shown in Figure 15.

Figure 16: Transition probability matrix

		To State						
		Begin	**1**	**2**	**3**	**End**	**A**	**B**
From State	**Begin**	0	P_{Begin1}	0	0	0	0	0
	1	0	0	P_{12}	0	0	P_{1A}	0
	2	0	0	0	P_{23}	0	P_{2A}	0
	3	0	P_{31}	0	0	P_{3End}	0	P_{3B}
	End	0	0	0	0	0	0	0
	A	0	0	0	0	0	0	0
	B	0	0	0	0	0	0	0

Sub-process 4: Risk Evaluation

Risk evaluation is the process to determine risk management priorities by comparing the levels of risk against predetermined standards, target risk levels, or other criteria. The risk evaluation sub-process is divided into five activities, which each having its own concern connected to it.

- **Activity 4.1: Determine Level of Risk** *(risk estimates concern).* The risk estimates concern documents the results from the risk-level determination.
- **Activity 4.2: Prioritize Risks** *(risk priority concern).* The risk priority concern documents the results from risk prioritization.
- **Activity 4.3: Categorise Risks** *(risk themes concern).* The risk themes concern documents the results from risk categorization.
- **Activity 4.4: Determine Interrelationships Among Risk Themes** *(risk themes relationship concern).* The risk themes relationship concern documents the results from identification of interrelationships among risk themes.
- **Activity 4.5: Prioritize the Resulting Risk Themes and Risks** *(risk theme priority concern).* The risk themes priority concern documents the results from the risk theme prioritization.

Sub-process 5: Risk Treatment

Risk treatment is the selection and implementation of appropriate options for dealing with risks. In this phase of the process, decisions need to be made about which treatments are affordable and which are not. These are important decisions that require a thorough understanding of the issues. Such choices are often made by decision-makers who often are in positions further removed from the system and its characteristics. This is one of the main reasons that the results of the assessment need to be presented in such a way that they are also readable for these stakeholders.

Activity 5.1: Identify treatment options

Treatments Concern

The treatment concern documents the results from the treatment identification. In connection with the treatments concern, two tables are used. One is the risk treatment table and the other is the risk *theme* treatment table.

In the *enterprise viewpoint*, treatment options may be described as use cases that prevent threats and protect assets. This is illustrated in Figure 17. The viewpoints and diagrams used for describing the treatment options in more detail will depend on the types of treatments as identified here:

- Security policies: Ponder (Damianou, 2000); class diagrams with OCL (OMG, 2001a) constraints; sequence, activity, and state diagrams describing procedures (*various viewpoints*).
- Security requirements: Use case diagrams; class diagrams; sequence diagrams (*enterprise viewpoint*).
- Security architecture: OCL; class diagrams; state diagrams; object diagrams; collaboration diagrams (*engineering viewpoint*).

Figure 17: Treatment options

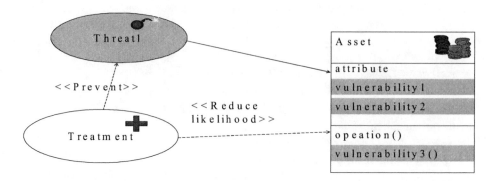

- Monitoring: State diagrams (*computational viewpoint*); deployment diagrams (*engineering viewpoint*).
- Testing: Sequence diagrams and TTCN test suites to describe the tests.

In the context of system development, the different types of treatment will have different importance during the different phases of UP:

- Security requirements are the dominating treatment in the risk assessment carried out after the inception phase.
- Security architecture and testing are the dominating treatments in the risk assessment after the elaboration phase.
- Testing and security policies are the dominating treatments in the risk assessment after the construction phase.
- Security policies and monitoring are the dominating treatments in the risk assessment after the transition phase.

In addition possible treatments may be:

- New iterations on specific parts before a new phase has been entered.
- Guidelines on what target of evaluation should be contained in the risk assessment after the next phase.

One way of specifying security architecture is to use object or collaboration diagrams with tags (Wimmel, 2002). In Table 2, some of these tags are proposed. Figure 18 shows an example using the tag <critical>. Here the server and the transmission channel are critical, while the client is non-critical.

Figure 18: Example of use of <critical>

Table 2: Tags to be applied for objects or collaboration diagrams

Tag	Description
critical	This part of the system contains data or information that should be protected against unauthorized operations. May be used on both components and data channels.
non-critical	Does not contain data or information that need to be protected. All parts of the system that are not tagged are non-critical by default.
private	A private channel is a dedicated connection between two components, and it may not be accessed by intruders. A channel without a tag is private by default.
public	A public channel may be accessed by intruders and must be considered to have an interface that an intruder may exploit.
replace	Is used on replaceable components. A component is replaceable if an intruder can replace it by another component and fool the other components into communicating with it.
node	Is used on components that only contain non-replaceable components and private channels.
secret	A secret channel may not be read by an intruder, but the intruder may write to it.
auth	Is used on authentic channels. An authentic channel may not be written on by an intruder, but the intruder may read the channel.

Figure 19 shows an example of the use of <public>. When a channel is public, it is interpreted as having an interface that an intruder could exploit. This is illustrated in Figure 20.

Figure 19: Example of use of <public>

Figure 20: Interpretation of <public>

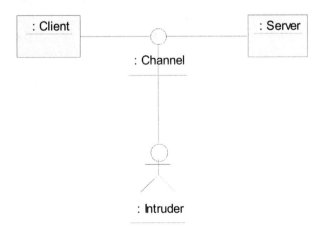

Figure 21: Example of use of <replace>

Figure 21 shows an example of the use of the tag <replace>. Here there is a possibility that the server may be replaced by a false server, and that the client could be fooled into communicating with this one instead of with the real server.

Activity 5.2: Assess alternative treatment approaches

Treatment Assessment Concern

The treatment assessment concern documents the results from the treatment assessment. For each risk and risk theme, the evaluation of the treatment option and approach is documented in two tables: one is the risk treatment evaluation table and the other is the risk *theme* treatment evaluation table.

Treatment Priority Cconcern

The treatment priority concern documents the results from the treatment prioritization. The risk treatment priority concern again makes use of two tables: the risk treatment priority table and the risk *theme* treatment priority table.

RELATED WORK

Since 1990, work has been going on to align and develop existing national and international schemes into one, mutually-accepted framework for testing IT security functionality. The Common Criteria (CC) (CCO, 2002) represents the outcome of this work. The Common Criteria project harmonizes the European "Information Technology Security Evaluation Criteria (ITSEC)" (Communications-Electronics Security Group, 2002), the Canadian "Canadian Trusted Computer Product Evaluation Criteria (CTCPEC)," and the American "Trusted Computer System Evaluation Criteria (TCSEC) and Federal Criteria (FC)." Increasingly, it is replacing national and regional criteria with a worldwide set accepted by the International Standards Organization (ISO15408) (ISO/IEC, 1999). The CC and CORAS are orthogonal approaches. The CC provides a common set of requirements for the security functions of IT products and systems as well as a common set of requirements for assurance measures that are applied to the IT functions of IT products and systems during a security evaluation. CORAS addresses and develops concrete specification technology to specifically address risk assessment.

Surety Analysis (SA) (Sandia National Laboratories, 2002), developed in Sandia National Laboratories, is a methodology based on the creation of an explicit model that covers several aspects of the system's behavior. The modeling framework in SA is proprietary, whereas CORAS uses the standardized RM-ODP as a common basis. SA supports modeling by means of basic techniques such as interaction and state and dataflow diagrams. CORAS aims to use the descriptive power of UML/OCL (Object

Constraint Language) and to investigate its enhancement with aspects of other modeling paradigms specific to security modeling.

RSDS (Reactive System Design Support) is a tool-supported methodology developed by King's College London and B-Core UK, ltd. The methodology has been applied in the specification and risk analysis of reactive systems in automated manufacturing and chemical process control. Both RSDS and CORAS aim to integrate object-oriented modeling and risk analysis for critical systems. However, CORAS focuses on security risk assessment whereas current work on RSDS focuses on safety and reliability analysis.

The Control Objectives for Information and related Technology (COBIT) (Control Objectives for Information and related Technology) addresses the management of IT. COBIT and CORAS are orthogonal approaches. COBIT focuses on control objectives defined in a process-oriented manner following the principles of business re-engineering. The IT process of assessing risks satisfies the business requirement of supporting management decisions through achieving IT objectives and responding to threats by reducing complexity, increasing objectivity, and identifying important decision factors. It is enabled by the organization engaging itself in IT risk-identification and impact analysis. CORAS provides a tight integration of viewpoint-oriented modeling in the whole risk management process, including the sub-processes of risk identification and risk analysis.

CCTA Risk Analysis and Management Methodology (CRAMM) (Barber, 1992) was developed by the British Government's Central Computer and Telecommunications Agency (CCTA) with the aim of providing a structured and consistent approach to computer security management for all systems. The UK National Health Service considers CRAMM to be the standard for risk analysis of information systems within health care establishments. CRAMM is an important source of inspiration for CORAS; and, aspects of CRAMM have been incorporated in CORAS. Contrary to CRAMM, CORAS provides a risk analysis process in which modeling is tightly integrated. CORAS also complies with state-of-the-art international standards for risk management, documentation, modeling, and development of systems.

CONCLUSIONS

Security and dealing with risk does not often get the attention it deserves: it is maybe even forgotten now and then. Apart from parachutists and base jumpers, it is likely that most people let security live its own life and just hope for the best. This natural attitude is probably necessary in our everyday life, but when it comes to IT systems, and especially security-critical IT systems, such an attitude could be fatal. We therefore need to break the habit of living on hope and turn it into informed, calculated, and constructive actions. To be able to do this, methods and tools are needed to guide us in our security analyses.

In this chapter, we have given insight into a methodology and a platform being developed in the CORAS project that provides guidelines on how risk assessment can become a natural part of the system development process. The length constraints imposed on this chapter limits us from presenting the full details, but it is clear that the use of UML in a risk assessment context contributes to understanding and communication during the process. The combination of risk assessment with UP makes security-related adjustments possible during all phases of the development process. However, this does not keep us from applying risk treatments after the system has been finished. This means that the method is also applicable during maintenance of existing systems.

We focus in this chapter on the process part of CORAS; another important part of the methodology is the implementation through the CORAS platform. Making the methodology executable in the form of a computerized tool is critical to its practical use.

Based on the current developments in the security field and the great interest in the CORAS project, it looks like businesses are becoming more aware of the importance of securing their IT systems. There is a long road ahead in the field of IT-security; however, with CORAS' methodology for model-based risk assessment of security critical systems, it provides a solid step in the right direction.

REFERENCES

Australian/New Zealand Standard AS/NZS 4360 (1999). Risk management.

Barber, B., & Davey, J. (1992). The use of the CCTA risk analysis and management methodology CRAMM. *Proc. MEDINFO92,* North Holland (pp. 1589–1593).

Bouti, A., & Ait Kadi, D. (1994). A state-of-the-art review of FMEA/FMECA. *International Journal of Reliability, Quality and Safety Engineering* 1 (pp. 515-543).

Clark, J. (November 1999). XSL transformations (XSLT) 1.0. *World Wide Web Consortium recommendation REC-xslt.*

Cockburn, A. (1997). Structuring use cases with goals. *Journal of Object-oriented Programming,* Sep/Oct: 35-40, Nov/Dec: 56-62.

Common Criteria Organization. (2002). Common criteria for information technology security evaluation. On the World Wide Web: http://www.commoncriteria.org

Communications-Electronics Security Group. (2002). Information security evaluation criteria. On the World Wide Web:: http://www.cesg.gov.uk/assurance/iacs/itsec/index.htm

Control objectives for information and related technology. *COBIT.* On the World Wide Web: http://www.isaca.org/ct_denld.htm

CORAS (2000). A platform for risk analysis of security critical systems. IST-2000-25031. On the World Wide Web: http://www.nr.no/coras/

Curry, D., & Debar Merrill Lynch, H. (December 28, 2001). Intrusion detection message exchange format (IDMEF). Working draft.

Damianou, N., Dulay, N., Lupu, E., & Sloman, M. (2000). Ponder: A language for specifying security and management policies for distributed systems. *The Language Specification - Version 2.2. Research Report DoC 2000/1*, Department of Computing, Imperial College, London.

Houmb, S. H. (2002). Stochastic models and mobile E-commerce: Are stochastic models usable in the analysis of risk in mobile c-commerce? *Unpublished Master's Thesis,* Østfold University College, Faculty of Computer Sciences, Halden, Norway.

IEC 1025. (1990). Fault tree analysis (FTA).

IEC 61508. (2000). Functional safety of electrical/electronic/programmable safety related systems.

ISO/IEC (1999). Information technology — Security techniques — *Evaluation Criteria for IT Security ISO/IEC,* 15408-1.

ISO/IEC 10746.(1995). Basic reference model of open distributed processing.

ISO/IEC TR 13335. (2001). Information technology – Guidelines for the management of IT security.

ISO/IEC 17799.(2000). Information technology – Code of practice for information security management.

Kruchten, P. (1999). The rational unified process, an introduction. Addison-Wesley.

Littlewood, B. (1975). A reliability model for systems with Markov structure. *Appl. Stat. 24* (pp. 172-177).

OMG. (1999). XML Metadata Interchange (XMI).

OMG. (2001a). Object constraint language specification. Part of the UML specification.

OMG. (2001b). Unified Modeling Language specification. Version 1.4.

Reactive System Design Support, RSDS. On the World Wide Web: http://www.dcs.kcl.ac.uk

Redmill, F., Chudleigh, M., & Catmur, J. (1999). Hazop and software Hazop. Wiley.

Sandia National Laboratories, Surety Analysis. Accessed in 2002 from the World Wide Web: http://www.sandia.gov

Schneider, G., & Winters, J. P. (1998). Applying use cases: a practical guide. Addison-Wesley.

Sindre, G., & Opdahl, A. L. (2000). Eliciting security requirements by misuse cases. *In Proc. TOOLS_PACIFIC 2000. IEEE Computer Society Press* (pp. 120-131).

Wimmel, G., & Wisspeintner, A. (2001). Extended description techniques for security engineering. *IFIP/SEC 2001 – 16th International Conference on Information Security*, Kluwer.

World Wide Web Consortium. (6 October, 2000). Extensible Markup Language (XML) v1.0, W3C recommendation (second edition).

Chapter XVIII

Towards a UML Profile for Building on Top of Running Software

Isabelle Mirbel
Laboratoire I3S, France

Violaine de Rivieres
Amadeus sas, France

ABSTRACT

Currently, fewer and fewer applications are developed from scratch. Therefore, with any development process, it is very important to determine during the analysis and design phases whether there are any applications that must be safeguarded and how this could be accomplished. Legacy applications, as well as Enterprise Resource Planning integration are typical examples of developments that deal with safeguarding. Indeed, safeguarding may be necessary for a specific piece of work involving the integration of new developments with different parts of running applications. To support such a difficult but fundamental task, we recommend a set of extensions through a UML profile. In this proposal, we highlight three aspects of safeguarding which have to be taken into account: the business expertise, the interfaces, and the code itself. We then present how this profile can be used along the different phases of analysis and design; applicable guidelines are provided to support software designers in their daily work.

INTRODUCTION

New applications are constantly built on top of running ones. Legacy applications and Enterprise Resource Planning (ERP) are typical examples of development on top of running applications or components. In such a context, it is very important to deal with any existing idiosyncrasies in the earliest stages of the development process, mostly during the analysis phase, in order to properly manage the potential risks inherent to this kind of development. Therefore, it is essential to have a clear understanding, as early as possible, what will be safeguarded from the running application, as well as why and how. Integration and interfacing aspects also have to be studied carefully.

We propose a UML profile to support people involved in development; to help them through their daily analysis and design activities. Given the complexity of developing software that will be built on top of a running application, we focus on both the concrete and ad hoc guidelines of the more critical aspects of the development.

The UML profile presented in this chapter is part of the JECKO methodology where a flexible approach is proposed for analysis and design with regards to the application context (Mirbel, 2002a; Mirbel, 2002b). The need for situation-specific approaches, to better satisfy particular situational requirements, has already been emphasized (Van Slooten, 1996; Ralyte, 2001a; Ralyte, 2001b). In JECKO, the application context is described through different criteria; to develop a new application on top of running applications is one such criterion. Flexibility is handled through the different modeling rules and guidelines proposed in each phase of the process. Some rules are useful regardless of the application context while other rules are dedicated to specific criteria. By situating the application in its context and by choosing the interesting modeling rules and guidelines, the process is tailored for the application under consideration in order to allow for a more efficient development process. The profile presented in this chapter is used within the modeling rules and guidelines that are dedicated to applications developed on top of running ones.

The chapter is organized as follows. First, the background of our work is presented. Then, we introduce our dedicated profile and we highlight the different aspects of safeguarding. We also show how this profile is used with the JECKO methodology. Finally, future trends are presented and a conclusion is given.

BACKGROUND

Many developments now start from running software rather than from scratch. This considerably changes the way analysis and design has to be handled: different aspects of the running software must be taken into consideration for the future development. In addition to the code itself, functional domain expertise (i.e., expertise taken from the functionalities, data, and screen shots) may also be of interest. Interfaces describing relationships that the running software has with other systems (software, databases, etc.) should also be taken into consideration early on in the software development process. But such a situation is rarely handled in the current analysis and design approaches (Spit, 1995).

Problems related to building on top of running software have been studied before, but only from the implementation point of view (Fowler, 1999; Beck, 1997; Opdyke, 1992). We believe that any issues should already be taken into consideration during the analysis phase. Undeniably, in addition to the code itself, the expertise regarding the functional domain and the interfaces (describing any relationships that the running application may have with other systems) may also be of interest, as will be exposed in this chapter.

UML (OMG; Rumbaugh, 1998; Booch, 1998) is an object-oriented, graphical language. It is now a standard notation used by programmers as well as by domain experts throughout the development cycle. UML is customizable through the notion of profile (Jacobson, 1998), which allows for the re-assembling of a set of extensions dedicated to a particular kind of application or development process: it has already been used in various domains (Nunes, 2000; Macona Kande, 2000). In this chapter, we present a profile that is dedicated to development on top of running software.

A PROFILE FOR BUILDING ON TOP OF RUNNING SOFTWARE

Our profile reassembles a set of stereotypes, which are defined to help cope with problems related to developments on top of running software, such as: maintaining a clear distinction between existing parts and new developments, presenting the software in a homogeneous way, and deciding how the elements must be safeguarded.

Use Case Stereotypes

The main interest of use case stereotypes is to make clear what is new in the software under development and what is safeguarded. Regarding the elements taken from the existing software, it is necessary to distinguish what is re-used "as-is" and what will be modified. It may also be interesting to include in the analysis models the description of elements that are not part of the software under development, but that may help to understand how the software will work. In this case, it is important to clearly indicate that these elements are included for clarification purposes only. The stereotypes dedicated to use cases are the following:

- **New:** A use case describing new functionalities.
- **To-be-modified:** A use case describing functionalities that already exist in the running software and that will be enhanced through the new development under consideration.
- **Re-use:** A use case describing existing functionalities that are re-used as they are.
- **Out-of-scope:** A use case describing functionalities that do not belong to the software under study, but are useful for understanding how the software works.

Constraints among stereotyped use cases: The "Well-FormednessRules" are expressed in OCL.

- If a use case *uc1* describing the running software is linked through an *inclusion* relationship to a use-case *uc2* stereotyped <<New>> or <<To-be-modified>>, then *uc1* must be stereotyped <<Re-use>> (and not <<Out-of-scope>>) because it is impacted by the new functionalities.

```
context Usecase inv:

self.stereotype.name="out-of-scope" implies

(self.include->forAll(uc|uc.stereotype.name <> "new"

and uc.stereotype.name <> "to-be-modified").
```

On the contrary, if *uc1* is related through an extension relationship to another use case *uc2*, then *uc1* might be stereotyped <<Out-of-scope>>, because *uc1* is not directly impacted by the new functionalities.

- A use case stereotyped <<re-use>> cannot include a use case stereotyped <<new>>.

```
context Usecase inv:

self.stereotype.name="re-use" implies

self.include.usecase->forAll (uc | uc.stereotype.name <>

"new").
```

Actor Stereotypes

When dealing with the requirements of software built on top of existing software, it is necessary to specify the actors already interacting with the running software (and who are still prepared to continue this interaction) from the actors involved in the new functionalities. Systems already involved in the running parts of the software must be identified to ensure compatibility with any interface that they may be using. These actors are a strong constraint on the new development. The proposed stereotypes help distinguish humans from systems and systems already interacting with the software from the other systems.

- **Human:** A person interacting with the software (through a human-computer interface).
- **System:** An actor interacting with the software as a system (not a person).
  - **New system:** A system that will use the services of the software under development.
  - **Dependent system:** A system already interacting with running software and to be maintained through the new software. It is called a dependent system because it already exists and has to be taken into account in the new development.
    - **Constraining system:** A system already interacting with the running software. This stereotype indicates that the actor will continue to

interact in exactly the same way: the interfaces it uses must be kept compatible. The actor imposes constraints on the software.

- **Collaborating system:** A system already interacting with the software. The actor will continue to interact with the software, but his or her interaction mode may be slightly modified.

Figure 1 shows the different stereotypes and their relationships as associated to actors.

Class Stereotypes

When dealing with classes and associations, as well as with attributes and operations, it is necessary to distinguish what has to be developed from what has to be safeguarded from running software. As done with the use cases, we distinguish classes that are re-used "as-is" from classes that are to be enhanced. We also provide additional information about classes that do not actually belong to the software under development, but help to understand it.

- **New:** A new class, association, attribute, or operation.
- **To-be-modified:** A class, association, attribute, or operation to be modified. In the case of attribute, operation, and association, a *note* has to be used to indicate what changes are to be made to the element and with what mapping (in regard to the safeguarding).
- **Re-use:** A class, association, attribute, or operation kept "as-is".
- **Out-of-scope:** A class, association, attribute, or operation described for only clarification purposes.

Figure 1: Actor stereotypes

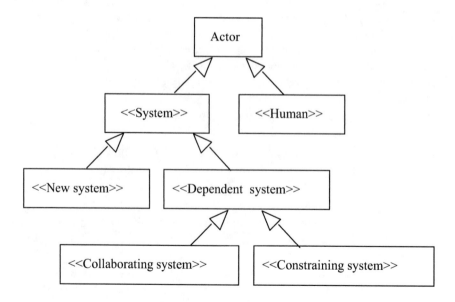

Constraints among stereotyped classes: The "Well-FormednessRules" are expressed in OCL.

- A Class *cl1* stereotyped <<out-of-scope>> or <<re-use>> cannot be the source of any association stereotyped <<new>> or <<to-be-modified>>:

```
context Class inv:

(self.stereotype.name="out-of-scope"   or

self.stereotype.name="re-use") implies

(self.association->forAll

(cl|cl.association.stereotype.name <> "new"

and cl.association.stereotype.name <> "to-be-modified").
```

Package Stereotypes

Additional information given for clarification purposes may be useful to help explain and justify the necessary development. Such information must be detached from the main part of the software in a particular package/set of packages stereotyped <<Out-of-scope>>.

- **Out-of-scope:** A package dealing with information associated to the software for clarification only.

Component Stereotypes

Stereotypes highlight the components kept "as-is" from the running software as well as the enhanced and new components.

- **New:** A new component of the software.
- **To-be-modified:** A component taken from a running software and modified through the new development.
- **Re-use:** A component taken from a running software and kept "as-is" in the new software.

Interface Stereotypes

Stereotypes highlight the interfaces from the running software that are maintained "as-is," as well as any new or enhanced interfaces.

- **New:** A new software interface.
- **To-be-modified:** An interface taken from running software and modified during the new development.
- **Re-use:** An interface taken directly from running software to be re-used "as-is" in the new software.

Table 1: UML stereotypes for building on top of running software

	Use-case	Class	Com-ponent	Packa-ge	Inter-face	Actors
<<New>>	X	X	X		X	<<New System>>
<<To-be-modified>>	X	X	X		X	<<Collaborating System>>
<<Re-use>>	X	X	X		X	<<Constraining System>>
<<Out-of-scope>>	X	X		X		

Table 1 summarizes the different stereotypes presented previously.

DEALING WITH RUNNING SOFTWARE

Different aspects of running software may be of interest throughout the analysis phase of the development process. In addition to the *code* itself, the expertise in the *functional domain* (taken from the functionalities, data, and screenshots of the software) may also be of interest. The *interfaces,* describing the relationships that running software may have with other systems (software, databases, etc.), may also be taken into consideration. By interfaces, we do not include human-computer interfaces, which are already included in the first aspect (dealing with the functional domain).

When dealing with legacy software, for instance, the most important aspects are the expertise in the functional domain and the code, which has to be safeguarded and encapsulated. On the contrary, when software is built with a Rapid Software Development tool, the code will not be safeguarded at all, but the expertise from the business, in addition to the human-computer interfaces, will be kept. When starting a new development, the standard situation consists of enhancing software in order to create a new version. In this case, the three aspects (functional domain, interfaces, and code) have to be taken into consideration.

The analysis phase is dedicated to clearly identifying what has to be safeguarded, while the design phase indicates how the safeguarding can be handled. To continue with this work, it is important to determine if the running part of the software:

- Has to be re-used "as-is", for instance, while interfacing an existing component without any possibility of modifying it (purchased component).
- Can be slightly modified, for instance, while interfacing an existing component developed by the company, but used by other softwares.
- Can be widely modified, for instance, when a software evolves into a new version (and the development team is the owner of the existing version).

The three aspects of safeguarding (functionalities, interfaces, and code) are modular, thus enabling optimum use during development. We qualify each of them by:

(i) *strong,* i.e., when no modification is allowed, (ii) *medium*, i.e., when modifications are allowed inside given boundaries, and (iii) *weak,* i.e., when modifications are allowed.

HANDLING SAFEGUARDING THROUGH THE JECKO METHODOLOGY

JECKO is a flexible approach to analysis and design. Analysis and design activities are adapted to the application context, which is specified through pre-defined basic criteria. Dealing with running software is one such criterion. Thanks to this context, suitable modeling rules and guidelines may be selected to better deal with the specificity of the software being considered. Furthermore, modeling rules and guidelines are sequentially organized into the JECKO framework. We distinguish *prime* modeling rules and guidelines from *specific* ones. *Prime* modeling rules and guidelines are used regardless of what the software context might be, while *specific* modeling rules and guidelines are associated with one of the pre-defined criteria. In this chapter, we focus on specific guidelines that are dedicated to applications built on top of running software. With these dedicated guidelines, the analysis and design activities are tailored to focus on the critical aspects of development on top of running software in order to better handle its complexity.

The JECKO standard process starts with the *Requirement Analysis* to formalize requirements. The second phase, the *Domain and Business Object Analysis*, focuses on the specification of the business covered by the software to be developed. The *Requirement Analysis* and *Domain and Business Object Analysis* phases may be processed in parallel. The third phase concentrates on the *System and Software Architecture.* The software is more and more complex, from both functional and technical viewpoints. Consequently, particular attention should be paid to the overall architecture in order to situate the software components on the different platforms and to ensure coherence between their dynamic interactions. In the fourth phase, the *Component Specification* handles the integration of the different components via the identification of their interfaces. Finally, it is during the *Internal Design* that the specification of each software element (component, class, and so on) is refined so as to cover the coding language constraints. JECKO phases are summarized in Figure 2.

Requirement Analysis

The *Requirement Analysis* deals with the formalization and organization of explicit requirements (expressed by the user) and implicit requirements (deduced by the analyst). Use cases enable the capture of functional or technical requirements. When building on top of running software, requirement analysis helps to identify the services already provided by the software and the enhancements that will have to be developed.

When functionalities and code are safeguarded: The focus of requirement analysis is to clearly distinguish the new functionalities from the ones already supported by the running part of the software. Regarding functionalities already supported, a distinction has to be made between the functionalities safeguarded as they are and functionalities that are enhanced during the new development. Functionalities not directly related to the software development may also be included for clarity. Needless to say, these descrip-

Figure 2: JECKO phases

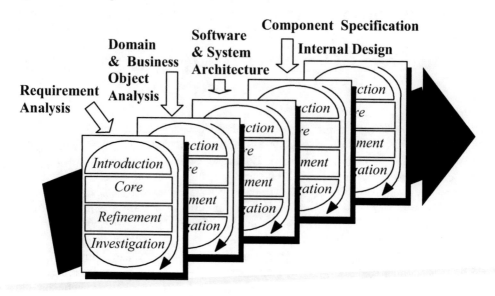

tions do not need to be as detailed as the descriptions concerning the main functionalities: They can even refer to existing documents (not necessarily written with UML) or the running software directly (if there is no existing document). One of the difficulties with the analysis work, in addition to clearly identifying and classifying the different functionalities, is to integrate all of them in a homogenized way.

The steps to follow are:

1. Place existing and new use cases in the same diagram according to functional domains. Distinguish them clearly through the stereotypes: <<New>>, <<To-be-modified>>, <<Re-use>>, and <<Out-of-scope>>.

2. Reorganize the use cases in the same diagram by using *generalization, inclusion,* or *extension* relationships; or, by splitting them (especially use cases describing existing functionalities) in order to enable the homogenization. It is important, while describing a <<To-be-modified>> use case, to let the new functionalities appear explicitly and to link them (through *extension, inclusion,* or *generalization* relationships) to the use case that describes the existing functionalities.

3. Check that the constraints related to the stereotypes are respected.

4. The split made to distinguish the safeguarded parts from the new part may lead to diagram(s) that are difficult to read and functionalities that are difficult to understand as the use case identification refinement has been driven by technical objectives rather than by pure end-user functional objectives. Therefore, activity diagram(s) should be provided in order to clarify the use case process where the use case ordering is not explicit. When the activity refers to the full use case behavior, it has to be named exactly as the use case it refers to.

5. Bring together all of the <<Out-of-scope>> use cases in a separate package; also stereotyped <<Out-of-scope>>.

The requirement analysis may lead to changes in stereotypes associated with use cases. For instance, a use case stereotyped <<Out-of-scope>> may finally appear as impacted by the new functionalities and therefore stereotyped <<Re-use>>.

A split may also lead to the discovery of <<Out-of-scope>> use cases. It is always important to keep in mind that the goal of the analysis is to isolate the impacted parts of the software from the non-impacted ones, and to clearly distinguish these two families through the use of <<Re-use>> and <<Out-of-scope>> stereotypes.

When interfaces are safeguarded: At this stage of analysis, the focus is on the actors using the interface. Only the actors representing systems (human actors interact with the software through human-computer interfaces studied in the functional domain aspect) are of interest. It is important to distinguish systems already interacting with the software from systems that will be interacting with the software. Indeed, dependent systems impose constraints and these constraints have to be identified during the *requirement analysis*. All systems already interacting with the running part of the software have to be identified because they may use an interface that cannot be subsequently changed. Indeed, these actors represent a strong constraint on the new development. The stereotypes presented in our profile help classify the different kinds of actors and highlight the constraints.

Domain and Business Objects Analysis

The *Domain and Business Object Analysis* focuses on the business description. Class diagrams and state chart diagrams enable the modeling of the business domain. Enhancements related to software domains are captured during this phase.

When functionalities are safeguarded: The business description is given through the existing functionalities (instead of being captured from the business domain). The work to be done is similar to what could be done for new software, but the input of the process is different.

When code is safeguarded: As during the *Requirement Analysis*, our process dealing with safeguarding is still driven by a clear differentiation between existing and new information.

With regards to the packages stereotyped <<Out-of-scope>>, the steps to follow are:
1.   Stereotype all included classes with <<Out-of-scope>>.

With regards to other packages, the steps to follow for each class are:
1.   Stereotype attributes and operations to clearly distinguish existing ones from new ones.
    For each existing element:
    a.   If the safeguarding is qualified as *strong*: use a <<Re-use>> stereotype.
    b.   If the safeguarding is qualified as *medium* or *weak*, choose whether to modify or not modify the element. To choose to safeguard the element leads to the use of the <<Re-use>> stereotype. To choose to modify the element consists of stereotyping it with <<To-be-modified>>.
    c.   Complete the element description with the characteristics taken from the running application (type, length, and so on.). With regards to operations, modifications have to be documented precisely.
    Stereotype new elements with <<New>>.

2.   Generalize the element stereotype to the class if all of the elements belonging to it share a common stereotype. Otherwise, try to isolate the <<Re-use>> elements from the <<To-be-modified>> and the <<New>> elements in order to associate a stereotype to the class by using the following relationships: *generalization, specialization, association,* and *composition.*

3.   Stereotype associations among classes as to the attributes, operations, and classes. Safeguarded characteristics of associations as well as modifications have to be documented.

4.   For each class stereotyped <<Re-use>> or <<To-be-modified>>, if a state-transition diagram is required (the class has a complex behavior, which must be described):

   a.   Save the diagram that documents the running software; or, if it does not exist, draw it.

   b.   If the class has a different behavior than the one described in the diagram that documents the running software, modify the diagram.

   It is important to note that a class "a-priori" stereotyped as <<Re-use>> may finally be modified (and therefore stereotyped <<To-be-modified>>) due to the fact that its state-transition diagram (i.e., its behavior) has changed in the software to be developed.

When interfaces are safeguarded: *Domain and Business Object Analysis* focuses on the description of constraints related to interactions between the software and the actors, especially the actors stereotyped as <<Constraining system>>. The system's actor is represented in the application to be developed by a set of classes that describe it; only classes interacting directly with the software under development are of interest. The main objective is to clearly distinguish the responsibility of services of the external system from the responsibility of services of the software under development. Therefore:

1.   For each actor stereotyped with <<System>>, document the classes that interact directly with the software. Of course, the classes must be linked to at least one class of the software under development; otherwise, there is no reason for the classes to appear in the diagrams.

2.   Stereotype each class with the name of the actor and document the stereotype.

3.   If required, use activity diagrams to document the interesting steps of the services provided by the actor. For instance, an external component may include verification, which is therefore not required in the current software. Activity diagrams allow for a justification of why services are or are not supported by the software under development. It may be especially useful to someone who is not involved in the analysis but is willing to participate in the forthcoming phases of the development.

4.   Use sequence diagrams to document the interaction between the actors and the software under development.

System and Software Architecture

Analysis of *System and Software Architecture* is a crucial phase. Software is more and more complex, therefore it is necessary to think about its logical architecture (documented with component diagrams). Currently, software is more often distributed, therefore it is also necessary to specify the physical architecture (documented with deployment diagrams). When building on top of running software, this work is even more crucial because in addition to relationships among components as well as among nodes of the software, relationships with running components have to be decided.

When functionalities are safeguarded: This has no impact on this step of the process.

When code is safeguarded: As with the previous steps, when building on top of running software, the goal of the system architecture step is to clearly distinguish existing components from new components and to highlight their relationships. We distinguish four cases:

- **Case 1:** The running software is safeguarded and new interfaces are added. For instance, this is the case for legacy software.
- **Case 2:** Modifications on running software are not very important. They are mostly safeguarded and new functionalities (easy to isolate) are added. In this case, the existing components are separately safeguarded from the new components. Existing components use services provided by new components.
- **Case 3:** Many new functionalities are integrated in the software. They cannot be isolated from existing components. This situation is called *re-design*.
- **Case 4:** The existing architecture is safeguarded and modifications (not very important) are integrated in it.

Figure 3 summarizes the different cases. Note that case 1 and 2 may coexist.

Each of these cases needs a suitable architecture. With regards to *case 1* and *2*, the steps to follow are:

1.   Organize classes stereotyped with <<Re-use>> into components; also stereotype them with <<Re-use>>. In *case 1*, the stereotype qualifying the running compo-

Figure 3: Component architecture

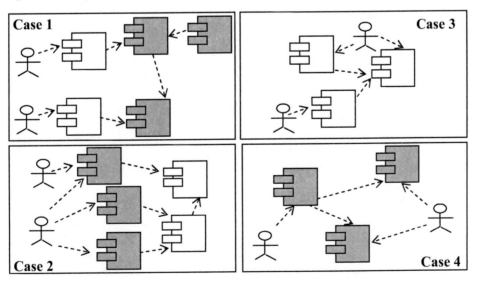

nents may be even better specified, for instance, with <<Encapsulated>>. If the software under study is a legacy software, then the stereotype may be named <<Legacy>> instead of <<Encapsulated>> to emphasize the software context.

2. Organize classes stereotyped <<New>> into components.
3. Identify links among components, especially between components stereotyped <<New>> and <<Re-use>>.

In *case 1*, check that:

a. Actors only interact with <<New>> components.
b. Relationships among <<Re-use>> components and <<New>> components always indicate that <<New>> components use services provided by <<Re-used>> components (and not the contrary).

In *case 2*, on the contrary, check that:

a. Actors interact only with <<Re-use>> components.
b. Relationships among <<Re-use>> components and <<New>> components always indicate that <<Re-use>> components use the services of <<New>> components (and not the contrary).

In *case 3*, the whole architecture is re-designed as if there was no existing architecture to start with. In this case, it is pointless to indicate at the component level if it includes classes stereotyped as <<New>>, <<To-be-modified>>, or <<Re-use>> because all of the components will have to be created (from existing code or not) and will therefore be considered as <<New>> ones.

In *case 4*, the steps to follow are:

1. Build the component diagram from the documentation related to the running software. If there is no documentation, the component diagram has to reflect the current architecture rather than the desired one.
2. Associate <<To-be-modified>> and <<Re-use>> classes to their components.
3. Place classes stereotyped <<New>> into existing components. This placement has to be driven by the relationships among the classes being studied. This work may lead to the conclusion that the architecture is not suitable and that it has to be changed (cf. *Case 2*).
4. Stereotype the components that require enhancements (through <<New>> or <<To-be-modified>> classes) with <<To-be-modified>> to highlight what will have to be taken into consideration during the development.

When interfaces are safeguarded:

1. When dealing with enhancements related to legacy applications, a reflection about the placement of each new service in the architecture of the application being developed has to be carried out. Three situations may be encountered:

    • *Situation 1:* The service is supported by the client of the legacy application, i.e., the actor communicating with the software. In this case, the service is considered as out of the scope of the software. It may be documented in a specific package, <<Out-of-scope>>, to help with the clarification.
    • *Situation 2:* The service is not supported by the legacy or by the actor and has to be implemented outside of the client and the legacy application.

- *Situation 3:* The service is supported by the legacy application and cannot be isolated from it.

The first situation corresponds to an enhancement, which does not impact the whole business and may therefore be only supported by the client using it. The second situation corresponds to an enhancement, which impacts the whole business and has therefore to be implemented outside of the client using it. If the client requiring the enhancement is the only client using the service, the modification may be isolated in a separate component. On the contrary, if the enhancement is required by several clients, modification may be integrated inside the legacy application: this corresponds to the third situation.

2. Verify that all safeguarded interfaces are represented in the component diagram. New interfaces may be added.
3. Stereotype new interfaces with <<New>> or safeguarded ones with <<Re-use>>, depending on whether it is more important to show the safeguarded interfaces or the new interfaces on the diagram.

Component Specification

When functionalities are safeguarded: This has no impact on this step of the process.

When code is safeguarded:

1. Whatever the case the architecture comes from, it is required at this stage of the process to:
    a. Specify the interfaces of <<To-be-modified>> and <<New>> components.
    b. Specify the interface of <<Re-use>> components.
2. With regards to legacy applications, if a new service has to be supported by the components of the legacy application, a reflection has to be carried out to decide either to place it in the core of the component or to place it in the interface. The last solution may be chosen if the change is a minor one (for instance, a data format length). The number and the kind of clients using the interface is also another aspect that has to be taken into consideration to decide whether to only modify the interface or to change it inside the code of the component.

When interfaces are safeguarded:

1. List all the existing interfaces taken from existing documentation or the running application. It is important at this stage of the process to properly identify the full interfaces dedicated to each actor stereotyped <<Dependent system>> appearing in the use case diagrams.
    If actors are constraining the dialogue, document it in order to check that the interfaces associated with the application will provide the services in the right dialogue mode.
2. Prioritize the interface previously listed, especially the actors stereotyped <<Con-straining system>> who have already been considered as essential for the new application. The interfaces they call have to be fully supported and therefore described.

3.   Select existing interfaces, which have to be kept. Note that when an actor is stereotyped <<Constraining system>>, the interface it uses has to be safeguarded "as-is". Therefore, the selection deals only with interfaces related to <<Collaborating system>> actors.

4.   Place the retained interfaces in the diagram(s). If the actor is a:
    a.   Constraining system, stereotype the interface with <<Re-use>>.
    b.   Collaborating system, choose between keeping and changing the interface and stereotype it, respectively, with <<Re-use>> or <<To-be-modified>>. In the last case, changes have to be clearly documented. If the safeguard is qualified by *strong*, stereotype interfaces as <<Re-use>>, otherwise, choose between <<Re-use>> and <<To-be-modified>> to stereotype the interfaces.

5.   Identify new interfaces from new actors or dependent actors requiring new interfaces.

6.   Place new interfaces as in the standard process. Stereotype them with <<New>>.

7.   For each component:
    a.   Check redundant interfaces and remove such redundancies (propose either one common interface or two distinct interfaces).
    b.   Merge interfaces that provide services closely related (i.e., that have similar main objectives) in order to reinforce coherence and consistency of the set of services published by the component.
    These operations have to be driven by the functional area.

8.   Check that all the required interfaces are provided and that dialogue modes are known in regards to the <<Constraining system>> actors.

Internal Design

1.   Select the components for which internal design will be required:
    a.   <<Re-use>> components do not need to be detailed through internal design.
    b.   Depending on the kind of modification to be done, <<To-be-modified>> components may or may not be detailed through internal design.

2.   Check that all services required by existing actors are supported by the software.

FUTURE TRENDS

In the future, we would like to enrich our profile and approach to the analysis and design of software built on top of running applications by mechanisms and artifacts that take into account software transformation through its different versions. For instance, part of the running application may be seen as being re-used in a first version of the new software and seen as "to-be-modified only" in a second version of the software.

We would also like to extend our approach to provide for re-use on top of running applications. In this chapter, we presented a profile to be used inside a project that is starting from running software. However, in a company, different projects may start from either one or from several of the same running applications and running components may be seen differently inside each project. Therefore, mechanisms have to be provided to support different views of the running application.

We would like to improve our modeling rules and guidelines to enrich the development context by integrating user feedback on our approach. In addition to the software criteria, information related to the project (e.g., time pressure and dependency with other projects) (Van Slooten 1996) may be taken into account.

We would like to enhance the JECKO framework by weighting the modeling rules and guidelines with regards to the designer's expertise to provide end-user adapted analysis and design activities. Depending on the person in charge of the analysis and design activities (junior or senior, business analyst, or technical analyst) the process may be slightly different.

Finally, we would like to improve the JECKO methodology and its associated profile to better highlight how incremental the process is and to handle traceability throughout the different steps and with regards to the guidelines that are provided by the methodology as well as through the different kinds of UML diagrams used during the development process.

CONCLUSION

In this chapter, we presented a UML profile for building on top of running software. We did not reduce the running software to only its code. We did take into consideration the expertise about the functional domain and the interfaces describing the relationships that the running software may have with other systems. The safeguarding is also qualified by *strong*, *medium*, or *weak*.

The profile presented in this chapter is part of the JECKO methodology used to propose a flexible approach for analysis and design with regards to software context. The profile is used throughout the modeling rules and guidelines of the methodology dedicated to software developed on top of running applications. By situating the software in its context, by choosing the interesting guidelines, and by using the dedicated profile, the development process is improved and its complexity is handled better.

REFERENCES

Beck, K. (1997). Smalltalk best practice patterns. Englewood Cliffs, NJ: Prentice Hall.

Booch, G., Rumbaugh, J., & Jacobson I. (1998). The Unified Modeling Language user guide. *Object Technology Series,* Addison-Wesley.

Fowler, M. (1999). Refactoring : Improving the design of existing code. *Object Technology Series,* Addison-Wesley,

Jacobson, I., Booch, G., & Rumbaugh, J. (1998). Unified software development process. *Object Technology Series,* Addison-Wesley.

Macona Kandé, M., & Strohmeier, A. (2000). Towards a UML profile for software architecture descriptions. *UML 2000* (pp. 513-527).

Mirbel, I., & De Rivière, V. (2002a). Introducing flexibility in the heart of analysis and design. *6th World Multi-conference on Systemics, Cybernetics and Informatics.*

Mirbel, I., & De Rivière, V. (2002b). Adapting analysis and design to software context: The JECKO approach. *8th International Conference on Object-Oriented Information Systems.*

Nunes, N.J., & Falcão e Cunha, J. (2000). Towards a UML profile for interaction design: the Wisdom approach. *UML 2000* (pp. 101-116).

Object Management Group. On the World Wide Web: http://www.omg.org/

Opdyke, W. (1992). Refactoring object-oriented frameworks. *Ph.D. Thesis,* Illinois.

Ralyte, J. (2001a). Ingénierie des méthodes à base de composants. *Ph.D. Thesis,* January, Université Paris I – Sorbonne.

Ralyte, J., & Rolland, C. (2001b). An assembly process model for method engineering. *CAISE 2001,* June (pp. 267-283).

Rumbaugh, J., Jacobson, I., & Booch, G. (1998). The Unified Modeling Language reference manual. *Object Technology Series*, Addison-Wesley.

Spit, M. (1995). Method modeling of Demeter – Describing comparing improving the Demeter Method for adaptative systems design. *Technical Report*, University of Twente.

Van Slooten, K., and Hodes, B. (1996). Characterizing IS development projects. *IFIP TC8, WG 8.1/8.2,* August (pp. 29-44).

Chapter XIX

A RUP-Based Software Process Supporting Progressive Implementation

Tiago Lima Massoni
Universidade Federal de Pernambuco (UFPE), Brazil

Augusto Cesar Alves Sampaio
Universidade Federal de Pernambuco (UFPE), Brazil

Paulo Henrique Monteiro Borba
Universidade Federal de Pernambuco (UFPE), Brazil

ABSTRACT

This chapter introduces an extension of the Rational Unified Process (RUP) with a method that supports the progressive, and separate, implementation of three different aspects: persistence, distribution, and concurrence control. This complements RUP with a specific implementation method, called Progressive Implementation Method (Pim), and helps to tame the complexity of applications that are persistent, distributed, and concurrent. By gradually and separately implementing, testing, and validating such applications, we obtain two major benefits: the impact caused by the requirements changes during development is reduced and testing and debugging are simplified. In addition, the authors hope to contribute to solving the lack of a specific implementation method in RUP.

INTRODUCTION

Software development has become a more complex activity over the last years. Clients have been increasingly demanding higher productivity, better software quality, and shorter time to market. Additional strain results from new, common requirements such as distribution and concurrent access. These non-functional issues complicate implementation, testing, and particularly, maintenance activities. Most human and financial resources are driven to maintenance activities (Pressman, 1997).

Industrial software processes, such as the Rational Unified Process (RUP), can be useful in dealing with this complexity. A software process defines a set of software construction, validation, and maintenance activities in order to discipline the overall software development practices in an organization. This is particularly true for RUP, which has been widely adopted by major software organizations (Ambler, 1999). It is a highly comprehensive and detailed process, yet focuses on requirements, analysis, and design activities.

Regarding the coding process, implementation methods are important to address the complexity of design decisions during coding activities, especially for non-functional concerns. In order to simplify those activities, we argue that it is useful to tackle functional and non-functional concerns separately. In fact, whereas architectural and design activities should jointly consider functional and non-functional concerns (Waldo et al., 1997), implementation activities can benefit from the separation of the two concerns.

In this context, an implementation method might help programmers to effectively achieve this separation. Therefore, we have defined the Progressive Implementation Method (Pim) (Borba et al., 1999), supporting a progressive approach for object-oriented implementation in Java (Gosgling et al.,1996) where persistence, distribution, and concurrence control aspects are not initially considered in the coding activities, but are gradually introduced. In this way, we can significantly reduce the impact caused by requirements changes during development and tame the complexity by gradually implementing and testing different aspects of code.

This progressive approach is possible because this method relies on the use of design patterns that provide a certain degree of modularity and separation of concerns (Parnas et al., 1972) in such a way that the different aspects can be implemented separately. However, other techniques and tools for separation of concerns might just as well be used, such as aspect-oriented programming (Kiczales et al., 1997).

The objectives of this chapter are:

- Present the basic concepts of the Progressive Implementation Method (Pim), defining a clear basis for our main goal, i.e., the RUP extension.
- Define the software process resulting from the inclusion of the method into RUP, providing proper implementation guidelines for RUP. Thus, we hope to support the progressive implementation of different aspects in software development projects where disciplined requirements, design, and test activities are essential (demanding a software process).

In the next sections, we present the main concepts of RUP and Pim, which are useful for a better understanding of our solution. We also outline the definition of RUPim, i.e., the proposed extension of RUP, and present some results obtained in simple practical experiments using RUPim. Finally, we present some conclusions, future trends, and related work.

BACKGROUND

Rational Unified Process

The Rational Unified Process (RUP) is an industrial software process, which is based on the work of Booch, Jacobson, and Rumbaugh in defining the Unified Process (Jacobson et al., 1999). RUP defines a process for component-based software development. In addition, RUP is focused on visual modeling based on the Unified Modeling Language (UML) (Booch et al., 1999), which includes visual abstractions representing requirements, design, implementation, and test models that simplify communication of software artifacts.

RUP is based on three key ideas (Krutchen, 1999):

- RUP's life cycle is use-case driven. Use cases outline interactions between the software system and its users (people or other systems), representing functional requirements. More than modeling requirements, use cases drive the whole development process (planning, design, implementation, testing and deployment). From use cases, software engineers create design and implementation models realizing use cases specifications and also generate test cases for each use case.

- RUP suggests an architecture-based approach. The guidelines enforce the early definition of a stable architecture supporting key use cases (including code for an architectural prototype), followed by the development of the remaining use cases that fill the earlier-defined architectural baseline.

- RUP defines an iterative and incremental life cycle for the software project. The project manager schedules several successive and dependent iterations for the whole development cycle. Each iteration develops a set of use cases, representing an increment to the final product.

RUP's iterative life cycle can be described in two dimensions that basically represent the dynamic and the static aspects of the process. The dynamic aspects of the process, as they are enacted, are represented by phases and iterations. The time life of a system is divided in life cycles, each of which yielding a new, ready-to-deliver version of the system. Each life cycle is expressed in terms of four serial phases, which are broken down into iterations.

First, in the inception phase, the life cycle objectives are defined, along with the business case and the scope of the system. Next, in the elaboration phase, the architectural baseline is developed and validated and becomes the basis for all of the following development activities. Then, in the construction phase, a software product that is ready for initial operation in the user environment is developed; this is often called a beta test release (Jacobson et al., 1999). Finally, in the transition phase, the product is established in the operational environment, i.e., delivered to the final user. Each iteration of every phase is a development effort that results in an executable subset of the final product. In addition, RUP provides a set of guidelines that define the most likely activities to be executed during iterations of the serialized phases. These guidelines are called iteration workflows, and RUP defines one for each phase.

On the other hand, the static aspects of the process are represented by activities, artifacts (project deliverables), workers (roles played by people who perform the activities), and workflows. Activities are the relevant units of work within the project, broken down into steps, which are usually performed together. Conceptually-related activities are grouped into workflows, which are organized into two groups: core workflows (business modeling, requirements, analysis and design, implementation, tests, and deployment) and support workflows (configuration and change management, project management and environment). According to the life cycle's phases, we choose which activities to be performed in each iteration. In order to group related activities within workflows, RUP defines workflow details, which are small sets of activities usually performed as a single activity.

Progressive Implementation Method

In a software project, addressing design-time decisions during coding activities is extremely complex. This is especially true when dealing with the non-functional aspects having impact on the software quality, such as persistence, distribution, and concurrence control. Therefore, methods that simplify the implementation tasks are highly appropriate as they separate concerns and address complexity.

Furthermore, analysis and design methods have been the focus of software engineering throughout the years, delegating less significance to implementation methods. Consequently, implementation efforts are mostly accomplished *ad hoc*, involving risks to software quality.

In order to approach these problems, the software community has tried to create new techniques, such as aspect-oriented programming (Kiczales et al., 1997) and subject-oriented programming (Ossher and Tarr, 1999). These techniques aim to overcome limitations of the object-oriented paradigm, allowing software developers to better represent design decisions concerning the non-functional aspects of the code. Although these benefits can be achieved, they can only be guaranteed by using these techniques as part of a well-defined implementation method.

In this context, the Progressive Implementation Method (Pim) guides the implementation of complex object-oriented applications in Java. Using this method, we do not initially consider persistence, distribution, and concurrence control in the implementation activities. Instead, we first build functional prototypes that evolve to a functionally-complete prototype. Then, the non-functional aspects are separately introduced. Figure 1 illustrates this progressive approach.

Although Figure 1 suggests an order for implementing each non-functional aspect, the order is not enforced by the method. In fact, the method only requires the different aspects to be separately implemented. In principle, one aspect could be implemented at

Figure 1: Progressive implementation method

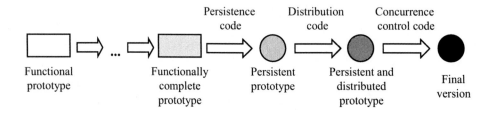

the same time as another one, because they are supported by a modular software architecture.

By initially abstracting from the non-functional code, developers can, for example, quickly develop and test local, sequential, and non-persistent prototypes that are useful in capturing and validating user requirements. As functional requirements become well understood and stable, non-persistent prototypes are used to derive a functionally-complete prototype. In this way, we can reduce the impact caused by requirements change during development, as most changes will likely occur before the functionally-complete prototype is transformed into the final version of the application. Moreover, the progressive approach naturally helps to tackle the complexity inherent to persistent and distributed applications by allowing for gradual testing of the various intermediate versions of the application (Borba et al., 1999).

In order to support this progressive approach, a separation of concerns principle must be applied to design activities. The software architecture must support the modular addressing of functional and non-functional aspects during coding activities. For the non-functional aspects considered here (persistence, distribution, and concurrence control), this can be achieved with architectural and design patterns (Alves and Borba, 2001; Massoni et al., 2001), imposing some constraints on design activities. These patterns were found in well-known software patterns throughout the literature, such as the "Layer" architectural pattern (Buschmann et al., 1996) and the "Façade" and "Abstract Factory" design patterns (Gamma et al., 1994).

The desired separation of concerns could also be achieved by using an aspect-oriented programming language, such as AspectJ (Kiczales et al., 2001). For instance, we could separate persistence-related code (as an aspect), from the business code. Additionally, the weaving of AspectJ would include persistence to the business code.

As Pim is just an implementation method, it should be carefully integrated to the design and testing activities of a software process in order to be used in practice. Consequently, we used Pim in the implementation activities of RUP; integrated to its analysis, design, and testing activities. The main contribution of our work is the extended software process resulting from this integration, i.e., RUPim.

RUPIM: THE INTEGRATED SOFTWARE PROCESS

The definition and enactment of a software process can help improve the quality and productivity in a software development's organization. This result can be obtained mainly due to the standardization of development activities, artifacts, and responsibilities, as well as to the notion of order among activities that are provided by the life cycle model.

In RUP and other popular software processes (Ambler, 1998; Graham and Henderson-Sellers, 1997), requirements, analysis, and design activities are usually clearly described and detailed. In addition, artifacts are unambiguously defined. RUP, for instance, provides specific guidelines for the production of UML models in the analysis and design workflow. In contrast, implementation activities are not described with that level of detail. Consequently, implementation practices are mostly *ad hoc*, or only guided by simple codification standards. However, the costly resources invested in requirements, analysis, and design may be wasted if the implementation process is neglected.

As a consequence, it is important to include implementation guidelines in a RUP process in order to tailor the process according to the chosen programming environment and to add discipline to the implementation process. Developers following RUP can also benefit from implementation methods such as Pim, which can offer, if correctly applied, less costly requirement changes and better tests.

This integration is also valuable from the point of view of Pim's research, since Pim must be integrated to the analysis, design and test methods (features of a software process) in order to be employed in real-world projects.

In order to address these needs, this work defines a tailored version of RUP, adding our method to RUP's implementation workflow. These changes affect other workflows as well. The resultant process is called RUPim, which is presented in the remainder of this section.

Considerations on the Integration

In order to extend RUP with Pim and obtain RUPim, we have to address some issues concerning both RUP and Pim. First, we have to precisely identify the constraints that Pim imposes on RUP. In particular, as Pim relies on a set of architectural and design patterns that provide for separation of concerns, RUP analysis and design activities should be adapted to conform to these patterns. This situation illustrates that more than the implementation aspects will be changed, since the system architecture will be affected as well.

Second, we have to identify the constraints that RUP imposes on Pim. For example, it is important to clearly define matches of corresponding concepts on both RUP and Pim, such as activities, tasks, and steps. In addition, the matching of Pim's sequential life cycle with RUP's iterative life cycle is critical to the success of the resultant process.

The modifications on RUP for addressing these issues can be classified as follows:

- Modifications concerning RUP's dynamic aspects: phases and iterations.
- Modifications concerning RUP's static aspects: workflows, workflow details, and activities.

Modifications Concerning RUP's Dynamic Aspects

As RUP promotes an iterative development, the inclusion of Pim's tasks to RUP's workflows is not enough to integrate Pim to the process. In fact, we have to adapt some RUP concepts in order to properly unify the Pim and RUP life cycles. The elaboration and construction phases receive the major modifications, whereas the inception phase was not significantly modified and receives only small changes related to project planning. The transition phase was not affected and has no direct impact on our integration.

Indeed, these modifications affect the entire scheduling of iterations in a development project and impact complex management issues. Thus, RUPim presents some alternatives which illustrate the iteration planning for the elaboration and construction phases. The iteration workflows for those phases receive several modifications in RUPim, since the iterations of these two phases are the most affected by Pim. The main modification is the split of a common RUP iteration into two types of iteration: *functional iterations* and *special iterations*.

In functional iterations, the scheduled use cases must be completely designed (as in RUP), but partially implemented. During the implementation activities, only business and user interface codes are considered. Data access code is implemented using volatile data structures. In addition, distribution and concurrency control are not considered, since the application will be executed in a single machine. During the elaboration phase, the architectural prototype built in functional iterations is a subset of the functionally-complete prototype as functional iterations of the construction phase complete it.

In contrast, special iterations basically contain only implementation and test activities. These activities deal with the implementation of non-functional aspects' code. Special iterations are also driven by use cases. For each use case, persistence, distribution, and concurrency control code is implemented, demanding changes to business code. These iterations must be accomplished in both the construction and elaboration phases as long as the implementation of the non-functional code involves the most important technical risks of the application, and as long as such risks are addressed on the definition of the architecture as well. This concern can guarantee a robust and comprehensive architectural baseline.

From the project manager's perspective, one or more special iterations can be scheduled for each non-functional code. However, general, special iterations can be defined to address all non-functional code in a parallel way. Although the latter approach can optimize the productivity of the development team, it is not always possible to isolate defects from different non-functional code in such a scenario, which increases complexity.

In addition, the project manager has to decide how many special iterations will be scheduled in the elaboration and construction phases and when the special iterations will be scheduled within each phase. RUPim suggests two alternatives that can be used to plan the special iterations, as shown in Figure 2.

Figure 2: Alternatives for scheduling special iterations

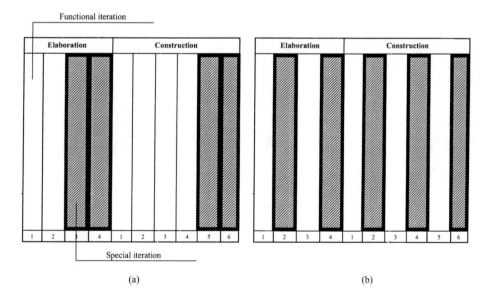

(a)   (b)

Figure 2(a) shows the first alternative for a sample project having four iterations in its elaboration phase and six iterations in its construction phase, in which the project manager must schedule the special iterations as the last of the corresponding phases. In such an approach, use cases will be partially implemented in functional iterations until all of the use cases planned for the elaboration and construction phases originate a functional prototype. This prototype will then evolve at the end of those phases into a persistent and distributed application with concurrence control along the special iterations.

Concerning the transition between such phases, the abstraction of the non-functional code is required. This is because persistence, distribution, and concurrence control code implemented in the elaboration phase cannot be considered in the functional iterations of the construction phase. Pim's design patterns can simplify this task considerably, allowing for effortless automation.

Using this approach, we can guarantee a reduced impact of functional requirements changes, since the later we implement non-functional code, the more we can reduce the impact of changing requirements. However, it may be difficult for the project manager to visualize progress in a project as long as the final version of a use case will be available only in the end of one of those phases. The non-functional code of the use cases is implemented only in the last iterations of the elaboration or construction phases.

Figure 2(b) shows the second alternative, in which the project manager plans interchangeable functional and special iterations during the elaboration and construction phases. Unlike the first alternative, subsets of use cases are completely implemented in their corresponding functional and special iterations. As an advantage, use cases are developed mainly once in the life cycle and through less iterations. Furthermore, the implementation effort for the non-functional code can be fragmented into several points during the phase. However, this approach has an important drawback. The changing requirements will have a greater impact on the code, since non-functional code will be implemented earlier in the life cycle.

Modifications Concerning RUP's Static Aspects

Concerning the RUP's static organization, some activities were created or modified in order to define RUPim. The modifications affected requirements, analysis and design, implementation, and workflow testing. Although activities from the configuration and change management workflows are closely related to implementation activities, they were not affected as the configuration management policies must be maintained despite the extension to the process.

There were two sorts of modifications made: first, we included steps and comments to the RUP activities and removed other steps and second, we included new activities to address specific implementation issues that were related directly to the use of Pim. For better clarity, some workflow details were also created or modified.

As the requirements and test workflows do not directly impact Pim, these were not significantly changed. In the former, RUPim includes guidelines on how to write code for user-interface prototypes. These guidelines state that if the programmer decides to implement part of the functional requirements in those prototypes, he must abstract them from non-functional code. This procedure can guarantee the isolation of the functional prototypes from Pim. In the latter, RUPim includes guidelines for designing tests in order to define different types of tests for considering functional and special iterations. Other test activities were maintained as stated for RUP.

On the other hand, the analysis and design, and implementation workflows received many modifications for the definition of RUPim, since these workflow types are directly affected by Pim's integration to RUP. The main modifications are presented in the following sections.

Analysis and design

This workflow is considerably affected since its activities are closely related to implementation activities. In order to use Pim, specific architectural and design patterns have to be applied for structuring the application; these impose restrictions on the analysis and design activities. Some of these modifications are presented as follows:

- In the activity, architectural design, the architect must define the architectural baseline and identify points where patterns can be used in order to structure the application. Therefore, RUPim guides the architect to incorporate the elements from Pim design patterns into the architecture of the application. In order to do this, Pim defines rules to transform conceptual classes from analysis into design classes and sub-systems. It also defines rules to divide the application in packages and sub-systems. In addition, RUPim guides the architect on how to document the structure and behavior of the design elements by stating the relationship between application classes (or sub-systems) and design elements from specific platforms. For example, developers may include classes from: RMI platform (Sun Microsystems, 1998) for distribution code or JDBC™ platform (Sun Microsystems, 2000) for persistence code if considering Java™ implementation.

- In the activity use case design, the designer must refine requirements in terms of the interactions of design elements. RUPim guides the designer to include all design elements defined in the activity architectural design into the use case design. This means that the use cases will be designed using elements from the design patterns in Pim and elements from specific platforms of non-functional aspects as previously structured and documented by the architect. It must be stressed that persistence, distribution, and concurrence control concerns are introduced according to the needs of business elements in the design activities; but, they are gradually introduced to code in the implementation activities.

Implementation

This workflow is the main focus of our extension, as long as our purpose is to integrate an implementation method to RUP. Beside changes in some activities, we created three new activities to address the implementation of non-functional code for persistence, distribution, and concurrence control, following guidelines defined in recent work (Alves and Borba, 2000; Soares and Borba, 2001; Viana, 2000). Some of the main modifications to this workflow are presented below:

- The original RUP's activity implement components has a different purpose in RUPim. Rather than implementing complete classes and sub-systems as they were designed, programmers must implement only business and user-interface code of the components from design that have been abstracted from non-functional code. The application at this point will be local and sequential and will use "in-memory" stored data. It can guarantee the correct use of Pim, which guides the initial abstraction of non-functional code in order to minimize the impact of changing requirements.

- RUPim includes the new activities: introduce persistence, introduce distribution, and introduce concurrence control. In each of these activities, steps are created that correspond to Pim tasks for introducing persistence, distribution, and concurrence control code, respectively. In general, these steps address the generation of code from design classes related to non-functional code, the implementation of the generated classes, the modification of some business classes, the documentation of code, etc. These activities are performed within the special iterations of the RUPim's life cycle.

Experiments

One way to evaluate a new software development method is to subject the method to some form of empirical study. Empirical studies are used in software engineering for studying questions that need practical results for analysis. Some empirical studies were performed in order to evaluate RUPim. These studies focused on implementation activities, since activities from the other workflows follow almost the same guidelines as in RUP. Hence, we consider this experiment as an evaluation of Pim, i.e., the implementation method integrated to RUPim.

In our simple empirical study, use cases from a real Web application were developed twice in two distinct projects: one guided by a RUP-based methodology and the other guided by a RUPim-based methodology. Implementation and test activities were observed and quantitative and qualitative data were collected. In implementation activities, we recorded the time used to read and understand the design and code, the number of lines of code, and the time spent for code writing. In test activities, the times for running tests were collected. Furthermore, we collected the times spent for finding and fixing defects and the lines of code changed for fixing defects.

Based on the results of these experiments, we compared software quality and productivity for the two approaches. Concerning software quality, we observed that following RUPim, the effort for changing functional requirements (measured at the point where the functionality was completed in the two projects), decreased 60% on average. Table 1 shows the results from the requirements changes that were applied during the study. In addition, the effort required for performing tests and fixing defects was

Table 1: Results from functional requirement changes

Modification	Project	Time	Number Classes	Lines of Code
Modification #1	RUP	0:21	16	50
	RUPim	0:15	12	25
Modification #2	RUP	0:52	25	135
	RUPim	0:29	17	91
Modification #3	RUP	0:08	3	41
	RUPim	0:03	2	24
Average	RUP	0:27	14.66	75.66
	RUPim	0:16	10.33	46.66

Table 2: Results from codification and integration tests effort

Project	Time	Lines of Code
RUP	37:05	5,494
RUPim	33:23	5,425

generally 30% lower, showing that the gradual testing along various intermediate versions of the application helped isolate business problems from aspects problems.

Concerning team productivity, we observed a total productivity gain following RUPim (approximately an 11% increase in terms of time) due to the lower test effort, even though programmers had to write more RUPim code (the test gain was significantly higher than the coding loss). These results are showed in Table 2. However, using RUPim, an application class was edited 50% more times (by successive modifications on the same class used for coding business rules and aspects) and the effort for coding test scripts was approximately 58% higher (by the testing of intermediate prototypes using in-memory data structures for storing and retrieving data). Future research will focus on specific tools for addressing productivity issues using RUPim to minimize the main disadvantages found in our approach.

It must be stressed that these results do not completely validate the benefits of our approach for industrial-strength software development. This can only be achieved by performing and analyzing more comprehensive experiments and case studies. In this way, we would be able to precisely validate the benefits and identify what must be improved in our new method.

CONCLUSION AND FUTURE TRENDS

In this chapter, we have proposed an extension of the Rational Unified Process (RUP) that supports progressive implementation. In fact, we integrated the Progressive Implementation Method (Pim) to RUP, modifying some aspects from the latter. These modifications consider dynamic aspects (new types of iterations) and static aspects (mainly implementation activities, with minor changes to the requirements, design, and tests activities). The resultant software process, RUPim, complements and improves RUP by allowing us to achieve the benefits of Pim in industrial development projects that are based on RUP.

We have also performed an empirical study to evaluate our approach. During this experiment, we collected qualitative and quantitative data from the implementation of a Web-based information system using two different approaches: first, a team of programmers implemented the application following RUP guidelines, including *ad hoc* implementation practices; next, the same team implemented the same application following RUPim guidelines.

When compared to RUP, RUPim helps to significantly reduce the impact of inevitable requirements changes during development. Indeed, most of the changes will likely occur before implementing the non-functional code (persistence, distribution, and concurrence control). Non-functional code is implemented only later in the project after validating a functionally-complete prototype with users and clients. Therefore, non-functional code, which might correspond to 47% of the complete application code, is only affected by very late requirements changes.

RUPim also shows benefit in taming the complexity of tests, since it allows for the gradual testing of the application by including or removing a different aspect of non-functional code one at a time. Hence, it is easier to locate and fix defects. However, more comprehensive experiments should be performed to better validate our approach.

Several languages and tools for separation of concerns have been proposed (Kiczales et al., 1997; Tarr et al., 1999) but associated processes have received less attention. Instead of using tools or new language constructs, RUPim is based on architectural and design patterns that try to achieve similar results for the three types of non-functional aspects considered here: persistence, distribution, and concurrency control. However, as better separation of concerns could be achieved with new language constructs and tools, it would be useful to adapt RUPim to support these as well. We believe that this is possible and useful for large software development projects.

Besides RUP, other modern software processes have been recently proposed (Ambler, 1998; Beck, 1999; Graham and Henderson-Sellers, 1997). OPEN and OOSP share many aspects with RUP and could be extended with Pim as well since these processes do not provide specific implementation methods. We chose RUP because it is widely used in industry today (Ambler, 1999). For example, Extreme Programming (XP) focuses on implementation activities rather than emphasizing analysis and design activities and artifacts. However, XP does not point any directions towards progressive implementation and it could be extended with Pim as well.

REFERENCES

Alves, V., & Borba P. (2001). An implementation method for distributed object-oriented applications. *In XV Brazilian Symposium of Software Engineering* (pp. 161-176).

Ambler, S. (1998). Process patterns: Building large-scale systems using object technology. Cambridge University Press, Cambridge, UK.

Ambler, S. (1999). Enhancing the unified process. *Software Development Magazine*, October.

Beck, K. (1999). Extreme programming explained: Embrace change. Reading, MA: Addison-Wesley,

Booch, G., et al. (1999). The Unified Modeling Language user guide. Reading, MA: Addison-Wesley.

Borba, P., Araujo, S., Bezerra, H., Lima, M., & Soares, S. (1999). Progressive implementation of distributed Java applications. *In Engineering Distributed Objects Workshop, 21st International Conference on Software Engineering* (pp. 40–47).

Buschmann, F., et al. (1996). Pattern oriented software architecture: A system of patterns. Hoboken, NJ: John Wiley and Sons.

Gamma, E., et al. (1994). Design patterns: Elements of reusable object-oriented software. Reading, MA: Addison-Wesley.

Gosgling, J., Joy, B., & Steele, G. (1996). The Java language specification. Reading, MA: Addison-Wesley.

Graham, I., & Henderson-Sellers, B. et al. (1997). The OPEN process specification. ACM Press, Reading, MA: Addison-Wesley.

Jacobson, I., et al. (1999). The unified software development process. Reading, MA: Addison- Wesley.

Kiczales, G., et al. (1997). Aspect-oriented programming. *In Proceedings of 11th European Conference on Object-Oriented Programming, ECOOP '97* (pp. 220–242).

Kiczales, G., et al. (2001). An overview of aspectJ. *In Proceedings of the 15th European Conference on Object-Oriented Programming, ECOOP 2001* (pp. 327–353).

Kruchten, P. (1999). Rational unified process - An introduction. Reading, MA: Addison-Wesley.

Massoni, T., Alves, V., Soares, S., & Borba, P. (2001). PDC: Persistent Data Collections pattern. *In First Latin American Conference on Pattern Languages Programming – SugarLoafPLoP*. To appear in UERJ Magazine: Special Issue on Software Patterns.

Ossher, H., & Tarr, P. (1999). Using subject-oriented programming to overcome common problems in object-oriented software development/evolution. *In 21st International Conference on Software Engineering* (pp. 688–698).

Parnas, D.L., et al. (1972). On the criteria to be used in decomposing systems into modules. *Communications of ACM*, 15(12) (pp.1053–58).

Pressman, R. S. (1997). Software engineering: A praticioner's approach. New York, NY: McGraw-Hill International Editions.

Soares, S., & Borba, P. (2001). Concurrence control with Java and relational databases (in Portuguese). *In V Brazilian Symposium of Programming Languages* (pp. 252–267).

Sun Microsystems (1998). Java remote method invocation specification.

Sun Microsystems (2000). Java database connectivity specification.

Tarr, P., et al. (1999). N degrees of separation: Multi–dimensional separation of concerns. *In 21st International Conference on Software engineering* (pp. 107–119).

Viana, E. (2000). Integrating Java with relational databases (in Portuguese). *Master's Thesis*, Centro de Informática, UFPE.

Waldo, J., et al. (1997). A note on distributed computing. *In Mobile Object Systems: Towards the Programmable Internet* (pp. 49–64), London: Springer-Verlag.

About the Authors

Liliana Favre is a full professor at the Computer Science Department in the Universidad Nacional del Centro de la Provincias de Buenos Aires, Argentina. She is a researcher of CIC ("Comisión de Investigaciones Científicas de la Provincia de Buenos Aires"). She has been working on several national projects about formal methods, software engineering methodologies, and software reusability. Currently, she is research leader of the "Software Technology" group at the Universidad Nacional del Centro de la Provincia de Buenos Aires. Her current research interests are focused on rigorous software and system engineering; mainly on the integration of algebraic techniques with UML.

*   *   *   *   *

Jan Øyvind Aagedal obtained his Ph.D. in computer science from the University of Oslo in 2001. He is a senior scientist at SINTEF (Norway), where he has been since 1993. His Ph.D. work focused on modeling of QoS in distributed systems. He has been the Norwegian technical expert in ISO JTC1/SC7/WG16 and WG17 (QoS in ODP systems and RM-ODP enterprise language, respectively). Dr. Aagedal has worked on a number of EU-projects and national research and industry projects, with the main focus on software development for middleware-based distributed systems. He has also authored a number of papers and reports in this area.

Edgardo Acosta was born in Río Cuarto, Córdoba. In 1996 he began his studies in computing sciences at the National University of Río Cuarto, Argentina. His interest has been in subjects such as modeling and formal system specification. He graduated in 2002 with his thesis "Extension of the UML Metamodel based on the Workflow Metamodel." His curiosity and vocation for investigation lead him to participate in teaching and diverse investigation projects.

Gabriel Baum is co-director of Lifia (Laboratorio de Investigacion y Formacion en Informatica), at the University of La Plata, Argentina. He is also vice-president of SADIO (Argentinean Society of Computer Science). He is professor for theoretical computer science, functional programming and formal languages at the University of La Plata, Argentina. He co-authored books and published numerous technical papers. His research interests comprise formal methods including specification and derivation of programs, calculus of program construction based on Fork algebras and generic programs, computability, abstract and concrete complexity, logics and algebra.

Paulo Borba obtained his doctoral degree in computing at Oxford University in 1995. He is an associate professor at the Informatics Center of the Federal University of Pernambuco, Brazil. His main research interest is on the definition and validation of theories, processes and tools for the implementation and refactoring of object-oriented and aspect-oriented applications.

Pere Botella is full professor at the UPC (Universitat Politècnica de Catalunya, Spain). He has been active in the software engineering field from more than 20 years. He has been dean of the Facultat d'Informàtica (1992-1998) and vicerector of the UPC (1982-1986; 1998-2002). He is also the author of more than 40 publications and program committee member of several international conferences, including ESEC, ICSE, RE, etc., including executive chair and co-editor of ESEC'95. Additionally, he is a member of the steering committees for ESEC-FSE and JISBD (the main Spanish event on software engineering) and has been coordinator in Spain for RENOIR (European Network of Excellence in Requirements Engineering).

Daniel Brandon, Jr. is a professor and department chairperson in the Information Technology Management (ITM) Department at Christian Brothers University (CBU) in Memphis, TN, USA. His education includes a B.S. degree in engineering from Case Western University, MSc in engineering from the University of Connecticut, and a Ph.D. from the University of Connecticut specializing in computer control and simulation. He also has the PMP (Project Management Professional) certification. His research interest is focused on software development, both on the technical side (analysis, design, and programming) and on the management side. In addition to his seven years at CBU, Dr. Brandon has over 20 years experience in the information systems industry, including experience in management, operations, research, and development. He was the director of information systems for the Prime Technical Contractor at the NASA Stennis Space Center for six years, MIS manager for Film Transit Corporation in Memphis for 10 years, and affiliated with Control Data Corporation in Minneapolis for six years in several positions, including manager of applications development. He has also been an independent consultant and software developer in a several industries including: medical, transportation/logistics, finance, law, and entertainment.

Stefan Conrad is a professor for Practical Computer Science at Heinrich-Heine-University Düsseldorf, Germany. From 1999 - 2002 he was associate professor at Ludwig-Maximilians-University Munich. His major research topic is the integration of heterogeneous databases and information systems. Furthermore he is working on database design and modeling languages. Dr. Conrad is member of several national and international organizations (e.g., ACM, IEEE Computer Society, GI-German Society for Computer Science). He is currently chair of the GI working group on foundations of information systems.

Ajantha Dahanayake is an associate professor in the Department of Information and Communication Technology at the Faculty of Technology, Policy and Management,

Delft University of Technology, The Netherlands. She previously served as an associate professor in the Department of Information Systems and Algorithms at the Faculty of Information Technology and Systems. She received her B.S. and M.Sc. in computer science from the University of Leiden and Ph.D. in information systems from Delft University of Technology. She has served in a number of Dutch research and academic institutions. Her research interests are distributed Web-enabled systems, CASE, methodology engineering, component-based development and m-business. She is the research director of the research program Building Blocks for Telematic Applications Development and Evaluation (BETADE).

Folker den Braber has an M.Sc. in computer science from the University in Leiden, The Netherlands. He has been working as a research scientist at SINTEF Telecom and Informatics since September 2001 at the department for Quality and Security Technologies. His main research interests are in semi-formal modeling, system architecture and development, and security analysis and architecture.

Violaine de Rivieres is a software engineer at Amadeus, France. Amadeus provides the most widely-used global distribution system (GDS) in the travel service industry. These solutions are based on the intelligent application of new technology; particularly in the object-oriented area. She is responsible for defining and enhancing the IT development process with state-of-the-art concepts in this domain, especially object-oriented technology using UML. Violaine also lectures at the University of Nice-Sophia, Antipolis.

Theo Dimitrakos has a Ph.D. in computing from the Imperial College, London, and a B.S. in mathematics from the University of Crete, Greece. He is currently a senior research scientist at the Business and Information Technology Department of the UK Central Laboratory of the Research Councils (CLRC), based at Rutherford Appleton Laboratory. He is leading research teams in the areas of trust management for dynamic open systems, service-oriented architectures for large scale distributed systems (GRIDs), and applications of distributed system technologies in e-business and e-learning. He is a member of IEEE, the Global Grid Forum (GGF), and the CLRC representative to ERCIM for the area of e-commerce. He has authored journal and conference papers in the areas of software engineering, distributed systems security, trust management, formal methods, and formal logic.

Ana María Funes is a teaching assistant at the Department of Computer Science of the National University of San Luis, San Luis, Argentina. Her research interests include formal techniques for object-oriented development and the use of formal methods for specification. She was a fellow at the International Institute for Software Technologies of the United Nations University (UNU/IIST) in Macau, from September 2001 to May 2002, where she worked on her master's thesis under the supervision of her adviser, Chris George.

José Luis Garbi is an advanced student at the National University of La Plata, Argentina. He has been a member of the UML group at LIFIA since 2000. His research interests include software development processes, formal methods and CASE tools.

Chris George has been a senior research fellow at UNU/IIST (Macau) from September 1994 through August 2003. He is one of the main contributors to RAISE, particularly the RAISE method, which remains his main research interest. Before coming to UNU/IIST, he worked for companies in the UK and Denmark.

Bjørn Axel Gran has a Ph.D. in industrial mathematics within the field of software reliability from the Norwegian Institute of Technology (NTNU), Trondheim 2002. In 1995 he joined the OECD Halden Reactor Project (Institutt for energiteknikk) where he was employed as as senior research scientist in the section for Safety and Reliability of Computerised Systems. His work has consisted of research within software dependability, and his main interest has been on the use of Bayesian Belief Networks for combining disparate sources of information in the safety assessment of software-based systems. He has also authored a number of papers and reports. Since 1996, he has also been treasurer for Scandinavian Reliability Engineers.

Audun Jensvoll is a civil engineer in computer science. He has worked as a research scientist in the Norwegian army, as a consultant at Telenor (a major Norwegian telecom company) and is currently working as a consultant within EDB4Tel. His major interest is software system methodology and component-based system development.

Seonwoo Kim is a doctoral student of the Department of Industrial Engineering at Seoul National University (SNU), Korea. He holds both a B.S. and MSc in industrial engineering from SNU. His research interest is in knowledge management systems.

John Krogstie is currently senior researcher at SINTEF Telecom and Informatics, which is part of Scandinavia's largest research institute. He also worked nine years for Andersen Consulting within the areas of development and deployment of methodology, knowledge management and process improvement. He has a Ph.D. and M.Sc. within information systems from NTNU, the Norwegian University of Science and Technology, where he also currently holds a position as adjunct professor. His main research areas are modeling of information systems, knowledge management and computer-supported cooperative work.

María Carmen Leonardi received her M.Sc. degree in software engineering at Universidad Nacional de La Plata, Argentina. Currently, she is a Ph.D. student at the same university. She is a also a teaching assistant in the Computer and Systems Department at Facultad de Ciencias Exactas, Universidad Nacional del Centro de la Provincia de Buenos Aires. Her research interests are focused on requirements engineering, conceptual models, natural language-based conceptual models, business rules, and object-oriented methodologies.

Mass Soldal Lund has an M.Sc. in computer science from the University of Oslo, Norway, specializing in formal methods. Since April 2002, he has been working as a research scientist at SINTEF Telecom and Informatics, situated in Oslo. Earlier, he had been a guest lecturer at the Norwegian School of Management BI. His main research interests are formal and semi-formal specification techniques, security modeling, and testing.

Tiago Lima Massoni is a software developer who spends most of his time studying software processes and object-oriented paradigm, particularly separation of concerns and design patterns. He holds a B.S. in computer science from the Federal University of Goias, Brazil, and an M.Sc. in computer science from the Federal University of Pernambuco, Brazil. He is currently on a one-year internship at IBM's Silicon Valley Lab in San Jose, CA, USA. Through this internship, he is able to combine software engineering with data management technologies such as relational databases and XML. Other interests include Java, aspect-oriented software development and Web development.

Paola Martellotto has a B.S. in computer science from Universidad Nacional de Rio Cuarto. She is a teaching assistant at Universidad Nacional de Rio Cuarto, Argentina. Ms. Martellotto's research focus is in systems verification and development into a relational environment. She has published papers on type theory, functional and imperative programming, and UML extensions.

Liliana Martínez is an assistant professor at UNCPBA (Universidad Nacional del Centro de la Pcia. de Buenos Aires) in Argentina. She is a researcher of the "Software Technology" group at UNCPBA. She is currently a master's degree student at the University of La Plata (Argentina). Her main research interests are in the areas of formal methods and software development methodologies.

Paula Mercado is an advanced student at the National University of La Plata, Argentina. She joined the UML group at LIFIA in 2000. Her research interests include software development processes, formal methods and CASE tools.

Isabelle Mirbel is an assistant professor of computer science at the University of Nice-Sophia in Antipolis, France. She received a Ph.D. in 1996 from the University of Nice-Sophia. Her research interest is in the integration of object-oriented design schemas. She is a member of the I3S Laboratory and has also been working at Politecnico di Milano in Italy with Professor Barbara Pernici on the WIDE ESPRIT Project (Workflow on Intelligent Distributed Database Environment) and in the CHOROCHRONOS TMR Project (a research network for spatio-temporal database systems).

German Montejano is a professor and research group director both at Universidad Nacional de San Luis, Argentina. Mr. Montejano holds a B.S. degree in computer science from Universidad Nacional de San Luis, Argentina. He is also a post-graduate student enrolled in the MSc program in software engineering at Universidad Nacional de San Luis, Argentina. Professor Montejano is an author/co-author of over 50 international publications in numerous refereed journals, conference proceedings, and book chapters. He has been working on research problems involving formal methods, UML, development process, workflow, and software quality assurance. He has very important experience in Information Technology.

Jon Oldevik is a research scientist in computer science. He has been working at SINTEF Telecom and Informatics in Norway since 1996. He received a MSc at the University of Oslo in 1996. His main research areas are tools, frameworks and methodologies for component-based, distributed systems. These include aspects of method and process development, tools for code generation and patterns.

Yongtae Park is associate professor of the Department of Industrial Engineering and associate director of Graduate Program of Technology Management at the Seoul National University (SNU), Korea. He holds a B.S. in industrial engineering from SNU. He also received both a, MSc and a Ph.D. in operations management from the University of Wisconsin-Madison. His research interests lie in the areas of industrial knowledge network, knowledge management system and on-line business modeling. Dr. Park has published numerous articles in publications that include *Technovation, International Journal of Production Research, Decision Sciences, Technology Analysis and Strategic Management, R&D Management* and *Technology in Society.*

Claudia Pereira is an assistant professor at UNCPBA (Universidad Nacional del Centro de la Pcia. de Buenos Aires) in Argentina. She is a researcher of the "Software Technology" Group at UNCPBA. She is currently a master's degree student at the University of La Plata (Argentina). Her interests focus on formal methods and object-oriented software engineering.

Claudia Pons is professor of logics and formal specification at the University of La Plata, Argentina. She obtained a Ph.D. in the application of formal methods to object-oriented modeling in 1999. She has participated in several research projects and has published papers in international conference proceedings and journals. She co-leads a research group on formal methods in software engineering at the Lifia (Laboratorio de Invetigacion y Formacion en Informatica), at the University of La Plata, Argentina. She works part time as a trainer and consultant in object-based development with Lifia.

Daniel Riesco is a professor and researcher at Universidad Nacional de San Luis and Universidad Nacional de Río Cuarto, Argentina. Professor Riesco holds a B.S. degree in computer science from Universidad Nacional de San Luis, Argentina and a MSc in knowledge engineering from Universidad Politécnica de Madrid, Spain. He is also a professor of the MSc program in software engineering at Universidad Nacional de San Luis, Universidad Nacional de Jujuy, and Universidad Nacional de Catamarca, Argentina. Professor Riesco is an author/co-author of over 50 publications in numerous refereed journals and conference proceedings. He has been working on research problems involving formal methods, UML, development process, workflow, and software quality assurance.

Peter Rittgen is currently acting professor at the Institute for Business Administration of Technical University Darmstadt in Germany. He earned a M.Sc. in computer science and computational linguistics from the University Koblenz-Landau in 1989 and a Ph.D. in economics and business administration from Frankfurt University in 1997. His dissertation was on *Process Theory of Scheduling and Planning* in the area of information systems. His current research focuses on business process modeling in conjunction with object-oriented and enterprise modeling.

Guadalupe Salazar-Zárate obtained a B.S. degree in computer science from Puebla University at Puebla, México, in 1989. She also earned an M.Sc. from Delft University of Technology in The Netherlands in 1996. She is currently working toward her Ph.D. at the Technical University of Catalonia in Barcelona, Spain. Her areas of interest are software engineering, requirements engineering, non-functional requirements' issues and information systems.

Augusto Cesar Alves Sampaio received his BSc degree in 1985 and his MSc in 1988, both in computer science, from the Federal University of Pernambuco, Brazil. He was awarded his doctorate in computing by the University of Oxford in 1993. Currently, he is an associate professor in computer science at the Federal University of Pernambuco, researching on formal methods, specification, design, refinement and formal refactoring of concurrent and object-oriented systems.

Devang Shah is currently working as a technical consultant with eXcelon Corp., USA. He received an M.Sc. in software engineering from Carnegie Mellon University in August 2000. Prior to his employment with eXcelon, he worked as a consultant with a number of companies including Oracle Corporation on the Oracle database and Oracle financials' suites of products. His areas of interest include software architecture, component- based development and product line practices, generative programming, UML, distributed databases and transaction processing systems.

Sandra Slaughter is an associate professor in the Graduate School of Industrial Administration at Carnegie Mellon University, USA. She obtained her Ph.D. from the University of Minnesota in 1995. Her research focuses on productivity and quality improvement in the development and maintenance of information systems and on effective management of information technology professionals. Currently, she is conducting research on software process improvement, the evolution of information systems in organizations, and the compensation, mobility and careers of information technology professionals. She has published articles in leading research journals in management and software engineering including: *Information Systems Research, Management Science, Communications of the ACM* and *IEEE Transactions on Software Engineering*.

Arnor Solberg is a research scientist in computer science. He has been working for SINTEF Telecom and Informatics since 1997. SINTEF is the largest independent institute for applied research in Norway and has approximately 1,800 employees. He finished his MSc in computer science at the Norwegian University of Science and Technology in Trondheim in December 1996. He has also worked as a system developer at Grøner Data for three years. His main research interests include model driven software system development, Model Driven Architectures (MDA), UML based object-oriented methodologies and quality specification in MDA-based system development.

Ketil Stølen obtained his Ph.D. in computer science from Manchester University in 1990. He has been employed as senior research scientist at SINTEF, Norway, since 1999. Since 1998, he has also been a part-time professor of computer science at the University of Oslo. After completing his Ph.D., Stølen was employed as a research associate at Manchester

University until 1991. From 1991 until 1996 he worked as a research scientist at the Technical University Munich. From 1996 until 1999 he was engaged at the OECD Halden Reactor Project. Stølen has broad experience ranging from formal specification and verification to development. His work has centered on distributed as well as safety-critical systems. He has authored a large number of papers and reports, and been involved in numerous research projects – both as a technical expert and as a project leader.

J. A. Sykes is a senior lecturer in the School of Information Technology at Swinburne University of Technology, Australia. He received a B.E. in electrical engineering from the University of Melbourne in 1969 and a Ph.D. from the University of New South Wales in 1974 for research on the use of computers for real-time fault protection of power transformers. In 1978, after several years as a lecturer in electrical engineering, he entered the IT industry, joining Control Data Australia initially as an analyst and later as a marketing representative. From 1982 he worked as a consultant and software developer where his experience included database design and software development for financial and stockbroking applications. He joined Swinburne University in 1989. His research now centres on the theory and application of modelling languages for information systems design and development, with special interests in component-based development, the Unified Modeling Language, and the role of natural language.

Andrew S. Targowski is a professor of computer information systems at Western Michigan University, USA. He received his Ph.D. from Warsaw Politechnic in 1969. His teaching and research interests are architectural systems development; global, national, local and enterprise information infrastructures development, and information civilization development. He is the author of numerous articles and books in the information management discipline. He is a chairman of the Advisory Council of the Information Resource Management Association.

Klaus Turowski holds the chair of business information systems at the University of Augsburg, Germany. Prior to assuming his current position, he was visiting professor at the University of the Federal Armed Forces in Munich and assistant professor at the University of Magdeburg. He received a M.Sc. in industrial engineering and management at the University of Karlsruhe and a Ph.D. in business information systems at the University of Münster. He was visiting professor at the University of Tartu (Estonia) and also taught at the universities of Darmstadt and Konstanz. In addition to his theoretical background, he has been working on various consulting projects.

Index

A

B

U.W.E.L. LEARNING RESOURCES